CITY OF HEROES

PRIMA'S OFFICIAL STRATEGY GUIDE

PRIMA GAMES
A DIVISION OF RANDOM HOUSE, INC.
3000 LAVA RIDGE COURT
ROSEVILLE, CA 95661
1-800-733-3000
WWW.PRIMAGAMES.COM

An Incan
Monkey God
Studios
Production

D0878739

CREDITS

WRITERS
Chris McCubbin
Christopher "MacAllen" Pinckard

EDITOR & STATS
David Ladyman

BOOK DESIGN & LAYOUT
Raini Madden

BEAUTIFUL GAME ART
Matt Harvey, *Concept Artist & City of Heroes Art Director*
Steve Stacy, Jeremy Mattson,
Chris Sutton, Christopher Chamberlain,
Nate Stephens, Jeff Jenkins, Ian Castaneda,
Doug Gaston, Kirk Young

MANY THANKS!
Many parts written by **Jack Emmert,**
City of Heroes *Lead Designer,*
from the incredibly detailed City of Heroes *Design Doc,*
along with Sean Michael Fish,
Jane Kalmes *(Thanks for all the review help, too, Jane!),*
and Al Rivera *(Thanks for the stat help, too, Al!)*

EXTRA SPECIAL PLACE IN OUR HEARTS FOR ...
Chris "The Answer Man" Julian
City of Heroes *Associate Producer*

AND, THE FOLKS WHO PUT
CREDIBILITY IN THE CREDITS ... OUR PANEL
Robert "abbobination" Parker,
Jeff "Almeric" Schuster, Scott "Archangel" Barber,
Mark "Biggs" Quesnel, Brent Copeland,
Eric "Bubski" Bramblett, Dave "i3ullseye" Maynor,
Chip "chabuhi" Henshaw, Tim "Dariuas" Slager,
Darren "darrenh" Huppert, Dave "Dave" Harrod,
Jason "Deimos" Reilly, Scott "DensityMan" Chevalier,
Michael "Dyn" Hampden, Ethan "Esis" Kidhardt,
Neill "GD" Balthis, John "Jaelk" Smith,
John "Jalimar" Leonard, Joseph "JoeBayley" Bayley,
Doug "Kaiser" Fernandes, Kristen "Katyara" Bates,
Kate "Kehly" Chappelle, Shawn "Kwip" Williams,
Matt "KyleOE" Shirley, Gary "Kylock" Morrow,
Ian "Lohengrin" Taylor, Mark "markbuck" Buckley,
Brian "PabloEx" Soles, Mike "Praxi" Lindsay,
Adam "priortuck" Fritz, Daniel "Rayzor" Coburn,
Ty "Ripley" Connor, Scott Wellman,
Jim "Singe" Boniface, Kevin "Skoriksis" Freet,
Nate "Stylean" Neiman, Steven "Torgen" Cochran,
Jacque "unitsi" English, Eric "VonAirik" Mickelson,
Eugene "Wolfgang" Vega, Dave "Wunderr" Powell,
Ernie "Zandarbar" Whited

Important:

Prima Games has made every effort to determine that the information contained in this book is accurate. However, the publisher makes no warranty, either expressed or implied, as to the accuracy, effectiveness, or completeness of the material in this book; nor does the publisher assume liability for damages, either incidental or consequential, that may result from using the information in this book. The publisher cannot provide information regarding game play, hints and strategies, or problems with hardware or software. Questions should be directed to the support numbers provided by the game and device manufacturers in their documentation. Some game tricks require precise timing and may require repeated attempts before the desired result is achieved.

ISBN: 0-7615-4516-6

Library of Congress Catalog Card Number: 2004100076

Printed in the United States of America

04 05 06 07 BB 10 9 8 7 6 5 4 3 2 1

Incan Monkey God Studios
www.incanmonkey.com

TABLE OF CONTENTS

DISCLAIMER

City of Heroes is a massive online game, or MOG. Like all games of this type, it is updated frequently and evolving constantly. Therefore, it is inevitable that some of the elements covered by this guide will change, some sooner than others. We have made this guide as accurate as possible as of its date of publication, and as useful as possible even as the game changes. Watch PRIMAGAMES.COM for updated versions of this guide.

Addenda: *As this guide was going to press, we received word that the Trial missions (described on pp. 272-281) would be changing drastically soon after publication. Unfortunately, it was not yet known exactly how they'd be changing, so it was not possible to incorporate any of these changes into this book.*

ARCHETYPES

Your archetype determines the nature of your powers. This choice will actually determine which power sets you can select for your primary and secondary powers.

BLASTER

Blasters are ranged power Heroes. They believe that the best defense is a strong offense. Most of their powers are centered around doing as much damage as possible before the villain can get close to melee range and start his serious attacks. Very low hit points and fragile defenses are the weaknesses of the Blaster.

Keeping the villains at range is the key to survival as a Blaster. Blasters use kiting or root blasting techniques to take villains down. Kiting is a tactic that involves constantly moving away from your enemy, letting him chase you while you blast away at him the whole time. When properly timed, you keep your distance and he eventually falls with minimal damage to you. The tricky thing about this tactic is keeping an eye out for other villains in the area. You could very easily run right into another group, and find yourself in more trouble than you can handle. Root blasting is a strong technique used when you do not want to constantly move

and run. You simply use a power that "roots" the target so he cannot move, then open fire with everything you've got. It's very effective, but you have to make sure the root stays on the target. Know how long the root lasts, and recast as needed.

The Blaster archetype has several complementary power sets built right into it. Ice, Fire and Energy are all represented with both an offensive "Blast" primary, and a defensive "Manipulation" secondary. The Ice Manipulation power set is great for fing down your enemy while you continue to pummel him with Ice Blast. The Fire power sets specialize in continuing to deal damage over time (DoT) to your enemy, while the Energy power sets knock your foes away from you with high Knockback bonuses.

Of course, it's always possible to combine your primary and secondary sets in more creative ways.

The Flight power pool is a natural for the Blaster. The first flight power, Hover, allows a Blaster to float above the villains out of melee range. Hover adds a defensive bonus and helps to minimize the damage on the Blaster. It does not give complete immunity to damage though — villains will find ways to harm you, with guns, blasts of their own, or even simply by throwing things at you. Villains can knock you out of the air. Other power pools that can offset the weakness of the Blaster include Fitness, which increases healing rates and reduces Endurance recharge times, Leadership, a great team assist that helps defenses, Accuracy and damage output, Fighting, which grants defensive toughness and weaving dodge, or Medicine, used to heal and cure negative effects.

Blasters are strong solo characters, who can take down villains at a rapid pace. Strong ranged attacks allow you to single out targets and eliminate them with formidable speed. To successfully solo with a Blaster you must learn to pull single villains. Solo Blasters defeat villains quickly, and this will needed if multiple foes are pulled. Blasters have very few hit points and are quite fragile. Rooting multiple foes helps to keep villains away from you while you take down your targets one at a time. The experience comes quickly, because villains die very fast due to your damage output. The slow down comes from the regeneration of Endurance. Blasters use a lot of Endurance. Among the first augmentations obtained should be Endurance reducing Enhancements to help keep this down time to a minimum.

In a group, Blasters are great at dishing out the damage, while Scrappers and Tanks take the brunt of the damage, and Controllers keep the extra villains occupied, and assist the group as a whole. The Blasters' function is to direct concentrated damage on the villains to take them down quickly and efficiently. Caution must be taken when using area effect damage. It is difficult for taunters and Controllers to keep villains off the Blaster who does too much damage to too many villains. Also, coordinate with mass mezmerizers to prevent frustration from damaging mezzed villains at the wrong time (mass mesmerized bad guys tend to wake up quickly when hit by an area attack, and they're usually annoyed). Blasters are very effective at stopping runners from escaping the scene. If a villain decides to run, a Blaster has the range and damage ability to quickly overtake, root and finish off any runner without attracting unwanted attention to the group.

Blasters appeal to the person who wants high ranged damage output. That is their strength. The weakness of a Blaster is his lack of defensive powers and the lowest level of hit points among the archetypes. If a villain is hitting you, there is little you can do about it, other than take down the villain before he can take you down. Watch your Endurance Bar, keep your Enhancements up to your current level, use Accuracy and Endurance reducing Enhancements — and, whenever possible, just stay out of reach. These things will help negate your high Endurance costs and help you dish out the needed damage that Blasters are known for.

Archetype researched by Unitsi

🔊 CONTROLLER

To other archetypes, Controllers are a bit of a mystery. Their specialty is crowd control — that is, making sure that large groups of enemies can only defend themselves in manageable numbers. The other players won't be oohing and aahing over the incredible damage that you deal as a Controller, but with the way you keep the bad guys at bay.

In situations where the team is up against twice the group's numbers, and the frontline fighters are thinking about bugging out, a Controller steps up and puts most of the creatures to Sleep using one power, then she starts locking down single targets so they can't move, while the rest of the team puts an end to their dastardly deeds. You have to love that feeling when your group accomplishes something only because you are there. Control freak? Nope, just a Controller.

"Well that sounds great!" you must be thinking. "So, where's the downside?" Well, one thing you will be missing is the damage output of your fellow Heroes who went the Blaster or Scrapper route. Yes, some of our abilities produce damage, but not in the serious amounts others can. So if you like seeing the big numbers, or dropping a few foes fast, then this is not the archetype for you.

Another downside to the archetype is that you will constantly be explaining things to your group: which mobs they can attack, and which ones they need to hold till last, so they don't wake them up. It

can be frustrating at times, especially when another Hero doesn't listen, but just be patient, explain it again, and just remember that they wouldn't be doing this nearly as easily without you.

Most of the Controller's powers deal with crowd control — keeping the bad guys from your party, or even turning them to your side to fight for you. There are plenty of different ways you can go about this, whether you would like to control things using the elements, tricking the mind, or creating something from thin air. Crowd control is truly an art form to master, and takes time and patience to learn your powers to be able to use them to the fullest.

Your secondary power choices mostly concentrate on healing and defensive powers. In fact, all of your secondary power sets are drawn from the Defender primary sets. Just remember that a primary set is always more powerful than a secondary set, even if their powers are otherwise identical, so don't expect to do everything with your secondary that a Defender can with the same set.

Archetype researched by Brent Copeland

DEFENDER

Defender. The name may not lead you to expect what you get. While Defenders can take some damage, and deal it out as well, their real strengths lie in augmenting other Heroes and hindering villains. Depending upon which route you decide to take, you can heal yourself and others, cause other Heroes to hit faster or harder, or improve the Accuracy or Defense of yourself and your allies. You can also do just the opposite to your enemies, Rooting them in place, Slowing their movement rate, Disorienting them enough to prevent them from causing harm, and Immobilizing them completely.

Defenders have, as perhaps their most important attribute, the capacity for healing. No other archetype can come close to matching it. However, Defenders have good hit points compared to Blasters or Controllers, and when there is no Hero in need of healing, Defenders can help out by directly attacking the foes.

The preferred range for Defender attacks is from a distance, where you have direct damage, as well as damage over time (DoT) powers. Defender attacks usually have additional effects as well, depending on the power set in play. In very general terms, Dark powers tend to lower Accuracy; Energy powers have a chance to knock your enemy back; Electricity powers lower Endurance and Endurance recovery; Psychic powers can bypass most defenses; and Radiation powers can lower Defense as well as bypass some defenses entirely.

However, the Defender is by no means a front-line fighter. In team play, they should stay behind the Tankers and Scrappers, providing healing support as needed.

It is quite possible to solo with a Defender, but the process may just seem a bit slower than it would for some other Heroes. The secret to being a Defender, or a Controller for that matter, is the ability to think on your feet and watch the big

picture. (Although, if you plan to do more than minimal soloing, you probably want to stay away from the Empathy power set, which is the most exclusively team-play-oriented set in the game.)

A well played Defender can be that silent force of the super team that holds the team together. You must have the patience to use your powers most effectively to turn the tide of a battle for you and your allies, not by blasting or striking, but through support and enhancement.

Archetype researched by Dave

SCRAPPERS

As the name implies, Scrappers are the warriors and martial artists of *City of Heroes*, the primary combatants who wade into melee and mix it up, delivering more damage per second than any other archetype. With excellent defenses available to them, they work well as both a solo character and as a team member. As with every archetype, they have advantages and disadvantages to consider before choosing which one to play.

Advantages

◆ Very high damage over a short period of time, allowing the Hero to solo a wide variety of opponents, with or without a team.

◆ Adequate defenses that allow the Hero to survive while delivering the above damage.

◆ Excellent solo archetype, for those looking for that style of play.

Disadvantages

◆ Poor aggro control. The Scrapper has an elevated aggro, meaning that opponents will defer their aggro to him over other, ranged Heroes, at least until the enemy actually takes damage from ranged combat. Once damaged by a ranged Hero, however, the opponents will leave the Scrapper and attack the source. The Scrapper must out-damage each individual target in order to hold their aggro.

◆ Poor crowd control. Given the above, Scrappers are ill-equipped to manage large groups of opponents, thereby keeping the ranged-power Heroes alive. This means that any group with a Scrapper needs some other way to control the targets.

◆ Minimal damage mitigation powers. Two of the six Scrapper power sets have Knockback or Disorient powers, while the rest have none until the highest levels. Damage mitigation powers incapacitate the target for a few seconds, during which they are not damaging anyone, reducing the total damage coming into the Hero team. While it is possible for a Scrapper to alleviate some of the above disadvantages through the use of pool powers like Manipulation, it is not advisable, due to the limited nature of the Scrapper's defenses. While the Tanker's focus is receiving/reducing damage to protect the other archetypes, the Scrapper's focus is delivering damage and, as such, you can easily be overwhelmed if too many opponents are focusing their attention on you. A Scrapper with Manipulation quickly draws all of the un-aggroed targets himself, and very likely goes down quickly.

◆ Limited team utility. Blasters, Tankers, Controllers and Defenders all have specific and narrowly defined functions in team combat, and their abilities seldom overlap. But the Scrapper is a hybrid. You can make a reasonable substitute for either a Tanker or a Blaster, but you can't really replace either one of the more specialized Heroes. To put it another way, given a similar degree of design and play skills, a team-up will always be better off with one Tanker and one Blaster than they would with two Scrappers. This isn't a huge drawback, but it can become a factor in your ability to find a good team, particularly at the highest levels.

Scrappers in a group are best suited to focusing their attention on eliminating targets quickly and surgically, especially those considered to be primary targets, and using powers like Taunt or Teleport Foe to pull targets to them when fighting solo, to avoid being overwhelmed by large groups.

TANKERS

The name says it all, really. A tank. The class has more hit points and more defenses, and is able to withstand beatings that would put almost anyone else into the pavement and then some. With more defensive choices then any other class, the Tanker is able to withstand a surprising amount of punishment, making you a key member in any group.

While damage output on the Tanker class isn't that high, you can still be quite effective at solo-ing. High hit points and defenses often let you survive the battle through sheer patience.

Defense is the key to a long-lived, healthy Tanker. If additional powers are chosen, complementary powers that increase your Hit Point or Endurance regeneration, or your defenses, are a sure bet, particularly for those Tankers who intend to specialize in team play, where defense is everything. For those who are interested in a damage Tanker, with more offensive punch, the Stone power sets (Stone Armor & Stone Melee) are a good choice.

Why You'll Love Being a Tanker

The ability to go head to head with almost everything in the game. Want to see that fiery power close up? With a Tanker you'll get to see every power in the game from a first-person perspective — In your face! You have the hit points to duke it out with multiple bad guys at once, and will become the main shield for your group. The bad guys need to get through you before they can go pick on that pencil-neck Blaster who's working behind you.

You'll have plenty of options with a Tanker, Whether it be a defensive Invulnerability Tanker, or a more offensively inclined Stone Tanker. Either way, it's pretty cool when you send a bad guy flying back almost 30 feet.

Why You'll Hate Being a Tanker

You can fight. And take punishment. That's about it. You don't have any abilities to hit bad guys at range, so you'll have to go to them or taunt them to you. You don't have any healing abilities, so it can take time to regenerate those bazillion health points you'll eventually have. If you want to do anything other then fight — like crowd control, ranged damage, heal or other cool powers — the Tanker class probably isn't for you.

Character Development

You're a Tanker. You fight. You probably will want to grab something that complements your fighting abilities or survival potential. Medicine is a good choice, as it will eventually let you heal your own wounds. The advanced travel powers such as fly and teleport are mostly wasted on a Tanker, (unless you want to be different or see the sights) as usually the ranged-power Heroes will have Group Flight or Teleport available. Leaping is good if you want something to cut down your personal travel time.

Archetype researched by Biggs

ORIGIN

Your origin is the source of your powers. Were you born with them, or did you study for long months and years to perfect them? Or perhaps you acquired them after some encounter with mysterious forces? Origin determines which Enhancements you can buy and therefore which stores you will use.

 ## MUTANT

Perhaps your parents were exposed to strange radiations, or maybe it's just the next leap forward in evolution, but your powers were encoded into your genes before you were born.

 ## SCIENCE

Exposure to chemicals, radiation or some other scientific process has left you changed, with new and mysterious abilities far beyond the mass of humanity.

 ## TECHNOLOGY

Unlike Science Heroes, whose bodies have been permanently changed by exposure to natural forces, as a Technology Hero you carry unique and advanced devices that allow you to produce superhuman effects.

 ## NATURAL

Your origin involves no mysterious forces or secret discoveries; you have simply used your remarkable talents to train yourself to the very pinnacle of human potential.

 ## MAGIC

"There are more things in heaven and earth" … supernatural forces are abroad in the world, and either through training and discipline, or simple chance, you have become a human nexus for them.

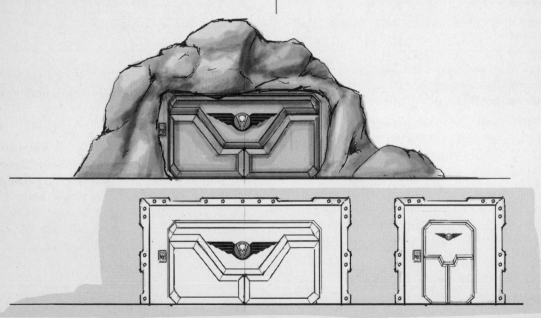

POWERS

POWER EFFECTS

Each power available to Heroes has one or more individual effects which create somewhat independent results. For example, Buckshot (Blaster Ranged: Assault Rifle) inflicts relatively high Lethal Damage when it hits, and can also inflict moderate Knockback, but only 25% of the time.

Chance is the base chance that an effect will trigger, *not* the chance that it will affect a target.

Some effects continue to inflict damage or have other effects over a period of time. (This includes DoT effects.) If there is a chance that an effect will cease before a power's normal duration, the effect is flagged with **Can Cancel**.

Since powers improve as the Hero gains levels, we did not try to list the numeric value of each power's effects, at each level, to avoid publishing a telephone book. We did give the relative strengths of each effect (Low, Moderate, High, and so forth).

Magnitude (Mag). Magnitude measures the intensity (not strength) of certain effects — generally Stun, Hold, Fear and other such effects. This intensity is cumulative between similar effects and Heroes. Each Hero and villain also has a base Magnitude value. The base Magnitude for all Heroes and minions is -1. For Lieutenants it's –2, and for Bosses it's -3.

For an effect with a Magnitude to take effect, the powers being used must raise the target's magnitude past 0. For example, to Stun a boss, one or more Heroes must hit him with a total combined Magnitude of more than 3. A Magnitude 3 Stun from Cobra Strike will not alone Stun a boss. If you or another Hero also activates Eagle Claw (Mag 3), making the Stun total Magnitude 6 , the boss will be Stunned.

The same power from the same Hero does not stack, but all others do, from the same or different players.

Note: Remember that the villains fight back with their own Magnitude powers. The Iron Will Inspiration series increases your base magnitude to -3, -6 and –11, respectively.

POWER STATS

Type. Toggle (turn on and off), Click (activate) or Auto (automatically functions). Abbreviations include **Togl** (Toggle) and **Clk** (Click).

Attacks (Acc). If a power attacks, the general type of attack is listed here. (If the power's chance of successful activation — not the chance it will actually hit — is higher or lower than normal, that increased or decreased Accuracy is also listed here.) Abbreviations include **Le**thal, **Sm**ash, **Fi**re, **En**ergy, **Me**lee, **NgEn** (Negative Energy), **Co**ld, **Psi**onic.

Cost. Cost in Endurance to activate the power. For Toggle powers, this is the cost per pulse of power.

Act. Time to activate the power, from the time you trigger it, in seconds.

Rech (Recharge) — time until a power's button becomes available again, in seconds.

Range. In feet.

Target. The possible target(s) for the power. If it creates a cone, the "radius" (length) and width of the cone are listed, in feet and degrees. If it creates a sphere, the radius of the sphere is listed.

Enhancements. Socketable Enhancements for this power. Abbreviations include **Acc**uracy, **Dam**age, **Dmg Resist**, **Defense+** (Defense Buff), **Defense–** (Defense Debuff), **End**urance **Drain**, **KB** (Knockback), **REC** (Reduce Endurance Cost), **Rng** (Range), **To Hit+** (To Hit Buff), **To Hit–** (To Hit Debuff), **Int**errupt, and **Rech**arge.

The strength rankings used reflect different things for different effects. With damage, the strength represents the amount of damage done relative to the norm for that archtype and level, which starts at different points and rises at different rates for each archetype. A Moderate attack inflicts damage close to the norm, while a Minor attack inflicts a fraction of that and an Extreme attack inflicts at least double the norm. With Knockback attacks, the strength rankings suggest how far the target will be knocked back. With other effects, like Stun, Taunt or Fear, they suggest the duration of the actual effect on the target.

BLASTER PRIMARY (RANGED)

ASSAULT RIFLE

Whether you want to be a 1920s G-man Hero or a 30th-century future trooper with a full arsenal all in one weapon, this could be the power set for you. Your Hero comes equipped with a Sniper Rifle for a long-range attack — in fact, the foe you're firing at may have to take the monorail just to get to you. Just kidding, but it is long range. While your foes are on their way to you, they can be blasted with a **Burst** of rounds, or even **Full Auto**, that does maximum damage at good range. You have a **Flamethrower** to roast villains like a marshmallow, and the **Ignite** option gives them a good hot foot with some damage over time from the heat. If by chance the foe is tough enough to make it through all that, you can use **Buckshot**, which can knock them off their feet. In an extreme case, when a whole pack of enemies is bearing down on you, the **M30 Grenade** can put them all on their backs. Of course the really tough guys will still keep coming, but **Full Auto** ought to be back up by then. In case you get a runner, you have a **Beanbag** that will Disorient him, making him wander aimlessly for a bit while you catch up. Usually you have time to get him before the effect wears off, and if not you can always sniper him.

The Assault Rifle Hero works well as a solo fighter. You have so many weapons once you collect the full set, you can use your powers to control the enemy, or just blast away until they're out of it. The set is well-balanced, so you'll always have good options against foes of your level. The best villains against the Assault Rifle are melee fighters, or "sitting ducks," but if the bad guys want to play ranged combat, hey, that's your specialty, and you can probably out-gun them. If you do get into trouble, you can always Sprint out as a last resort. In a group you have the ability to pull and to inflict major damage, taking a big burden off the group Tankers or Scrappers. Keep your Inspiration slots full of Endurance, Heal and Revive boosters. Endurance insures you still have lead in your pencil, Heal makes sure the lead can be delivered and Revive keeps you at the site to take revenge on the foe that got in a lucky punch.

Power researched by Zandarbar.

Assault Rifle Effects

Burst

Lethal Damage (Minor)
Defense Debuff (Moderate)

Slug

Lethal Damage (High)
Knockback (Moderate; 25% chance)

Buckshot

Lethal Damage (Moderate)
Knockback (Moderate; 50% chance)

M30 Grenade

Smashing Damage (Minor)
Lethal Damage (Moderate)
Knockback (High; 50% chance)

Beanbag

Smashing Damage (Minor)
Stun (High) Mag 3

Sniper Rifle

Lethal Damage (Very High)
Knockback (Moderate; 50% chance)

Flamethrower

Fire Damage (Minor)

Ignite

Summons (Flame Accelerant)

Full Auto

Lethal Damage (Minor)
Lethal Damage (Moderate; 10% chance)

ASSAULT RIFLE STATS

Name	Type	Attacks (Acc)	Cost	Act	Rech	Range	Target	Enhancements
Burst	Clk	Le (+5% Acc)	6.0	2.2	4	90	Foe	Acc, Dam, REC, Rng, Defense−, Rech
Slug	Clk	Le (+5% Acc)	9.8	1.9	8	100	Foe	Acc, Dam, REC, Rng, KB, Rech
Buckshot	Clk	Le (+5% Acc)	11.8	1.9	8	—	Foe (40', 30° cone)	Acc, Dam, Rech, REC, KB, cone
M30 Grenade	Clk	Le, Sm (+5% Acc)	17.5	1.9	16	80	Foe (15' sphere)	Acc, Dam, Rech, REC, Rng
Beanbag	Clk	Sm (+5% Acc)	11.8	1.9	20	60	Foe	Acc, Dam, Rech, REC, Rng, Stun
Sniper Rifle	Clk	Le (+25% Acc)	16.6	1.9	12	150	Foe	Acc, Dam, Rech, REC, Rng, KB, Int
Flamethrower	Clk	Fi (+30% Acc)	25.2	3.5	20	—	Foe (40', 45° cone)	Acc, Dam, Rech, REC, cone
Ignite	Clk	(+100% Acc)	6.0	4.0	3	30	Location	Acc, REC, Rng, Rech, Dam
Full Auto	Clk	Le (+35% Acc)	30.0	6.0	25	—	Foe (80', 10° cone)	Acc, Dam, Rech, REC, cone

Type: Togl (Toggle); **Clk** (Click)
Attacks: Lethal, **Sm**ash, **Fi**re, **En**ergy, **Me**lee, **NgEn** (Negative Energy), **Co**ld, **Psi**onic
Rech: Recharge Time
Enhancements: Accuracy, **Dam**age, **Dmg Resist**, **Defense+** (buff), **Defense−** (debuff), **End**urance **Drain**, **KB** (Knockback), **REC** (Reduce Endurance Cost), **Rng** (Range), **To Hit+** (buff), **To Hit−** (debuff), **Int**errupt, and **Rech** (recharge)

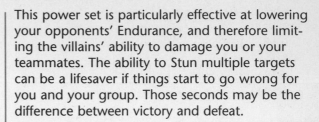

ELECTRICAL BLAST

Thunder and lightning! Feeling the crackle of electricity in your hand, and the smell of ozone in your nostrils makes for one of the most exciting power sets you can choose.

The Electrical Blaster has a formidable array of powers that not only damage opponents, but drain Endurance and Stun them as well! From a well placed sniper **Zapp** to a multi-target **Ball Lightning**, or even a well timed **Short Circuit** Stun, you can be effective both solo and in groups.

As a solo Hero, you can use your ranged attacks in concert with Stun effects or crowd control secondary powers to effectively fight multiple opponents. Not only does the long range of some of your blasts allow single pull, it also allows you to hit a target multiple times before taking damage yourself, when a lot of damage is necessary. You can do damage over time to multiple targets at an early level, but this works best with a secondary power set that involves Endurance regeneration, because sending out electrical bolts is hard work!

In a team, your powers enable you to really contribute. Electrical Blast has a large array of single-target blasts allowing for nearly nonstop damage as you gain more and different abilities through the levels. By standing back, you can get the most out of your considerable damage potential.

This power set is particularly effective at lowering your opponents' Endurance, and therefore limiting the villains' ability to damage you or your teammates. The ability to Stun multiple targets can be a lifesaver if things start to go wrong for you and your group. Those seconds may be the difference between victory and defeat.

Power researched by Wunderr.

Electrical Blast Effects

Charged Bolts
Energy Damage (Moderate)
End Drain (Minor)
Endurance Recovery (None; 20% chance)

Lightning Bolt
Energy Damage (High)
End Drain (Minor)
Endurance Recovery (None; 30% chance)

Ball Lightning
Energy Damage (Minor)
Energy Damage (Minor)
End Drain (Minor)
Endurance Recovery (None; 30% chance)

Short Circuit
Energy Damage (Minor)
End Drain (Very High)
Endurance Recovery (None)

Aim

- To Hit Buff (Very High)
- Add Smash Damage (Extreme)
- Add Lethal Damage (Extreme)
- Add Fire Damage (Extreme)
- Add Cold Damage (Extreme)
- Add Energy Damage (Extreme)
- Add Neg.Energy Damage (Extreme)
- Add Psionic Damage (Extreme)

Zapp

- Energy Damage (Very High)
- End Drain (High)
- Endurance Recovery (None; 50% chance)

Tesla Cage

- Heal (High) Mag 3
- Energy Damage (Minor)

- End Drain (Minor)
- Endurance Recovery (None)

Voltaic Sentinel

- Summons (Electric Field)

Thunderous Blast

- Smashing Damage (Moderate)
- Energy Damage (High)
- Energy Damage (Moderate; 75% chance)
- Energy Damage (Moderate; 50% chance)
- End Drain (Extreme)
- End Drain (Very High; 30% chance)
- End Drain (Very High; 30% chance)
- Endurance Recovery (None)
- Endurance Recovery (None)
- Endurance Cost (Extreme)
- Stun (Very High) Mag 2

ELECTRICAL BLAST STATS

Name	Type	Attacks (Acc)	Cost	Act	Rech	Range	Target	Enhancements
Charged Bolts	Clk	En	6.0	2.1	4	70	Foe	Acc, Dam, REC, Rng, Drain End, Rech
Lightning Bolt	Clk	En	9.8	2.0	8	80	Foe	Acc, Dam, Rech, REC, Rng, Drain End
Ball Lightning	Clk	En	17.5	1.1	16	80	Foe (15' sphere)	Acc, Dam, Rech, REC, Rng, Drain End
Short Circuit	Clk	En (+20% Acc)	18.0	3.0	20	–	Foe (20' sphere)	Acc, Dam, Rech, REC, Drain End
Aim	Clk		6.0	1.2	30	–	Self	REC, Rech, To Hit+
Zapp	Clk	En (+20% Acc)	16.6	1.3	12	150	Foe	Acc, Dam, Rech, REC, Rng, Drain End, Int
Tesla Cage	Clk	En	7.9	2.2	10	60	Foe	Acc, Dam, Rech, REC, Rng, Hold, Drain End
Voltaic Sentinel	Clk	(+100% Acc)	30.0	3.1	120	60	Location	Rech, REC, Rng, Dam, Drain End, Acc
Thunderous Blast	Clk	En (+30% Acc)	36.0	3.7	240	60	Foe (25' sphere)	Acc, Dam, Rech, REC, Drain End

Type: Togl (Toggle); **Clk** (Click)
Attacks: Lethal, **Sm**ash, **Fi**re, **En**ergy, **Me**lee, **NgEn** (Negative Energy), **Co**ld, **Psi**onic
Rech: Recharge Time
Enhancements: Accuracy, **Dam**age, **Dmg Resist, Defense+** (buff), **Defense–** (debuff), **End**urance **Drain**, **KB** (Knockback), **REC** (Reduce Endurance Cost), **Rng** (Range), **To Hit+** (buff), **To Hit-** (debuff), **Int**errupt, and **Rech** (recharge)

ENERGY BLAST

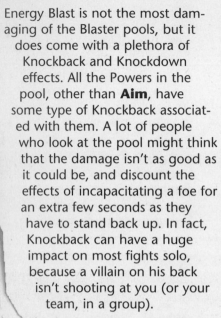

Energy Blast is not the most damaging of the Blaster pools, but it does come with a plethora of Knockback and Knockdown effects. All the Powers in the pool, other than **Aim**, have some type of Knockback associated with them. A lot of people who look at the pool might think that the damage isn't as good as it could be, and discount the effects of incapacitating a foe for an extra few seconds as they have to stand back up. In fact, Knockback can have a huge impact on most fights solo, because a villain on his back isn't shooting at you (or your team, in a group).

Power Burst and **Power Blast** are the main single-target high-damage dealers of the set. Power Burst is a short-range attack, so it's good to start with it, knock a foe back, then follow up with Power Bolt, due to its longer range.

Power Bolt is fairly fast, but low on damage. It makes a good filler attack. **Power Push** is mainly used to keep melee foes out of range, or keep a ranged foe on the ground. It does very little damage, but considerable Knockback.

Power Burst, **Power Blast** and **Power Bolt** are all going to want significant Enhancement slots as your main attacks. Accuracy, recharge time, damage and Endurance cost need to be on your radar, with maybe an extra helping of damage to make up for the lower damage from the pool. Power Blast and Power Bolt can both benefit from range enhancers, but that probably shouldn't be your main concern.

As far as area of effect (AoE) goes for this pool, you're looking at **Energy Torrent** (short-ranged cone), **Explosive Blast** (Normal ranged AoE), and **Nova** (PBAoE with a self Stun and self Endurance drain). **Energy Torrent** and **Explosive Blast** are fairly light on damage, but heavy on the Knockback. Nova, being the highest power in the pool, is heavy on damage *and* heavy on Knockback. If you're using AoE a lot, you'll definitely want damage enhancers in these powers, probably doubled up. **Energy Torrent** could use cone range increase, along with Accuracy. **Explosive Blast** definitely needs Accuracy and damage to be effective. Nova is all about Accuracy and damage.

Overall the pool is a good balance of damage and secondary effects. It offers good rewards in combat, and is very entertaining.

Power researched by Praxi.

Energy Blast Effects

Power Bolt

> Smashing Damage (Minor)
> Energy Damage (Moderate)
> Knockback (Moderate; 20% chance)

Power Blast

> Smashing Damage (Moderate)
> Energy Damage (Moderate)
> Knockback (Moderate; 30% chance)

Energy Torrent

> Smashing Damage (Minor)
> Energy Damage (Moderate)
> Knockback (High; 60% chance)

Power Burst

Smashing Damage (Moderate)
Energy Damage (Moderate)
Knockback (High; 60% chance)

Sniper Blast

Smashing Damage (Moderate)
Energy Damage (High)
Knockback (Moderate; 50% chance)

Aim

To Hit Buff (Very High)
Add Smash Damage (Extreme)
Add Lethal Damage (Extreme)
Add Fire Damage (Extreme)
Add Cold Damage (Extreme)
Add Energy Damage (Extreme)
Add Neg.Energy Damage (Extreme)
Add Psionic Damage (Extreme)

Power Push

Smashing Damage (Minor)
Energy Damage (Minor)
Knockback (Very High)

Explosive Blast

Smashing Damage (Minor)
Energy Damage (Minor)
Knockback (High; 50% chance)

Nova

Smashing Damage (Moderate)
Energy Damage (High)
Energy Damage (Moderate; 75% chance)
Energy Damage (Moderate; 50% chance)
Knockback (Very High)
Endurance Recovery (None)
Endurance Cost (Extreme)
Stun (Very High) Mag 2

ENERGY BLAST STATS

Name	Type	Attacks (Acc)	Cost	Act	Rech	Range	Target	Enhancements
Power Bolt	Clk	Sm, En	6.0	2.0	4	80	Foe	Acc, Dam, REC, Rng, KB, Rech
Power Blast	Clk	Sm, En	9.8	1.7	8	80	Foe	Acc, Dam, Rech, REC, Rng, KB
Energy Torrent	Clk	Sm, En	13.7	1.1	12	–	Foe (40', 45° cone)	Acc, Dam, Rech, REC, KB, cone
Power Burst	Clk	Sm, En	12.0	2.0	10	20	Foe	Acc, Dam, Rech, REC, Rng, KB
Sniper Blast	Clk	Sm, En (+20% Acc)	16.6	1.3	12	150	Foe	Acc, Dam, Rech, REC, Rng, KB, Int
Aim	Clk		6.0	1.2	30	–	Self	REC, Rech, To Hit+
Power Push	Clk	Sm, En (+40% Acc)	9.8	1.1	8	70	Foe	Acc, Dam, Rech, REC, Rng, KB
Explosive Blast	Clk	Sm, En	17.5	1.7	16	80	Foe (15' sphere)	Acc, Dam, Rech, REC, Rng, KB
Nova	Clk	Sm, En (+40% Acc)	36.0	3.0	240	–	Foe (25' sphere)	Acc, Dam, Rech, REC, KB

Type: **Togl** (Toggle); **Clk** (Click)
Attacks: **Le**thal, **Sm**ash, **Fi**re, **En**ergy, **Me**lee, **NgEn** (Negative Energy), **Co**ld, **Psi**onic
Rech: Recharge Time
Enhancements: **Acc**uracy, **Dam**age, **Dmg Resist**, **Defense+** (buff), **Defense–** (debuff), **End**urance Drain, **KB** (Knockback), **REC** (Reduce Endurance Cost), **Rng** (Range), **To Hit+** (buff), **To Hit–** (debuff), **Int**errupt, and **Rech** (recharge)

FIRE BLAST

Why be a Fire Blaster?

A Fire Blaster has excellent area of effect damage.

You have moderately good range, and are able to inflict damage quickly.

You have crowd control, in a sense, with certain powers. Depending on your secondary choice of powers, however, you will most definitely have access to a power which will allow you to keep a villain in his tracks while you set them aflame.

Why not be a Fire Blaster?

You are able to dish out damage, granted. In the long run however, it is not massive damage. You will have access to very few direct damage powers, which means you will have a tough time soloing groups at the higher levels. In deciding your secondary power set, remember the soul of a Blaster is range — damage from afar is the motto.

Since you are not able to heal yourself, it can get time-consuming to stay in solo combat. If you want to go head to head with villains and be able to take out large groups with reasonable ease, then Fire Blast is not for you.

Combat. With the ability to damage entire groups of villains at one time, low-level combat will come very easy. However, at higher levels your powers can come up short if not used wisely. It is suggested you make use of whatever snare powers come in your secondary power set. For example, **Fire Blast** and **Fire Manipulation** will give you **Ring of Fire**, a snare power, meaning it will stop a foe in his tracks. Since most of your powers will cause DoT (damage over time) you will always be dealing damage.

Note: Most DoT is not high — it will range from 1-30 damage per attack, every couple of seconds

Team Ups. Often, in a team, you will be the designated puller, which means you will always be the one to take the first hit. The way you develop your Fire Blaster will determine on the best course of action to take once you pull. When you pull — and you will — do not use an AoE power such as **Fire Ball**. Instead use **Flares**, or **Fire Blast** — a direct-damage power, and very accurate. These two powers are also very quick to recharge. By the time you have used both Flares and Fire Blast, one of the two will be recharged or close to it, and ready to be unleashed once again. If you decide to choose Flight as a transportation power pool, **Hover** will become your best friend. It gives you a defense against being hit, plus it can give you a quick escape from that first hit. Nine times out of ten, you will not deal the most damage in large groups, but of course this depends on the makeup of your current team.

Power researched by Dariuas.

Fire Blast Effects

Flares

Fire Damage (Minor)
Fire Damage (Minor)

Fire Blast

Fire Damage (Moderate)
Fire Damage (Minor; 80% chance) Can Cancel

Fire Ball

Smashing Damage (Minor)
Fire Damage (Moderate)
Fire Damage (Minor; 80% chance) Can Cancel

Rain of Fire

Summons (Fire Storm)

Fire Breath

Fire Damage (Moderate)

Aim

To Hit Buff (Very High)
Add Smash Damage (Extreme)
Add Lethal Damage (Extreme)
Add Fire Damage (Extreme)
Add Cold Damage (Extreme)
Add Energy Damage (Extreme)
Add Neg.Energy Damage (Extreme)
Add Psionic Damage (Extreme)

Blaze

Fire Damage (High)
Fire Damage (Minor; 80% chance) Can
Cancel

Blazing Bolt

Fire Damage (Very High)
Fire Damage (Minor; 80% chance) Can
Cancel

Inferno

Smashing Damage (Moderate)
Fire Damage (High)

Fire Damage (Moderate; 75% chance)
Fire Damage (Moderate; 50% chance)
Fire Damage (Minor; 99% chance) Can
Cancel
Endurance Recovery (None)
Endurance Cost (Extreme)
Stun (Very High) Mag 2

FIRE BLAST STATS

Name	Type	Attacks (Acc)	Cost	Act	Rech	Range	Target	Enhancements
Flares	Clk	Fi	4.1	2.2	2.18	60	Foe	Acc, Dam, REC, Rng, Rech
Fire Blast	Clk	Fi	9.8	1.2	4	80	Foe	Acc, Dam, Rech, REC, Rng
Fire Ball	Clk	Fi	17.5	1.0	16	80	Foe (15' sphere)	Acc, Dam, Rech, REC, Rng
Rain of Fire	Clk	(+100% Acc)	30.0	2.0	60	60	Location	Rech, REC, Rng, Dam
Fire Breath	Clk	Fi (+20% Acc)	17.5	2.7	16	—	Foe (40', 30° cone)	Acc, Dam, Rech, REC, cone
Aim	Clk		6.0	1.2	30	—	Self	REC, Rech, To Hit+
Blaze	Clk	Fi	12.0	1.0	10	20	Foe	Acc, Dam, Rech, REC, Rng
Blazing Bolt	Clk	Fi (+20% Acc)	16.6	1.7	12	150	Foe	Acc, Dam, Rech, REC, Rng, Int
Inferno	Clk	Fi (+40% Acc), Sm	36.0	3.0	240	—	Foe (25' sphere)	Acc, Dam, Rech, REC

Type: Togl (Toggle); **Clk** (Click)
Attacks: Lethal, **Sm**ash, **Fi**re, **En**ergy, **Me**lee, **NgEn** (Negative Energy), **Co**ld, **Psi**onic
Rech: Recharge Time
Enhancements: Accuracy, **Dam**age, **Dmg Resist**, **Defense+** (buff), **Defense–** (debuff), **End**urance **Drain**, **KB** (Knockback), **REC** (Reduce Endurance Cost), **Rng** (Range), **To Hit+** (buff), **To Hit-** (debuff), **Int**errupt, and **Rech** (recharge)

ICE BLAST

Ice Blast is a precision power set. Your attacks are designed to shut down a foe's ability to fight back while still dealing a reasonable amount of damage. Most of your powers are meant for single targets, and your damage mostly comes from a two-fold attack of Smashing and Cold. The great side effect of this is that you also leave a lasting chill on your target, making the recharge rate for their attacks take longer.

Your first two powers, **Ice Bolt** and **Ice Blast**, both have this effect. Both are single target attacks that also lower your target's recharge rate. These two will be a great one-two punch that you'll use regularly throughout your heroic career. Combined with **Bitter Ice Blast** that you can pick up later, you can dish out a lot of damage in a hurry.

Frost Breath, is your first attack that can hit multiple targets in a cone shape in front of you. This attack does decent damage and hits several times in a short period of time.

Aim is a great power to have. It doesn't last a long time, but the ability to effectively have an Accuracy Inspiration available whenever you need it can be a life saver.

Freeze Ray is the first of your two crowd control powers. It will put your foe to Sleep by encasing him in a block of ice. Be careful, though, as any attack initiated against him will wake him up. Keep that in mind if you start an attack that takes a while to complete. Later you can get **Bitter Freeze Ray**, which not only puts your target to Sleep, but also lets you damage them without waking them.

Ice Storm is your sixth attack power. Finally, you get an area of effect attack! Initiate this attack, select where you want to aim it, and watch them run. Ice Storm is very effective if you can combine it with another attack that Slows movement, so

your foes won't have a chance to escape the full effect of the Ice Storm. **Blizzard** is your upgrade to this power, but it can leave you feeling a little dazed after using it, so be careful.

If you enjoy picking apart your opponents piece by piece, the Ice Blast power set is for you.

Power researched by Skoriksis.

Ice Blast Effects

Ice Bolt

>   Smashing Damage (Minor)
>   Cold Damage (Moderate)
>   Run Speed (Slow)
>   Fly Speed (Very Slow)
>   Recharge Time (Slowest)

Ice Blast

>   Smashing Damage (Moderate)
>   Cold Damage (Moderate)
>   Run Speed (Slow)
>   Fly Speed (Very Slow)
>   Recharge Time (Slowest)

Frost Breath

>   Cold Damage (Moderate)
>   Recharge Time (Slowest)
>   Run Speed (Slow)
>   Fly Speed (Very Slow)

Aim

>   To Hit Buff (Very High)
>   Add Smash Damage (Extreme)
>   Add Lethal Damage (Extreme)
>   Add Fire Damage (Extreme)
>   Add Cold Damage (Extreme)
>   Add Energy Damage (Extreme)
>   Add Neg.Energy Damage (Extreme)
>   Add Psionic Damage (Extreme)

Freeze Ray

Cold Damage (Minor)
Hold (High) Mag 3
Resist Knockback (Moderate)
Resist Knockup (Moderate)

Ice Storm

Summons (Ice Storm)

Bitter Ice Blast

Smashing Damage (Moderate)
Cold Damage (Moderate)
To Hit Debuff (Moderate)
Recharge Time (Slowest)
Run Speed (Slow)
Fly Speed (Very Slow)

Bitter Freeze Ray

Cold Damage (Moderate)
Recharge Time (Slowest)
Run Speed (Slow)
Fly (Very Slow)
Hold (High) Mag 3
Resist Knockback (Moderate)
Resist Knockup (Moderate)

Blizzard

Summons (Blizzard)
Endurance Recovery (None)
Endurance Cost (Extreme)
Stun (Very High) Mag 2

ICE BLAST STATS

Name	Type	Attacks (Acc)	Cost	Act	Rech	Range	Target	Enhancements
Ice Bolt	Clk	Sm, Co	6.0	1.2	4	80	Foe	Acc, Dam, Rech, REC, Rng
Ice Blast	Clk	Sm, Co	9.8	1.0	8	80	Foe	Acc, Dam, Rech, REC, Rng
Frost Breath	Clk	Co (+20% Acc)	17.5	2.7	16	40	Foe (40', 30° cone)	Acc, Dam, Rech, REC, cone
Aim	Clk		6.0	1.2	30	–	Self	REC, Rech, To Hit+
Freeze Ray	Clk	Co	7.9	1.0	10	60	Foe	Acc, Dam, Rech, REC, Rng, Hold
Ice Storm	Clk	(+100% Acc)	30.0	2.0	60	60	Location	Rech, REC, Rng, Dam, Slow
Bitter Ice Blast	Clk	Sm, Co	15.0	1.1	12	50	Foe	Acc, Dam, Rech, REC, Rng, To Hit–
Bitter Freeze Ray	Clk	Co	17.5	3.7	20	80	Foe	Acc, Dam, Rech, REC, Rng, Hold
Blizzard	Clk	(+100% Acc)	48.0	2.0	120	60	Location	Rech, REC, Rng, Dam, Slow, To Hit–

Type: Togl (Toggle); **Clk** (Click)
Attacks: **Le**thal, **Sm**ash, **Fi**re, **En**ergy, **Me**lee, **NgEn** (Negative Energy), **Cold**, **Psi**onic
Rech: Recharge Time
Enhancements: Accuracy, **Dam**age, **Dmg Resist**, **Defense+** (buff), **Defense–** (debuff), **End**urance **Drain**, **KB** (Knockback), **REC** (Reduce Endurance Cost), **Rng** (Range), **To Hit+** (buff), **To Hit-** (debuff), **Int**errupt, and **Rech** (recharge)

BLASTER SECONDARY (SUPPORT)

DEVICES

The Devices power set is for those mechanically minded Heroes. In general, this set's powers will increase your damage output, as well as Slow your foes down.

The first power you get is **Web Grenade**. You throw a grenade at a targeted foe and attempt to form a web around his feet, so he cannot run, though he can still attack while he's webbed. The Web Grenade works great in keeping foes who lack effective long-range attacks out of your hair while you finish up other foes, as well as a way to keep runners from running.

The **Caltrops** power throws a handful of caltrops at a targeted location. Any foes moving through this area will have his movement rate Slowed and also take a small amount of damage. A great tactic is to throw these between a group of foes and yourself, and then pull the foes through them.

The **Taser** power will cause a slight amount of damage, and will also cause a foe to become Disoriented. Foes will not be able to attack back during this time. This power really helps when you need to make a getaway, and it's also a good way to lower the amount of damage a foe will be able to hit you with.

Targeting Drone causes a small drone to circle your head, emitting lights and lasers to help improve the Accuracy of your attacks. While active, the drone uses Endurance. This power reduces the need for Accuracy Inspirations, freeing up those slots for other useful Inspirations.

The **Smoke Grenade** power creates an area filled with smoke around a target. Most foes within the smoke won't be able to see past melee range, unless they are attacked, and even then they'll have a harder time hitting you.

Power researched by Brent Copeland.

Cloaking Device also makes you hard to see, though you will be seen if you get too close to the enemy. With this power active, even if spotted you will still be harder to attack. You can use this power to bypass many foes to get to the final part of a mission, or just to make travel safer.

The **Trip Mine** power causes you to kneel down and set a trip mine. Any foe crossing the trip mine will set it off, doing damage to all foes nearby. You can be interrupted while trying to use this power. It is always best to set a trip mine between a group of foes and yourself. Then you can pull the foes, causing the trip mine to explode.

Time Bomb is similar to Trip Mine. It takes longer to set, but instead of going off when a foe gets into range, it has a set timer of 15 seconds. The explosion is larger than the trip mine. It is hard to get close enough to villains to make this attack effective, and it is best used either before a group of foes is pulled, or while other group members have the attention of the foes.

A good combination to use is to set a Trip Mine between yourself and a group of foes. Then, back up to max range of one of their distance attacks and start setting a Time Bomb, then pull. The foes should be knocked back from the Trip Mine blast, and give the Hero just enough time to set the Time Bomb, dealing quite a bit of area-of-effect damage.

The **Auto Turret** power places a stationary turret on the ground, which fires on any foes that come into its range. The turret is armored, but can be destroyed. It will stay in place and fire until the foe leaves the area, or it is destroyed. It is always good to protect the turret by keeping foes at bay so they cannot destroy it. The longer a turret is up, the more damage it will deal out. When a foe is in range of an auto turret, try to keep him in place with a web grenade, so he can't escape the damage.

Devices Effects

Web Grenade

Immobilize (High) Mag 3
Recharge Time (Very Slow)
Run Speed (Slower)
Fly (Slower)
Resist Knockback (Moderate)
Resist Knockup (Moderate)
Jump (Reduced)
Fly (Stopped)

Caltrops

Summons (Caltrops)

Taser

Energy Damage (Minor)
Stun (High) Mag 3

Targeting Drone

To Hit Buff (High) Can Cancel

Smoke Grenade

Perception Radius

Cloaking Device

Stealth (Moderate)
Melee Defense (Moderate)
Translucent
Ranged Defense (Moderate)

Trip Mine

Summons (Mine)

Time Bomb

Summons (Bomb)

Auto Turret

Summons (Turret)

DEVICES STATS

Name	Type	Attacks (Acc)	Cost	Act	Rech	Range	Target	Enhancements
Web Grenade	Clk	Co	9.0	1.4	4	50	Foe	Acc, Rech, REC, Immobilize, Rng
Caltrops	Clk		9.0	1.1	45	25	Location	Rech, REC, Rng, Dam, Slow
Taser	Clk	Me, Sm	11.8	1.4	20	5	Foe	Acc, Dam, Rech, REC, Stun
Targeting Drone	Togl		0.2	1.2	10	–	Self	REC, Rech, To Hit+
Smoke Grenade	Clk		9.0	1.4	15	70	Foe (35' sphere)	Rech, REC, To Hit–
Cloaking Device	Togl		0.2	0.7	20	–	Self	Rech, REC, Defense
Trip Mine	Clk		15.0	–	30	–	Self	Acc, Rech, REC, Dam, KB
Time Bomb	Clk		30.0	–	240	–	Self	Acc, Rech, REC, Dam, KB
Auto Turret	Clk		45.0	–	180	–	Location	Acc, Rech, REC, Dam,

Type: Togl (Toggle); **Clk** (Click)
Attacks: Lethal, **Sm**ash, **Fi**re, **En**ergy, **Me**lee, **NgEn** (Negative Energy), **Co**ld, **Psi**onic
Rech: Recharge Time
Enhancements: Accuracy, **Dam**age, **Dmg Resist, Defense+** (buff), **Defense–** (debuff), **End**urance **Drain, KB** (Knockback), **REC** (Reduce Endurance Cost), **Rng** (Range), **To Hit+** (buff), **To Hit-** (debuff), **Int**errupt, and **Rech** (recharge)

ELECTRICITY MANIPULATION

Arcing loops of electricity Hold your opponent tight, leaving him weakened and vulnerable to your onslaught!

Electricity Manipulation provides a multitude of abilities as a secondary power set. In the beginning it allows for Immobilization of enemies while slowly draining off their Endurance. Later it enables you to literally leech Endurance away from an adversary and transfer it to yourself. Add in Stun effects and increase damage powers, and you've got a nice addition to any Hero's arsenal.

As a Blaster, getting hit is a luxury you can rarely afford. Your ability to take damage is very limited, so what good is it to be able to dish it out if you're lying in a coma in the nearest hospital? This is where Electricity Manipulation comes into play. To start, you get **Electric Fence**, a basic target Immobilization field. This lets you keep the villain at a distance as you destroy him with your ranged powers. Does the evildoer have ranged weapons also? That's just fine; your Electric Fence is draining his Endurance as it Holds him in place. Have your opponents overwhelmed you and gotten into melee range? That's ok, too! Summon a **Lightning Field** and damage all of your attackers at once.

Later on as your powers mature, you get **Power Sink**, the ability to drain an enemy's Endurance for your own use. As your Endurance gets low, target a thug and get the boost you need to do real damage! Even further down the line, you can drain Endurance from multiple targets, powering yourself up and making them helpless at the same time. And some of the later powers have a Stun effect associated with them, against both single and multiple targets.

This power set is mainly for the Blaster Hero who envisions himself in a minor crowd control and debuff role. While it is not strong on healing, it can effectively reduce the need for healing, by

significantly reducing the damage potential of your opponent. Electricity Manipulation as a secondary power is best used by the solo Hero, or in a group that has a healer or a strong melee contingent on board.

Power researched by Wunderr.

Electricity Manipulation Effects

Electric Fence

Energy Damage (Minor)
Immobilize (High) Mag 3
End Drain (Minor)
Run Speed (Slower)
Fly (Slower)
Resist Knockback (Moderate)
Resist Knockup (Moderate)
Endurance Recovery (None; 20% chance)

Charged Brawl

Smashing Damage (Moderate)
Energy Damage (Minor)
End Drain (Minor)
Endurance Recovery (None; 20% chance)

Lightning Field

Energy Damage (Minor)
End Drain (Minor)

Havoc Punch

Smashing Damage (Moderate)
Energy Damage (Moderate)
Knockback (Moderate; 30% chance)
End Drain (Minor)
Endurance Recovery (None; 30% chance)

Build Up

To Hit Buff (High)
Add Smash Damage (Extreme)
Add Lethal Damage (Extreme)

Add Fire Damage (Extreme)
Add Cold Damage (Extreme)
Add Energy Damage (Extreme)
Add Neg.Energy Damage (Extreme)
Add Psionic Damage (Extreme)

Lightning Clap

Stun (Moderate; 50% chance) Mag 2
Knockback (Moderate)

Thunder Strike

Smashing Damage (High)
Stun (Moderate; 50% chance) Mag 3
Summons (Thunder Strike)
Knockback (High)
Endurance Recovery (None; 40% chance)

Power Sink

End Drain (Very High)
Endurance Recovery (None; 30% chance)
Endurance Bonus (Very High)

Shocking Grasp

Energy Damage (Minor)
Hold (High) Mag 3
End Drain (Minor)
Endurance Recovery (None; 50% chance)

ELECTRICITY MANIPULATION STATS

Name	Type	Attacks (Acc)	Cost	Act	Rech	Range	Target	Enhancements
Electric Fence	Clk	En	9.0	1.2	4	50	Foe	Acc, Dam, Rech, REC, Immobilize, Rng, Drain End
Charged Brawl	Clk	Me, Sm, En	6.0	0.6	4	5	Foe	Acc, Dam, Rech, REC, Stun, Drain End
Lightning Field	Togl	En	2.4	2.0	10	–	Foe (20' sphere)	Acc, Dam, Rech, REC, Drain End
Havoc Punch	Clk	Me, Sm, En	9.8	1.5	8	5	Foe	Acc, Dam, Rech, REC, Drain End, KB
Build Up	Clk		6.0	1.2	45	–	Self	REC, Rech, To Hit+
Lightning Clap	Clk	En	15.0	1.2	30	–	Foe (15' sphere)	Acc, Rech, REC, Stun, KB
Thunder Strike	Clk	Me, Sm, En	21.4	3.3	20	5	Foe	Acc, Dam, Rech, REC, Stun, KB
Power Sink	Clk	En	15.0	2.0	60	–	Foe (10' sphere)	REC, Rech, Drain End, End.Rec.
Shocking Grasp	Clk	En	21.0	1.0	15	5	Foe	Acc, Dam, Rech, REC, Hold, Drain End

Type: Togl (Toggle); **Clk** (Click)
Attacks: Lethal, **Sm**ash, **Fi**re, **En**ergy, **Me**lee, **NgEn** (Negative Energy), **Co**ld, **Psi**onic
Rech: Recharge Time
Enhancements: Accuracy, **Dam**age, **Dmg Resist**, **Defense+** (buff), **Defense–** (debuff), **End**urance **Drain**, **KB** (Knockback), **REC** (Reduce Endurance Cost), **Rng** (Range), **To Hit+** (buff), **To Hit-** (debuff), **Int**errupt, and **Rech** (recharge)

ENERGY MANIPULATION

The Energy Manipulation pool is a Hero's friend, with all its secondary effects. The majority of the secondary effects are some type of damage avoidance (either through Knockback, Disorient or Stun). Most of the damaging powers are mid-to-low damage. When you use a power from this pool, you are probably hoping to avoid taking damage, as your damage will usually come from your primary pool. Other than **Bone Smasher**, the only decent damage power in the pool, most of the powers just need Accuracy, recharge timer, and Endurance cost reduction Enhancements. Along with those, Bone Smasher deserves a damage add and Disorient duration also.

One of the nice things you can do with these effects is lightweight crowd control. Fighting in door missions or hard-to-reach spots, you can often knock an unwanted opponent off a building or terrace, so he has to waste time running back up to you while you or your team finishes off his friends. Or put a good duration Stun or Disorient on a few villains to keep the crowd at bay and buy more time. **Power Thrust**, Bone Smasher, and **Stun** work quite well for accomplishing those tasks. Solo, these abilities can make the difference between downtime and no downtime. A word of caution; having a lot of these abilities eats Endurance quickly — invest heavily in some way to reduce that cost or recover Endurance more quickly.

Non-damaging powers in this pool can have impressive effects, by increasing your damage output, reducing cost, increasing range, reducing recharge time, or some combination of those abilities. You will have to make careful choices about what powers to take from all your pools, so the more advanced powers in Energy Manipulation often get overlooked. **Conserve Power** fits in well with most pool schemes. **Boost Range** is a good all-around power, but tends to be more useful solo.

Overall, the Energy Manipulation pool is widely varied in what it can do: good damage, good self buffs, great secondary effects. The hard part is figuring out what to skip to get the powers you want.

Power researched by Praxi.

Energy Manipulation Effects

Power Thrust

Smashing Damage (Minor)
Energy Damage (Minor)
Knockback (Very High)

Energy Punch

Smashing Damage (Moderate)
Energy Damage (Minor)
Stun (Moderate; 30% chance) Mag 2

Build Up

To Hit Buff (High)
Add Smash Damage (Extreme)
Add Lethal Damage (Extreme)
Add Fire Damage (Extreme)
Add Cold Damage (Extreme)
Add Energy Damage (Extreme)
Add Neg.Energy Damage (Extreme)
Add Psionic Damage (Extreme)

Bone Smasher

Smashing Damage (Moderate)
Energy Damage (Moderate)
Stun (Moderate; 60% chance) Mag 3

Conserve Power

Stun (Moderate)

Stun

Smashing Damage (Minor)
Energy Damage (Minor)
Stun (High) Mag 3

Power Boost

Boost Stun (Moderate)
Boost Sleep (Moderate)
Boost Confused (Moderate)
Boost Fear (Moderate)
Boost Immobilize (Moderate)
Boost Hold (Moderate)
Boost Knockback (Moderate)
Boost Knockup (Moderate)
Boost Repel (Moderate)
Boost Speed (Moderate)
Boost Fly (Moderate)
Boost Defense (Moderate)
Boost Melee (Moderate)
Boost Ranged (Moderate)

Boost AoE (Moderate)
Boost Smashing (Moderate)
Boost Lethal (Moderate)
Boost Fire (Moderate)
Boost Cold (Moderate)
Boost Energy (Moderate)
Boost Neg.Energy (Moderate)
Boost Psionic (Moderate)
Boost To Hit (Moderate)
Boost Endurance (Moderate)

Boost Range

Boost Range (Moderate)

Total Focus

Smashing Damage (Moderate)
Energy Damage (Very High)
Hold (High) Mag 4
Stun (Moderate) Mag 2

ENERGY MANIPULATION STATS

Name	Type	Attacks (Acc)	Cost	Act	Rech	Range	Target	Enhancements
Power Thrust	Clk	Me, Sm, En	7.9	1.0	6	5	Foe	Acc, Dam, Rech, REC, KB
Energy Punch	Clk	Me, Sm, En	6.0	0.6	4	5	Foe	Acc, Dam, Rech, REC, Stun
Build Up	Clk		6.0	1.2	45	–	Self	REC, Rech, To Hit+
Bone Smasher	Clk	Me, Sm, En	9.8	1.5	8	5	Foe	Acc, Dam, Rech, REC, Stun
Conserve Power	Clk		9.0	1.2	600	–	Self	REC, Rech
Stun	Clk	Me, Sm, En	11.8	1.8	20	5	Foe	Acc, Dam, Rech, REC, Stun
Power Boost	Clk		9.0	1.2	60	–	Self	REC, Rech
Boost Range	Clk		15.0	1.2	60	–	Self	REC, Rech
Total Focus	Clk	Me, Sm, En	21.4	3.3	20	5	Foe	Acc, Dam, Rech, REC, Hold

Type: Togl (Toggle); **Clk** (Click)
Attacks: Lethal, **Sm**ash, **Fi**re, **En**ergy, **Me**lee, **NgEn** (Negative Energy), **Co**ld, **Psi**onic
Rech: Recharge Time
Enhancements: Accuracy, **Dam**age, **Dmg Resist**, **Defense+** (buff), **Defense–** (debuff), **End**urance **Drain**, **KB** (Knockback), **REC** (Reduce Endurance Cost), **Rng** (Range), **To Hit+** (buff), **To Hit-** (debuff), **Int**errupt, and **Rech** (recharge)

FIRE MANIPULATION

Even a good Blaster can't keep all of the villains at bay forever. Sooner or later, you're going to get caught in some tight quarters and be face-to-face with a guy wielding a sledgehammer and bad intentions, so you're going to need some up close and personal protection.

Fire Manipulation has some nice advantages to give you a little help when you have to fight in close quarters, plus a couple of ranged abilities thrown in as well.

First of all, one of the greatest things about fire is that it burns. Many of these powers not only have an initial effect, but can burn your foes for a little extra damage after first contact. That little bit of extra damage over time can be just the edge you need.

Many of the powers have a point-blank area of effect that allows you to dish out damage to multiple enemies at the same time. A few of the powers are used as single-target powers, but definitely have their uses. As a Blaster, the last thing you really want is to be completely surrounded by enemies.

Ring of Fire is invaluable for helping to put some distance between you and a foe, or perhaps stop a purse snatcher from getting away. It's also great for helping to thin out multiple enemies that are chasing you, as

well as providing a little extra damage. This is one power that you will keep using for a long time.

Fire Sword is another valuable tool when you need to dish out some good damage to a villain right in front of you. It also allows for a very quick one-two combo with Brawl.

Combustion and **Fire Sword Circle** are basically the same, except that Fire Sword Circle does more damage, while Combustion has better range and recharge rate. Both powers are nice for hitting multiple enemies at the same time.

Build Up is another excellent power. It is like having access to a Damage Inspiration whenever the power is charged up. Excellent for helping to enhance your primary Blaster skills! While it might not last a long time, the damage increase is well worth it against bosses and lieutenants.

Add in **Consume, Burn** and **Hot Feet,** and you have a well rounded set of defensive powers.

Power researched by Skoriksis.

Fire Manipulation Effects

Ring of Fire

Fire Damage (Minor)
Immobilize (High) Mag 3
Resist Knockback (Moderate)
Resist Knockup (Moderate)

Fire Sword

Lethal Damage (Minor)
Fire Damage (Moderate)
Fire Damage (Minor; 80% chance) Can Cancel

Combustion

Fire Damage (Minor)

Fire Sword Circle

Lethal Damage (Moderate)
Fire Damage (Moderate)
Fire Damage (Minor; 80% chance) Can
Cancel

Build Up

To Hit Buff (High)
Add Smash Damage (Extreme)
Add Lethal Damage (Extreme)
Add Fire Damage (Extreme)
Add Cold Damage (Extreme)
Add Energy Damage (Extreme)
Add Neg.Energy Damage (Extreme)
Add Psionic Damage (Extreme)

Blazing Aura

Fire Damage (Minor)

Consume

Fire Damage (Minor)
Endurance Bonus (High)

Burn

Summons (Burn)
Resist Immobilize (Moderate)

Hot Feet

Fire Damage (Minor; 75% chance)
Fear (Moderate) Mag 3
Run Speed (Slower)

FIRE MANIPULATION STATS

Name	Type	Attacks (Acc)	Cost	Act	Rech	Range	Target	Enhancements
Ring of Fire	Clk	Fi	9.0	1.2	4	50	Foe	Acc, Dam, Rech, REC, Immobilize, Rng
Fire Sword	Clk	Me, Le, Fi	7.9	1.8	6	5	Foe	Acc, Dam, REC, Rech
Combustion	Clk	Fi	10.2	3.0	12	–	Foe (15' sphere)	Acc, Dam, REC, Rech
Fire Sword Circle	Clk	Me, Fi, Le	21.4	4.2	20	–	Foe (10' sphere)	Acc, Dam, Rech, REC
Build Up	Clk		6.0	1.2	45	–	Self	REC, Rech, To Hit+
Blazing Aura	Togl	Fi	1.8	2.0	2	–	Foe (8' sphere)	Acc, Rech, REC, Dam
Consume	Clk	Fi	0.6	2.0	180	–	Foe (20' sphere)	Acc, Rech, REC, Dam, End.Rec.
Burn	Clk	(+100% Acc)	18.0	2.0	4	–	Location	REC, Rech, Dam
Hot Feet	Togl	Fi	2.4	1.5	20	–	Foe (20' sphere)	Dam, Rech, REC, Slow

Type: Togl (Toggle); **Clk** (Click)
Attacks: Lethal, **Sm**ash, **Fi**re, **En**ergy, **Me**lee, **NgEn** (Negative Energy), **Co**ld, **Psi**onic
Rech: Recharge Time
Enhancements: Accuracy, **Dam**age, **Dmg Resist**, **Defense+** (buff), **Defense−** (debuff), **End**urance **Drain**, **KB** (Knockback), **REC** (Reduce Endurance Cost), **Rng** (Range), **To Hit+** (buff), **To Hit-** (debuff), **Int**errupt, and **Rech** (recharge)

ICE MANIPULATION

Ice Manipulation is mostly a defensive power set. While some of the powers can inflict decent damage, most are meant to Slow down your opponents and give you enough time to either finish them off or at least put some distance between you and them.

Chilblain is the first power in the set, and it's a must-have! It stops the villain dead in his tracks. And while he can still shoot at you, he won't be moving in any closer.

Frozen Fists and **Ice Sword** are the two damage-dealing powers you have in this set. Both require you to be in melee range and both slow the recharge rate of your foe.

Chilling Embrace is nice, because you can constantly leave it on, since it doesn't drain too much Endurance. It helps Slow down the movement and recharge rate of anyone who's foolish enough to get close to you.

Build Up will temporarily boost your damage output and slightly raise your Accuracy. It works great in conjunction with your damaging powers.

Ice Patch is a lifesaver, and it has so many uses! It forms a patch of ice under you that can cause any foe walking over it to fall down. It's great to use in small corridors, placing it down, then taking a few steps back and pulling your enemy through it. This gives you some extra time and some free hits. Just be sure that your feet are on the ground when you use this power, as it won't work if you're airborne.

Shiver is another great power to have. Use it to Slow down a group of foes' movement and recharge rate, and then unleash an AoE attack on them. It keeps them from running out of range as fast!

Freezing Touch and **Frozen Aura** will help keep foes under control, but you'll need to be within melee range to use them.

Ice Manipulation is a great power set to have to give you some control over your foes and give you that extra time to dish out some major damage with your primary power set.

Power researched by Skoriksis.

Ice Manipulation Effects

Chilblain

Cold Damage (Minor)
Immobilize (High) Mag 3
Run Speed (Very Slow)
Fly (Very Slow)
Recharge Time (Slowest)
Resist Knockback (Moderate)
Resist Knockup (Moderate)
Fly (Stopped)

Frozen Fists

Smashing Damage (Minor)
Cold Damage (Moderate)
Run Speed (Slower)
Fly Speed (Very Slow)
Recharge Time (Slowest)

Ice Sword

Lethal Damage (Minor)
Cold Damage (Moderate)

Run Speed (Slower)
Fly Speed (Very Slow)
Recharge Time (Slowest)

Chilling Embrace

Run Speed (Slow)
Recharge Time (Slow)
Fly (Slow)

Build Up

To Hit Buff (High)
Add Smash Damage (Extreme)
Add Lethal Damage (Extreme)
Add Fire Damage (Extreme)
Add Cold Damage (Extreme)
Add Energy Damage (Extreme)
Add Neg.Energy Damage (Extreme)
Add Psionic Damage (Extreme)

Ice Patch

Summons (Ice Patch)

Shiver

Recharge Time (Slower)
Run Speed (Slower)
Fly (Slower)

Freezing Touch

Cold Damage (Minor)
Hold (High) Mag 3
Resist Knockback (Moderate)
Resist Knockup (Moderate)

Frozen Aura

Sleep (Very High) Mag 2

ICE MANIPULATION STATS

Name	Type	Attacks (Acc)	Cost	Act	Rech	Range	Target	Enhancements
Chilblain	Clk	Co	9.0	1.2	4	50	Foe	Acc, Dam, Rech, REC, Immobilize, Rng
Frozen Fists	Clk	Co, Me, Sm	5.0	1.3	3	5	Foe	Acc, Dam, REC, Slow, Rech
Ice Sword	Clk	Me, Le, Co	7.9	1.8	6	5	Foe	Acc, Dam, REC, Slow, Rech
Chilling Embrace	Togl	Co	0.2	0.7	2	—	Foe (10' sphere)	REC, Rech
Build Up	Clk		6.0	1.2	45	—	Self	REC, Rech, To Hit+
Ice Patch	Clk	(+100% Acc)	12.0	2.0	35	—	Self	Rech, REC
Shiver	Clk	Co	12.0	2.2	12	—	Foe (60', 135° cone)	Acc, Rech, REC, cone, Slow
Freezing Touch	Clk	Me, Co	11.8	1.0	10	5	Foe	Acc, Dam, Rech, REC, Hold
Frozen Aura	Clk		15.0	2.1	20		Foe (10' sphere)	Acc, Sleep, Rech, REC

Type: Togl (Toggle); **Clk** (Click)
Attacks: Lethal, **Sm**ash, **Fi**re, **En**ergy, **Me**lee, **NgEn** (Negative Energy), **Co**ld, **Psi**onic
Rech: Recharge Time
Enhancements: Accuracy, **Dam**age, **Dmg Resist**, **Defense+** (buff), **Defense–** (debuff), **End**urance **Drain**, **KB** (Knockback), **REC** (Reduce Endurance Cost), **Rng** (Range), **To Hit+** (buff), **To Hit-** (debuff), **Int**errupt, and **Rech** (recharge)

CONTROLLER PRIMARY (CONTROL)

EARTH CONTROL

Put your Accuracy Enhancements into **Stone Cages**, **Salt Crystals** and **Stalagmites** to affect as many foes as possible with these AoE powers.

If you're a solo player, invest in **Salt Crystals**, but this power is hard to use without coordination in a team with lots of AoE damage powers.

Volcanic Gasses can be very powerful. Be sure to pump lots of Hold Enhancements into this one. Since only some of the targets will be held some of the time, putting Hold Enhancements in Volcanic Gases will cause the Holds to overlap and Hold more targets at once .

Earthquake is great for placing at bottlenecks like doorways.

Get **Animate Stone** as soon as possible. Enhancements in this power are passed along to the stone golem.

Earth Control Effects

Stone Prison

Smashing Damage (Minor)
Immobilize (High) Mag 4
Resist Knockback (Moderate)
Resist Knockup (Moderate)
Defense Debuff (High)
Fly (Stopped)

Fossilize

Hold (High; 20% chance) Mag 1
Defense Debuff (High)
Smashing Damage (Moderate)

Stone Cages

Smashing Damage (Minor)
Immobilize (High; 50% chance) Mag 1
Resist Knockback (Moderate)
Resist Knockup (Moderate)
Defense Debuff (High)
Fly (Stopped)

Quicksand

Summons (Quicksand)

Salt Crystals

Sleep (High) Mag 3
Sleep (High; 50% chance) Mag 1

Stalagmites

Stun (High) Mag 3
Lethal Damage (Minor)
Stun (Moderate; 50% chance) Mag 1

Earthquake

Summons (Earthquake)

Volcanic Gasses

Summons (Volcanic Gasses)

Animate Stone

Summons (Animate Stone)

EARTH CONTROL STATS

Name	Type	Attacks (Acc)	Cost	Act	Rech	Range	Target	Enhancements
Stone Prison	Clk	Sm (+20% Acc)	11.3	1.9	4	80	Foe	Acc, Dam, Rech, REC, Rng, Immobilize
Fossilize	Clk	(+20% Acc)	12.3	2.1	8	80	Foe	Acc, Rech, REC, Rng, Hold, Dam
Stone Cages	Clk	Sm (-10% Acc)	22.5	2.8	8	80	Foe (30' sphere)	Acc, Dam, Rech, REC, Rng, Immobilize
Quicksand	Clk		60.0	3.1	45	60	Location	Rech, REC, Rng, Slow
Salt Crystals	Clk	(-20% Acc)	22.5	1.1	45	–	Foe (30' sphere)	Acc, Rech, REC, Sleep
Stalagmites	Clk	Le (-20% Acc)	15.0	2.1	45	70	Foe (25' sphere)	Acc, Rech, REC, Rng, Stun, Dam
Earthquake	Clk		15.0	2.0	45	60	Location	Rech, REC, Rng, KB, Defense–, To Hit–
Volcanic Gasses	Clk		45.0	1.2	120	60	Location	Rech, REC, Rng, Dam, Hold
Animate Stone	Clk		37.5	3.2	240	60	Location	Rech, REC, Rng, Stun, Dam, KB, Acc

Type: Togl (Toggle); **Clk** (Click)
Attacks: Lethal, **Sm**ash, **Fi**re, **En**ergy, **Me**lee, **NgEn** (Negative Energy), **Co**ld, **Psi**onic
Rech: Recharge Time
Enhancements: Accuracy, **Dam**age, **Dmg Resist**, **Defense+** (buff), **Defense–** (debuff), **End**urance Drain, **KB** (Knockback), **REC** (Reduce Endurance Cost), **Rng** (Range), **To Hit+** (buff), **To Hit-** (debuff), **Int**errupt, and **Rech** (recharge)

FIRE CONTROL

Put your Accuracy Enhancements into **Fire Cages**, **Flashfire** and **Cinders** to affect as many foes as possible with these AoE powers.

 If you're a solo player, invest in **Smoke**, but this power is hard to use without coordination in a team with lots of AoE damage powers.

Putting too many Slow boosts into **Hot Feet** will assure more damage, but will effectively negate the Fear effect.

Bonfire is great for placing at congested bottle-necks like doorways.

Get **Fire Imps** as soon as possible. Enhancements in this power are passed along to the Imp.

Fire Control Effects

Ring of Fire

Fire Damage (Minor)
Immobilize (High; 20% chance) Mag 1
Resist Knockback (Moderate)
Resist Knockup (Moderate)

Char

Hold (High; 20% chance) Mag 1
Fire Damage (Minor)

Fire Cages

Fire Damage (Minor)
Immobilize (High) Mag 3
Resist Knockback (Moderate)
Resist Knockup (Moderate)

Smoke

Perception Radius

Hot Feet

Fire Damage (Minor; 75% chance)
Fear (Moderate) Mag 3
Run Speed (Slower)

Flashfire

Fire Damage (Minor)
Stun (High) Mag 3
Stun (Moderate; 50% chance) Mag 1

Cinders

Hold (Very High) Mag 3
Hold (High; 50% chance) Mag 1

Bonfire

Summons (Bonfire)

Fire Imps

Summons (Fire Imps)

FIRE CONTROL STATS

Name	Type	Attacks (Acc)	Cost	Act	Rech	Range	Target	Enhancements
Ring of Fire	Clk	Fi (+20% Acc)	11.3	1.2	4	80	Foe	Acc, Dam, Rech, REC, Rng, Immobilize
Char	Clk	Fi (+20% Acc)	12.3	1.1	8	80	Foe	Acc, Rech, REC, Rng, Hold, Dam
Fire Cages	Clk	Fi (-10% Acc)	22.5	1.0	8	80	Foe (30' sphere)	Acc, Dam, Rech, REC, Rng, Immobilize
Smoke	Clk		11.3	1.2	15	80	Foe (35' sphere)	Rech, REC, To Hit–
Hot Feet	Togl	Fi	3.0	1.5	20	–	Foe (20' sphere)	Dam, Rech, REC, Slow
Flashfire	Clk	Fi (-20% Acc)	22.5	2.4	45	70	Foe (25' sphere)	Acc, Dam, Rech, REC, Rng, Stun
Cinders	Clk		22.5	1.1	120	–	Foe (30' sphere)	Acc, Rech, REC, Rng, Hold
Bonfire	Clk	(+100% Acc)	18.8	3.1	60	70	Location	Rech, REC, Rng, Dam, KB
Fire Imps	Clk	(+100% Acc)	37.5	2.0	240	60	Location	Rech, REC, Rng, Dam, Acc

Type: **Togl** (Toggle); **Clk** (Click)
Attacks: **Le**thal, **Sm**ash, **Fi**re, **En**ergy, **Me**lee, **NgEn** (Negative Energy), **Co**ld, **Psi**onic
Rech: Recharge Time
Enhancements: **Acc**uracy, **Dam**age, **Dmg Resist**, **Defense+** (buff), **Defense–** (debuff), **End**urance **Drain**, **KB** (Knockback), **REC** (Reduce Endurance Cost), **Rng** (Range), **To Hit+** (buff), **To Hit-** (debuff), **Int**errupt, and **Rech** (recharge)

GRAVITY CONTROL

Control is everything. Gravity gives you many options to Hold an enemy in place without his being able to counterstrike. This Hold does not break as he takes damage, like some other forms of control.

With good Hold Duration Enhancements you can actually keep more than one opponent completely neutralized while your group fights other enemies. And while they are held, you are actually contributing damage to the battle at the same time.

With Gravity control … you get to throw forklifts and cars! I mean, how cool is that? You can throw cars!

Put your Accuracy Enhancements into **Crushing Field** and **Gravity Distortion Field** to affect as many foes as possible with these area of effect powers.

You have powers in this set that alleviate the need for some of the abilities you would normally have to assign pool power slots to. Namely, you can make an ally intangible, and you can summon your group to you.

Dimension Shift is no good to the solo player, but a great power to rescue allies in trouble.

Fold Space is the ultimate regrouping power and can rescue a fallen Teammate who is deep in enemy territory. Combined with another Hero who can teleport allies, this power can be used to coordinate effective hit and run tactics (everyone in — BAM — everyone out).

Wormhole can be used to remove a troublesome villain from an encounter.

Gravity Control Effects

Crush

Smashing Damage (Minor)
Immobilize (High; 20% chance) Mag 1
Run Speed (Slower)
Fly (Slower)
Fly (Stopped)

Lift

Knockup (Moderate)
Smashing Damage (Moderate)
Fly (Stopped)

Gravity Distortion

Hold (Very High) Mag 3
Hold (High; 20% chance) Mag 1
Smashing Damage (Minor)
Run Speed (Slower)
Fly (Slower)
Resist Knockback (Moderate)
Resist Knockup (Moderate)

Propel

Smashing Damage (Moderate)
Knockback (High)

Crushing Field

Smashing Damage (Minor)
Immobilize (High; 50% chance) Mag 1
Run Speed (Slower)
Fly (Stopped)

Dimension Shift

Translucent
Stealth (Moderate)
Intangible (Moderate) Mag 3
Untouchable (Moderate) Mag 3

Gravity Distortion Field

Hold (Very High) Mag 3
Hold (High; 50% chance) Mag 1
Run Speed (Slower)
Fly (Slower)
Resist Knockback (Moderate)
Resist Knockback (Moderate)

Fold Space

Translucent
Teleport

Wormhole

Translucent
Teleport Mag 3
Stun (High) Mag 3
Knockback (Very High)

GRAVITY CONTROL STATS

Name	Type	Attacks (Acc)	Cost	Act	Rech	Range	Target	Enhancements
Crush	Clk	Sm (+20% Acc)	11.3	3.1	4	80	Foe	Acc, Dam, REC, Rng, Immobilize, Rech
Lift	Clk	Sm	9.9	1.0	6	80	Foe	Acc, Dam, Rech, REC, Rng, KB
Gravity Distortion	Clk	Sm (+20% Acc)	12.3	3.2	8	80	Foe	Acc, Rech, REC, Rng, Hold, Dam
Propel	Clk	Sm	13.5	3.5	8	60	Foe	Acc, Dam, Rech, REC, Rng, KB
Crushing Field	Clk	Sm (-10% Acc)	22.5	3.1	8	80	Foe (30' sphere)	Acc, Dam, Rech, REC, Rng, Immobilize
Dimension Shift	Clk		30.0	1.2	30	30	Ally	Rech, REC, Rng, Intangible
Gravity Distortion Field	Clk	(-20% Acc)	22.5	3.2	120	80	Foe (20' sphere)	Acc, Rech, REC, Rng, Hold
Fold Space	Clk		71.3	1.9	60	—	Ally (10000' sphere)	Rech, REC, Rng
Wormhole	Clk		22.5	3.0	20	60	Foe	Acc, Rech, REC, Rng, KB, Stun

Type: **Togl** (Toggle); **Clk** (Click)
Attacks: **Le**thal, **Sm**ash, **Fi**re, **En**ergy, **Me**lee, **NgEn** (Negative Energy), **Co**ld, **Psi**onic
Rech: Recharge Time
Enhancements: **Acc**uracy, **Dam**age, **Dmg Resist**, **Defense+** (buff), **Defense−** (debuff), **End**urance Drain, **KB** (Knockback), **REC** (Reduce Endurance Cost), **Rng** (Range), **To Hit+** (buff), **To Hit−** (debuff), **Int**errupt, and **Rech** (recharge)

ICE CONTROL

Put your Accuracy Enhancements into **Frostbite**, **Shiver**, **Flash Freeze** and **Glacier**, to affect as many foes as possible with these AoE powers.

If you're a solo player, invest in **Flash Freeze**, but this power is hard to use without coordination in a team with lots of AoE damage powers.

Arctic Air can be a bread and butter Defense Buff. Put lots of Buff Defense Enhancements in this one.

Pumping lots of Slow Enhancements into **Shiver** can turn this power into a quasi-Cone Hold attack on your enemy.

Ice Slick is great for placing at congested bottlenecks like doorways.

Get **Jack Frost** as soon as possible. Enhancements in this power are passed along to the Jack.

Ice Control Effects

Chilblain

Cold Damage (Minor)
Immobilize (High; 20% chance) Mag 4
Run Speed (Very Slow)
Fly (Very Slow)
Recharge Time (Slowest)
Resist Knockback (Moderate)
Resist Knockup (Moderate)
Fly (Stopped)

Block of Ice

Hold (Very High; 20% chance) Mag 3
Run Speed (Very Slow)
Fly (Very Slow)
Recharge Time (Very Slow)
Resist Knockback (Moderate)
Resist Knockup (Moderate)
Cold Damage (Moderate)

Frostbite

- Cold Damage (Minor)
- Immobilize (High; 50% chance) Mag 3
- Run Speed (Very Slow)
- Fly (Very Slow)
- Recharge Time (Slowest)
- Resist Knockback (Moderate)
- Resist Knockup (Moderate)
- Fly (Stopped)

Arctic Air

- Stealth (High)
- Melee Defense (Moderate)
- Ranged Defense (Moderate)
- Run Speed (Very Slow)
- Fly (Very Slow)

Shiver

- Recharge Time (Slower)
- Run Speed (Slower)
- Fly (Slower)

Ice Slick

- Summons

Flash Freeze

- Lethal Damage (Minor)
- Cold Damage (Minor)
- Sleep (High; 50% chance) Mag 3

Glacier

- Hold (Very High) Mag 3
- Hold (High; 50% chance) Mag 1
- Resist Knockback (Moderate)
- Resist Knockup (Moderate)
- Run Speed (Slower)
- Fly (Slower)
- Recharge Time (Very Slow)

Jack Frost

- Summons (Jack Frost)

ICE CONTROL STATS

Name	Type	Attacks (Acc)	Cost	Act	Rech	Range	Target	Enhancements
Chilblain	Clk	Co (+20% Acc)	11.3	1.2	4	80	Foe	Acc, Dam, Rech, REC, Rng, Immobilize
Block of Ice	Clk	Co (+20% Acc)	12.3	1.9	8	80	Foe	Acc, Rech, REC, Rng, Hold, Dam
Frostbite	Clk	Co (-10% Acc)	22.5	2.1	8	80	Foe (30' sphere)	Acc, Dam, Rech, REC, Rng, Immobilize
Arctic Air	Togl		0.3	2.0	15	–	Hero/Self (40' sphere)	Rech, REC, Defense
Shiver	Clk		15.0	2.2	12	–	Foe (60', 135° cone)	Acc, Rech, REC, cone, Slow
Ice Slick	Clk		15.0	3.1	45	60	Location	Rech, REC, Rng
Flash Freeze	Clk	Co (-20% Acc)	22.5	2.4	45	60	Foe (25' sphere)	Acc, Dam, Rech, REC, Rng, Sleep
Glacier	Clk	(-20% Acc)	22.5	2.0	120	–	Foe (30' sphere)	Acc, Rech, REC, Hold
Jack Frost	Clk		37.5	1.9	240	60	Location	Rech, REC, Rng, Hold, Dam, Acc

Type: Togl (Toggle); **Clk** (Click)
Attacks: Lethal, **Sm**ash, **Fi**re, **En**ergy, **Me**lee, **NgEn** (Negative Energy), **Cold**, **Psi**onic
Rech: Recharge Time
Enhancements: Accuracy, **Dam**age, **Dmg Resist**, **Defense+** (buff), **Defense–** (debuff), **End**urance **Drain**, **KB** (Knockback), **REC** (Reduce Endurance Cost), **Rng** (Range), **To Hit+** (buff), **To Hit-** (debuff), **Int**errupt, and **Rech** (recharge)

ILLUSION CONTROL

Illusion Controllers play differently from any other Controller power set. Most of the damage you deal out is all in your target's mind — soon, they realize that they aren't really severely wounded, and most of the "damage" melts away. While your attacks may do more than many other Controller attacks, you'd better finish your foe quickly. So, why pick an Illusion Controller? If you're willing to pay your dues, you become arguably the "flashiest" Controller, with the best solo ability at high levels.

Unlike other Controllers, who get multiple powers to control whole groups of foes at once, your only AoE power, **Flash**, is on a long timer. You need a secondary power set that will give you more crowd control options. Good choices for this are Storm Summoning and Kinetics. As you get into the higher levels, you will have to be a crowd control expert, whether in a group of players or for your "pets."

Blind and Flash can't be cancelled by other players' attacks. Use this to sell yourself to groups. At Level 18 you gain access to your first "pet power" — **Phantom Army**. Phantom Army summons two to four temporary illusions to attack your foes. You now have your own temporary "group" — run crowd control for them like you would a regular team up.

Fire, Ice and Earth Controllers get a single pet at Level 32. You'll be getting your second pet then — **Phantasm**. Phantasm is a long-term pet that will summon intangible duplicates of itself during battle. Where the Phantom Army is indestructible, Phantasm can be healed, buffed — and killed! Since Phantasm can be targeted, you can use Teleport Friend on it to help it through indoor missions or plant it in a group of enemies without getting into aggro range yourself.

With both pet powers, you should be able to solo groups of white minions with yellow and orange Lieutenants, or even take out pairs of purple foes, … or even two orange bosses with some difficulty. If you plan to stick with it, an Illusion Controller is worth the early pain.

Here's the run-down on the Illusion powers:

Spectral Wounds. Spectral Wounds convinces the target he has taken severe damage. Most of this is in his mind, and about 1/3 of the damage soon fades away. Finish the job before that happens. This is your main damage power until Level 18.

Blind. Blind renders the enemy helpless and stationary, unable to react to attacks. When you finish the tutorial, you should take Blind as your next power. This and Spectral Wounds will be your "one-two" punch.

Deceive. This tricks an enemy into attacking his friends. While useful for thinning a large group of foes, you get no experience for the damage or kills the deceived enemy does.

Flash. An upgraded Blind, Flash is another often-used power. Flash has the chance to lock down every enemy near you, but it requires you to get close to the enemy group for it to work.

Superior Invisibility. A toggled power, Invisibility continually drains Endurance, but makes you almost impossible to detect. While invisible, you cannot attack or affect others at all.

Group Invisibility. Also a toggled power, it makes your teammates invisible, but does not affect you yourself. Even if detected, invisible teammates are much harder to hit.

Phantom Army. This is where becoming an Illusion Controller starts to pay off. This power summons a short-lived group of 2 to 4 indestructible decoys that spectacularly attack your enemies. Like Spectral Wounds, most of the damage is illusory, fading within a few seconds, but the phantoms can often take down even-level foes before it wears off. Both Phantom Army and the later Phantasm are independent pets. They will follow you, but cannot be commanded.

Spectral Terror. A stationary "pet" that will cause foes to flee in terror. This power will activate Fear powers at any enemy in the vicinity as long as it is still active.

Phantasm. The top Illusion power, and worth it! The Phantasm is a long-term pet that can be healed, buffed, even teleported, attacking your foes with force powers. It will summon intangible clones to assist in the battle, but they quickly fade. Unlike Phantom Army, the Phantasm (but not its clones) can be killed. Most of the damage done, as with many other Illusion powers, is all "in the mind," and will fade after a short time.

Power researched by Steven Cochran.

Illusion Control Effects

Spectral Wounds

Psionic Damage (High)

Blind

Hold (High) Mag 3
Hold (Moderate; 20% chance) Mag 1
Psionic Damage (Moderate)
Summons

Deceive

Confusion (20% chance) Mag 3

Flash

Hold (Very High; 50% chance) Mag 3

Superior Invisibility

Stealth (Extreme)
Melee Defense (High)
Ranged Defense (High)
Translucent

Group Invisibility

Stealth (Very High)
Melee Defense (Moderate)
Ranged Defense (Moderate)
Translucent

Phantom Army

Summons (Decoys)

Spectral Terror

Summons (Spectral Terror)

Phantasm

Summons (Phantasm)

ILLUSION CONTROL STATS

Name	Type	Attacks (Acc)	Cost	Act	Rech	Range	Target	Enhancements
Spectral Wounds	Clk	Psi (+10% Acc)	9.9	1.1	6	80	Foe	Acc, Dam, Rech, REC, Rng
Blind	Clk	Psi (+10% Acc)	12.3	1.7	9	80	Foe	Acc, Dam, REC, Rng, Sleep, Rech, Hold
Deceive	Clk	(+20% Acc)	12.3	5.9	8	80	Foe	Acc, Rech, REC, Rng, Confuse
Flash	Clk	(-20% Acc)	22.5	3.0	120	—	Foe (30' sphere)	Acc, Rech, REC, Hold
Superior Invisibility	Togl		0.8	0.7	15	—	Self	REC, Rech, Defense
Group Invisibility	Clk		15.0	2.0	240	—	Ally/Self (25' sphere)	REC, Rech, Defense
Phantom Army	Clk		37.5	3.1	240	80	Location	Rech, REC, Rng, Dam, Acc
Spectral Terror	Clk		24.0	3.2	45	60	Location	Rech, REC, Rng, Fear, Acc
Phantasm	Clk		37.5	2.0	240	60	Location	Rech, REC, Rng, Dam, KB, Flying, Acc

Type: Togl (Toggle); **Clk** (Click)
Attacks: Lethal, **Sm**ash, **Fi**re, **En**ergy, **Me**lee, **NgEn** (Negative Energy), **Co**ld, **Psi**onic
Rech: Recharge Time
Enhancements: Accuracy, **Dam**age, **Dmg Resist**, **Defense+** (buff), **Defense–** (debuff), **End**urance **Drain**, **KB** (Knockback), **REC** (Reduce Endurance Cost), **Rng** (Range), **To Hit+** (buff), **To Hit-** (debuff), **Int**errupt, and **Rech** (recharge)

CITY OF HEROES

MIND CONTROL

The Mind Control primary power set uses mental powers to control the will of your foes. You will be able to render your victims useless in combat, or even have them fight on your side.

Mesmerize is one of the first powers you can get. This power will damage the target slightly, and then put him to Sleep for a short duration, or until he's attacked.

Levitate will be your primary attack power. It lifts a target into the air, dropping him to the ground and causing damage. This power does not work on flying foes.

You can grant the power of flight to a targeted ally with the **Telekinesis** power. The power can be interrupted if you're attacked.

One of the best powers in the set is **Dominate**. This power will be used quite a bit. You can dominate the target with this power and render him helpless. Attacking a foe that is affected by this power will not wake him up. This power also causes damage, so it is possible to activate it over and over on the same target and take him out without ever letting him fight back.

Mass Hypnosis works like Mesmerize. It will put a group of foes to Sleep in a small area. If they are attacked, they will wake up. It has a long duration. This power causes no damage.

Confuse will cause a targeted foe to start attacking other foes close by. The amount of experience you will get for defeating the foe under attack will go down in proportion to how much damage the Confused foe deals. You can use this power to get through entire missions, or even defeat a difficult boss.

Total Domination is the AoE version of the power Dominate.

Terrify can be used to send foes running. It is a cone-effect power affecting only foes that are in front of you.

Mass Confusion is the area of effect version of Confuse. You can clear out large areas of foes with this power. Once again, you will get less experience for every point of damage a foe does to another foe. If a foe kills another foe, you get no experience for that kill.

Power researched by Brent Copeland.

Mind Control Effects

Mesmerize

Sleep (Very High) Mag 3
Psionic Damage (Moderate)
Sleep (High; 20% chance) Mag 1

Levitate

Knockup (Moderate)
Smashing Damage (Moderate)
Fly (Stopped)

Dominate

Hold (Very High; 20% chance) Mag 3
Psionic Damage (Moderate)

Confuse

Confusion (20% chance) Mag 3

Mass Hypnosis

Sleep (High; 50% chance) Mag 3

Telekinesis

Fly

Total Domination

Hold (Very High; 50% chance) Mag 3

Terrify

Fear (Very High; 20% chance) Mag 3

Mass Confusion

Confusion (50% chance) Mag 3

MIND CONTROL STATS

Name	Type	Attacks (Acc)	Cost	Act	Rech	Range	Target	Enhancements
Mesmerize	Clk	Psi (+10% Acc)	7.5	1.7	6	100	Foe	Acc, Dam, REC, Rng, Sleep
Levitate	Clk		9.9	1.9	6	80	Foe	Acc, Dam, Rech, REC, Rng, KB
Dominate	Clk	Psi (+20% Acc)	12.3	1.1	8	80	Foe	Acc, Rech, REC, Rng, Hold, Dam
Confuse	Clk	(+20% Acc)	12.3	5.9	8	80	Foe	Acc, Rech, REC, Rng, Confuse
Mass Hypnosis	Clk	(-20% Acc)	22.5	2.0	45	80	Foe (25' sphere)	Acc, Rech, REC, Rng, Sleep
Telekinesis	Togl		0.6	0.3	20	5000	Ally	Rech, REC, Rng
Total Domination	Clk	(-20% Acc)	22.5	2.0	120	80	Foe (20' sphere)	Acc, Rech, REC, Rng, Hold
Terrify	Clk	(-10% Acc)	30.0	2.0	20	60	Foe (60', 90° cone)	Acc, Rech, REC, Rng, Fear, To Hit–, cone
Mass Confusion	Clk	(-20% Acc)	37.5	1.7	240	80	Foe (25' sphere)	Acc, Rech, REC, Rng, Confuse

Type: Togl (Toggle); **Clk** (Click)
Attacks: Lethal, **Sm**ash, **Fi**re, **En**ergy, **Me**lee, **NgEn** (Negative Energy), **Co**ld, **Psi**onic
Rech: Recharge Time
Enhancements: Accuracy, **Dam**age, **Dmg Resist**, **Defense+** (buff), **Defense–** (debuff), **End**urance **Drain**, **KB** (Knockback), **REC** (Reduce Endurance Cost), **Rng** (Range), **To Hit+** (buff), **To Hit-** (debuff), **Int**errupt, and **Rech** (recharge)

CONTROLLER SECONDARY (BUFF)

EMPATHY

Empathy is the ultimate party support power. More than any other ability, Empathy will earn you a place in just about any team up you come across. While other powers allow Heroes to take or dish out massive amounts of damage, Empathy is focused on keeping those same Heroes alive long enough to use those powers.

In addition to being able to heal Heroes, you will also gain the ability to restore their Endurance, and even take one Hero and make him nearly unstoppable for a short period of time. You can clear many debuffs from your allies, and with the proper pacing in a good group, you'll have very little downtime. When disaster strikes and one of your teammates is struck down, you'll be able to resurrect him and save him a trip to the hospital.

The downside, however, is that you have very limited power to protect or help yourself with Empathy. You have some power to heal yourself, but the main focus of this power pool will always be on keeping your teammates alive and fighting at their best. Your group should be aware of this, and do their best to draw any anger away from you and onto members better able to take punishment. And, of course, if you select a primary power set that's also exclusively focused on helping others, you're going to be left with little or no ability to function solo.

Empathy isn't a cure-all power; if your group is taking too much punishment, you will quickly run out of Endurance and won't be able to keep them all alive. Some of the enemies you come across will deal out massive amounts of damage, so you won't be able to just hit your group heal every few minutes and consider your work done. Getting to know what sort of Heroes you're fighting alongside is important as well — you need to

understand what sort of damage each different Hero will be able to take.

In intense fights, your Endurance will burn down rapidly. As you gain more Powers, you'll want to keep track of their cost. Keeping all your buffs up might help your teammates, but burning up your Endurance so that you have nothing left to spend on heals overshadows any good the buffs did. Learn to balance the benefits of the buffs so that you have enough Endurance to spend on your heals — that's the main focus of Empathy, so make sure you keep that as your top priority in combat.

It is always a good idea to plan out your character's progression early, so as to avoid any power choice mistakes that may come back to haunt you in later levels, and this is especially true with Empathy. This is the single most group-oriented power set in the game, and oddly it is the one you might be best dedicating the least power choices to early on. As the only power that can aid you in those early levels, for which you will likely spend the majority of your time solo, you may want to focus on **Healing Aura**, and then dedicate the rest of your early power choices to your secondary set to get combat abilities, and pick up your travel power (and other pool powers) early.

Healing Aura. This is an AoE power that heals you and all allies within a radius.

Heal Other. Heals a single targeted Hero ally.

Absorb Pain. This power has only a tiny Endurance cost, but dramatically heals an ally's wounds by sacrificing some of your own hit points. Absorbing someone's pain can be quite traumatic, and afterwards you will be unable to heal your own wounds by any means for a short while.

Resurrect. Revive a fallen Hero with full hit points, but no Endurance. This power should be performed away from combat, as it can be interrupted (and the patient will be pretty helpless for awhile after he wakes up).

Clear Mind. Frees an ally from any Immobilize, Sleep, Disorient and Hold effects, and leaves him resistant to such effects for a good while.

Fortitude. Fortitude immensely enhances a single targeted ally's Accuracy, damage potential and Defense. The target Hero takes less damage from those few attacks that do hit him. Fortitude even protects the Hero from Psionic attacks and damage.

Recovery Aura. Emits an aura that increases the Endurance recovery rate of all nearby Heroes.

Regeneration Aura. Emits an aura that increases the healing rate of all nearby Heroes.

Adrenaline Boost. Empowers another Hero with virtually unlimited Endurance for a limited time, but leaves you Disoriented.

General Tips. Heal will tend to be a more effective Enhancement than Recharge Rate. Bigger heals are better than more frequent heals most of the time, and the amount of added healing averages higher than the healing over time provided by the faster firing of the same power.

While it may not be efficient to swoop in with Flight and try to hit your target, and then get out of their range, it is very effective to rush in to heal your tanks and Scrappers and then fade back out.

The assist and targeting code is a huge boon to healers, so use it. If you target your main Tanker, any attack you send automatically launches at his target. Since they are already hitting it, this prevents you from drawing aggro from a target who has yet to be hit. If you do have an enemy targeted, your heals will automatically be applied to the Hero that villain currently has targeted for attack.

Don't be scared to get in there with your fists from time to time. As long as your Tankers and Scrappers keep the aggro, you have medium hit points and can deal just as much damage as most others with your basic Brawl ability. And while you are in close melee range, your Healing Aura is then getting the most effectiveness it can during the combat.

Grabbing a low-level sidekick allows you to overcome your biggest weakness, since all of your heals and buffs require a friendly crime fighter to be effective. But on a two-man team, even with basic Brawl as your team's best offensive power, your heals and fortitude can make a normal man into a titan.

When in a group, don't be afraid to take charge and dictate the pace of the battles. No one will be more aware of what you can or can not handle than you. When the chaos ensues, your ability to keep your allies healed will often be the single deciding factor in determining whether you retreat or fight on.

You *never* want to be low on Endurance. It will happen … It will happen a *lot* … but you want to avoid it whenever possible. Reduce Endrance Cost enhancers are never a bad choice for any of your powers, but especially heals. The Fitness pool of powers can eventually increase your natural health and Endurance recovery, and is a great asset to this path also.

Power researched by i3ullseye.

Empathy Effects

Healing Aura

Heal (Moderate)

Heal Other

Heal (High)

Absorb Pain

Heal (Extreme)
Regeneration (None)

Resurrect

Heal (Moderate)
Revive

Clear Mind

Resist Stun (Moderate)
Resist Sleep (Moderate)
Resist Immobilize (Moderate)
Resist Hold (Moderate)
Resist Confusion (Moderate)
Resist Fear (Moderate)

Fortitude

To Hit Buff (Moderate)
Add Smash Damage (High)
Add Lethal Damage (Very High)
Add Fire Damage (High)

Add Cold Damage (High)
Add Energy Damage (High)
Add Neg Damage (High)
Add Psionic Damage (High)
Smashing Defense (Moderate)
Lethal Defense (Moderate)
Fire Defense (Moderate)
Cold Defense (High)
Energy Defense (Moderate)
Neg.Energy Defense (Moderate)
Psionic Defense (Moderate)

Recovery Aura

Endurance Recovery (High)

Regeneration Aura

Regeneration (Very High)

Adrenaline Boost

Endurance Recovery (Extreme)
Stun Self (Very High) Mag 2

EMPATHY STATS

Name	Type	Attacks (Acc)	Cost	Act	Rech	Range	Target	Enhancements
Healing Aura	Clk		26.3	2.0	8	–	Ally/Self (25' sphere)	Rech, REC, Heal
Heal Other	Clk		22.5	2.3	4	80	Ally	REC, Heal, Rng, Rech
Absorb Pain	Clk		0.8	2.3	15	80	Ally	Rech, REC, Heal, Rng
Resurrect	Clk		73.5	3.2	180	15	Downed Hero	Rech, REC, Heal, Rng, Int
Clear Mind	Clk		14.7	3.1	8	70	Hero	Rech, REC, Rng
Fortitude	Clk		15.0	2.3	60	80	Ally	Rech, REC, Rng, Defense, To Hit+
Recovery Aura	Clk		37.5	2.0	500	–	Ally/Self (25' sphere)	Rech, REC, End.Rec.
Regeneration Aura	Clk		37.5	2.0	500	–	Ally/Self (25' sphere)	Rech, REC, Heal
Adrenaline Boost	Clk		15.0	2.3	300	80	Ally	Rech, REC, Rng, End.Rec.

Type: Togl (Toggle); **Clk** (Click)
Attacks: Lethal, **Sm**ash, **Fi**re, **En**ergy, **Me**lee, **NgEn** (Negative Energy), **Co**ld, **Psi**onic
Rech: Recharge Time
Enhancements: Accuracy, **Dam**age, **Dmg Resist**, **Defense+** (buff), **Defense–** (debuff), **End**urance Drain, **KB** (Knockback), **REC** (Reduce Endurance Cost), **Rng** (Range), **To Hit+** (buff), **To Hit-** (debuff), **Int**errupt, and **Rech** (recharge)

FORCE FIELD

Personal Force Field has lots of uses. Pump lots of Defense and Endurance discount Enhancements into this one. Although you can't attack well when it is up, your survivability is greatly increased while it is up … just don't wait until you're down to 1 HP to turn it on.

Putting multiple **Deflection Shields** on a target won't increase your allies' Defense, but if two different Heroes put a Deflection Shield on the same target, the effect will stack. The same holds true for **Insulation Shield**.

Detention Shield won't work on a boss, but it will take a troublesome lieutenant (like a Sorcerer, Reaper or Witchdoctor) out of a fight long enough for you to gain control of the situation.

Take **Dispersion Bubble** as soon as possible, and slot as many Enhancement into it as you can. Then fill it with Defense and Endurance discount Enhancements. This is the first Force Field power that you can use on your teammates and yourself, and it has very good defensive capability, as well as high resistance to Hold, Disorient and Immobilization. You will use this one a lot.

Repulsion Bomb is great for rescuing an ally who is surrounded.

Repulsion Field is a toggle, but it is expensive, so don't leave it on in a combat situation. However, it can be very effective when used in short, controlled, on-and-off bursts.

Force Bubble has lots of unique uses. Try shoving an entire force of enemies off a cliff. Force Bubble can severely reduce the need for melee teammates. Your Blaster allies will love you for it.

Force Field Effects

Personal Force Field

To Hit Debuff (Extreme)
Defense (Extreme)

Deflection Shield

Smashing Defense (High)
Lethal Defense (High)

Force Bolt

Smashing Damage (Minor)
Knockback (Very High)

Insulation Shield

Fire Defense (High)
Cold Defense (High)
Energy Defense (High)
Neg.Energy Defense (High)

Refraction Shield

Untouchable (Moderate) Mag 3
Immobilize (Moderate) Mag 3

Dispersion Bubble

Smashing Defense (Moderate)
Lethal Defense (Moderate)
Fire Defense (Moderate)
Cold Defense (High)
Energy Defense (Moderate)
Neg.Energy Defense (Moderate)
Resist Hold (Moderate)
Resist Stun (Moderate)
Resist Immobilize (Moderate)

Repulsion Field

Knockback (High)
Endurance Cost (Moderate)

Repulsion Bomb

Smashing Damage (Minor)
Knockback (Very High)

Force Bubble

Repel (Moderate)
To Hit Debuff (High) Can Cancel

FORCE FIELD STATS

Name	Type	Attacks (Acc)	Cost	Act	Rech	Range	Target	Enhancements
Personal Force Field	Togl		0.9	2.0	10	–	Self	Rech, REC, Defense
Deflection Shield	Clk		11.3	2.1	2	80	Ally	REC, Defense, Rng, Rech
Force Bolt	Clk	Sm (+40% Acc)	7.5	1.1	4	80	Foe	Acc, Dam, Rech, REC, Rng, KB
Insulation Shield	Clk		11.3	2.1	2	80	Ally	REC, Defense, Rng, Rech
Refraction Shield	Clk	(+40% Acc)	18.0	2.1	40	80	Foe	REC, Rng, Rech
Dispersion Bubble	Togl		0.4	1.1	15	–	Ally/Self (25' sphere)	Rech, REC, Defense
Repulsion Field	Togl		0.6	2.0	20	–	Foe (7' sphere)	Rech, REC, KB
Repulsion Bomb	Clk	Sm (+20% Acc)	15.0	3.1	10	70	Foe (12' sphere)	Acc, Dam, Rech, REC, Rng, KB
Force Bubble	Togl		0.6	1.1	15	–	Foe (50' sphere)	Rech, REC, To Hit–

Type: **Togl** (Toggle); **Clk** (Click)
Attacks: **Le**thal, **Sm**ash, **Fi**re, **En**ergy, **Me**lee, **NgEn** (Negative Energy), **Co**ld, **Psi**onic
Rech: Recharge Time
Enhancements: **Acc**uracy, **Dam**age, **Dmg Resist**, **Defense+** (buff), **Defense–** (debuff), **End**urance **Drain**, **KB** (Knockback), **REC** (Reduce Endurance Cost), **Rng** (Range), **To Hit+** (buff), **To Hit-** (debuff), **Int**errupt, and **Rech** (recharge)

KINETICS

Siphon Speed can be used as a travel power and an escape power. Be sure to put lots of Accuracy Enhancements into this one so you don't miss when you need to get away. Because of Siphon Speed and **Inertial Reduction**, a Kinetics Hero doesn't really need to invest in a travel power, so this will allow you to invest in other pool powers.

Transfusion can heal you and your allies, but it is best for supporting melee Heroes.

Remember, **Increase Density** can free an ally from Hold, Immobilization and Disorient effects, as well as make him resistant to such effects.

You can never get enough Endurance, so be sure to take **Transference** as soon as possible and put lots of Accuracy and Recovery Enhancements into it.

Fulcrum Shift is good, but it becomes *uber* powerful when there are *lots* of enemies all close to your team. Each affected foe is drained, and passes power to each of your teammates, and a single teammate can get double, triple, quadruple (whatever) buffs for each foe that is drained, provided everyone is in close proximity. Be sure to coordinate with your team to pack everyone as close together as possible before activating this power. Help from other Heroes with powers like Tar Patch, Quicksand, Chilling Embrace, Mudpots or other snaring powers can make Fulcrum Shift more effective.

Kinetics Effects

Transfusion

Summons (Transfusion)
End Drain (High)
Immobilize (Minor) Mag 10

Siphon Power

Smash Dmg Debuff (High)
Lethal Dmg Debuff (High)
Fire Dmg Debuff (High)
Cold Dmg Debuff (High)
Energy Dmg Debuff (High)
Neg Dmg Debuff (High)
Psionic Dmg Debuff (High)

Repel

Knockback (High)
Endurance Cost (Moderate)

Siphon Speed

Run Speed Self (Moderate)
Run Speed Target (Slow)
Fly Self (Moderate)
Fly Target (Slow)

Increase Density

Resist Smashing (High)
Resist Energy (High)
Resist Stun (Moderate)
Resist Hold (Moderate)
Resist Immobilize (Moderate)
Resist Knockback (Moderate)
Resist Knockup (Moderate)
Resist Repel (Moderate)
Fly (Very Slow)
Run Speed (Very Slow)

Speed Boost

Recharge Increase (High)
Endurance Recovery (Moderate)
Run Speed (Slower)
Fly (Slower)

Inertial Reduction

Leap (Moderate)

Transference

End Drain (High)
Immobilize (Minor) Mag 10

Kinetic Transfer

Smash Dmg Debuff (High)
Lethal Dmg Debuff (High)
Fire Dmg Debuff (High)
Cold Dmg Debuff (High)
Energy Dmg Debuff (High)
Neg Dmg Debuff (High)
Psionic Dmg Debuff (High)

KINETICS STATS

Name	Type	Attacks (Acc)	Cost	Act	Rech	Range	Target	Enhancements
Transfusion	Clk		7.5	1.2	8	60	Foe	Rech, REC, Rng, Drain End, Acc, Heal
Siphon Power	Clk		15.0	1.9	20	80	Foe	Rech, REC, Rng, Acc
Repel	Togl		0.6	1.1	20	—	Foe (7' sphere)	Rech, REC, KB
Siphon Speed	Clk		11.3	4.7	60	80	Foe	Rech, REC, Rng, Run
Increase Density	Clk		18.0	2.1	3	70	Hero	Rech, REC, Rng, Dmg Resist
Speed Boost	Clk		15.0	1.0	2	50	Ally	Rech, REC, Rng, Run, End.Rec.
Inertial Reduction	Clk		33.8	2.0	60	—	Ally/Self (25' sphere)	REC, Jump, Rech
Transference	Clk		3.8	2.3	30	60	Foe	Rech, REC, Rng, Drain End, Acc, End.Rec.
Kinetic Transfer	Clk		22.5	2.2	60	60	Foe (30' sphere)	Rech, REC, Rng, Acc

Type: Togl (Toggle); **Clk** (Click)
Attacks: Lethal, **Sm**ash, **Fi**re, **En**ergy, **Me**lee, **NgEn** (Negative Energy), **Co**ld, **Psi**onic
Rech: Recharge Time
Enhancements: Accuracy, **Dam**age, **Dmg Resist**, **Defense+** (buff), **Defense−** (debuff), **End**urance **Drain**, **KB** (Knockback), **REC** (Reduce Endurance Cost), **Rng** (Range), **To Hit+** (buff), **To Hit−** (debuff), **Int**errupt, and **Rech** (recharge)

RADIATION EMISSION

Be sure to stick your **Radiation Infection** and **Enervating Field** on the toughest enemy. Then don't defeat that foe until the end, to ensure the effect will harm as many foes as possible. If the target is defeated, you will have to re-activate these powers, wasting valuable time, so let your team know.

Accelerate Metabolism is an awesome power. Fill this one with lots of Enhancement slots.

Mutation resurrects a fallen Hero with *uber* buffs, turning him into a killing machine. But warn your teammates to use this advantage right away and be prepared, because it wears off quickly and leaves your ally very weak.

Pump lots of Accuracy Enhancements into **Lingering Radiation** to ensure lots of targets are affected, then top it off with a couple of Slow Enhancements.

You can't put Accuracy Enhancements into **Choking Cloud**, but you can put Hold Enhancements into this power. Since Choking Cloud Holds about half the targets for five seconds and then rotates to Hold another random group for five seconds, increasing the duration of the Holds with Hold Enhancements will cause this effect to overlap, eventually allowing you to Hold most, if not all, foes in the affected area.

Radiation Emission Effects

Radiation Emission

Heal (Moderate)

Radiation Infection

To Hit Debuff (High)
Defense Debuff (High)

Accelerate Metabolism

Add Smash Damage (High)
Add Lethal Damage (High)
Add Fire Damage (High)
Add Cold Damage (High)
Add Energy Damage (High)
Add Neg Damage (High)
Add Psionic Damage (High)
Resist Hold (Moderate)
Resist Stun (Moderate)
Resist Sleep (Moderate)
Resist Immobilize (Moderate)
Recharge Increase (Moderate)
Endurance Recovery (Minor)
Fly (Minor)
Running (Minor)

Enervating Field

Smash Dmg Debuff (High)
Lethal Dmg Debuff (High)
Fire Dmg Debuff (High)

Cold Dmg Debuff (High)
Energy Dmg Debuff (High)
Neg Dmg Debuff (High)
Psionic Dmg Debuff (High)
Energy Damage (Minor; 75% chance)

Mutation

Heal (Moderate)
Endurance Bonus (Minor)
Endurance Recovery (High)
Add Smash Damage (Extreme)
Add Lethal Damage (Extreme)
Add Fire Damage (Extreme)
Add Cold Damage (Very High)
Add Energy Damage (Very High)
Add Neg Damage (Extreme)
Add Psionic Damage (Extreme)
To Hit Buff (Very High)
Smash Dmg Debuff (Extreme)
Lethal Dmg Debuff (Extreme)
Fire Dmg Debuff (Extreme)
Cold Dmg Debuff (Very High)
Energy Dmg Debuff (Very High)

Neg Dmg Debuff (Extreme)
Psionic Dmg Debuff (Extreme)
To Hit Debuff (Very High)
Stun (Very High) Mag 3

Lingering radiation

Run Speed (Slower)
Recharge Time (Slower)
Fly (Slower)

Choking Cloud

Hold (Moderate; 40% chance) Mag 2

Fallout

Energy Damage (Very High)

EMP Pulse

Hold (Extreme; 50% chance) Mag 3; Can Cancel
Stun (High) Mag 3; Can Cancel
Endurance Recovery (None)

RADIATION EMISSION STATS

Name	Type	Attacks (Acc)	Cost	Act	Rech	Range	Target	Enhancements
Radiation Emission	Clk		26.3	2.0	8	–	Ally/Self (25' sphere)	Rech, REC, Heal
Radiation Infection	Togl		0.4	3.1	8	70	Foe (15' sphere)	Rech, REC, Defense–, To Hit–, Rng
Accelerate Metabolism	Clk		22.5	2.0	300	–	Ally/Self (25' sphere)	Rech, REC, Run, End.Rec.
Enervating Field	Togl	En	3.0	1.5	8	70	Foe (15' sphere)	Rech, REC, Dam
Mutation	Clk		56.3	3.2	180	15	Downed Hero	Rech, REC, Rng, End.Rec., Int
Lingering radiation	Clk		22.5	1.5	25	80	Foe (25' sphere)	Rech, REC, Slow
Choking Cloud	Togl		6.0	2.0	90	–	Foe (15' sphere)	Rech, REC, Hold
Fallout	Clk	En	0.0	1.2	300	–	Foe (20' sphere)	Rech, REC, Dam
EMP Pulse	Clk		30.0	2.9	300	–	Foe (80' sphere)	Rech, REC, Hold

Type: Togl (Toggle); **Clk** (Click)
Attacks: Lethal, **Sm**ash, **Fi**re, **En**ergy, **Me**lee, **NgEn** (Negative Energy), **Co**ld, **Psi**onic
Rech: Recharge Time
Enhancements: Accuracy, **Dam**age, **Dmg Resist**, **Defense+** (buff), **Defense–** (debuff), **End**urance **Drain**, **KB** (Knockback), **REC** (Reduce Endurance Cost), **Rng** (Range), **To Hit+** (buff), **To Hit–** (debuff), **Int**errupt, and **Rech** (recharge)

STORM SUMMONING

This power set is good for Controllers who would like a combination of extra damage, healing abilities and defensive abilities.

The first power from Storm Summoning is **O2 Boost**. O2 Boost is used to heal allies and can be quite useful. The O2 boost can also protect a targeted ally Hero from Sleep and Stun effects. The amount O2 Boost heals will increase as you level up. This is the only heal power in the Storm Summoning set.

For the defensive abilities, Storm Summoning starts out with **Gale** which, when activated, will attempt to knock down foes, causing minor damage. The Gale radiates from you in a cone.

Later, a similar power, **Hurricane**, will form a storm around you. When a foe tries to get to you through this hurricane, he has a chance of being knocked back out of range. It also reduces the range and Accuracy of nearby foes.

For damage, Storm Summoning offers a choice of powers. Starting off with **Snowstorm**, you can call a snowstorm to a targeted location, which will damage all foes in an area around that target area. Any foe running into that area will be damaged as the snow falls down. It will also Slow the attack and movement of those foes.

Another power that not only helps with Defense, but also looks really cool, is **Tornado**. This power creates a tornado that jumps around, throwing foes up into the air and hurling them great distances. It also has a chance to create panic and scare away foes.

The **Steamy Mist** power creates a mist of steam around you and your allies. Steamy Mist helps protect against Fire, Cold and Energy-based attacks, reducing the damage from those types of powers.

The **Fog** power creates a fog around you and your allies. It makes you harder to see and increases your Defense. It will have the negative side effect of reducing movement speed.

Thunderclap is an AoE power that renders foes helpless and can really increase your crowd control potential. It affects a wide area, and has a long duration.

Lightning Storm creates a dark cloud overhead that sends bolts of lightning arcing into any foes within range. It can also create Fear in foes, scaring them away. Lightning bolts will continue to strike for the duration of the storm.

Power researched by Brent Copeland.

Storm Summoning Effects

Gale

> Smashing Damage (Minor)
> Knockback (Very High)

O2 Boost

> Heal (Moderate)
> Resist Stun (Moderate)
> Resist Sleep (Moderate)

Snow Storm

> Run Speed (Slower)
> Recharge Time (Very Slow)
> Fly (Slower)
> Fly (Stopped)

Steamy Mist

> Stealth (Moderate)
> Melee Defense (Moderate)
> Ranged Defense (Moderate)
> Run Speed (Very Slow)
> Fly (Very Slow)
> Resist Fire (Very High)
> Resist Cold (Very High)
> Resist Energy (Very High)
> Summons (Fog)

Freezing Rain

Cold Damage (Minor)
Multiple Resistances Debuff (High)
Slow (Moderate)
Summons (Freezing Rain)

Hurricane

Range Reduce
To Hit Debuff (Very High)
Repel (Moderate)
Knockback (Very High; 5% chance)

Thunder Clap

Stun (High) Mag 2; Can Cancel

Tornado

Summons (Tornado)
Smashing Damage (Minor)
Disorient (Moderate; 30% chance)

Lightning Storm

Summons (Lightning Storm)

STORM SUMMONING STATS

Name	Type	Attacks (Acc)	Cost	Act	Rech	Range	Target	Enhancements
Gale	Clk	Sm (-10% Acc)	11.3	2.2	8	50	Foe (50', 80° cone)	Acc, REC, Rech, Dam, KB, cone
O2 Boost	Clk		7.5	2.3	4	80	Ally	REC, Heal, Rng, Rech
Snow Storm	Togl		0.4	2.0	10	80	Foe (25' sphere)	REC, Rech, Slow
Steamy Mist	Togl		0.4	1.9	15	–	Ally/Self (40' sphere)	Rech, REC, Defense, Dmg Resist
Freezing Rain	Clk	Co (+100% Acc)	21.0	2.0	60	60	Location	Rech, REC, Rng, Dam, Slow, Defense–
Hurricane	Togl		0.2	2.0	10	–	Foe (25' sphere)	REC, Rech, To Hit–, KB
Thunder Clap	Clk	(-32% Acc)	15.0	2.4	45	–	Foe (25' sphere)	REC, Rech, Stun
Tornado	Clk	Sm	30.0	1.2	60	60	Location	REC, Rech, Rng, Dam, Defense–, Stun, KB
Lightning Storm	Clk	(+100% Acc)	45.0	2.0	90	–	Self	REC, Rech, Dam, KB, Drain End, Acc

Type: Togl (Toggle); **Clk** (Click)
Attacks: Lethal, **Sm**ash, **Fi**re, **En**ergy, **Me**lee, **NgEn** (Negative Energy), **Cold, Psi**onic
Rech: Recharge Time
Enhancements: Accuracy, **Dam**age, **Dmg Resist, Defense+** (buff), **Defense–** (debuff), **End**urance **Drain, KB** (Knockback), **REC** (Reduce Endurance Cost), **Rng** (Range), **To Hit+** (buff), **To Hit-** (debuff), **Int**errupt, and **Rech** (recharge)

DEFENDER PRIMARY (BUFF)

DARK MIASMA

The Dark Miasma power set is a very versatile, with cool graphics and side effects which typically lower an enemy's Accuracy.

Twilight Grasp is a group heal, with a limited range, and it requires a target from which to "drain the power." When using it, be sure to try to center yourself on your group, or stand near the Hero you want healed.

Tar Patch is a good way to defeat a villain using your secondary power sets to wear it down. Drop a patch by your target, and run around it blasting as your power recycles.

Darkest Night is a ranged AoE that will lower the damage output of the villains. You should target the weakest villain, and take out the tougher ones while the power is toggled so that it remains active for the duration of the battle.

Howling Twilight is a resurrect with a twist. It is an AoE resurrect, which targets a group of villains. It will damage them, Disorient them, Slow them and slow their recharge rate. All Heroes that have fallen within the AoE will be resurrected with very little side effects — the more villains you target, the higher the hit points of your allies.

Shadow Fall will grant your team stealth, which is not invisibility, but makes them less likely to be noticed, as well as giving a bonus to Defense and resistances to Energy, Negative Energy and Psionic damage.

Fearsome Stare is a Fear-type ability. Use Fearsome Stare to force villains to run away. They will stop to use their ranged attacks when they recharge, but if they run out of range, they just continue to run.

Petrifying Gaze is a ranged Hold. It Roots them in place and Stuns them so they do not use ranged

or melee attacks on you.

Black Hole is a ranged AoE which will make your target and several foes around him intangible. This is good against several targets when you are solo, as it takes several out of the fight, leaving only a few who make the save. In desperate situations, you can force your target intangible and use your rest ability to get your bearings.

Dark Servant will summon an intangible mass that has all the Dark Miasma abilities (save Dark Servant) and will use them in battle with you. When this power uses Twilight Grasp, it will heal group members as well, so it is a good idea to put it up within range of the villains, but also within range of the Heroes.

Power researched by Dave.

Dark Miasma Effects

Twilight Grasp

Summons (Twilight Grasp)
Immobilize (Minor) Mag 10
Immobilize (Moderate) Mag 0
To Hit Debuff (Moderate)
Smash Dmg Debuff (Moderate)
Lethal Dmg Debuff (Moderate)
Fire Dmg Debuff (Moderate)
Cold Dmg Debuff (Moderate)
Energy Dmg Debuff (Moderate)
Neg.Energy Dmg Debuff (Moderate)
Psionic Dmg Debuff (Moderate)

Tar Patch

Summons (Tar Patch)

Darkest Night

Smash Dmg Debuff (Very High)

Lethal Dmg Debuff (Very High)
Fire Dmg Debuff (Very High)
Cold Dmg Debuff (Very High)
Energy Dmg Debuff (Very High)
Neg.Energy Dmg Debuff (Very High)
Psionic Dmg Debuff (Very High)

Howling Twilight

Run Speed (Slower)
Recharge Time (Very Slow)
Fly (Slower)
Neg.Energy Damage (Minor)
Stun (High) Mag 2
Fear (High) Mag 3
Immobilize (Moderate) Mag 10
Immobilize (Moderate) Mag 10
Summons (Howling Twilight)

Shadow Fall

Stealth (Moderate)
Melee Defense (Moderate)
Ranged Defense (Moderate)

Run Speed (Very Slow)
Fly (Very Slow)
Resist Psionic (Very High)
Resist Energy (Very High)
Resist Neg.Energy (Very High)

Fearsome Stare

Fear (Very High) Mag 3
To Hit Debuff (Very High; 20% chance) Mag 1

Petrifying Gaze

Hold (Very High) Mag 3

Black Hole

Translucent
Intangible (Moderate) Mag 3
Untouchable (Moderate) Mag 3
Immobilize (Very High) Mag 3

Dark Servant

Summons (Chill of the Night)

DARK MIASMA STATS

Name	Type	Attacks (Acc)	Cost	Act	Rech	Range	Target	Enhancements
Twilight Grasp	Clk		15.0	3.7	8	80	Foe	Rech, REC, Rng, Acc, To Hit–, Heal
Tar Patch	Clk		15.0	3.1	45	60	Location	Rech, REC, Rng, Slow
Darkest Night	Togl		0.4	3.2	10	70	Foe (25' sphere)	Rech, REC, Rng
Howling Twilight	Clk	NgEn	37.5	3.2	180	20	Foe (15' sphere)	Rech, REC, Slow, Stun, Dam, Rng, Heal, End.Rec.
Shadow Fall	Togl		0.4	2.0	15	–	Ally/Self (40' sphere)	REC, Rech, Defense
Fearsome Stare	Clk		12.3	2.0	12	–	Foe (70', 45° cone)	Acc, Rech, REC, To Hit–, Fear, cone
Petrifying Gaze	Clk		11.3	1.7	8	70	Foe	Acc, Rech, REC, Rng, Hold
Black Hole	Clk		37.5	1.0	45	50	Foe (20' sphere)	Acc, Rech, REC, Rng, Intangible
Dark Servant	Clk	(+100% Acc)	45.0	3.2	180	60	Location	Rech, REC, To Hit–, Heal, Fear, Acc, Immobilize

Type: Togl (Toggle); **Clk** (Click)
Attacks: Lethal, **Sm**ash, **Fi**re, **En**ergy, **Me**lee, **NgEn** (Negative Energy), **Co**ld, **Psi**onic
Rech: Recharge Time
Enhancements: Accuracy, **Dam**age, **Dmg Resist**, **Defense+** (buff), **Defense–** (debuff), **End**urance **Drain**, **KB** (Knockback), **REC** (Reduce Endurance Cost), **Rng** (Range), **To Hit+** (buff), **To Hit-** (debuff), **Int**errupt, and **Rech** (recharge)

EMPATHY

Empathy is the ultimate party support power. More than any other ability, Empathy will earn you a place in just about any team up you come across. While other powers allow Heroes to take or dish out massive amounts of damage, Empathy is focused on keeping those same Heroes alive long enough to use those powers.

In addition to being able to heal Heroes, you will also gain the ability to restore their Endurance, and even take one Hero and make him nearly unstoppable for a short period of time. You can clear many debuffs from your allies, and with the proper pacing in a good group, you'll have very little downtime. When disaster strikes and one of your teammates is struck down, you'll be able to resurrect him and save him a trip to the hospital.

The downside, however, is that you have very limited power to protect or help yourself with Empathy. You have some power to heal yourself, but the main focus of this power pool will always be on keeping your teammates alive and fighting at their best. Your group should be aware of this, and do their best to draw any anger away from you and onto members better able to take punishment.

Empathy isn't a cure-all power; if your group is taking too much punishment, you will quickly run out of Endurance and won't be able to keep them all alive. Some of the enemies you come across will deal out massive amounts of damage, so you won't be able to just hit your group heal every few minutes and consider your work done. Getting to know what sort of Heroes you're fighting alongside is important as well — you need to understand what sort of damage each different Hero will be able to take.

In intense fights, your Endurance will burn down rapidly. As you gain more powers, you'll want to keep track of their cost. Keeping all your buffs up might help your teammates, but burning up your Endurance so that you have nothing left to spend on heals overshadows any good the buffs did. Learn to balance the benefits of the buffs so that you have enough Endurance to spend on your heals — that's the main focus of Empathy, so make sure you keep that as your top priority in combat.

It is always a good idea to plan out your character's progression early, so as to avoid any power choice mistakes that may come back to haunt you in later levels, and this is especially true with Empathy. This is the single most group-oriented power set in the game, and oddly it is the one you might be best dedicating the least power choices to early on. As the only power that can aid you in those early levels, for which you will likely spend the majority of your time solo, you may want to focus on Healing Aura, and then dedicate the rest of your early power choices to your secondary set to get combat abilities, and pick up your travel power (and other pool powers) early.

Healing Aura. This is an AoE power that heals you and all allies within a radius.

Heal Other. Heals a single targeted Hero ally.

Absorb Pain. This power has only a tiny Endurance cost, but dramatically heals an ally's wounds by sacrificing some of your own hit points. Absorbing someone's pain can be quite traumatic, and afterwards you will be unable to heal your own wounds by any means for a short while.

Resurrect. Revive a fallen Hero with full hit points, but no Endurance. This power should be performed away from combat, as it can be interrupted (and the patient will be pretty helpless for awhile after he wakes up).

Clear Mind. Frees an ally from any Immobilize, Sleep, Disorient and Hold effects, and leaves him resistant to such effects for a good while.

Fortitude. Fortitude immensely enhances a single targeted ally's Accuracy, damage potential and Defense. The target Hero even takes less damage from those few attacks that do hit him. Fortitude even protects the Hero from Psionic attacks and damage.

Regeneration Aura. Emits an aura that increases the healing rate of all nearby Heroes.

Recovery Aura. Emits an aura that increases the Endurance recovery rate of all nearby Heroes.

Adrenaline Boost. Empowers another Hero with virtually unlimited Endurance for a limited time, but leaves you Disoriented.

General Tips. Heal will tend to be a more effective Enhancement than Recharge Rate. Bigger heals are better than more frequent heals most of the time, and the amount of added healing averages higher than the healing over time provided by the faster firing of the same power.

While it may not be efficient to swoop in with Flight and try to hit your target, and then get out of its range, it is very effective to rush in to heal your Tankers and Scrappers and then fade back out.

The assist and targeting code is a huge boon to healers, so use it. If you target your main Tanker, any attack you send automatically launches at his target. Since they are already hitting it, this prevents you form drawing aggro from a target who has yet to be hit. If you *do* have an enemy targeted, your heals will automatically be applied to the Hero that villain currently has targeted for attack.

Don't be scared to get in there with your fists from time to time. As long as your Tankers and Scrappers keep the aggro, you have medium hit points and can deal just as much damage as most others with your basic Brawl ability. And while you are in melee range, your Healing Aura is then getting the most effectiveness it can during the combat.

Grabbing a low-level sidekick allows you to overcome your biggest weakness, since all of your heals and buffs require a friendly crime fighter to be effective. But on a two-man team, even with basic Brawl as your team's best offensive power, your heals and fortitude can make a normal man into a titan.

When in a group, don't be afraid to take charge and dictate the pace of the battles. No one will be more aware of what you can or can not handle than you. When the chaos ensues, your ability to keep your allies healed will often be the single most important factor in determining whether you retreat or fight on.

You *never* want to be low on Endurance. It will happen … It will happen a *lot* … but you want to avoid it whenever possible. Reduce Endurance Cost Enhancements are never a bad choice for any of your powers, but especially heals. The Fitness pool of powers can eventually increase your natural health and Endurance recovery, and is a great asset to this path also.

Power researched by i3ullseye.

Empathy Effects

Healing Aura

Heal (Moderate)

Heal Other

Heal (High)

Absorb Pain

Heal (Extreme)
Regeneration (None)
Heal (Moderate)

Resurrect

Heal (Moderate)
Revive

Clear Mind

Resist Stun (Moderate)
Resist Sleep (Moderate)
Resist Immobilize (Moderate)
Resist Hold (Moderate)
Resist Confusion (Moderate)
Resist Fear (Moderate)

Fortitude

To Hit Buff (Moderate)
Add Smash Damage (High)
Add Lethal Damage (Very High)
Add Fire Damage (High)

Add Cold Damage (High)
Add Energy Damage (High)
Add Neg.Energy Damage (High)
Add Psionic Damage (High)
Smashing Defense (Moderate)
Lethal Defense (Moderate)
Fire Defense (Moderate)
Cold Defense (High)
Energy Defense (Moderate)
Neg.Energy Defense (Moderate)
Psionic Defense (Moderate)

Recovery Aura

Endurance Recovery (High)

Regeneration Aura

Regeneration (Very High)

Adrenaline Boost

Endurance Recovery (Extreme)
Stun Self (Very High) Mag 2

EMPATHY STATS

Name	Type	Attacks (Acc)	Cost	Act	Rech	Range	Target	Enhancements
Healing Aura	Clk		26.3	2.0	8	–	Ally/Self (25' sphere)	Rech, REC, Heal
Heal Other	Clk		18.8	2.3	4	80	Ally	REC, Heal, Rng, Rech
Absorb Pain	Clk		0.8	2.3	15	80	Ally	Rech, REC, Heal, Rng
Resurrect	Clk		73.5	3.2	180	15	Downed Hero	Rech, REC, Heal, Rng, Int
Clear Mind	Clk		14.7	3.1	8	70	Hero	Rech, REC, Rng
Fortitude	Clk		15.0	2.3	60	80	Ally	Rech, REC, Rng, Defense, To Hit+
Recovery Aura	Clk		37.5	2.0	500	–	Ally/Self (25' sphere)	Rech, REC, End.Rec.
Regeneration Aura	Clk		37.5	2.0	500	–	Ally/Self (25' sphere)	Rech, REC, Heal
Adrenaline Boost	Clk		15.0	2.3	300	80	Ally	Rech, REC, Rng, End.Rec

Type: Togl (Toggle); **Clk** (Click)
Attacks: Lethal, **Sm**ash, **Fi**re, **En**ergy, **Me**lee, **NgEn** (Negative Energy), **Co**ld, **Psi**onic
Rech: Recharge Time
Enhancements: Accuracy, **Dam**age, **Dmg Resist, Defense+** (buff), **Defense–** (debuff), **End**urance **Drain**, **KB** (Knockback), **REC** (Reduce Endurance Cost), **Rng** (Range), **To Hit+** (buff), **To Hit-** (debuff), **Int**errupt, and **Rech** (recharge)

FORCE FIELD

Personal Force Field has lots of uses. Pump lots of Defense and Endurance discount Enhancements into this one. Although you can't attack well when it is up, your survivability is greatly increased … just don't wait until you're down to 1 HP to turn it on.

Putting multiple **Deflection Shields** on a target won't increase your allies' Defense, but if two different Heroes put a Deflection Shield on the same target, the effect will stack. The same holds true for the **Insulation Shield** power.

Detention Shield won't work on a Boss, but it will take a troublesome Lieutenant (like a Sorcerer, Reaper or Witchdoctor) out of a fight long enough for you to gain control of the situation.

Take **Dispersion Bubble** as soon as possible, and put as many Enhancement slots into this one as you can. Then fill it with Defense and Endurance discount Enhancements. This is the first Force Field power that can be used on your teammates and yourself, and it has very good defensive capability, as well as high resistance to Hold, Disorient and Immobilization. You will use this one a lot.

Repulsion Bomb is great for rescuing an ally who is surrounded.

Repulsion Field is a toggle, but it is expensive, so don't leave it on in a combat situation. It can be very effective when used in short, controlled, on/off bursts.

Force Bubble has lots of unique uses. Try shoving an entire force of enemies off a cliff. Force Bubble can severely reduce the need for melee teammates. Your Blaster allies will love you for it.

Force Field Effects

Personal Force Field

To Hit Debuff (Extreme)
Defense (Extreme)

Deflection Shield

Smashing Defense (High)
Lethal Defense (High)

Force Bolt

Smashing Damage (Minor)
Knockback (Very High)

Insulation Shield

Fire Defense (High)
Cold Defense (High)
Energy Defense (High)
Neg.Energy Defense (High)

Detention Field

Untouchable (Moderate) Mag 3
Immobilize (Very High) Mag 3

Dispersion Bubble

Smashing Defense (Moderate)
Lethal Defense (Moderate)
Fire Defense (Moderate)
Cold Defense (High)
Energy Defense (Moderate)
Neg.Energy Defense (Moderate)
Resist Hold (Moderate)
Resist Stun (Moderate)
Resist Immobilize (Moderate)

Repulsion Field

Knockback (High)
Endurance Cost (Moderate)

Repulsion Bomb

Smashing Damage (Minor)
Knockback (Very High)

Force Bubble

Repel (Moderate)
To Hit Debuff (High) Can Cancel

FORCE FIELD STATS

Name	Type	Attacks (Acc)	Cost	Act	Rech	Range	Target	Enhancements
Personal Force Field	Togl		0.9	2.0	10	–	Self	Rech, REC, Defense
Deflection Shield	Clk		11.3	2.1	2	80	Ally	REC, Defense, Rng, Rech
Force Bolt	Clk	Sm (+40% Acc)	7.5	1.1	4	80	Foe	Acc, Dam, Rech, REC, Rng, KB
Insulation Shield	Clk		11.3	2.1	2	80	Ally	REC, Defense, Rng, Rech
Detention Field	Clk	(+40% Acc)	18.0	2.1	40	80	Foe	REC, Rng, Rech
Dispersion Bubble	Togl		0.4	1.1	15	–	Ally/Self (25' sphere)	Rech, REC, Defense
Repulsion Field	Togl		0.6	2.0	20	–	Foe (7' sphere)	Rech, REC, KB
Repulsion Bomb	Clk	Sm (+20% Acc)	15.0	3.1	10	70	Foe (12' sphere)	Acc, Dam, Rech, REC, Rng, KB
Force Bubble	Togl		0.6	1.1	15	–	Foe (50' sphere)	Rech, REC, To Hit–

Type: **Togl** (Toggle); **Clk** (Click)
Attacks: **Le**thal, **Sm**ash, **Fi**re, **En**ergy, **Me**lee, **NgEn** (Negative Energy), **Co**ld, **Psi**onic
Rech: Recharge Time
Enhancements: **Acc**uracy, **Dam**age, **Dmg Resist**, **Defense+** (buff), **Defense–** (debuff), **End**urance **Drain**, **KB** (Knockback), **REC** (Reduce Endurance Cost), **Rng** (Range), **To Hit+** (buff), **To Hit–** (debuff), **Int**errupt, and **Rech** (recharge)

KINETICS

Siphon Speed can be used as a travel power and an escape power. Be sure to put lots of Accuracy Enhancements into this one so you don't miss when you need to get away. Because of Siphon Speed and **Inertial Reduction**, a Kinetics Hero doesn't really need to invest in a travel power, so this will allow you to invest in other pool powers.

Transfusion can heal you and your allies, but it is best for supporting melee Heroes.

Remember, **Increase Density** can free an ally from Hold, Immobilization and Disorient effects, as well as make him resistant to such effects.

You can never get enough Endurance, so be sure to take **Transference** as soon as possible and put lots of Accuracy and recovery Enhancements into it.

Fulcrum Shift is good, but it becomes *uber* powerful when there are *lots* of enemies all close to your team. Each affected foe is drained, and passes power to each of your teammates. A single teammate can get double, triple, quadruple (whatever) buffs for each foe that is drained, provided everyone is in close proximity. Be sure to coordinate with your team to pack everyone as close together as possible before activating this power. Help from other Heroes with powers like Tar Patch, Quicksand, Chilling Embrace, Mudpots or other snaring powers can make Fulcrum Shift more effective.

Kinetics Effects

Transfusion

> End Drain (High)
> Immobilize (Minor) Mag 10

Siphon Power

> Smash Dmg Debuff (High)
> Lethal Dmg Debuff (High)
> Fire Dmg Debuff (High)
> Cold Dmg Debuff (High)
> Energy Dmg Debuff (High)
> Neg.Energy Dmg Debuff (High)
> Psionic Dmg Debuff (High)

Repel

> Knockback (High)
> Endurance Cost (Moderate)

Siphon Speed

Run Speed Self (Moderate)
Run Speed Target (Slow)
Fly Self (Moderate)
Fly Target (Slow)

Increase Density

Resist Smashing (High)
Resist Energy (High)
Resist Stun (Moderate)
Resist Hold (Moderate)
Resist Immobilize (Moderate)
Resist Knockback (Moderate)
Resist Knockup (Moderate)
Resist Repel (Moderate)
Fly (Very Slow)
Run Speed (Very Slow)

Speed Boost

Recharge Increase (High)
Endurance Recovery (Moderate)

Run Speed (Slower)
Fly (Slower)

Inertial Reduction

Leap (Moderate)

Transference

End Drain (High)
Immobilize (Minor) Mag 10

Fulcrum Shift

Summons (Kinetic Transfer)
Smash Dmg Debuff (High)
Lethal Dmg Debuff (High)
Fire Dmg Debuff (High)
Cold Dmg Debuff (High)
Energy Dmg Debuff (High)
Neg.Energy Dmg Debuff (High)
Psionic Dmg Debuff (High)

KINETICS STATS

Name	Type	Attacks (Acc)	Cost	Act	Rech	Range	Target	Enhancements
Transfusion	Clk		7.5	1.2	8	60	Foe	Rech, REC, Rng, Drain End, Acc, Heal
Siphon Power	Clk		15.0	1.9	20	80	Foe	Rech, REC, Rng, Acc
Repel	Togl		0.6	1.1	20	—	Foe (7' sphere)	Rech, REC, KB
Siphon Speed	Clk		11.3	4.7	60	80	Foe	Rech, REC, Rng, Run
Increase Density	Clk		18.0	2.1	3	70	Hero	Rech, REC, Rng, Dmg Resist
Speed Boost	Clk		15.0	1.0	2	50	Ally	Rech, REC, Rng, Run, End.Rec.
Inertial Reduction	Clk		33.8	2.0	60	—	Ally/Self (25' sphere)	REC, Jump, Rech
Transference	Clk		3.8	2.3	30	60	Foe	Rech, REC, Rng, Drain End, Acc, End.Rec.
Fulcrum Shift	Clk	(-10% Acc)	22.5	2.2	60	60	Foe (30' sphere)	Rech, REC, Rng, Acc

Type: Togl (Toggle); **Clk** (Click)
Attacks: Lethal, **Sm**ash, **Fi**re, **En**ergy, **Me**lee, **NgEn** (Negative Energy), **Co**ld, **Psi**onic
Rech: Recharge Time
Enhancements: Accuracy, **Dam**age, **Dmg Resist**, **Defense+** (buff), **Defense–** (debuff), **End**urance **Drain**, **KB** (Knockback), **REC** (Reduce Endurance Cost), **Rng** (Range), **To Hit+** (buff), **To Hit-** (debuff), **Int**errupt, and **Rech** (recharge)

RADIATION EMISSION

Be sure to stick your **Radiation Infection** and **Enervating Field** on the toughest enemy. Then don't defeat that foe until the end, to ensure the effect will harm as many foes as possible. If the target is defeated, you will have to re-activate these powers, wasting valuable time, so let your team know.

Accelerate Metabolism is an awesome power. Fill this one with lots of Enhancement slots.

Mutation resurrects a fallen Hero with *uber* buffs, turning him into a killing machine. But warn your teammates to use this advantage right away and be prepared, because it wears off quickly and leaves your ally very weak.

Pump lots of Accuracy Enhancements into **Lingering Radiation** to ensure lots of targets are affected, then top it off with a couple of Slow Enhancements.

You can't put Accuracy Enhancements into **Choking Cloud**, but you can put Hold Enhancements into this power. Since Choking Cloud Holds about half the targets for five seconds and then rotates to Hold another random group for five seconds, increasing the duration of the Holds with Hold Enhancements will cause this effect to overlap, eventually allowing you to Hold most, if not all, foes in the affected area.

Radiation Emission Effects

Radiation Emission

Heal (Moderate)

Radiation Infection

To Hit Debuff (High)
Defense Debuff (High)

Accelerate Metabolism

Add Smash Damage (High)
Add Lethal Damage (High)
Add Fire Damage (High)
Add Cold Damage (High)
Add Energy Damage (High)
Add Neg.Energy Damage (High)
Add Psionic Damage (High)
Resist Hold (Moderate)
Resist Stun (Moderate)
Resist Sleep (Moderate)
Resist Immobilize (Moderate)
Recharge Increase (Moderate)
Endurance Recovery (Minor)
Fly (Very Slow)
Running (Very Slow)

Enervating Field

Smash Dmg Debuff (High)
Lethal Dmg Debuff (High)
Fire Dmg Debuff (High)
Cold Dmg Debuff (High)
Energy Dmg Debuff (High)
Neg.Energy Dmg Debuff (High)
Psionic Dmg Debuff (High)
Energy Damage (Minor; 75% chance)

Mutation

Heal (Moderate)
Endurance Bonus (Minor)
Endurance Recovery (High)
Add Smash Damage (Extreme)
Add Lethal Damage (Extreme)
Add Fire Damage (Extreme)
Add Cold Damage (Very High)
Add Energy Damage (Very High)
Add Neg.Energy Damage (Extreme)
Add Psionic Damage (Extreme)
To Hit Buff (Very High)

Smash Dmg Debuff (Extreme)
Lethal Dmg Debuff (Extreme)
Fire Dmg Debuff (Extreme)
Cold Dmg Debuff (Very High)
Energy Dmg Debuff (Very High)
Neg.Energy Dmg Debuff (Extreme)
Psionic Dmg Debuff (Extreme)
To Hit Debuff (Very High)
Stun (Very High) Mag 3

Lingering Radiation

Run Speed (Slower)
Recharge Time (Slower)
Fly (Slower)

Choking Cloud

Hold (Moderate; 40% chance) Mag 2

Fallout

Energy Damage (Very High)

EMP Pulse

Hold (Extreme; 50% chance) Mag 1; Can Cancel
Stun (High) Mag 3; Can Cancel
Endurance Recovery (None)

RADIATION EMISSION STATS

Name	Type	Attacks (Acc)	Cost	Act	Rech	Range	Target	Enhancements
Radiation Emission	Clk		26.3	2.0	8	–	Ally/Self (25′ sphere)	Rech, REC, Heal
Radiation Infection	Togl		0.4	3.1	8	70	Foe (15′ sphere)	Rech, REC, Defense–, To Hit–, Rng
Accelerate Metabolism	Clk		22.5	2.0	300	–	Ally/Self (25′ sphere)	Rech, REC, Run, End.Rec.
Enervating Field	Togl	En	3.0	1.5	8	70	Foe (15′ sphere)	Rech, REC, Dam
Mutation	Clk		56.3	3.2	180	15	Downed Hero	Rech, REC, Rng, End.Rec., Int
Lingering Radiation	Clk		22.5	1.5	25	80	Foe (25′ sphere)	Rech, REC, Slow
Choking Cloud	Togl		6.0	2.0	90	–	Foe (15′ sphere)	Rech, REC, Hold
Fallout	Clk	En	0.0	1.2	300	–	Foe (20′ sphere)	Rech, REC, Dam
EMP Pulse	Clk		30.0	2.9	300	–	Foe (80′ sphere)	Rech, REC, Hold

Type: Togl (Toggle); **Clk** (Click)
Attacks: Lethal, **Sm**ash, **Fi**re, **En**ergy, **Me**lee, **NgEn** (Negative Energy), **Co**ld, **Psi**onic
Rech: Recharge Time
Enhancements: Accuracy, **Dam**age, **Dmg Resist**, **Defense+** (buff), **Defense–** (debuff), **End**urance **Drain**, **KB** (Knockback), **REC** (Reduce Endurance Cost), **Rng** (Range), **To Hit+** (buff), **To Hit-** (debuff), **Int**errupt, and **Rech** (recharge)

STORM SUMMONING

This power set is good for Defenders who would like a combination of extra damage, healing abilities and defensive abilities.

The first power from Storm Summoning is **O2 Boost**. O2 Boost is used to heal allies and can be quite useful. The O2 boost can also protect a targeted ally Hero from Sleep and Stun effects. The amount O2 Boost heals will increase as you level up. This is the only heal power in the Storm Summoning set.

For defensive abilities, Storm Summoning starts out with **Gale** which, when activated, will attempt to knock down foes and cause minor damage. The Gale radiates from you in a cone.

Later, a similar power, **Hurricane**, will form a storm around you. When a foe tries to get to you through this hurricane, he has a chance of being knocked back out of range. It will also reduce the range and Accuracy of nearby foes.

For damage, Storm Summoning offers a choice of powers. Starting off with **Snowstorm**, you can

call a Snowstorm to a targeted location, which will damage all foes in an area around that location. Any foe running into that area will be damaged as the snow falls down. It will also Slow the attack and movement of those foes.

Another power that not only helps with Defense, but also looks really cool, is **Tornado**. This power will create a tornado that jumps around, throwing foes up into the air and hurling them great distances. It also has a chance to create panic and scare away foes.

The **Steamy Mist** power creates a mist of steam around you and your allies. Steamy Mist helps protect against Fire, Cold and Energy-based attacks, reducing the damage your team takes from those types of powers.

The **Fog** power creates a fog around you and your allies. It makes you harder to see and increases your Defense. It will have the negative side effect of reducing movement speed.

Thunderclap is an AoE power that renders foes helpless and can really increase your crowd control potential. It affects a wide area, and has a long duration.

Lightning Storm creates a dark cloud overhead that sends bolts of lightning arcing into any foes within range. It can also create Fear in foes, scaring them away. Lightning bolts will continue to strike for the duration of the storm.

Power researched by Brent Copeland.

Storm Summoning Effects

Gale

Smashing Damage (Minor)
Knockback (Very High)

O2 Boost

- Heal (Moderate)
- Resist Stun (Moderate)
- Resist Sleep (Moderate)

Snow Storm

- Run Speed (Slower)
- Recharge Time (Very Slow)
- Fly (Slower)
- Fly (Stopped)

Steamy Mist

- Stealth (Moderate)
- Melee Defense (Moderate)
- Ranged Defense (Moderate)
- Run Speed (Very Slow)
- Fly (Very Slow)
- Resist Fire (Very High)
- Resist Cold (Very High)
- Resist Energy (Very High)

Freezing Rain

- Summons (Fog)

Hurricane

- Range Reduce
- To Hit Debuff (Very High)
- Repel (Moderate)
- Knockback (Very High; 5% chance)

Thunder Clap

- Stun (High) Mag 2; Can Cancel

Tornado

- Summons (Tornado)

Lightning Storm

- Summons (Lightning Storm)

STORM SUMMONING STATS

Name	Type	Attacks (Acc)	Cost	Act	Rech	Range	Target	Enhancements
Gale	Clk	Sm (-10% Acc)	11.3	2.2	8	50	Foe (50 (80° cone)	Acc, REC, Rech, Dam, KB, cone
O2 Boost	Clk		11.3	2.3	4	80	Ally	REC, Heal, Rng, Rech
Snow Storm	Togl		0.4	2.0	10	80	Foe (25' sphere)	REC, Rech, Slow
Steamy Mist	Togl		0.4	1.9	15	–	Ally/Self (40' sphere)	Rech, REC, Defense, Dmg Resist
Freezing Rain	Clk	(+100% Acc)	21.0	2.0	60	60	Location	Rech, REC, Rng, Dam, Slow, Defense–
Hurricane	Togl		0.2	2.0	10	–	Foe (25' sphere)	REC, Rech, To Hit–, KB
Thunder Clap	Clk	(-32% Acc)	15.0	2.4	45	–	Foe (25' sphere)	REC, Rech, Stun
Tornado	Clk		30.0	1.2	60	60	Location	REC, Rech, Rng, Dam, Defense–, Stun, KB
Lightning Storm	Clk	(+100% Acc)	45.0	2.0	90	–	Self	REC, Rech, Dam, KB, Drain End, Acc

Type: Togl (Toggle); **Clk** (Click)
Attacks: **Le**thal, **Sm**ash, **Fi**re, **En**ergy, **Me**lee, **NgEn** (Negative Energy), **Co**ld, **Ps**ionic
Rech: Recharge Time
Enhancements: Accuracy, **Dam**age, **Dmg Resist, Defense+** (buff), **Defense–** (debuff), **End**urance **Drain, KB** (Knockback), **REC** (Reduce Endurance Cost), **Rng** (Range), **To Hit+** (buff), **To Hit-** (debuff), **Int**errupt, and **Rech** (recharge)

DEFENDER SECONDARY (RANGED)

DARK BLAST

Dark Blast is one of the more sinister power sets available to a Defender. Each attack not only damages the villain, but most also have a debilitating effect that debuffs the target's Accuracy, reducing his ability to hit your team.

This set offers many other effects that can limit your target's ability to damage you. There are AoE attacks that Immobilize a target, cone attacks that knock targets back, and burst attacks that can confuse foes. This line includes damage over time effects for more efficient damage vs. the Endurance spent, and even a long range sniper attack that has damage comparable to most Blaster attacks.

All in all, Darkness is one of the most versatile offensive sets available, and with a high Endurance drain attack that can also channel the opponent's life to your own health bar, it can be one of the most self-sufficient and survivable lines any Hero can acquire.

When fighting it is sometimes better to hit every opponent you can at least once just to lower their Accuracy, and then focus on one target to eliminate him. Be cautious of doing this when not in a group.

This line has many AoE attacks — use them with great caution if you are fighting solo.

Dark Blast. A long-range blast of dark Energy that deals moderate damage and reduces the target's chance to hit.
Gloom. Gloom slowly drains a target of life and reduces his chance to hit. Slower than Dark Blast, but deals more damage over time.
Moonbeam. An extremely long-range, slender beam of Negative Energy that reduces the target's chance to hit. This is a sniper attack, and like most sniper attacks, it is best fired from a distance, as it can be interrupted. Solo, it is great to pull with; in a group it is a great finishing shot if the enemy is locked onto one of your teammates, but be careful of the aggro it generates.

Dark Pit. Envelopes the targeted foe and any nearby enemies in a pit of Negative Energy. The attack deals no damage, but Disorients all those affected for some time.
Tenebrous Tentacles. Cone blast that envelopes all foes in oily tentacles. Affected foes are slowly drained of life while the tentacles Immobilize them and reduce their ability to hit.
Night Fall. Unleashes a burst of netherworld particles in a narrow cone at modest range. All targets in the cone area take damage and have a reduced chance to hit.
Torrent. You summon a wave of mire that sweeps away foes within its arc. The attack deals minimal damage, but sends them flying and reduces their chance to hit.
Life Drain. You tap the powers of the netherworld to steal some life from a target foe and reduce his chance to hit. Some of that life is transferred to you.
Black Star. You unleash a devastating blast of Negative Energy around yourself, dealing massive amounts of Negative Energy damage and reducing the foes' ability to hit. Activating this power costs a lot of Endurance, and afterward leaves you drained, Disoriented and unable to recover any Endurance for a while.

Power researched by i3ullseye.

Dark Blast Effects

Dark Blast

> Neg.Energy Damage (Moderate)
> To Hit Debuff (Moderate)

Gloom

> Neg.Energy Damage (Minor)
> To Hit Debuff (Moderate)

Moonbeam

Neg.Energy Damage (Very High)
To Hit Debuff (Moderate)

Dark Pit

Stun (High) Mag 2

Tenebrous Tentacles

Smashing Damage (Minor)
Neg.Energy Damage (Minor)
To Hit Debuff (Moderate)
Immobilize (High) Mag 3

Night Fall

Neg.Energy Damage (Minor)
To Hit Debuff (Moderate)

Torrent

Smashing Damage (Minor)

Knockback (Very High)
To Hit Debuff (Moderate)

Life Drain

Neg.Energy Damage (Moderate)
Heal (Moderate)
To Hit Debuff (Moderate)

Blackstar

Smashing Damage (Moderate)
Neg.Energy Damage (High)
Neg.Energy Damage (Moderate; 75% chance)
Neg.Energy Damage (Moderate; 50% chance)
To Hit Debuff (High)
Endurance Recovery (None)
Endurance Cost (Extreme)
Stun (Very High) Mag 2

DARK BLAST STATS

Name	Type	Attacks (Acc)	Cost	Act	Rech	Range	Target	Enhancements
Dark Blast	Clk	NgEn	7.5	1.0	4	80	Foe	Acc, Dam, Rech, REC, Rng, To Hit–
Gloom	Clk	NgEn	12.3	1.1	8	80	Foe	Acc, Dam, REC, Rng, To Hit–
Moonbeam	Clk	NgEn	20.7	1.3	12	175	Foe	Acc, Dam, Rech, REC, Rng, To Hit–, Int
Dark Pit	Clk	(-32% Acc)	18.8	1.1	30	70	Foe (20' sphere)	Acc, Rech, REC, Rng, Stun
Tenebrous Tentacles	Clk	NgEn, Sm	14.7	1.7	10	–	Foe (40', 40° cone)	Acc, Dam, Rech, REC, To Hit–, Immobilize, cone
Night Fall	Clk	NgEn	18.9	2.0	10	–	Foe (60', 20° cone)	Acc, Dam, Rech, REC, To Hit–, cone
Torrent	Clk	Sm	20.7	1.0	15	–	Foe (80', 30° cone)	Acc, Dam, Rech, REC, To Hit–, KB, cone
Life Drain	Clk	NgEn	22.5	1.9	15	60	Foe	Acc, Dam, Rech, REC, Rng, To Hit–, Heal
Blackstar	Clk	Sm, NgEn (+40% Acc)	45.0	3.0	240	–	Foe (25' sphere)	Acc, Dam, Rech, REC, To Hit–

Type: Togl (Toggle); **Clk** (Click)
Attacks: Lethal, **Sm**ash, **Fi**re, **En**ergy, **Me**lee, **NgEn** (Negative Energy), **Co**ld, **Psi**onic
Rech: Recharge Time
Enhancements: Accuracy, **Dam**age, **Dmg Resist, Defense+** (buff), **Defense–** (Debuff), **End**urance **Drain, KB** (Knockback), **REC** (Reduce Endurance Cost), **Rng** (Range), **To Hit+** (buff), **To Hit–** (Debuff), **Int**errupt, and **Rech** (recharge)

ELECTRICAL BLAST

Thunder and lightning! Feeling the crackle of electricity in your hand and the smell of ozone in your nostrils makes for one of the most exciting power sets you can choose.

The Electrical Blaster has a formidable array of powers that not only damage an opponent, but drain Endurance and Stun them as well! From a well placed sniper **Zapp** to a multi-target **Ball Lightning**, or even a well timed **Short Circuit** Stun, you can be effective both solo and in groups.

As a solo Hero, you can use your ranged attacks in concert with Stun effects or crowd control secondary powers to effectively fight multiple opponents. Not only does the long range of some of your blasts allow single pull, it also allows you to hit a target multiple times before taking damage yourself, when a lot of damage is necessary. You can do damage over time to multiple targets at an early level, but this works best with a primary power set that involves Endurance regeneration, because sending out electrical bolts is hard work!

In a team, your powers enable you to really contribute. Electrical Blast has a large array of single target blasts allowing for nearly nonstop damage as you gain more and different abilities through the levels. By standing back, you can get the most out of your considerable damage potential. This power set is particularly effective at lowering your opponents' Endurance, and therefore limiting the villains' ability to damage you or your teammates. The ability to Stun multiple targets can be a lifesaver if things start to go wrong for you and your group. Those seconds may be the difference between victory and defeat.

Power researched by Wunderr.

Electrical Blast Effects

Charged Bolts

Energy Damage (Moderate)
End Drain (Minor)
Endurance Recovery (None; 20% chance)

Lightning Bolt

Energy Damage (High)
End Drain (Minor)
Endurance Recovery (None; 30% chance)

Ball Lightning

Energy Damage (Minor)
Energy Damage (Minor)
End Drain (Minor)
Endurance Recovery (None; 30% chance)

Short Circuit

Energy Damage (Minor)
End Drain (Very High)
Endurance Recovery (None)

Aim

To Hit Buff (Very High)
Add Smash Damage (Extreme)
Add Lethal Damage (Extreme)
Add Fire Damage (Extreme)
Add Cold Damage (Extreme)
Add Energy Damage (Extreme)
Add Neg.Energy Damage (Extreme)
Add Psionic Damage (Extreme)

Zapp

Energy Damage (Very High)
End Drain (High)
Endurance Recovery (None; 50% chance)

Tesla Cage

Hold (High) Mag 3
Energy Damage (Minor)
End Drain (Minor)
Endurance Recovery (None)

Voltaic Sentinel

Summons (Voltaic Sentinel)

Thunderous Blast

Smashing Damage (Moderate)
Energy Damage (High)
Energy Damage (Moderate; 75% chance)
Energy Damage (Moderate; 50% chance)
End Drain (Extreme)
End Drain (Very High; 30% chance)
Endurance Recovery (None)
Endurance Recovery (None)
Endurance Cost (Extreme)
Stun Self (Very High) Mag 2

ELECTRICAL BLAST STATS

Name	Type	Attacks (Acc)	Cost	Act	Rech	Range	Target	Enhancements
Charged Bolts	Clk	En	7.5	2.1	4	70	Foe	Acc, Dam, REC, Rng, Drain End, Rech
Lightning Bolt	Clk	En	12.3	2.0	8	80	Foe	Acc, Dam, Rech, REC, Rng, Drain End
Ball Lightning	Clk	En	21.9	1.1	16	80	Foe (15' sphere)	Acc, Dam, Rech, REC, Rng, Drain End
Short Circuit	Clk	En	22.5	3.0	20	—	Foe (20' sphere)	Acc, Dam, Rech, REC, Drain End
Aim	Clk		7.5	1.2	30	—	Self	REC, Rech, To Hit+
Zapp	Clk	En (+20% Acc)	20.7	1.3	12	150	Foe	Acc, Dam, Rech, REC, Rng, Drain End, Int
Tesla Cage	Clk	En	7.9	2.2	10	60	Foe	Acc, Dam, Rech, REC, Rng, Hold, Drain End
Voltaic Sentinel	Clk	(+100% Acc)	37.5	3.1	60	60	Location	Rech, REC, Rng, Dam, Drain End, Acc
Thunderous Blast	Clk	Sm, En (+30% Acc)	45.0	3.7	240	60	Foe (25' sphere)	Acc, Dam, Rech, REC, Drain End

Type: **Togl** (Toggle); **Clk** (Click)
Attacks: **Le**thal, **Sm**ash, **Fi**re, **En**ergy, **Me**lee, **NgEn** (Negative Energy), **Co**ld, **Psi**onic
Rech: Recharge Time
Enhancements: **Acc**uracy, **Dam**age, **Dmg Resist**, **Defense+** (buff), **Defense–** (Debuff), **End**urance **Drain**, **KB** (Knockback), **REC** (Reduce Endurance Cost), **Rng** (Range), **To Hit+** (buff), **To Hit–** (Debuff), **Int**errupt, and **Rech** (recharge)

ENERGY BLAST

Energy Blast is not the most damaging of the Blaster pools, but it does come with a plethora of Knockback and Knockdown effects. All the Powers in the pool, other than **Aim**, have some type of Knockback associated with them. A lot of people who look at the pool might think that the damage isn't as good as it could be, and discount the effects of incapacitating a foe for an extra few seconds as they have to stand back up. In fact, Knockback can have a huge impact on most solo fights, because a villain on his back isn't shooting at you (or your team, in a group).

Power Burst and **Power Blast** are the main single-target high-damage dealers of the group. Power Burst is a short-range attack, so it's good to start with it, knock a foe back, then follow up with Power Bolt, due to its longer range.

Power Bolt is fairly fast, but low on damage. It makes a good filler attack. **Power Push** is mainly used to keep melee foes out of range, or keep a ranged foe on the ground. It does very little damage, but considerable Knockback.

Power Burst, Power Blast and Power Bolt are all going to want significant Enhancement slots as your main attacks. Accuracy, recharge time, damage and Endurance cost need to be on your radar, with maybe an extra helping of damage to make up for the lower damage from the pool. Power Blast and Power Bolt can both benefit from range enhancers, but that probably shouldn't be your main concern.

As far as the AoE aspects of this set, you're looking at **Energy Torrent** (short-ranged cone), **Explosive Blast** (mid-range AoE), and **Nova** (PBAoE with a self Stun and self Endurance drain). Energy Torrent and Explosive Blast are fairly light on damage, but heavy on the Knockback. Nova, being the highest power in the pool, is heavy on

damage *and* Knockback. If you're using AoE powers a lot, you'll definitely want damage enhancers in these powers, probably doubled up. Energy Torrent could use cone range increase, along with Accuracy. Explosive Blast definitely needs Accuracy and damage to be effective. Nova is all about Accuracy and damage.

Overall the pool is a good balance of damage and secondary effects. It offers good rewards in combat, and is very entertaining.

Power researched by Praxi.

Energy Blast Effects

Power Bolt

Smashing Damage (Minor)
Energy Damage (Moderate)
Knockback (Moderate; 20% chance)

Power Blast

Smashing Damage (Moderate)
Energy Damage (Moderate)
Knockback (Moderate; 30% chance)

Energy Torrent

Smashing Damage (Minor)
Energy Damage (Moderate)
Knockback (High; 50% chance)

Power Burst

Smashing Damage (Moderate)
Energy Damage (Moderate)
Knockback (High; 60% chance)

Sniper Blast

Smashing Damage (Moderate)
Energy Damage (High)
Knockback (Moderate; 50% chance)

Aim

To Hit Buff (Very High)
Add Smash Damage (Extreme)
Add Lethal Damage (Extreme)
Add Fire Damage (Extreme)
Add Cold Damage (Extreme)
Add Energy Damage (Extreme)
Add Neg Damage (Extreme)
Add Psionic Damage (Extreme)

Power Push

Smashing Damage (Minor)
Energy Damage (Minor)
Knockback (Very High)

Explosive Blast

Smashing Damage (Minor)
Energy Damage (Minor)
Knockback (High; 50% chance)

Nova

Smashing Damage (Moderate)
Energy Damage (High)
Energy Damage (Moderate; 75% chance)
Energy Damage (Moderate; 25% chance)
Knockback (Very High)
Endurance Recovery (None)
Endurance Cost (Extreme)
Stun (Very High) Mag 2

ENERGY BLAST STATS

Name	Type	Attacks (Acc)	Cost	Act	Rech	Range	Target	Enhancements
Power Bolt	Clk	Sm, En	7.5	2.0	4	80	Foe	Acc, Dam, REC, Rng, KB, Rech
Power Blast	Clk	Sm, En	12.3	1.7	8	80	Foe	Acc, Dam, Rech, REC, Rng, KB
Energy Torrent	Clk	Sm, En	12.3	1.1	8	40	Foe (40', 45° cone)	Acc, Dam, Rech, REC, KB, cone
Power Burst	Clk	Sm, En	15.0	2.0	10	20	Foe	Acc, Dam, Rech, REC, Rng, KB
Sniper Blast	Clk	Sm, En (+20% Acc)	20.7	1.3	12	150	Foe	Acc, Dam, Rech, REC, Rng, KB, Int
Aim	Clk		7.5	1.2	30	–	Self	REC, Rech, To Hit+
Power Push	Clk	Sm, En (40% Acc)	12.3	1.1	8	70	Foe	Acc, Dam, Rech, REC, Rng, KB
Explosive Blast	Clk	Sm, En	21.9	1.7	16	80	Foe (15' sphere)	Acc, Dam, Rech, REC, Rng, KB
Nova	Clk	Sm, En (40% Acc)	45.0	3.0	240	–	Foe (25' sphere)	Acc, Dam, Rech, REC, KB

Type: Togl (Toggle); **Clk** (Click)
Attacks: Lethal, **Sm**ash, **Fi**re, **En**ergy, **Me**lee, **NgEn** (Negative Energy), **Co**ld, **Psi**onic
Rech: Recharge Time
Enhancements: Accuracy, **Dam**age, **Dmg Resist**, **Defense+** (buff), **Defense–** (Debuff), **End**urance **Drain**, **KB** (Knockback), **REC** (Reduce Endurance Cost), **Rng** (Range), **To Hit+** (buff), **To Hit-** (Debuff), **Int**errupt, and **Rech** (recharge)

PSYCHIC BLAST

This set has a variety of different effects. Most of these powers can slow the recharge time of the target. This effect can stack, so once you have multiple powers that can do this, be sure to keep attacking the same target and you can seriously reduce the target's attack rate.

Be sure to put lots of Accuracy Enhancements into **Psychic Scream**, **Psionic Tornado** and **Psychic Wail**, to affect as many foes as possible in these AoE powers.

Remember, humanoid foes are rarely resistant to Psionic damage, but targets without brains usually take less damage from these powers.

Don't use Psychic Wail until you have put a couple of damage and Accuracy Enhancements into it. It is devastating, but you don't want to be left alone, surrounded by any surviving villains after you use this. Fire it off when most of the enemy has taken some damage. Better yet, sneak in (stealth/teleport) and have a teammate teleport you out after you activate this.

Psychic Blast Effects

Mental Blast

Psionic Damage (Moderate)
Recharge Time (Very Slow)

Subdue

Psionic Damage (Moderate)
Immobilize (Moderate; 80% chance) Mag 3;
Can Cancel

Psionic Lance

Psionic Damage (Very High)
Recharge Time (Slowest)

Psychic Scream

Psionic Damage (Moderate)
Recharge Time (Very Slow)

Telekinetic Blast

Smashing Damage (Moderate)
Psionic Damage (Moderate)
Knockback (Very High; 60% chance)

Will Domination

> Psionic Damage (High)
> Sleep (Moderate; 80% chance) Mag 3; Can Cancel

Psionic Tornado

> Psionic Damage (Minor)
> Recharge Time (Very Slow)
> Knockup (Moderate; 50% chance)

Scramble Thoughts

> Psionic Damage (Minor)
> Stun (High) Mag 3; Can Cancel

Psychic Wail

> Psionic Damage (Very High)
> Psionic Damage (Moderate; 75% chance)
> Psionic Damage (Moderate; 50% chance)
> Stun (High) Mag 3

> Endurance Recovery (None)
> Endurance Cost (Extreme)
> Stun (Very High) Mag 2

PSYCHIC BLAST STATS

Name	Type	Attacks (Acc)	Cost	Act	Rech	Range	Target	Enhancements
Mental Blast	Clk	Psi	7.5	2.7	4	100	Foe	Acc, Dam, REC, Rng, Rech
Subdue	Clk	Psi	12.3	1.7	8	100	Foe	Acc, Dam, Rech, REC, Rng, Immobilize
Psionic Lance	Clk	Psi (+20% Acc)	20.7	1.0	12	175	Foe	Acc, Dam, Rech, REC, Rng, Int
Psychic Scream	Clk	Psi	17.1	2.7	12	–	Foe (60', 30° cone)	Acc, Dam, Rech, REC, cone
Telekinetic Blast	Clk	Sm, Psi	12.3	1.0	8	100	Foe	Acc, Dam, Rech, REC, Rng, KB
Will Domination	Clk	Psi	14.7	1.1	14	100	Foe	Acc, Dam, Rech, REC, Rng, Sleep
Psionic Tornado	Clk	Psi	26.7	2.4	20	100	Foe (20' sphere)	Acc, Dam, Rech, REC, Rng, KB
Scramble Thoughts	Clk	Psi	15.0	3.0	20	100	Foe	Acc, Dam, Rech, REC, Rng, Stun
Psychic Wail	Clk	Psi (+50% Acc)	45.0	2.0	240	–	Foe (25' sphere)	Acc, Dam, Rech, REC, KB

Type: Togl (Toggle); **Clk** (Click)
Attacks: Lethal, **Sm**ash, **Fi**re, **En**ergy, **Me**lee, **NgEn** (Negative Energy), **Co**ld, **Psi**onic
Rech: Recharge Time
Enhancements: Accuracy, **Dam**age, **Dmg Resist, Defense+** (buff), **Defense–** (Debuff), **End**urance **Drain, KB** (Knockback), **REC** (Reduce Endurance Cost), **Rng** (Range), **To Hit+** (buff), **To Hit–** (Debuff), **Int**errupt, and **Rech** (recharge)

RADIATION BLAST

Radiation Blast is a very accurate power set. Combined with its inherent ability to reduce a target's Defense, multiple hits on the same target with powers in this set can be very effective.

Put your Accuracy Enhancements into **Irradiate, Electron Haze, Neutron Bomb** and **Atomic Blast** to affect as many foes as possible in these AoE powers.

Don't use Atomic Blast until you have put a couple of Damage and Accuracy Enhancements into it. It is devastating, but you don't want to be left alone, surrounded by any surviving villains after you use this. Fire it off when most of the enemy has taken some damage. Better yet, sneak in (stealth/teleport) and have a teammate teleport you out after you activate this.

Radiation Blast Effects

Neutrino Bolt

Energy Damage (Moderate)
Defense Debuff (Moderate) Can Cancel

X-Ray Beam

Energy Damage (Moderate)
Defense Debuff (High)

Irradiate

Energy Damage (Minor)
Defense Debuff (Extreme)

Electron Haze

Energy Damage (Moderate)
Defense Debuff (High)
Knockback (Moderate; 25% chance)

Proton Volley

Energy Damage (Moderate)
Defense Debuff (Extreme) Can Cancel

Aim

To Hit Buff (Very High)
Add Smash Damage (Extreme)
Add Lethal Damage (Extreme)
Add Fire Damage (Extreme)
Add Cold Damage (Extreme)
Add Energy Damage (Extreme)
Add Neg Damage (Extreme)
Add Psionic Damage (Extreme)

Cosmic Burst

Energy Damage (High)
Stun (Moderate) Mag 3
Defense Debuff (Extreme) Can Cancel

Neutron Bomb

Energy Damage (Moderate)
Defense Debuff (High)

Atomic Blast

Smashing Damage (Moderate)
Energy Damage (High)
Energy Damage (Moderate; 75% chance)
Energy Damage (Moderate; 50% chance)
Immobilize (Very High) Mag 3
Defense Debuff (Extreme)
Endurance Recovery (None)
Endurance Cost (Extreme)
Stun (Very High) Mag 2

RADIATION BLAST STATS

Name	Type	Attacks (Acc)	Cost	Act	Rech	Range	Target	Enhancements
Neutrino Bolt	Clk	En	4.5	1.0	1.5	80	Foe	Acc, Dam, REC, Rng, Defense–, Rech
X-Ray Beam	Clk	En (+10% Acc)	7.5	1.7	4	80	Foe	Acc, Dam, REC, Rng, Defense–, Rech
Irradiate	Clk	En (+10% Acc)	26.7	1.1	20	–	Foe (20' sphere)	Acc, Dam, Rech, REC, Defense–
Electron Haze	Clk	En (+10% Acc)	20.7	2.4	16	–	Foe (40', 30° cone)	Acc, Dam, Rech, REC, KB, cone, Defense–
Proton Volley	Clk	En (+20% Acc)	20.7	1.3	12	150	Foe	Acc, Dam, Rng, REC, Rech, Defense–, Int
Aim	Clk		7.5	1.2	30	–	Self	Rech, REC, To Hit+
Cosmic Burst	Clk	En	15.0	2.1	10	20	Foe	Acc, Dam, Rech, REC, Rng, Stun, Defense–
Neutron Bomb	Clk	En (+10% Acc)	21.9	1.7	16	80	Foe (15' sphere)	Acc, Dam, Rech, REC, Rng, Defense–
Atomic Blast	Clk	Sm, En (+30% Acc)	45.0	2.9	240	–	Foe (25' sphere)	Acc, Dam, Rech, REC, Defense–

Type: Togl (Toggle); **Clk** (Click)
Attacks: Lethal, **Sm**ash, **Fi**re, **En**ergy, **Me**lee, **NgEn** (Negative Energy), **Co**ld, **Psi**onic
Rech: Recharge Time
Enhancements: Accuracy, **Dam**age, **Dmg Resist**, **Defense+** (buff), **Defense–** (Debuff), **End**urance **Drain**, **KB** (Knockback), **REC** (Reduce Endurance Cost), **Rng** (Range), **To Hit+** (buff), **To Hit–** (Debuff), **Int**errupt, and **Rech** (recharge)

SCRAPPER PRIMARY (MELEE)

BROADSWORD

Be sure to have your sword out before entering combat. Avoid taking pool attack powers that will cause you to put your sword away. Broadsword has enough attack powers, so you don't need to add more.

Put your Accuracy Enhancements into **Slice** and **Whirling Sword** to affect as many foes as possible with these AoE powers.

Hack and **Slash** are your bread and butter, so open up all the Enhancement slots in these two.

Disembowel and **Head Splitter** are devastating, so you don't want to miss with these. Be mindful of a good balance of Accuracy, recharge, Endurance discount and damage Enhancements in these two.

Broadsword Effects

Hack

Lethal Damage (High)
Defense Debuff (Moderate) Can Cancel

Slash

Lethal Damage (Moderate)
Defense Debuff (Moderate) Can Cancel

Slice

Lethal Damage (Moderate)
Defense Debuff (Moderate) Can Cancel

Build Up

To Hit Buff (High)
Add Smash Damage (Extreme)
Add Lethal Damage (Extreme)
Add Fire Damage (Extreme)
Add Cold Damage (Extreme)

Add Energy Damage (Extreme)
Add Neg. Energy Damage (Extreme)
Add Psionic Damage (Extreme)

Taunt

Taunt (Very High) Mag 4

Parry

Lethal Damage (Minor)
Melee Defense (High)

Whirling Sword

Lethal Damage (Moderate)
Lethal Damage (Minor)

Disembowel

Lethal Damage (High)
Knockup (Moderate; 75% chance)
Defense Debuff (Moderate) Can Cancel

Head Splitter

Lethal Damage (Very High)
Knockback (Moderate; 60% chance)
Lethal Damage (High; 15% chance)
Defense Debuff (Moderate) Can Cancel

BROADSWORD STATS

Name	Type	Attacks (Acc)	Cost	Act	Rech	Range	Target	Enhancements
Hack	Clk	Me, Le (+5% Acc)	7.5	1.8	8	5	Foe	Acc, Dam, Rech, REC, Defense–
Slash	Clk	Me, Le (+5% Acc)	12.3	1.4	4	5	Foe	Acc, Dam, Rech, REC, Defense–
Slice	Clk	Me, Le (+5% Acc)	12.3	2.3	8	–	Foe (5', 130° cone)	Acc, Dam, Rech, REC, Defense–
Build Up	Clk	(+5% Acc)	7.5	1.2	45	–	Self	REC, Rech, To Hit+
Taunt	Clk	(+5% Acc)	0.0	2.2	3	70	Foe	Rng, Taunt, Rech
Parry	Clk	Me, Le (+5% Acc)	12.3	2.9	3	5	Foe	Acc, Dam, REC, Defense, Rech
Whirling Sword	Clk	Me, Le (+5% Acc)	18.8	2.9	14	–	Foe (8' sphere)	Acc, Dam, Rech, REC, Defense–
Disembowel	Clk	Me, Le (+5% Acc)	12.3	2.9	10	5	Foe	Acc, Dam, Rech, REC, Defense–, KB
Head Splitter	Clk	Me, Le (+5% Acc)	19.5	2.9	14	5	Foe	Acc, Dam, Rech, REC, Defense–, KB

Type: Togl (Toggle); **Clk** (Click)
Attacks: Lethal, **Sm**ash, **Fi**re, **En**ergy, **Me**lee, **NgEn** (Negative Energy), **Co**ld, **Psi**onic
Rech: Recharge Time
Enhancements: Accuracy, **Dam**age, **Dmg Resist**, **Defense+** (buff), **Defense–** (Debuff), **End**urance **Drain**, **KB** (Knockback), **REC** (Reduce Endurance Cost), **Rng** (Range), **To Hit+** (buff), **To Hit-** (Debuff), **Int**errupt, and **Rech** (recharge)

CLAWS

Claws are a vicious attack power set for the Scrapper, allowing you to deliver Lethal damage to your target. It's not the most damaging of the Scrapper offensive power sets, but still effective for a number of reasons.

The Pros of Claws:

◆ Claws' Lethal damage is resisted by enemies significantly less often than Smashing damage is, making Claws powers more effective, generally, than Smashing powers.

◆ Two Knockdown powers — excellent for damage mitigation (a knocked down target is not attacking you, he's getting up).

◆ Fast recharge speeds on most of the attacks.

◆ **Slash** lowers the target's Defense, which benefits everyone else attacking the target.

◆ Multiple multi-target attacks, allowing you to damage more than one target at a time.

Cons:

◆ Only moderate damage, compared to other Scrapper power sets like Martial Arts.

◆ Burns through Endurance very quickly, forcing you to focus on filling Enhancement slots with Enhancements that lower Endurance cost of the powers, versus using them to increase damage or Accuracy.

As mentioned in the cons, focus on keeping the Endurance cost of the powers down. You cycle through your attacks very fast, which means you burn through Endurance just as quickly. Given how fast the Claws attack buttons recharge, there is little need to get other combat powers, like Jumping: Jump Kick or Fighting: Boxing, as you'll always have a Claw attack up and available to be used, and they're far more effective than the secondary pool powers. Fitness makes an excellent addition to this power set, as Stamina helps offset some of the Endurance cost issues.

Claws Effects

Swipe

Lethal Damage (Minor)
Lethal Damage (Minor)

Strike

Lethal Damage (Moderate)

Slash

Lethal Damage (Moderate)
Defense Debuff (Moderate)

Spin

Lethal Damage (Moderate)

Taunt

Taunt (Very High) Mag 4

Follow Up

Lethal Damage (Moderate)
To Hit Buff (High)

Add Smash Damage (Very High)
Add Lethal Damage (Very High)
Add Fire Damage (Very High)
Add Cold Damage (Very High)
Add Energy Damage (Very High)
Add Neg.Energy Damage (Very High)
Add Psionic Damage (Very High)

Focus

Lethal Damage (High)
Knockback (Moderate)

Eviscerate

Lethal Damage (High)
Lethal Damage (Moderate; 5% chance)

Shockwave

Lethal Damage (Moderate)
Knockback (Moderate)

CLAWS STATS

Name	Type	Attacks (Acc)	Cost	Act	Rech	Range	Target	Enhancements
Swipe	Clk	Me, Le	4.9	2.4	1.8	5	Foe	Acc, Dam, REC, Rech
Strike	Clk	Me, Le	6.5	1.3	3.2	5	Foe	Acc, Dam, Rech, REC
Slash	Clk	Me, Le	8.5	2.4	4.8	5	Foe	Acc, Dam, Rech, REC, Defense–
Spin	Clk	Me, Le	19.5	2.1	14	—	Foe (8' sphere)	Acc, Dam, Rech, REC
Taunt	Clk		0.0	2.4	3	70	Foe	Rng, Taunt, Rech
Follow Up	Clk	Me, Le	11.3	1.6	12	5	Foe	Acc, Dam, Rech, REC, To Hit+
Focus	Clk	Le	10.4	1.5	6.4	40	Foe	Acc, Dam, Rech, REC, KB, Rng
Eviscerate	Clk	Me, Le	14.7	2.2	10	—	Foe (5', 90° cone)	Acc, Dam, Rech, REC
Shockwave	Clk	Me, Le	26.0	1.5	13.5	—	Foe (30', 90° cone)	Acc, Dam, Rech, REC, KB, Rng

Type: Togl (Toggle); **Clk** (Click)
Attacks: Lethal, **Sm**ash, **Fi**re, **En**ergy, **Me**lee, **NgEn** (Negative Energy), **Co**ld, **Psi**onic
Rech: Recharge Time
Enhancements: Accuracy, **Dam**age, **Dmg Resist**, **Defense+** (buff), **Defense–** (Debuff), **End**urance **Drain**, **KB** (Knockback), **REC** (Reduce Endurance Cost), **Rng** (Range), **To Hit+** (buff), **To Hit–** (Debuff), **Int**errupt, and **Rech** (recharge)

DARK MELEE

Unlike most other Scrapper power sets, Dark Melee has fewer direct attacks and more methods of dealing with difficult situations. It is an excellent choice for the brooding, lone-wolf Hero. The Dark Energy punches also have the added benefit of lowering your target's Accuracy for a short time.

Shadow Punch. Your basic attack. It does only medium damage, but recharges quickly.

Smite. Another basic attack, Smite does more damage than Shadow Punch, but takes longer to recharge.

Shadow Maul. Your most damaging attack for many levels, this maneuver performs many punches in a row, and will stop an opponent fast. Best of all, if you have multiple enemies in very close proximity to each other, you can often hit more than one person simultaneously.

Touch of Fear. A successful strike will make your opponent run away. Although chasing a running foe isn't always fun, this provides an easy way to thin out a tough fight against multiple foes.

Taunt. You can use this to pull an enemy off of a teammate, but it is also an excellent soloing tool. Stand back and use Taunt to convince an enemy to leave his friends and attack you alone.

Siphon Life. This attack does a high amount of damage to a foe, and then heals you with a good portion of that Energy. It has a high Endurance cost, but Endurance recovers more quickly than hit points do, so use this to save yourself in a tough fight, or even just to top off your health toward the end of the battle.

Dark Consumption. Dark Consumption is an AoE attack that will hit all nearby enemies. They take only a small amount of damage, but each opponent affected will fill up a significant portion of your Endurance Bar, allowing you to keep going in a long fight.

Soul Drain. Another AoE attack, Soul Drain also does a small amount of damage to everyone directly around you, but in this case you receive an increase to your Accuracy and damage in future attacks for each affected enemy. This allows you to take down a handful of enemies a lot faster than you'd otherwise be able to.

Midnight Grasp. This attack serves two purposes: First, a successful strike does a high amount of damage to a villain, and continues to damage him through the duration of the power, making this easily your most damaging option. Secondly, that villain will be unable to move for quite some time while you pummel him or his friends.

Power researched by Almeric.

Dark Melee Effects

Shadow Punch

Smashing Damage (Minor)
Neg.Energy Damage (Minor)
To Hit Debuff (Moderate)

Smite

Smashing Damage (Minor)
Neg.Energy Damage (Moderate)
To Hit Debuff (Moderate)

Shadow Maul

Smashing Damage (Minor)
Neg.Energy Damage (Minor)
To Hit Debuff (Moderate)

Touch of Fear
Fear (Very High) Mag 3
To Hit Debuff (High)

Taunt
Taunt (Very High) Mag 4

Siphon Life
Neg.Energy Damage (Moderate)
Heal (Moderate)
To Hit Debuff (Moderate)

Dark Consumption
Neg.Energy Damage (Moderate)
Endurance Bonus (Very High)

Soul Drain
Neg.Energy Damage (Moderate)
To Hit Buff (Moderate)
Add Smash Damage (Moderate)
Add Lethal Damage (Moderate)
Add Fire Damage (Moderate)
Add Cold Damage (Moderate)
Add Energy Damage (Moderate)
Add Neg.Energy Damage (Moderate)
Add Psionic Damage (Moderate)

Midnight Grasp
Neg.Energy Damage (Moderate)
Immobilize (High) Mag 3
To Hit Debuff (Moderate)
Neg.Energy Damage (Minor)

DARK MELEE STATS

Name	Type	Attacks (Acc)	Cost	Act	Rech	Range	Target	Enhancements
Shadow Punch	Clk	Me, Sm, NgEn	6.3	0.6	3	5	Foe	Acc, Dam, Rech, REC, To Hit–
Smite	Clk	Me, Sm, NgEn	9.9	1.0	6	5	Foe	Acc, Dam, Rech, REC, To Hit–
Shadow Maul	Clk	Me, Sm, NgEn	12.3	3.1	8	–	Foe (5', 45° cone)	Acc, Dam, Rech, REC, To Hit–
Touch of Fear	Clk	(+20% Acc)	12.3	1.2	8	5	Foe	Acc, Rech, REC, To Hit–, Fear
Taunt	Clk		0.0	1.7	3	70	Foe	Rng, Taunt
Siphon Life	Clk	Me, NgEn	22.5	1.9	15	5	Foe	Acc, Dam, Rech, REC, To Hit–
Dark Consumption	Clk	NgEn	0.8	1.0	180	–	Foe (8' sphere)	Acc, Dam, Rech, End.Rec.
Soul Drain	Clk	NgEn (+20% Acc)	22.5	2.4	120	–	Foe (10' sphere)	Acc, Dam, Rech, REC, To Hit+
Midnight Grasp	Clk	Me, NgEn	17.3	2.1	15	5	Foe	Acc, Dam, Rech, REC, To Hit–, Immobilize

Type: Togl (Toggle); **Clk** (Click)
Attacks: Lethal, **Sm**ash, **Fi**re, **En**ergy, **Me**lee, **NgEn** (Negative Energy), **Co**ld, **Psi**onic
Rech: Recharge Time
Enhancements: Accuracy, **Dam**age, **Dmg Resist**, **Defense+** (buff), **Defense–** (Debuff), **End**urance **Drain**, **KB** (Knockback), **REC** (Reduce Endurance Cost), **Rng** (Range), **To Hit+** (buff), **To Hit-** (Debuff), **Int**errupt, and **Rech** (recharge)

KATANA

The Katana power set is very heavily weighted towards offense. It contains a multitude of powerful attacks, but they tend to go off rather slowly. You will absolutely need to develop your defensive secondary wisely if you want to survive with Katana as a primary. The Fitness power pool, with its free and continuous combat buffs, is also a good friend to the Katana fighter.

Endurance Enhancements are paramount to the Katana fighter, but damage, Accuracy and recharge rate are also vital. Basically, you need to keep all your attacks as fully buffed as possible.

The Katana set works well for solo play, though it's a bit one-dimensional to be the perfect solo power set. It's a good choice for a frontline team fighter, particularly if the group is short on Blasters.

Hack and **Slash** will be with you from the start, and they'll never let you down. Their balance between damage potential and recharge speed is pretty close to ideal, particularly when they're both fully enhanced.

The real secret to effective Katana play, however, is learning how to make the best of the AoE attacks, **Slice** and **Whirling Sword**. These attacks recharge more slowly, but if used effectively they can be real lifesavers in combat against groups. In addition to its base damage, Whirling Sword also includes a brief damage over time (DoT) effect. Slice is a cone effect, and you'll soon become adept in lining up as many enemies as possible right in front of you. Whirling Sword, bless it, has a 360-degree effect. Its biggest drawback is that it takes a long time to actually complete the attack.

Parry is a very useful combat asset. It only does about half the damage of a successful Slash, but

it gives you a nice defensive bonus when it goes off. The Defense buff doesn't last long, but Parry recharges quickly so it's easy to renew.

Other than that, your only significant non-damage tools are **Taunt**, which is useful in group play and can help you thin out the ranks of enemies when solo, and **Build Up**, a good all-around buff that doesn't hang around for very long.

At the top end of the set are the serious damage dealers, **Disembowel** and **Head Splitter**, both of which combine really impressive damage with the ability to knock the enemy for a loop. Recharge times, of course, are substantial for these attacks.

A fully developed Katana Hero attacking a group of enemies solo might start off by trying to Taunt the stragglers away from the group to take them out quietly. Then she could hit Build Up and rush the body of enemies, hitting the toughest foe in the bunch with Head Splitter and Disembowel, to try to take him out in one or two strikes. By the time those attacks go off, the enemy will be bunching around her, so she'll unleash her Whirling Sword and Slice for effect against the maximum number of foes. By now Build Up is probably wearing off and she's beginning to take damage, so she starts mixing Parry into her attack sequence, followed by quick Hack and Slash attacks. Now her major damage attacks are recharged, and her AoE powers are well on their way, so she can start all over again …

Katana Effects

Hack

Lethal Damage (Moderate)
Defense Debuff (Moderate) Can Cancel

Slash

Lethal Damage (Moderate)
Defense Debuff (Moderate) Can Cancel

Slice

Lethal Damage (Moderate)
Defense Debuff (Moderate) Can Cancel

Build Up

To Hit Buff (High)
Add Smash Damage (Extreme)
Add Lethal Damage (Extreme)
Add Fire Damage (Extreme)
Add Cold Damage (Extreme)
Add Energy Damage (Extreme)
Add Neg.Energy Damage (Extreme)
Add Psionic Damage (Extreme)

Taunt

Taunt (Very High) Mag 4

Parry

Lethal Damage (Minor)
Melee Defense (High)

Whirling Sword

Lethal Damage (Moderate)
Lethal Damage (Minor)

Disembowel

Lethal Damage (High)
Knockup (Moderate; 75% chance)
Defense Debuff (Moderate) Can Cancel

Head Splitter

Lethal Damage (High)
Knockback (Moderate; 60% chance)
Lethal Damage (High; 15% chance)
Defense Debuff (Moderate) Can Cancel

KATANA STATS

Name	Type	Attacks (Acc)	Cost	Act	Rech	Range	Target	Enhancements
Hack	Clk	Me, Le (+5% Acc)	6.3	1.8	5	5	Foe	Acc, Dam, Rech, REC, Defense–
Slash	Clk	Me, Le (+5% Acc)	8.7	1.4	3	5	Foe	Acc, Dam, Rech, REC, Defense–
Slice	Clk	Me, Le (+5% Acc)	9.9	2.3	6	–	Foe (5′ 130° cone)	Acc, Dam, Rech, REC, Defense–
Build Up	Clk		7.5	1.2	45	–	Self	REC, Rech, To Hit+
Taunt	Clk	(+5% Acc)	0.0	2.2	3	70	Foe	Rng, Taunt, Rech
Parry	Clk	Me, Le (+5% Acc)	12.3	2.9	3	5	Foe	Acc, Dam, REC, Defense, Rech
Whirling Sword	Clk	Me, Le (+5% Acc)	18.8	2.9	14	–	Foe (8′ sphere)	Acc, Dam, Rech, REC, Defense–
Disembowel	Clk	Me, Le (+5% Acc)	13.5	2.9	9	5	Foe	Acc, Dam, Rech, REC, Defense–, KB
Head Splitter	Clk	Me, Le (+5% Acc)	17.1	2.9	12	5	Foe	Acc, Dam, Rech, REC, Defense–, KB

Type: **Togl** (Toggle); **Clk** (Click)
Attacks: **Le**thal, **Sm**ash, **Fi**re, **En**ergy, **Me**lee, **NgEn** (Negative Energy), **Co**ld, **Psi**onic
Rech: Recharge Time
Enhancements: **Acc**uracy, **Dam**age, **Dmg Resist**, **Defense+** (buff), **Defense–** (Debuff), **End**urance **Drain**, **KB** (Knockback), **REC** (Reduce Endurance Cost), **Rng** (Range), **To Hit+** (buff), **To Hit–** (Debuff), **Int**errupt, and **Rech** (recharge)

MARTIAL ARTS

Martial Arts offers a wide array of strong attacks. Some are pure damage, but there are also some useful tools for dealing with multiple attackers and bosses.

Thunder Kick. A basic, solid, fast attack that can always be relied on to help finish off an opponent.

Storm Kick. This attack deals heavy damage via a stream of many kicks. This will be your strongest attack for a long time. The only drawbacks to this move are that it takes a while to perform, which leaves you open to extra damage from secondary opponents, and that it's an all-or-nothing attack, meaning that either all attacks hit, or they all miss. Still, two Thunder Kicks with a Storm Kick in the middle will finish off many lower-level minions.

Cobra Strike. Cobra Strike does almost no damage to a foe, but will leave him Disoriented and unable to strike back through your next several attacks. You can use this for crowd control, but this is still a great tool against single targets — *especially* bosses. Bosses can do a lot of awful things to you, but if they're Disoriented they can't do anything at all. This power has a fairly long recharge time, so bring extra Accuracy Enhancements, because you might not get a second chance! Note, a boss is resistant to Stun and a single Cobra Strike is not enough to Stun him. However, Thunder Kick also has a chance to Stun, and the two powers back to back can Stun virtually anything that can be Stunned.

Focus Chi. For a brief time, Focus Chi increase the damage done by each successful attack, and make your attacks more accurate. You'll only have time for about three attacks before it wears off, but the Endurance you save by taking out the enemy more quickly is well worth the trouble.

Crane Kick. Crane Kick packs a huge punch, and has a very good chance of knocking your opponent to the ground. Since you're still standing, you can easily get an extra attack in on him while he's getting up, *or* you can turn your attention to other foes. The high damage output alone is worth keeping this attack in your repertoire no matter the circumstance.

Crippling Axe Kick. This is a low damage attack, but it will Slow your opponent down for a short time. This is useful for stopping fleeing enemies, and it also Slows down an opponent's attack rate.

Warrior's Challenge. You can use this to pull an enemy off of a teammate, but this is also an excellent soloing tool. Stand back and you can taunt an enemy to leave his friends and attack you alone.

Dragon's Tail. An excellent crowd control tool, use this power when numbers are against you. You'll have a good chance of knocking nearby opponents to the ground, which will give you a moment to regroup.

Eagle's Claw. This is another attack that specializes in Disorienting an opponent, but unlike Cobra Strike it is also useful for damage. Since Cobra Strike won't have reset when its Disorientation effect wears off, you can use Eagle's Claw to ensure a strong foe won't get many attacks in!

Power researched by Almeric.

Martial Arts Effects

Thunder Kick

Smashing Damage (Moderate)
Stun (Moderate) Mag 1

Storm Kick

Smashing Damage (Minor)

Cobra Strike

Smashing Damage (Minor)
Stun (High) Mag 3

Focus Chi

To Hit Buff (High)
Add Smash Damage (Extreme)
Add Lethal Damage (Extreme)
Add Fire Damage (Extreme)
Add Cold Damage (Extreme)
Add Energy Damage (Extreme)
Add Neg.Energy Damage (Extreme)
Add Psionic Damage (Extreme)

Warriors Challenge

Taunt (Very High) Mag 4

Crane Kick

Smashing Damage (High)
Knockback (High; 60% chance)

Crippling Axe Kick

Smashing Damage (Minor)
Immobilize (Moderate) Mag 2
Slow (Moderate; 50% chance) Mag 1
Run Speed (Slower)

Dragons Tail

Smashing Damage (Moderate)
Knockback (Moderate; 50% chance)

Eagles Claw

Smashing Damage (High)
Stun (Moderate; 60% chance) Mag 3
Lethal Damage (Moderate; 15% chance)

MARTIAL ARTS STATS

Name	Type	Attacks (Acc)	Cost	Act	Rech	Range	Target	Enhancements
Thunder Kick	Clk	Me, Sm (+10% Acc)	7.5	1.1	4	5	Foe	Acc, Dam, Rech, REC, Stun
Storm Kick	Clk	Me, Sm (+10% Acc)	10.1	4.2	4	5	Foe	Acc, Dam, Rech, REC
Cobra Strike	Clk	Me, Sm (+10% Acc)	14.6	3.0	20	5	Foe	Acc, Dam, Rech, REC, Stun
Focus Chi	Clk		7.5	1.2	45	–	Self	REC, Rech, To Hit+
Warriors Challenge	Clk	(+10% Acc)	0.0	2.7	3	70	Foe	Rng, Taunt, Rech
Crane Kick	Clk	Me, Sm (+10% Acc)	12.3	3.0	7	5	Foe	Acc, Dam, REC, KB, Rech
Crippling Axe Kick	Clk	Me, Sm (+10% Acc)	7.5	2.2	4	5	Foe	Acc, Dam, REC, Immobilize, Rech
Dragons Tail	Clk	Me, Sm (+10% Acc)	18.8	2.8	14	–	Foe (8' sphere)	Acc, Dam, Rech, REC, KB
Eagles Claw	Clk	Me, Sm (+10% Acc)	15.0	4.6	10	5	Foe	Acc, Dam, REC, Stun, Rech

Type: Togl (Toggle); **Clk** (Click)
Attacks: Lethal, **Sm**ash, **Fi**re, **En**ergy, **Me**lee, **NgEn** (Negative Energy), **Co**ld, **Psi**onic
Rech: Recharge Time
Enhancements: Accuracy, **Dam**age, **Dmg Resist**, **Defense+** (buff), **Defense–** (Debuff), **End**urance **Drain**, **KB** (Knockback), **REC** (Reduce Endurance Cost), **Rng** (Range), **To Hit+** (buff), **To Hit-** (Debuff), **Int**errupt, and **Rech** (recharge)

SPINES

The Spine power set is designed for the Scrapper that wants to be a bit different. We all know of fictional Heroes who are really strong, or have claws, but there are very few that use spines. Spines also have a unique look, in that the quills don't only grow from your character's hands, but all over the body, creating an impressive array of spikes.

The Spines power set is a lot like Claws in many ways. Both powers involve "growing" weapons from your body in order to deal damage. The Spines are described as hollow tubes that inject poison into a target, causing damage and Slowing or Immobilizing the target.

The basic Spine attacks involve stabbing your target in quick bursts, which individually don't deal a lot of damage, but the quick recharge time means you can throw several of these attacks out in a short space of time. When you mix in the other Spines powers that deal high amounts of damage, but with a much longer recharge rate, the power set is quite an impressive damage dealer.

As a Scrapper, you want to maximize the amount of damage you inflict in the shortest possible time. Luckily, you can do that easily as the Spines attacks recharge very quickly, and with a few Enhancements you can chain your attacks so that by the time you're hitting your third power, your first one is charged and waiting for use.

A good combo at lower levels is to open with **Barb Swipe**, then **Lunge**, followed with a normal Brawl. By the time your punch gets off, Barb Swipe is ready for use again and you can simply repeat until victory is yours. **Taunt** becomes available to pull targets off of allies or from a group, and later Impale allows you to do a large mount of damage and Hold your target, preventing him from moving or attacking.

At later levels, the **Build Up** power can be used to great effect against tougher enemies, as it boosts your damage output and increases your Accuracy. Although it only has a short duration, you can complete one run of Barb Swipe, Lunge and Brawl easily, causing serious damage to your opponent.

If you're in a group, the **Throw Spines, Ripper** or **Quills** powers can effectively Slow your enemies, as these attacks are AoE, and hurt many enemies at once. The other bonus for these powers is that they can Slow your targets, giving you an easier time chasing after the ones that decided to run away.

Power researched by JoeBayley.

Spines Effects

Barb Swipe

Lethal Damage (Minor)
Lethal Damage (Minor)
Run Speed (Very Slow)
Fly (Very Slow)
Recharge Time (Slowest)
Immobilize (Moderate) Mag 0.67

Lunge

Lethal Damage (Moderate)
Run Speed (Very Slow)
Fly (Very Slow)
Recharge Time (Slowest)
Immobilize (Moderate) Mag 0.67; Can Cancel

Spine Burst

Lethal Damage (Moderate)
Run Speed (Very Slow)
Fly (Very Slow)
Recharge Time (Slowest)
Immobilize (High) Mag 0.67; Can Cancel

Build Up

- To Hit Buff (High)
- Add Smash Damage (Extreme)
- Add Lethal Damage (Extreme)
- Add Fire Damage (Extreme)
- Add Cold Damage (Extreme)
- Add Energy Damage (Extreme)
- Add Neg.Energy Damage (Extreme)
- Add Psionic Damage (Extreme)

Taunt

- Taunt (Very High) Mag 4

Impale

- Lethal Damage (High)
- Immobilize (High) Mag 3; Can Cancel
- Run Speed (Very Slow)
- Fly (Very Slow)
- Recharge Time (Slowest)

Quills

- Lethal Damage (Minor)
- Immobilize (Moderate) Mag 0.67; Can Cancel
- Recharge Time (Slowest)
- Fly (Very Slow) Can Cancel
- Run Speed (Very Slow) Can Cancel

Ripper

- Lethal Damage (High)
- Knockback (Moderate; 60% chance)
- Recharge Time (Slowest)
- Recharge Time (Slowest)
- Fly (Very Slow) Can Cancel
- Immobilize (High) Mag 0.67; Can Cancel

Throw Spines

- Lethal Damage (Moderate)
- Run Speed (Slower)
- Fly (Slower)
- Recharge Time (Slowest)
- Immobilize (High) Mag 0.67; Can Cancel

SPINES STATS

Name	Type	Attacks (Acc)	Cost	Act	Rech	Range	Target	Enhancements
Barb Swipe	Clk	Me, Le	5.1	2.4	2	5	Foe	Acc, Dam, REC, Rech
Lunge	Clk	Me, Le	7.5	1.6	4	5	Foe	Acc, Dam, Rech, REC, Slow
Spine Burst	Clk	Le	21.9	3.0	16	–	Foe (15' sphere)	Acc, Dam, Rech, REC, Rng, Slow
Build Up	Clk		7.5	0.7	45	–	Self	REC, Rech, To Hit+
Taunt	Clk		0.0	2.7	3	70	Foe	Rng, Taunt, Rech
Impale	Clk	Le	7.5	2.4	8	20	Foe	Acc, Dam, Rech, REC, Defense–, Immobilize
Quills	Togl	Le	2.3	0.7	15	–	Foe (8' sphere)	Acc, Dam, Rech, REC
Ripper	Clk	Me, Le	15.9	2.2	11	–	Foe (5', 90° cone)	Acc, Dam, Rech, REC, KB
Throw Spines	Clk	Le	18.8	1.6	12	–	Foe (30', 90° cone)	Acc, Dam, Rech, REC, Rng, Slow

Type: Togl (Toggle); **Clk** (Click)
Attacks: Lethal, **Sm**ash, **Fi**re, **En**ergy, **Me**lee, **NgEn** (Negative Energy), **Co**ld, **Psi**onic
Rech: Recharge Time
Enhancements: Accuracy, **Dam**age, **Dmg Resist**, **Defense+** (buff), **Defense–** (Debuff), **End**urance **Drain**, **KB** (Knockback), **REC** (Reduce Endurance Cost), **Rng** (Range), **To Hit+** (buff), **To Hit–** (Debuff), **Int**errupt, and **Rech** (recharge)

SCRAPPER SECONDARY (DEFENSE)

DARK ARMOR

The Dark Armor power set is a mixed bag of defense powers and self buffs, but you pay a price for this flexibility.

In the Dark Armor power set, you get everything you need to keep yourself alive, and your enemies weakened, either by boosting your damage output, harming all nearby foes, or by causing them to run away in terror. The number of options you get with these powers is impressive.

Unfortunately, this power has a price.

As the powers are mystical in nature, you have to activate them when you need them. This means you have to keep a close eye on your Endurance Bar, and not try to have everything running at the same time. Forgetting this means a quick ticket to the hospital.

Another thing you need to watch for is enemies that Stun, as this will cancel all your activated powers, leaving you quite vulnerable.

The powers are very cool though, with effects ranging from self invisible (**Cloak of Darkness**) to self resurrection (**Soul Transfer,** very handy if out of Revive Inspirations). At higher levels you can keep Cloak of Darkness on en route, which makes travel a whole lot safer.

Despite the trade-offs, the flexibility offered by Dark Armor does make it an attractive power set for the Hero who wants to be able to adapt to any situation.

Power researched by JoeBayley.

Dark Armor Effects

Dark Embrace

Resist Smashing (Very High)
Resist Lethal (Very High)
Resist Neg.Energy (High)

Death Shroud

Neg.Energy Damage (Minor)

Murky Cloud

Resist Fire (Very High)
Resist Cold (Very High)
Resist Energy (Very High)
Resist Neg.Energy (High)

Obsidian Shield

Resist Psionic (Extreme)
Resist Stun (Moderate)
Resist Sleep (Moderate)

Dark Regeneration

Neg.Energy Damage (Minor)
Heal (Very High)

Cloak of Darkness

Stealth (Moderate)
Melee Defense (Moderate)
Translucent
Ranged Defense (Moderate)

Cloak of Fear

Fear (Moderate) Mag 3

Oppressive Gloom

Stun (Moderate) Mag 2; Can Cancel

Soul Transfer

Neg.Energy Damage (Moderate)
Heal (Very High)
Endurance Bonus (High)

DARK ARMOR STATS

Name	Type	Attacks (Acc)	Cost	Act	Rech	Range	Target	Enhancements
Dark Embrace	Togl		0.2	1.2	4	–	Self	REC, Rech, Dmg Resist
Death Shroud	Togl	NgEn	2.3	1.2	4	–	Foe (8' sphere)	Acc, Rech, REC, Dam
Murky Cloud	Togl		0.2	1.2	4	–	Self	REC, Rech, Dmg Resist
Obsidian Shield	Togl		0.2	1.2	4	–	Self	REC, Rech, Dmg Resist
Dark Regeneration	Clk	NgEn	48.8	1.2	30	–	Foe (20' sphere)	REC, Acc, Rech, Heal, Dam
Cloak of Darkness	Togl		0.2	1.2	20	–	Self	REC, Rech, Defense
Cloak of Fear	Togl	(+20% Acc)	0.4	1.2	4	–	Foe (8' sphere)	Acc, Rech, REC, To Hit–, Fear
Oppressive Gloom	Togl		0.2	1.2	8	–	Foe (8' sphere)	Acc, Rech, REC, Rech, Stun
Soul Transfer	Clk	NgEn	0.0	1.2	300	–	Foe (20' sphere)	Rech, Heal, Dam

Type: **Togl** (Toggle); **Clk** (Click)
Attacks: **Le**thal, **Sm**ash, **Fi**re, **En**ergy, **Me**lee, **NgEn** (Negative Energy), **Co**ld, **Psi**onic
Rech: Recharge Time
Enhancements: **Acc**uracy, **Dam**age, **Dmg Resist**, **Defense+** (buff), **Defense–** (Debuff), **End**urance Drain, **KB** (Knockback), **REC** (Reduce Endurance Cost), **Rng** (Range), **To Hit+** (buff), **To Hit–** (Debuff), **Int**errupt, and **Rech** (recharge)

INVULNERABILITY

Invulnerability isn't as flashy as some of the defensive powers sets out there, like Fire or Ice Armor, but it does the job, and remarkably well. There isn't any super defense vs any one type of damage, but instead it offers the ability to become resistant to all damage types (except Psionics).

The powers in the set are mostly passive powers, which means that if you're dazed, you don't instantly lose all your defenses. *Focus* on the passive defenses. Make sure you get them early and assign slots to them for Enhancements. Keep them enhanced with the best bonuses you can find (dual-Origin as soon as you can afford them, then single-Origin), and keep them green so they offer the highest bonus to the powers. The more enhanced your defenses are, the less damage you are taking, and every point counts.

On the downside, the damage reduction rate is relatively flat, while damage received from villains ramps up, meaning you take progressively more damage as you advance, and your defenses do not rise at the same rate to compensate. Also, the only defenses that actually prevent blows from landing in the first place are at the highest levels, so you're being hit as often as any Blaster or Controller — you're just taking less damage from the hits.

Two Origins can take the Invulnerability power set; The Tanker and the Scrapper. It's almost a purely defensive power, with very little offensive use. Invulnerability for the Scrapper is identical to the same power set for the Tanker, with one important difference: For the Scrappers, it's a secondary power set; while for the Tankers it's a primary. This means that not only do the powers become available to you at a much slower rate, but the powers are, in general, less effective than their Tanker counterparts. Therefore, all things being equal (level, enhancers, etc.), an invulnerable Tanker is more invulnerable than a like-powered Scrapper.

Both Origins can benefit from any of the powers in the power set, but you may want to consider different priorities depending on your Origin.

Dull Pain is a must for the Scrapper. With your low Hit Points and low tolerance to damage, anything that boosts your Hit Points is a great choice. The resists are good for you, But **Temp Invulnerability** and eventually **Invincibility** are probably your goals, You're a straight-up damage dealer. While the resists look attractive, your goal is to beat the bad guy into the ground before he can hurt you — well, much.

Something that's worth repeating — *don't* overlook the benefit of Dull Pain. There aren't very many hit point enhancing powers in the game, and anything that improves your total is a definite winner. **Dull Pain** has two uses: a temporary hit point bonus, *and* a quick heal. Used at the right time, it can be the difference between a victory and a trip to the hospital.

Power researched by Biggs.

Invulnerability Effects

Resist Physical Damage

Resist Smashing (Moderate)
Resist Lethal (Moderate)

Temporary Invulnerability

Resist Smashing (Very High)
Resist Lethal (Very High)

Dull Pain

Give Hitpoints (Moderate)
Heal (Extreme)

Resist Elements

Resist Fire (Moderate)
Resist Cold (Moderate)

Unyielding Stance

Resist Knockback (Moderate)
Resist Knockup (Moderate)
Resist Repel (Moderate)
Resist Stun (Moderate)
Resist Hold (Moderate)
Resist Sleep (Moderate)
Immobilize Self (Minor) Mag 100

Resist Energies

Resist Energy (Moderate)
Resist Neg.Energy (Moderate)

Invincibility

Taunt (Moderate) Mag 3; Can Cancel
To Hit Buff (Moderate)
Smashing Defense (Moderate)
Lethal Defense (Moderate)
Fire Defense (Moderate)
Cold Defense (Moderate)
Energy Defense (Moderate)
Neg.Energy Defense (Moderate)

Tough hide

Smashing Defense (Moderate)
Lethal Defense (Moderate)
Fire Defense (Moderate)
Cold Defense (Moderate)
Energy Defense (Moderate)
Neg.Energy Defense (Moderate)

Unstoppable

Resist Smashing (Extreme)
Resist Lethal (Extreme)
Resist Fire (Extreme)
Resist Cold (Extreme)
Resist Energy (Extreme)
Resist Neg.Energy (Extreme)
Endurance Recovery (Moderate)
Resist Knockback (Moderate)
Resist Knockup (Moderate)
Resist Repel (Moderate)
Resist Stun (Moderate)
Resist Hold (Moderate)
Resist Sleep (Moderate)
Resist Immobilize (Moderate)
Endurance Cost (Minor)
Stun (Very High) Mag 4

INVULNERABILITY STATS

Name	Type	Attacks (Acc)	Cost	Act	Rech	Range	Target	Enhancements
Resist Physical Damage	Auto		0.0	–	–	–	Self	Dmg Resist
Temp Invulnerability	Clk		18.8	0.7	360	–	Self	REC, Rech, Dmg Resist
Dull Pain	Clk		15.0	0.7	360	–	Self	REC, Rech, Heal
Resist Elements	Auto		0.0	–	–	–	Self	Dmg Resist
Unyielding Stance	Togl		0.2	2.3	10	–	Self	REC, Rech
Resist Energies	Auto		0.0	0.5	–	–	Self	Dmg Resist
Invincibility	Togl		0.2	3.0	10	–	Self	REC, Rech, Defense, To Hit+
Tough hide	Auto		0.0	–	–	–	Self	Defense
Unstoppable	Clk		7.5	3.1	300	–	Self	REC, Rech, Dmg Resist, End.Rec.

Type: **Togl** (Toggle); **Clk** (Click)
Attacks: **Le**thal, **Sm**ash, **Fi**re, **En**ergy, **Me**lee, **NgEn** (Negative Energy), **Co**ld, **Psi**onic
Rech: Recharge Time
Enhancements: **Acc**uracy, **Dam**age, **Dmg Resist**, **Defense+** (buff), **Defense–** (Debuff), **End**urance **Drain**, **KB** (Knockback), **REC** (Reduce Endurance Cost), **Rng** (Range), **To Hit+** (buff), **To Hit–** (Debuff), **Int**errupt, and **Rech** (recharge)

REGENERATION

This power set works well for a Scrapper, because Scrappers start out with lower HP than a Tanker, and this set can make up for that. Your ability to keep healing and recovering Endurance even during battle will greatly enhance your combat effectiveness and survivability.

This power set is great for the player type that likes to get in there and mix it up face to face — maybe just a bit over your head. The best thing about this set is that it doesn't take a lot ofEnhancement slots to cover the Enhancements that can be used. Make sure you have plenty of Endurance recovery Enhancements, and of course plenty of Healing Enhancements.

If power leveling is your thing, this pool makes for quick recoveries and constant fighting. With the power to **Revive** yourself and then continue battle after a brief respite, any foe should fear you. At the top end this set is almost like being able to fight in perpetual motion. With the healing and recovery abilities, plus the resist powers, you can become nearly invincible for your level — which makes this a fun Hero to play with.

This is also a great power pool to have when you fight with a group. You are self sufficient and your need for a caretaker is minimal. If you have a Defender and a Tanker on your team, you can step right up and deal great damage and keep pushing the edge of the envelope.

Fast Healing and **Quick Recovery** are auto-run on self, meaning that they work in the background constantly and don't use up your Endurance. **Reconstruction** is your heal self power, and Dull Pain is a heal self plus a hit point self buff (very good to use in battle when you take a couple of critical hits and need to grab some points quickly).

The high end healing power is **Instant Healing**, which is a toggled power that you can turn on

and off, letting you regenerate automatically while you fight. The downside is it uses Endurance as it works.

At the top end of the set are **Revive** and **Moment of Glory**. Revive means that when you fall in battle, you can resurrect yourself and save a couple extra spots in your Inspiration slots for other useful boosts. As with all rezzes, Revive will leave you Disoriented and low on Endurance for awhile after you wake up, so don't try to use it in the middle of a crowd of enemies. Moment of Glory is a short-term mega-buff that leaves you very low on Hit Points when it wears off.

The power set also offers **Resist Disorientation** and **Integration**. Resist Disorientation is really helpful in keeping your Scrapper alive, because you can resist the powers that make your Hero wander around aimlessly while the foe puts the smack down on him. This is a toggle power that uses Endurance constantly while on, so make sure you put a good reduce Endurance cost Enhancement on it and keep it up to level. Integration is a short-duration resist power, good against Knockback, Disorient, Sleep, Hold and Immobilization.

Power researched by Zandarbar.

Regeneration Effects

Fast Healing

Regeneration (Minor)

Reconstruction

Heal (Very High)

Quick Recovery

Endurance Recovery (Minor)

Resist Disorientation
Resist Stun (High)
Resist Stun (Moderate)

Integration
Resist Knockback (Moderate)
Resist Knockup (Moderate)
Resist Stun (Moderate)
Resist Hold (Moderate)
Resist Immobilize (Moderate)
Resist Sleep (Moderate)

Dull Pain
Give Hitpoints (Moderate)
Heal (Very High)

Instant Healing
Regeneration (Extreme)

Revive
Heal (Extreme)

Moment of Glory
Heal (Extreme)
Endurance Recovery (Moderate)
Regeneration (None)
Resist Stun (Moderate)
Resist Immobilize (Moderate)
Resist Sleep (Moderate)
Defense (Extreme)
Resist Smashing (Extreme)
Resist Lethal (Extreme)
Resist Fire (Extreme)
Resist Cold (Extreme)
Resist Energy (Extreme)
Resist Neg.Energy (Extreme)

REGENERATION STATS

Name	Type	Attacks (Acc)	Cost	Act	Rech	Range	Target	Enhancements
Fast Healing	Auto		0.0	—		—	Self	Heal
Reconstruction	Clk		15.0	0.7	60	—	Self	REC, Rech, Heal
Quick Recovery	Auto		0.0	—		—	Self	Recovery
Resist Disorientation	Togl		0.1	0.7	10	—	Self	REC, Rech
Integration	Clk		15.0	3.1	40	—	Self	REC, Rech
Dull Pain	Clk		21.0	0.7	360	—	Self	REC, Rech, Heal
Instant Healing	Togl		0.8	3.0	300	—	Self	Heal
Revive	Clk		0.0	4.3	300	—	Self	Rech, Heal
Moment of Glory	Clk		15.0	2.6	300	—	Self	REC, Rech, Heal, Defense, Dmg Resist, End.Rec.

Type: **Togl** (Toggle); **Clk** (Click)
Attacks: **Le**thal, **Sm**ash, **Fi**re, **En**ergy, **Me**lee, **NgEn** (Negative Energy), **Cold**, **Psi**onic
Rech: Recharge Time
Enhancements: **Acc**uracy, **Dam**age, **Dmg Resist**, **Defense+** (buff), **Defense−** (Debuff), **End**urance **Drain**, **KB** (Knockback), **REC** (Reduce Endurance Cost), **Rng** (Range), **To Hit+** (buff), **To Hit−** (Debuff), **Int**errupt, and **Rech** (recharge)

SUPER REFLEXES

Super Reflexes is unique among the defensive power sets in that its focus is damage avoidance instead of damage resistance. In other words, while all of the other defensive power sets allow your Hero to be hit as often as an undefended Hero, but reduce the damage he takes, Reflexes focuses on avoiding the hits in the first place.

The Pros to this are quite obvious:

◆ Avoiding the damage, i.e. effectively reducing it to zero, is (at least when it works) superior to attempting to soak and reduce the damage, especially at higher levels when the incoming damage can come in multiples of 100.

◆ There are inspirations that further increase this power set's effectiveness.

There are, however, Cons as well:

◆ Super Reflexes offers little defense vs. AoE attacks until past 30th level, where the damage reduction power sets reduce the damage, regardless of where it came from.

◆ There are minimal defenses vs. Psionic attacks, which puts the Super Reflexes Hero at a disadvantage versus factions such as the Lost.

◆ The most effective defenses in this power set are active, which means if you're Stunned or Disoriented in the middle of a melee those defense will drop, making you vulnerable. Also, taking time to turn them back on before re-engaging in the fight is inconvenient.

The greatest strength of this power set is its passive defenses, and it is highly recommended that, through the course of time, a Hero with this set make sure he chooses those powers over the active ones, as early as possible. Additionally, putting at least two Enhancement slots into these passive powers, filling them with the best enhancers possible (dual-Origin as soon as they are available, then singles) and keeping them green (maximum effectiveness) further increases their effectiveness. Doing the same with the active powers is advised but, as mentioned above, being knocked silly turns those off and leaves the Hero relying solely upon his passive defenses, so the more effective they are, the better.

Super Reflexes Effects

Focused Fighting

Melee Defense (Moderate)

Focused Senses

Ranged Defense (Moderate)

Agile

Ranged Defense (Moderate)

Practiced Brawler

Resist Knockback (Moderate)
Resist Knockup (Moderate)
Resist Stun (Moderate)
Resist Hold (Moderate)
Resist Immobilize (Moderate)
Resist Sleep (Moderate)

Dodge

Melee Defense (Moderate)

Quickness

Recharge Increase (Minor)
Run Speed (Minor)

Lucky

AoE Defense (Moderate)

Evasion

AoE Defense (Moderate)

Elude

Melee Defense (Extreme)
Ranged Defense (Extreme)
AoE Defense (Extreme)
Jump (Moderate)
Run Speed (Moderate)

SUPER REFLEXES STATS

Name	Type	Attacks (Acc)	Cost	Act	Rech	Range	Target	Enhancements
Focused Fighting	Togl		0.2	0.7	4	–	Self	REC, Rech, Defense
Focused Senses	Togl		0.2	2.0	4	–	Self	REC, Rech, Defense
Agile	Auto		0.0	–	–	–	Self	Defense
Practiced Brawler	Clk		15.0	1.5	40	–	Self	REC, Rech
Dodge	Auto		0.0	–	–	–	Self	Defense
Quickness	Auto		0.0	–	–	–	Self	Run
Lucky	Auto		0.0	–	–	–	Self	Defense
Evasion	Togl		0.2	3.0	4	–	Self	REC, Rech, Defense
Elude	Togl		0.9	2.0	10	–	Self	REC, Rech, Defense, Run

Type: Togl (Toggle); **Clk** (Click)
Attacks: Lethal, **Sm**ash, **Fi**re, **En**ergy, **Me**lee, **NgEn** (Negative Energy), **Co**ld, **Psi**onic
Rech: Recharge Time
Enhancements: Accuracy, **Dam**age, **Dmg Resist, Defense+** (buff), **Defense–** (Debuff), **End**urance **Drain, KB** (Knockback), **REC** (Reduce Endurance Cost), **Rng** (Range), **To Hit+** (buff), **To Hit-** (Debuff), **Int**errupt, and **Rech** (recharge)

TANKER PRIMARY (DEFENSE)

FIERY AURA

Flashy and effective, the Fiery Aura power set is one of the cooler looking ones. It's also extremely versatile and allows you to recharge yourself in the middle of combat, increasing your survivability.

Pros

- **Healing Flames** gives you a very effective self-heal that damages your foes.

- **Consume** gives you a great Endurance recharge, again damaging your foes.

- Lots of point-blank area-of-effect (PBAoE) defenses that also damage foes.

Cons

- Minimal passive defenses, so being Stunned/mesmerized/Sleep/Disoriented means you're as defenseless as any Blaster.

- All active defenses means you burn Endurance like mad against complex foes like the Skulls, which do Smashing damage (Fire Shield) and Negative Energy damage (Plasma Shield) from the same attacks.

- Zero resistance to Psionics.

- Minimal resistance to Disorient, Sleep, Stun or mesmerization attacks.

The least Tanker-like of the Tanker primaries, Fire Tankers can not stand and face the same amounts of damage that the other Tankers can. This is balanced, however, by the fact that almost everything they do damages their foes — even their defenses — so they are almost Scrapper-like in their damage output, with better defenses than most Scrappers.

As with all archetypes that are heavy on active defenses, Endurance plays a big factor in the Fire Tanker's tactics. This means combining Defense with Endurance Enhancements to make sure the powers are effective *and* that you can keep them online. Powers like Healing Flames and Consume have very long recharge times, so sticking one or two recharge Enhancements in them would increase their usefulness.

Fiery Aura Effects

Blazing Aura

Fire Damage (Minor)

Fire Shield

Resist Smashing (Very High)
Resist Lethal (Very High)
Resist Fire (High)
Resist Cold (Moderate)

Healing Flames

Heal (High)
Resist Stun (Moderate)

Temperature Protection

Resist Cold (Moderate)
Resist Fire (High)

Consume

Fire Damage (Minor)
Endurance Bonus (High)

Plasma Shield

Resist Energy (Very High)
Resist Neg.Energy (Very High)
Resist Fire (High)

Burn

Summons (Burn)
Resist Immobilize (Moderate)

Fiery Embrace

Add Fire Damage (Extreme)

Rise of the Phoenix

Heal (Extreme)
Endurance Recovery (None)
Stun (Very High) Mag 2

FIERY AURA STATS

Name	Type	Attacks (Acc)	Cost	Act	Rech	Range	Target	Enhancements
Blazing Aura	Togl	Fi	2.3	2.0	4	–	Foe (8' sphere)	Acc, Rech, REC, Dam
Fire Shield	Togl		0.2	1.7	2	–	Self	REC, Rech, Dmg Resist
Healing Flames	Clk		15.0	3.3	60	–	Self	REC, Heal, Rech
Temperature Protection	Auto		0.0	–	–	–	Self	Dmg Resist
Consume	Clk	Fi	0.8	2.0	180	–	Foe (20' sphere)	Acc, Rech, REC, Dam, End.Rec.
Plasma Shield	Togl		0.2	3.0	2	–	Self	REC, Rech, Dmg Resist
Burn	Clk		22.5	2.0	4	–	Location	REC, Rech, Dam
Fiery Embrace	Clk		11.3	0.7	180	–	Self	REC, Rech
Rise of the Phoenix	Clk		0.0	4.3	300	–	Self	Heal, Rech

Type: **Togl** (Toggle); **Clk** (Click)
Attacks: **Le**thal, **Sm**ash, **Fi**re, **En**ergy, **Me**lee, **NgEn** (Negative Energy), **Cold**, **Psi**onic
Rech: Recharge Time
Enhancements: **Acc**uracy, **Dam**age, **Dmg Resist**, **Defense+** (buff), **Defense–** (Debuff), **End**urance **Drain**, **KB** (Knockback), **REC** (Reduce Endurance Cost), **Rng** (Range), **To Hit+** (buff), **To Hit-** (Debuff), **Int**errupt, and **Rech** (recharge)

ICE ARMOR

Ice Armor offers good resistance to Cold damage.

Collect lots of Endurance discount, Defense and damage resistance Enhancements for this set.

Be mindful that many of the armors in this set cannot be activated at the same time.

Chilling Embrace is very handy, and can be used with any armor. Put lots of Endurance discount Enhancements in this one.

When going up against foes that can Hold, Immobilize or Disorient you, turn on **Wet Ice**. You will be protected from these effects and the power has good damage resistance.

Although **Hoarfrost** can be used as a heal power, it is more effective to use Hoarfrost before a battle than at the end of a battle. You will get more HP that way.

Putting lots of recharge Enhancements into **Energy Absorption** can cause this power to overlap. If you do this, the buff can stack!

Ice Armor Effects

Frozen Armor

Smashing Defense (Moderate)
Lethal Defense (Moderate)
Resist Cold (Moderate)

Hoarfrost

Give Hitpoints (Moderate)
Heal (Extreme)

Chilling Embrace

Run Speed (Slow)
Recharge Time (Slow)
Fly (Slow)

Wet Ice

Resist Knockback (Moderate)
Resist Knockup (Moderate)
Resist Stun (Extreme)
Resist Hold (Moderate)
Resist Immobilize (Moderate)
Resist Cold (High)
Smashing Defense (Moderate)
Lethal Defense (Moderate)
Fire Defense (Moderate)
Cold Defense (Moderate)
Energy Defense (Moderate)
Neg. Energy Defense (Moderate)

Permafrost

Resist Cold (High)
Resist Fire (Moderate)

Icicles

Lethal Damage (Minor)

Glacial Armor

Energy Defense (High)
Neg.Energy Defense (High)
Resist Cold (Moderate)
Translucent

Energy Absorption

End Drain (Very High)
Smashing Defense (Moderate)
Lethal Defense (Moderate)
Fire Defense (Moderate)
Cold Defense (High)
Energy Defense (Moderate)
Neg.Energy Defense (Moderate)

Hibernate

Untouchable (Moderate)
Immobilized
Endurance Discount (Very High)
Regeneration (Extreme)

ICE ARMOR STATS

Name	Type	Attacks (Acc)	Cost	Act	Rech	Range	Target	Enhancements
Frozen Armor	Togl		0.2	0.7	2	–	Self	REC, Rech, Defense, Dmg Resist
Hoarfrost	Clk		21.0	0.7	360	–	Self	REC, Rech, Heal
Chilling Embrace	Togl		0.2	0.7	2	–	Foe (10' sphere)	REC, Rech
Wet Ice	Togl		0.2	0.7	2	–	Self	REC, Rech, Defense
Permafrost	Auto		0.0	–	–	–	Self	Dmg Resist
Icicles	Togl	Me, Le	2.3	1.7	4	–	Foe (8' sphere)	Acc, Rech, REC, Dam
Glacial Armor	Togl		0.2	2.0	2	–	Self	REC, Rech, Defense, Dmg Resist
Energy Absorption	Clk		18.8	0.7	60	–	Foe (10' sphere)	REC, Rech, Defense, Drain End
Hibernate	Togl		0.0	2.0	60	–	Self	REC, Rech

Type: **Togl** (Toggle); **Clk** (Click)
Attacks: **Le**thal, **Sm**ash, **Fi**re, **En**ergy, **Me**lee, **NgEn** (Negative Energy), **Cold**, **Psi**onic
Rech: Recharge Time
Enhancements: **Acc**uracy, **Dam**age, **Dmg Resist**, **Defense+** (buff), **Defense–** (Debuff), **End**urance **Drain**, **KB** (Knockback), **REC** (Reduce Endurance Cost), **Rng** (Range), **To Hit+** (buff), **To Hit–** (Debuff), **Int**errupt, and **Rech** (recharge)

INVULNERABILITY

Invulnerability isn't as flashy as some of the defensive powers sets out there, like Fire or Ice Armor, but it does the job, and remarkably well. It doesn't have a super defense vs. any one type of damage, but instead it offers the ability to become resistant to all damage types (except Psionics).

The powers in the set are mostly passive powers, which means that if you're dazed, you don't instantly lose all your defenses. *Focus* on the passive defenses. Make sure you get them early and assign slots to them for Enhancements. Keep them enhanced with the best bonuses you can find (dual-Origin as soon as you can afford them, then single-Origin), and keep them green so they offer the highest bonus to the powers. The more enhanced your defenses are, the less damage you are taking, and every point counts.

On the downside, the damage reduction rate is relatively flat, while damage received from villains ramps up, meaning you take progressively more damage as you advance, and your defenses do not rise at the same rate to compensate. Also, the only defenses that actually prevent blows from landing in the first place are at the highest levels, so you're being hit as often as any Blaster or Controller, you're just taking less damage from the hits.

Two Origins can take the Invulnerability power set; The Tanker and the Scrapper. It's almost a purely defensive power, with very little offensive use. Invulnerability for the Tanker is identical to the same power set for the Scrapper, with one important difference: For the Scrappers, it's a secondary power set; while for the Tankers it's a primary. This means that not only do the powers become available to you at a much faster rate, but the powers are, in general, more effective than their Scrapper counterparts. Therefore, all things being equal (level, enhancers, etc.), an

invulnerable Tanker is more invulnerable than a like-powered Scrapper.

Both Origins can benefit from any of the powers in the power set, but you may want to consider different priorities depending on your Origin.

Look seriously at all the resists: **Dull Pain**, **Tough Hide**, and **Invincibility**. **Temporary Invulnerability** and **Unstoppable** are optional. Tankers are not primary damage dealers — their object is to act as a shield for the rest of the party and take the beating that is meant for others. Not very glamorous but, hey, it's what you're paid for.

Something that's worth repeating — *don't* overlook the benefit of Dull Pain. There aren't very many hit point enhancing powers in the game, and anything that improves you total is a definite winner. **Dull Pain** has two uses: a temporary hit point bonus *and* a quick heal. Used at the right time, it can be the difference between a victory and a trip to the hospital.

Power researched by Biggs.

Invulnerability Effects

Resist Physical Damage

Resist Smashing (Moderate)
Resist Lethal (Moderate)

Temporary Invulnerability

Resist Smashing (Very High)
Resist Lethal (Very High)

Dull Pain

Give Hitpoints (Moderate)

Resist Elements

Resist Fire (Moderate)
Resist Cold (Moderate)

Unyielding Stance

Resist Knockback (Moderate)
Resist Knockup (Moderate)
Resist Repel (Moderate)
Resist Stun (Moderate)
Resist Hold (Moderate)
Resist Sleep (Moderate)
Immobilize Self (Minor) Mag 100

Resist Energies

Resist Energy (Moderate)
Resist Neg.Energy (Moderate)

Invincibility

Taunt (Moderate) Mag 3; Can Cancel
To Hit Buff (Moderate)
Smashing Defense (Moderate)
Lethal Defense (Moderate)
Fire Defense (Moderate)
Cold Defense (Moderate)
Energy Defense (Moderate)
Neg.Energy Defense (Moderate)

Tough Hide

Smashing Defense (Moderate)
Lethal Defense (Moderate)
Fire Defense (Moderate)
Cold Defense (Moderate)
Energy Defense (Moderate)
Neg.Energy Defense (Moderate)

Unstoppable

Resist Smashing (Extreme)
Resist Lethal (Extreme)
Resist Fire (Extreme)
Resist Cold (Extreme)
Resist Energy (Extreme)
Resist Neg.Energy (Extreme)
Endurance Recovery (Moderate)
Resist Knockback (Moderate)
Resist Knockup (Moderate)
Resist Repel (Moderate)
Resist Stun (Extreme)
Resist Sleep (High)
Resist Hold (High)
Resist Immobilize (Moderate)
Endurance Cost (Minor)

INVULNERABILITY STATS

Name	Type	Attacks (Acc)	Cost	Act	Rech	Range	Target	Enhancements
Resist Physical Damage	Auto		0.0	–	–	–	Self	Dmg Resist
Temporary Invulnerability	Togl		18.8	0.7	360	–	Self	REC, Rech, Dmg Resist
Dull Pain	Clk		21.0	0.7	360	–	Self	REC, Rech, Heal
Resist Elements	Auto		0.0	–	–	–	Self	Dmg Resist
Unyielding Stance	Togl		0.2	2.3	10	–	Self	REC, Rech
Resist Energies	Auto		0.0	0.5	–	–	Self	Dmg Resist
Invincibility	Togl		0.2	3.0	10	–	Foe (10' sphere)	REC, Rech, Defense, To Hit+
Tough Hide	Auto		0.0	–	–	–	Self	Defense
Unstoppable	Clk		7.5	3.1	300	–	Self	REC, Rech, Dmg Resist, End.Rec.

Type: Togl (Toggle); **Clk** (Click)
Attacks: Lethal, **Sm**ash, **Fire**, **En**ergy, **Me**lee, **NgEn** (Negative Energy), **Co**ld, **Psi**onic
Rech: Recharge Time
Enhancements: Accuracy, **Dam**age, **Dmg Resist**, **Defense+** (buff), **Defense–** (Debuff), **End**urance **Drain**, **KB** (Knockback),
REC (Reduce Endurance Cost), **Rng** (Range), **To Hit+** (buff), **To Hit-** (Debuff), **Int**errupt, and **Rech** (recharge)

STONE ARMOR

Stone Armor is one of the best defensive power sets available. Not only does it give one of the highest defenses against damage, is it the only set that gives defense against Psionic attacks, as well as granting offensive and healing powers.

The various "Armor" powers grant you defenses against different kinds of attacks. They are mutually exclusive, but you can switch between them with a single keystroke, quickly adjusting to the attacks of your opponents.

This power set lets you choose a permanent damage resistant power at character creation. **Stone Skin** is vitally important, because it is always on and requires no Endurance.

Earth's Embrace is extremely useful in those long fights, as it heals more than 50% of your maximum hit points, and even increases your maximum hit points temporarily.

Mud Pots gives you the ability to snare all opponents within melee range, *and* does damage to them. This is a great way to build up opponent anger. Couple it with a damage-increasing Inspiration or buff, and you can take down whole groups of foes without lifting a finger.

There are two downsides to this power set:

All of the powers except **Stone Skin** are active, so they stop working when you are Stunned or Disoriented, leaving you vulnerable to attack.

And, for what it's worth, all of the Armors turn you into a walking, humanoid, rough-hewn statue, so no one can see your costume while they are active, nor can you be made invisible by any power, including your own, while they are up.

Endurance is your friend. Buy Endurance-reducing Enhancements every chance you get, as all these powers are a steady drain, and a naked Tanker is not very helpful.

Set one of your attacks to auto-attack. Don't worry about the amount of damage you do; focus on keeping as many attackers attacking *you* as possible. Let the rest of the group defeat them.

Keep Endurance Inspirations handy. You'll need them more than heals or revives.

Turn off Sprint and other travel powers while you're in combat. They just drain Endurance you need for your defensive powers.

Power researched by Bubski.

Stone Armor Effects

Rock Armor

Smashing Defense (High)
Lethal Defense (High)
Translucent (Off)

Stone Skin

Resist Smashing (Moderate)
Resist Lethal (Moderate)

Earth's Embrace

Give Hitpoints (High)
Heal (Extreme)

Mud Pots

Run Speed (Slower)
Immobilize (Moderate) Mag 2
Fire Damage (Minor; 75% chance)

Rooted

Immobilize (Moderate)
Resist Knockup (Moderate)
Resist Knockback (Moderate)
Resist Repel (Moderate)
Resist Stun (Moderate)
Resist Sleep (Moderate)
Resist Hold (Moderate)
Immobilize Self (Minor) Mag 100

Brimstone Armor

Resist Fire (Extreme)
Resist Cold (Extreme)
Translucent (Off)

Mineral Armor

Psionic Defense (High)
Translucent (Off)

Crystal Armor

Resist Energy (High)
Resist Neg.Energy (Extreme)
Translucent (Off)

Granite Armor

Resist Smashing (Moderate)
Resist Lethal (Moderate)
Resist Fire (Moderate)
Resist Cold (Moderate)
Resist Energy (Moderate)
Resist Neg.Energy (Moderate)
Resist Stun (Moderate)
Resist Knockback (Moderate)
Resist Knockup (Moderate)
Resist Repel (Moderate)
Running (Slowest)
Jump (Reduced)
Translucent (Off)

STONE ARMOR STATS

Name	Type	Attacks (Acc)	Cost	Act	Rech	Range	Target	Enhancements
Rock Armor	Togl		0.2	0.7	4	–	Self	REC, Rech, Defense
Stone Skin	Auto		0.0	–	–	–	Self	Dmg Resist
Earth's Embrace	Clk		15.0	2.0	360	–	Self	REC, Heal, Rech
Mud Pots	Togl	Fi	2.3	2.0	4	–	Foe (8' sphere)	REC, Rech, Dam, Slow
Rooted	Togl		0.2	1.2	10	–	Self	REC, Rech
Brimstone Armor	Togl		0.2	0.7	4	–	Self	REC, Rech, Dmg Resist
Mineral Armor	Togl		0.2	0.7	4	–	Self	REC, Rech, Defense
Crystal Armor	Togl		0.2	2.0	4	–	Self	REC, Rech, Defense, Dmg Resist
Granite Armor	Togl		0.8	0.7	4	–	Self	REC, Rech, Dmg Resist

Type: Togl (Toggle); **Clk** (Click)
Attacks: Lethal, **Sm**ash, **Fi**re, **En**ergy, **Me**lee, **NgEn** (Negative Energy), **Co**ld, **Psi**onic
Rech: Recharge Time
Enhancements: Accuracy, **Dam**age, **Dmg Resist**, **Defense+** (buff), **Defense–** (Debuff), **End**urance **Drain**, **KB** (Knockback), **REC** (Reduce Endurance Cost), **Rng** (Range), **To Hit+** (buff), **To Hit–** (Debuff), **Int**errupt, and **Rech** (recharge)

TANKER SECONDARY (MELEE)

BATTLEAXE

The Battleaxe power set is one of the hardest-hitting melee sets. Almost every move has some degree of Knockdown potential, and deals a sizable amount of damage.

Keeping your foes flying across the room and grievously wounded comes at a weighty price. Battleaxe is also the slowest to recharge and has one of the larger Endurance costs. Battleaxers can hack an even-level minion to the quick in two or three swings, but their powers can also leave them winded in any longer-lasting combat.

Enhancers can help to offset the Endurance drain and slower recharge, but Axers will always seem like spectators next to speedy Scrappers. The ax animations are quite fast to fire off, compared to some like Superstrength or Stone Melee, which have noticeable wind-up animations. Though quick to fire on the front end, their cost comes in the delay waiting for the power to reset. Go into this power set with these points in mind to avoid frustration. Accept it and enjoy the huge hits and the ability to slap villains across the street.

For a solo-minded Hero, Battleaxe is a solid choice. In a large group where combat is hot and fast, it can be discouraging. The Battleaxe power set excels at taking low numbers of foes and defeating them with apparent ease. All offensive moves in Battleaxe benefit from adding reduce Endurance and recharge Enhancements. Damage and Accuracy shouldn't be neglected, but Battleaxe can get away with only a nod towards either, though missing swings can be painful. Adding Knockback seems almost redundant, given how often Knockdown occurs with the Battleaxe power set. Taking the Fitness power pool is strongly recommended. Endurance is heavenly, and six slots of Endurance regen enhancers make Battleaxers unholy whirlwinds of criminal jurisprudence.

Gash. Moderate damage with a decent Knockback chance. Add recharge and Endurance reduction Enhancements — this will be a common theme throughout the set.

Chop. As Gash, with better damage. Add Accuracy Enhancements to avoid misses. A weeping Hero with a large axe is a sad thing ... don't let it happen to you.

Taunt. The same power found throughout the Scrapper and Tanker sets, Battleaxe comes into it earlier than some.

Beheader. Yes, even larger amounts of damage in this power, plus more Knockback. Sing along, you know the words ... Recharge and End reduction enhancers!

Build Up. Another common power for offensive power sets. Stacks with Inspirations and buffs. Orange boss? Build Up, Damage Inspiration, Beheader, good night.

Swoop. An upswing that throws your opponent straight up into the air. Good for knocking down or interrupting.

Whirling Axe. Like Chop ... only to everything around you. Full spinning axe move that deals the Battleaxe damage you have come to love to all villains surrounding you, throwing some back out of the fight. Would mention Endurance reduction here, but you probably saw that coming. Recharge enhancer isn't as needed, on the theory that Heroes should not be surrounded so often they need this power back quickly.

Cleave. The hardest hitting swing in the arsenal. Extreme damage, slow recharge, huge Endurance drain. Battleaxe personified.

Pendulum. Cutting arc that damages and throws opponents in a cone in front of the Hero. Perfect to clear a path through the enemy.

Power researched by Lohengrin.

Battleaxe Effects

Gash
Smashing Damage (Moderate)
Knockback (High; 40% chance)
Taunt (Moderate) Mag 4

Chop
Lethal Damage (High)
Knockback (Moderate; 50% chance)
Taunt (Moderate) Mag 4

Taunt
Taunt (Very High) Mag 4

Beheader
Smashing Damage (High)
Knockback (High; 50% chance)
Taunt (Moderate) Mag 4

Build Up
To Hit Buff (High)

Add Smash Damage (Extreme)
Add Lethal Damage (Extreme)
Add Fire Damage (Extreme)
Add Cold Damage (Extreme)
Add Energy Damage (Extreme)
Add Neg.Energy Damage (Extreme)
Add Psionic Damage (Extreme)

Swoop
Lethal Damage (High)
Knockup (Moderate; 70% chance)
Taunt (Moderate) Mag 4

Whirling Axe
Smashing Damage (Moderate)
Knockback (High; 50% chance)
Taunt (Moderate) Mag 4

Cleave
Smashing Damage (Very High)
Knockback (Very High; 80% chance)
Taunt (Moderate) Mag 4

Pendulum
Lethal Damage (High)
Knockback (High; 50% chance)
Taunt (Moderate) Mag 4

BATTLEAXE STATS

Name	Type	Attacks (Acc)	Cost	Act	Rech	Range	Target	Enhancements
Gash	Clk	Me, Le (+5% Acc)	7.5	1.8	4	5	Foe	Acc, Dam, REC, Rech, KB
Chop	Clk	Me, Le (+5% Acc)	12.3	1.8	8	5	Foe	Acc, Dam, REC, Rech, KB
Taunt	Clk	(+5% Acc)	0.0	2.2	3	70	Foe	Rng, Taunt, Rech
Beheader	Clk	Me, Le (+5% Acc)	14.7	1.4	10	5	Foe	Acc, Dam, REC, Rech, KB
Build Up	Clk	(+5% Acc)	7.5	1.2	45	–	Self	REC, Rech, To Hit+
Swoop	Clk	Me, Le (+5% Acc)	1.7	2.9	12	5	Foe	Acc, Dam, REC, Rech, KB
Whirling Axe	Clk	Me, Le (+5% Acc)	18.8	2.9	14	–	Foe (8' sphere)	Acc, Dam, Rech, REC, KB
Cleave	Clk	Me, Le (+5% Acc)	20.7	2.9	15	5	Foe	Acc, Dam, REC, Rech, KB
Pendulum	Clk	Me, Le (+5% Acc)	20.7	2.3	15	–	Foe (5', 180° cone)	Acc, Dam, REC, Rech, KB

Type: Togl (Toggle); **Clk** (Click)
Attacks: Lethal, **Sm**ash, **Fi**re, **En**ergy, **Me**lee, **NgEn** (Negative Energy), **Cold**, **Psi**onic
Rech: Recharge Time
Enhancements: Accuracy, **Dam**age, **Dmg Resist, Defense+** (buff), **Defense–** (Debuff), **End**urance **Drain**, **KB** (Knockback), **REC** (Reduce Endurance Cost), **Rng** (Range), **To Hit+** (buff), **To Hit–** (Debuff), **Int**errupt, and **Rech** (recharge)

ENERGY MELEE

The most useful part of the Energy Melee power set is that every power in your arsenal, (except **Taunt**, of course), has a chance to Disorient a foe upon successful contact. Not only does this give you a huge advantage over the enemy, due to the obvious fact that he is no longer attacking you, but it also gives a teammate a chance to get away from him if, for example, a Controller is being pummeled by a boss. This power set allows Tankers the ability to take out a couple of targets early in on the fight, while keeping the bigger ones occupied and on them. During a fight it is usually beneficial to try to keep a number of targets Disoriented, so that your group, and you, will take a lot less damage over time. It is also good for the Energy melee Tanker to bounce from enemy to enemy, trying to Disorient them all while the damage dealers take them out. This tactic seems to work really effectively up to Level 24 or so.

One thing Energy Melee lacks at the earlier levels is damage output. Simply put, you will be doing sub-par damage when compared to other melee power sets. Where Energy Melee has other sets beat is in the Disorient ability. When a foe is unable to attack you or your teammates, you can take all the time in the world and beat him down slowly. Once you receive **Energy Transfer** and **Total Focus,** this all changes. Energy Transfer immediately becomes your bread and butter attack. Placing a couple recharge reduction, Accuracy, and damage Enhancements on it makes it the best overall power you will get in this set. Its damage is unmatched when compared to the other Energy Melee powers, and it doesn't have any negative effects like Total Focus does. Total Focus, like many other the final powers, offers great damage, but at a price. Using it will require good knowledge of the situation, or else once it's

used you may be sorry for it.

A major problem for Energy Melee, as well as other melee power sets, is the lack of range. A Tanker who chooses Energy Melee as his main attack will never do a lot of damage, and will find soloing very slow and tedious. It doesn't make soloing any more dangerous, since most Tankers can solo even-fight enemies relatively easily, but it increases your time to kill each enemy. Without the range, enemies like Tsoo sorcerers will give the Tanker a hard time while he runs around the map trying to catch up to them. Energy Melee Tankers have one advantage here, in their potential to Disorient that foe so that he stays put for at least a couple of seconds while you beat him to the ground.

Power researched by Kylock.

Energy Melee Effects

Barrage

> Smashing Damage (Minor)
> Energy Damage (Minor)
> Stun (Moderate) Mag 1
> Taunt (Moderate) Mag 4

Energy Punch

> Smashing Damage (Moderate)
> Energy Damage (Minor)
> Stun (Moderate; 30% chance) Mag 2
> Taunt (Moderate) Mag 4

Taunt

> Taunt (Very High) Mag 4

Bone Smasher

> Smashing Damage (Moderate)

Energy Damage (Moderate)
Stun (Moderate; 60% chance) Mag 3
Taunt (Moderate) Mag 4

Whirling Hands

Smashing Damage (Moderate)
Energy Damage (Minor)
Stun (Moderate; 30% chance) Mag 2
Taunt (Moderate) Mag 4

Stun

Smashing Damage (Minor)
Energy Damage (Minor)
Stun (High) Mag 3
Taunt (Moderate) Mag 4

Build Up

To Hit Buff (High)
Add Smash Damage (Extreme)

Add Lethal Damage (Extreme)
Add Fire Damage (Extreme)
Add Cold Damage (Extreme)
Add Energy Damage (Extreme)
Add Neg.Energy Damage (Extreme)
Add Psionic Damage (Extreme)

Energy Transfer

Smashing Damage (High)
Energy Damage (Very High)
Heal (Minor)
Taunt (Moderate) Mag 4

Total Focus

Smashing Damage (Moderate)
Energy Damage (Very High)
Hold (High) Mag 4
Stun (Moderate) Mag 2
Taunt (Moderate) Mag 4

ENERGY MELEE STATS

Name	Type	Attacks (Acc)	Cost	Act	Rech	Range	Target	Enhancements
Barrage	Clk	Me, Sm, En	5.1	1.3	2	5	Foe	Acc, Dam, REC, Stun, Rech
Energy Punch	Clk	Me, Sm, En	7.5	0.6	4	5	Foe	Acc, Dam, Rech, REC, Stun
Taunt	Clk		0.0	2.7	3	70	Foe	Rng, Taunt, Rech
Bone Smasher	Clk	Me, Sm, En	12.3	1.5	8	5	Foe	Acc, Dam, Rech, REC, Stun
Whirling Hands	Clk	Me, Sm, En	18.8	1.7	14	–	Foe (8' sphere)	Acc, Dam, Rech, REC, Stun
Stun	Clk	Me, Sm, En	14.7	1.8	20	5	Foe	Acc, Dam, Rech, REC, Stun
Build Up	Clk		7.5	1.2	45	–	Self	REC, Rech, To Hit+
Energy Transfer	Clk	Me, Sm, En	14.7	1.0	20	5	Foe	Acc, Dam, Rech, REC
Total Focus	Clk	Me, Sm, En	26.7	3.3	20	5	Foe	Acc, Dam, Rech, REC, Hold

Type: **Togl** (Toggle); **Clk** (Click)
Attacks: **Le**thal, **Sm**ash, **Fi**re, **En**ergy, **Me**lee, **NgEn** (Negative Energy), **Co**ld, **Psi**onic
Rech: Recharge Time
Enhancements: **Acc**uracy, **Dam**age, **Dmg Resist**, **Defense+** (buff), **Defense–** (Debuff), **End**urance **Drain**, **KB** (Knockback), **REC** (Reduce Endurance Cost), **Rng** (Range), **To Hit+** (buff), **To Hit-** (Debuff), **Int**errupt, and **Rech** (recharge)

FIERY MELEE

Flashy and extremely damaging, the Fiery Melee power set is one of the most damaging power sets in the Tanker arsenal, especially looking at the bigger picture — that is, taking damage over time (DoT) into account.

Pros

◆ Almost every power does damage over time, increasing the actual damage done by the powers beyond the initial attack.

◆ Few enemies are Fire resistant, making this power more effective than Smashing or Lethal attacks in many situations.

◆ Several Point Blank Area of Effect (PBAoE) attacks, damaging multiple foes, are included. These attacks inflict DoT as well.

◆ Many attacks have moderate-to-quick recharge rates, so you don't find yourself waiting on an attack button to come up before you can strike again.

Cons

◆ No damage mitigation of any kind. No Knockback, no Stun, no Disorient. No way to force a foe to not be able to attack you for a period of time while you are attacking them.

This is a relatively balanced power set when it comes to applying Enhancements. The attack animations are not overly long, making Accuracy a bit less of a priority. They have quick recharge rates, so no need to focus on that. Endurance can be tight, but no more than any other power set. You're best advised to just balance out your Enhancements, and any extra slots should go to damage, especially on the big-damage powers like **Fire Sword** and **Breath of Fire**. The great thing about damage Enhancements for this power set is that the bonus from the Enhancement also impacts the DoT, further adding to the overall damage done.

Fiery Melee Effects

Scorch

Fire Damage (Moderate)
Fire Damage (Minor; 80% chance) Can Cancel
Taunt (Moderate) Mag 4

Fire Sword

Lethal Damage (Minor)
Fire Damage (Moderate)
Fire Damage (Minor; 80% chance) Can Cancel
Taunt (Moderate) Mag 4

Taunt

Taunt (Very High) Mag 4

Combustion

Fire Damage (Minor)
Taunt (Moderate) Mag 4

Breath of Fire

Fire Damage (Moderate)
Fire Damage (Minor; 80% chance) Can Cancel
Taunt (Moderate) Mag 4

Build Up

To Hit Buff (High)
Add Smash Damage (Extreme)
Add Lethal Damage (Extreme)

Add Fire Damage (Extreme)
Add Cold Damage (Extreme)
Add Energy Damage (Extreme)
Add Neg.Energy Damage (Extreme)
Add Psionic Damage (Extreme)

Fire Sword Circle

Lethal Damage (Moderate)
Fire Damage (Moderate)
Fire Damage (Minor; 80% chance) Can Cancel
Taunt (Moderate) Mag 4

Incinerate

Fire Damage (Minor)
Taunt (Moderate) Mag 4

Greater Fire Sword

Lethal Damage (Moderate)
Fire Damage (Moderate)
Fire Damage (Minor; 80% chance) Can Cancel
Taunt (Moderate) Mag 4

FIERY MELEE STATS

Name	Type	Attacks (Acc)	Cost	Act	Rech	Range	Target	Enhancements
Scorch	Clk	Me, Fi	6.3	1.7	3	5	Foe	Acc, Dam, REC, Rech
Fire Sword	Clk	Me, Le, Fi	9.9	1.8	6	5	Foe	Acc, Dam, REC, Rech
Taunt	Clk		0.0	2.7	3	70	Foe	Rng, Taunt, Rech
Combustion	Clk	Fi	12.8	3.0	12	—	Foe (15' sphere)	Acc, Dam, REC, Rech
Breath of Fire	Clk	Fi	14.7	2.7	10	—	Foe (15', 30° cone)	Acc, Dam, Rech, REC, cone
Build Up	Clk		7.5	1.2	45	—	Self	REC, Rech, To Hit+
Fire Sword Circle	Clk	Me, Fi, Le	26.7	4.2	20	—	Foe (10' sphere)	Acc, Dam, Rech, REC
Incinerate	Clk	Me, Fi	9.9	1.7	10	5	Foe	Acc, Dam, Rech, REC
Greater Fire Sword	Clk	Me, Le, Fi	18.3	3.0	12	5	Foe	Acc, Dam, Rech, REC

Type: Togl (Toggle); **Clk** (Click)
Attacks: Lethal, **Sm**ash, **Fi**re, **En**ergy, **Me**lee, **NgEn** (Negative Energy), **Cold**, **Psi**onic
Rech: Recharge Time
Enhancements: Accuracy, **Dam**age, **Dmg Resist**, **Defense+** (buff), **Defense–** (Debuff), **End**urance Drain, **KB** (Knockback), **REC** (Reduce Endurance Cost), **Rng** (Range), **To Hit+** (buff), **To Hit-** (Debuff), **Int**errupt, and **Rech** (recharge)

ICE MELEE

Put your Accuracy Enhancements into **Frost** and **Frozen Aura** to affect as many foes as possible in these AoE powers.

The Slow effect of all the attack powers in this set can stack, so be sure to keep attacking the same target to see optimal effect.

Make sure you have a lot of foes in melee before activating Frozen Aura. Then attack any foes that are not affected to avoid freeing the frozen foes.

Ice Patch will stay where you place it, so it can be used in doorways or other bottlenecks to Slow foes from coming through.

Ice Melee Effects

Frozen Fists

> Smashing Damage (Minor)
> Cold Damage (Moderate)
> Run Speed (Minor)
> Fly Speed (Very Slow)
> Recharge Time (Slowest)
> Taunt (Moderate) Mag 4

Ice Sword

> Lethal Damage (Minor)
> Cold Damage (Moderate)
> Run Speed (Minor)
> Fly Speed (Very Slow)
> Recharge Time (Slowest)
> Taunt (Moderate) Mag 4

Taunt

Taunt (Very High) Mag 4

Frost

Cold Damage (Minor)
Recharge Time (Slowest)
Run Speed (Slow)
Fly Speed (Very Slow)
Taunt (Moderate) Mag 4

Build Up

To Hit Buff (High)
Add Smash Damage (Extreme)
Add Lethal Damage (Extreme)
Add Fire Damage (Extreme)
Add Cold Damage (Extreme)
Add Energy Damage (Extreme)
Add Neg.Energy Damage (Extreme)
Add Psionic Damage (Extreme)

Ice Patch

Summons (Ice Patch)

Freezing Touch

Cold Damage (Minor)
Hold (High) Mag 3
Resist Knockback (Moderate)
Resist Knockup (Moderate)
Taunt (Moderate) Mag 4

Greater Ice Sword

Lethal Damage (Moderate)
Cold Damage (Moderate)
Recharge Time (Slowest)
Run Speed (Minor)
Fly Speed (Very Slow)
Taunt (Moderate) Mag 4

Frozen Aura

Sleep (Very High) Mag 2
Taunt (Moderate) Mag 4

ICE MELEE STATS

Name	Type	Attacks (Acc)	Cost	Act	Rech	Range	Target	Enhancements
Frozen Fists	Clk	Me, Sm, Co	6.3	1.3	3	5	Foe	Acc, Dam, REC, Slow, Rech
Ice Sword	Clk	Me, Le, Co	9.9	1.8	6	5	Foe	Acc, Dam, Rech, REC, Slow
Taunt	Clk		0.0	2.7	3	70	Foe	Rng, Taunt, Rech
Frost	Clk	Co	15.9	2.3	11	–	Foe (7', 90° cone)	Acc, Dam, Rech, REC, Slow, cone
Build Up	Clk		7.5	1.2	45	–	Self	REC, Rech, To Hit+
Ice Patch	Clk	(+100% Acc)	15.0	2.0	35	–	Self	Rech, REC
Freezing Touch	Clk	Me, Co	14.7	1.0	16	5	Foe	Acc, Dam, Rech, REC, Hold
Greater Ice Sword	Clk	Me, Le, Co	14.7	2.7	10	5	Foe	Acc, Dam, Rech, RECSlow
Frozen Aura	Clk		18.8	2.1	20	–	Foe (10' sphere)	Acc, Sleep, Rech, REC

Type: Togl (Toggle); **Clk** (Click)
Attacks: Lethal, **Sm**ash, **Fi**re, **En**ergy, **Me**lee, **NgEn** (Negative Energy), **Co**ld, **Psi**onic
Rech: Recharge Time
Enhancements: Accuracy, **Dam**age, **Dmg Resist**, **Defense+** (buff), **Defense–** (Debuff), **End**urance **Drain**, **KB** (Knockback), **REC** (Reduce Endurance Cost), **Rng** (Range), **To Hit+** (buff), **To Hit–** (Debuff), **Int**errupt, and **Rech** (recharge)

STONE MELEE

Stone Fist. A medium-damage hit, with a fast recharge timer and relatively low Endurance cost, makes this a staple of the power set. It will quickly replace Brawl as your security level advances. Stone Fist has a very low chance to Stun, so relying on that effect isn't a good plan. When adding Enhancements, Heroes should concentrate on damage and Accuracy, with at least one for recharge and Endurance reduction.

Stone Mallet. Solid damage with a decent chance to Knockback — this is another power that will be part of your routine attack combo. Stone Mallet has a moderate Endurance cost and a slower recharge, and benefits greatly from a recharge and Endurance reduction Enhancement. Including Knockback Enhancements in the mix isn't necessary, but it can be amusing to throw villains for a 50-yard loss.

Taunt. As found in many other Tanker and Scrapper power sets, the only difference being when this power becomes available. Stone Melee receives it fairly early compared to other sets. Can be used to great effect for pulling single enemies, above and beyond its intended use. Adding a Range Enhancement can further that usefulness.

Heavy Mallet. High damage and high Knockback chance, balanced by high Endurance cost and slow recharge.

Build Up. Another power shared with other offensive power sets. For a short duration, it dramatically increases damage and Accuracy. Will stack alongside Accuracy and damage Inspirations for truly sick amounts of smackdown.

Fault. Enemies on their backs have a difficult time fighting back. Will Knockdown villains in an area, with a small chance to Stun. Very useful. Between Stone Mallet, Heavy Mallet and Fault,

the determined Hero can keep villains on their backs for entire combats.

Hurl Boulder. Tankers with ranged attacks! Ranged attacks that have a chance to Knockdown … even better. Slap on some damage and Accuracy Enhancements and start ripping up sidewalks in the name of justice.

Tremor. Causes a moderate amount of damage in a decent area around you, with a huge chance to knock enemies down. Slow recharge time and hefty Endurance costs make this a power to use deliberately.

Seismic. Inflicts a huge amount of damage with a Hold effect, effectively shutting down the opponent for the duration. If it's a minion, it's probably another notch on your super belt.

Power researched by Lohengrin.

Stone Melee Effects

Stone Fist

Smashing Damage (Moderate)
Stun (Moderate; 10% chance) Mag 2
Taunt (Moderate) Mag 4

Stone Mallet

Smashing Damage (High)
Knockback (Moderate; 50% chance)
Taunt (Moderate) Mag 4

Taunt

Taunt (Very High) Mag 4

Heavy Mallet

Smashing Damage (High)
Knockback (High; 75% chance)
Taunt (Moderate) Mag 4

Build Up

To Hit Buff (High)
Add Smash Damage (Extreme)
Add Lethal Damage (Extreme)
Add Fire Damage (Extreme)
Add Cold Damage (Extreme)
Add Energy Damage (Extreme)
Add Neg.Energy Damage (Extreme)
Add Psionic Damage (Extreme)

Fault

Knockup (Moderate)
Stun (Moderate; 50% chance) Mag 2
Taunt (Moderate) Mag 4

Hurl Boulder

Smashing Damage (High)
Knockback (High; 50% chance)
Taunt (Moderate) Mag 4

Tremor

Smashing Damage (Moderate)
Knockback (High; 80% chance)
Taunt (Moderate) Mag 4

Seismic Smash

Smashing Damage (Very High)
Hold (High; 40% chance) Mag 4
Taunt (Moderate) Mag 4

STONE MELEE STATS

Name	Type	Attacks (Acc)	Cost	Act	Rech	Range	Target	Enhancements
Stone Fist	Clk	Me, Sm	7.5	0.6	4	5	Foe	Acc, Dam, Rech, REC, Stun
Stone Mallet	Clk	Me, Sm	11.9	3.7	6	5	Foe	Acc, Dam, REC, KB, Rech
Taunt	Clk		0.0	2.7	3	70	Foe	Rng, Taunt, Rech
Heavy Mallet	Clk	Me, Sm	17.9	3.7	11.1	5	Foe	Acc, Dam, Rech, REC, KB
Build Up	Clk		7.5	1.2	45	—	Self	REC, Rech, To Hit+
Fault	Clk		14.7	2.1	20	20	Foe (15' sphere)	Acc, Rech, REC, KB, Rng, Stun,
Hurl Boulder	Clk	Sm	13.5	3.8	8	40	Foe	Acc, Dam, REC, KB, Rng, Rech
Tremor	Clk	Sm	19.5	3.3	14	—	Foe (15' sphere)	Acc, Dam, Rech, REC, KB
Seismic Smash	Clk	Me, Sm	26.7	1.5	20	5	Foe	Acc, Dam, Rech, REC, Hold

Type: Togl (Toggle); **Clk** (Click)
Attacks: Lethal, **Sm**ash, **Fi**re, **En**ergy, **Me**lee, **NgEn** (Negative Energy), **Co**ld, **Psi**onic
Rech: Recharge Time
Enhancements: Accuracy, **Dam**age, **Dmg Resist, Defense+** (buff), **Defense−** (Debuff), **End**urance **Drain, KB** (Knockback), **REC** (Reduce Endurance Cost), **Rng** (Range), **To Hit+** (buff), **To Hit-** (Debuff), **Int**errupt, and **Rech** (recharge)

SUPER STRENGTH

Super Strength gives you the power to inflict a reasonable amount of damage on your opponents. You will never do as much damage as a Scrapper or Blaster, but that's OK. It's your job to take more damage than you give.

Most of the Super Strength powers have the ability to knock down or Stun your opponents. This causes them to lose at least one attack when you're successful.

Many of the Super Strength powers are area attacks, giving you a chance to injure, knock down and/or Stun all opponents near you. Not only does this cause them to lose attacks, but it builds their anger toward you (which, as a Tanker, is something you want).

Use your attacks sparingly when teamed up. Only attack to acquire and maintain anger, and to stop your opponents from attacking your teammates.

Power researched by Bubski.

Super Strength Effects

Jab

Smashing Damage (Moderate)
Stun (Moderate; 10% chance) Mag 2
Taunt (Moderate) Mag 4

Punch

Smashing Damage (Moderate)
Knockback (Moderate; 30% chance)
Taunt (Moderate) Mag 4

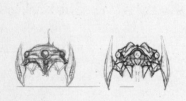

Set one of these powers to auto-attack, then don't worry about it. Focus on targeting opponents who are *not* attacking you, and convincing them that you're the best target. (Of course, if you're soloing, you may want to be a bit more cautious.)

Use Endurance reducing Enhancements to buy these powers down as much as possible. You need to save your Endurance for your defensive powers.

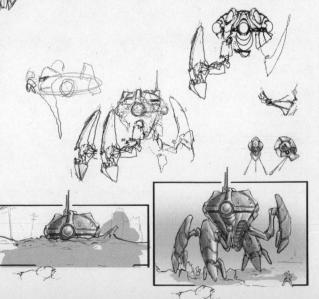

Taunt

Taunt (Very High) Mag 4

Haymaker

Smashing Damage (High)
Knockback (Very High; 60% chance)
Taunt (Moderate) Mag 4

Hand Clap

Stun (Moderate; 50% chance) Mag 2
Knockback (Moderate)
Taunt (Moderate) Mag 4

Knockout Blow

Smashing Damage (Moderate)
Stun (High) Mag 3
Knockup (Moderate)
Taunt (Moderate) Mag 4

Rage

To Hit Buff (High)
Add Smash Damage (Extreme)
Add Lethal Damage (Extreme)
Add Fire Damage (Extreme)
Add Cold Damage (Extreme)
Add Energy Damage (Extreme)
Add Neg.Energy Damage (Extreme)
Add Psionic Damage (Extreme)
Defense Debuff (High)
Stun (High) Mag 10

Hurl

Smashing Damage (High)
Knockback (High; 50% chance)
Taunt (Moderate) Mag 4

Foot Stomp

Smashing Damage (Moderate)
Knockback (High; 80% chance)
Taunt (Moderate) Mag 4

SUPER STRENGTH STATS

Name	Type	Attacks (Acc)	Cost	Act	Rech	Range	Target	Enhancements
Jab	Clk	Me, Sm	5.1	1.1	2	5	Foe	Acc, Dam, REC, Stun, Rech
Punch	Clk	Me, Sm	7.5	1.2	4	5	Foe	Acc, Dam, Rech, REC, KB
Taunt	Clk		0.0	2.7	3	70	Foe	Rng, Taunt, Rech
Haymaker	Clk	Me, Sm	12.3	1.5	8	5	Foe	Acc, Dam, Rech, REC, KB
Hand Clap	Clk		18.8	1.2	30	–	Foe (15' sphere)	Acc, Rech, REC, Stun, KB
Knockout Blow	Clk	Me, Sm	18.8	2.2	25	13.2	Foe	Acc, Dam, Rech, REC, KB, Hold
Rage	Clk		18.8	1.2	240	1	Self	REC, Rech, To Hit+
Hurl	Clk	Sm	13.5	3.8	8	40	Foe	Acc, Dam, Rech, REC, KB, Rng
Foot Stomp	Clk	Sm	26.7	2.1	20	–	Foe (15' sphere)	Acc, Dam, Rech, REC, KB

Type: Togl (Toggle); **Clk** (Click)
Attacks: Lethal, **Sm**ash, **Fi**re, **En**ergy, **Me**lee, **NgEn** (Negative Energy), **Co**ld, **Psi**onic
Rech: Recharge Time
Enhancements: Accuracy, **Dam**age, **Dmg Resist, Defense+** (buff), **Defense–** (Debuff), **End**urance Drain, **KB** (Knockback), **REC** (Reduce Endurance Cost), **Rng** (Range), **To Hit+** (buff), **To Hit–** (Debuff), **In**terrupt, and **Rech** (recharge)

WAR MACE

Be sure to have your weapon out before entering combat. Avoid taking pool attack powers that will cause you to put your mace away. War Mace has enough attack powers, so you don't need to add more.

Put your Accuracy Enhancements into **Crowd Control** and **Whirling Mace**, to affect as many foes as possible with these AoE powers.

Bash and **Pulverize** are your bread and butter so open up all the Enhancement slots in these two.

Take **Clobber** as soon as possible. Use it to mitigate damage. Clobber one target and then take out another.

Jawbreaker, **Shatter** and Crowd Control are devastating, but you don't want to miss with

these. Be mindful of a good balance of recharge, Endurance discount and damage Enhancements in these three.

War Mace Effects

Bash

Smashing Damage (Moderate)
Stun (Moderate; 10% chance) Mag 2
Taunt (Moderate) Mag 4

Pulverize

Smashing Damage (High)
Stun (Moderate; 20% chance) Mag 2
Taunt (Moderate) Mag 4

Taunt

Taunt (Very High) Mag 4

Clobber

Smashing Damage (Minor)
Stun (High) Mag 3
Taunt (Moderate) Mag 4

Build Up

To Hit Buff (High)
Add Smash Damage (Extreme)
Add Lethal Damage (Extreme)
Add Fire Damage (Extreme)
Add Cold Damage (Extreme)
Add Energy Damage (Extreme)
Add Neg.Energy Damage (Extreme)
Add Psionic Damage (Extreme)

Jawbreaker

Smashing Damage (High)
Knockup (Moderate; 75% chance)
Taunt (Moderate) Mag 4

Whirling Mace

Smashing Damage (Moderate)
Stun (Moderate; 30% chance) Mag 2
Taunt (Moderate) Mag 4

Shatter

Smashing Damage (High)
Knockback (High; 80% chance)
Taunt (Moderate) Mag 4

Crowd Control

Smashing Damage (High)
Knockback (High; 60% chance)
Taunt (Moderate) Mag 4

WAR MACE STATS

Name	Type	Attacks (Acc)	Cost	Act	Rech	Range	Target	Enhancements
Bash	Clk	Me, Sm (+5% Acc)	7.5	1.4	4	5	Foe	Acc, Dam, Rech, REC, Stun
Pulverize	Clk	Me, Sm (+5% Acc)	12.3	1.8	8	5	Foe	Acc, Dam, Rech, REC, Stun
Taunt	Clk	(+5% Acc)	0.0	2.2	3	70	Foe	Rng, Taunt, Rech
Clobber	Clk	Me, Sm (+5% Acc)	14.7	1.8	20	5	Foe	Acc, Dam, Rech, REC, Stun
Build Up	Clk	(+5% Acc)	7.5	1.2	45	–	Self	REC, Rech, To Hit+
Jawbreaker	Clk	Me, Sm (+5% Acc)	12.3	2.9	10	5	Foe	Acc, Dam, Rech, REC, KB
Whirling Mace	Clk	Me, Sm (+5% Acc)	18.8	2.9	14	–	Foe (8' sphere)	Acc, Dam, Rech, REC, Stun
Shatter	Clk	Me, Sm (+5% Acc)	17.1	2.9	12	5	Foe	Acc, Dam, Rech, REC, KB
Crowd Control	Clk	Me, Sm (+5% Acc)	17.1	2.3	12	–	Foe (5', 180° cone)	Acc, Dam, Rech, REC, KB

Type: Togl (Toggle); **Clk** (Click)
Attacks: Lethal, **Sm**ash, **Fi**re, **En**ergy, **Me**lee, **NgEn** (Negative Energy), **Cold**, **Psi**onic
Rech: Recharge Time
Enhancements: Accuracy, **Dam**age, **Dmg Resist**, **Defense+** (buff), **Defense–** (Debuff), **End**urance **Drain**, **KB** (Knockback), **REC** (Reduce Endurance Cost), **Rng** (Range), **To Hit+** (buff), **To Hit-** (Debuff), **Int**errupt, and **Rech** (recharge)

POWER POOLS

CONCEALMENT

Stealth is the first choice in the power set. It makes you less likely to be seen, but does not grant complete invisibility. While using Stealth, you have a bonus to Defense and can use powers on villains, on yourself and on other Heroes, but if you approach too close to a villain, you can be seen and attacked. Stealth is good for a Hero who wants to sneak around with the benefit of a Defense bonus, but doesn't want to keep switching the power on and off.

Grant Invisibility is similar to Stealth, in that it provides partial invisibility to the targeted Hero (one of your allies). The Hero has a bonus to Defense, and is more difficult to see. The power has a limited duration, and wears off after a set amount of time. While in stealth mode, the Hero can use powers for himself and other Heroes, and against villains.

Invisibility grants you complete invisibility from villains and partial invisibility to other Heroes. While invisible, you can only activate self-only powers, such as healing, Defense buffs or travel powers. You cannot even use your powers to help other Heroes. Invisibility is a good power for when you wish to explore your surroundings. It is also good to use when you need to see around corners, or as a reconnaissance tool to gather information.

Phase Shift is a self-only ability that combines some of the features of Invisibility and Stealth. Phase Shift makes you intangible. While intangible, you're harder to see and cannot be harmed by villains, as you actually shift your body to an alternate plane. While intangible, you can only use self powers. You can, however, use this ability to provide a distraction to allow other Heroes to

revive a fallen Hero, move to another location, or single out a villain to defeat.

Power researched by Dave.

Concealment Effects

Stealth

> Stealth (Moderate)
> Melee Defense (Moderate)
> Run Speed (Very Slow)
> Fly (Very Slow)
> Ranged Defense (Moderate)
> Translucent

Grant Invisibility

> Stealth (High)
> Melee Defense (Moderate)
> Ranged Defense (Moderate)
> Translucent

Invisibility

> Stealth (High)
> Melee Defense (Moderate)
> Ranged Defense (Moderate)
> Translucent

Phase Shift

> Translucent
> Stealth (Moderate)
> Intangible (Moderate) Mag 3
> Untouchable (Moderate) Mag 3

CONCEALMENT STATS

Name	Type	Attacks (Acc)	Cost	Act	Rech	Range	Target	Enhancements
Stealth	Togl		0.2	0.7	20	–	Self	Rech, REC, Defense
Grant Invisibility	Clk		18.0	1.2	3	40	Ally	REC, Rech, Defense, Rng
Invisibility	Togl		0.8	0.7	20	–	Self	REC, Rech, Defense
Phase Shift	Togl		1.5	3.0	20	–	Self	REC, Rech

Type: Togl (Toggle); **Clk** (Click)
Attacks: Lethal, **Sm**ash, **Fi**re, **En**ergy, **Me**lee, **NgEn** (Negative Energy), **Co**ld, **Psi**onic
Rech: Recharge Time
Enhancements: Accuracy, **Dam**age, **Dmg Resist, Defense+** (buff), **Defense–** (Debuff), **End**urance **Drain, KB** (Knockback), **REC** (Reduce Endurance Cost), **Rng** (Range), **To Hit+** (buff), **To Hit-** (Debuff), **Int**errupt, and **Rech** (recharge)

FIGHTING

The first two powers in this set are really helpful for Heroes with few attacks (like a Controller). On the other hand, the last two, **Tough** and **Weave**, are quite useful to Tankers and Scrappers. This is because the defense abilities of these powers can stack with your Tanker/Scrapper defense powers. With a few Enhancements, you can significantly augment your defense.

Fighting Effects

Boxing

Smashing Damage (Moderate)
Stun (Moderate; 20% chance) Mag 2

Kick

Smashing Damage (Moderate)
Knockback (Moderate; 20% chance)

Tough

Resist Smashing (High)
Resist Lethal (High)

Weave

Melee Defense (Moderate)
Ranged Defense (Moderate)

FIGHTING STATS

Name	Type	Attacks (Acc)	Cost	Act	Rech	Range	Target	Enhancements
Boxing	Clk	Me, Sm	5.1	1.1	2.5	5	Foe	Acc, Dam, REC, Rech, Stun
Kick	Clk	Me, Sm	5.7	1.8	3	5	Foe	Acc, Dam, REC, Rech, KB
Tough	Togl		0.1	3.1	10	–	Self	REC, Rech, Dmg Resist
Weave	Togl		0.1	0.7	10	–	Self	REC, Rech, Defense

Type: Togl (Toggle); **Clk** (Click)
Attacks: Lethal, **Sm**ash, **Fi**re, **En**ergy, **Me**lee, **NgEn** (Negative Energy), **Co**ld, **Psi**onic
Rech: Recharge Time
Enhancements: Accuracy, **Dam**age, **Dmg Resist, Defense+** (buff), **Defense–** (Debuff), **End**urance **Drain, KB** (Knockback), **REC** (Reduce Endurance Cost), **Rng** (Range), **To Hit+** (buff), **To Hit-** (Debuff), **Int**errupt, and **Rech** (recharge)

FITNESS

Every Hero starts out humble, and in time they develop amazing powers. But all of them have the same basic traits in common at the start of their crime-fighting careers. All of them will run before they can fly, all of them will jump small cars before they can leap tall buildings, all of them will need to recover the damage they take from the villains of the world … and all of them will get tired.

So what could be better than a pool set that enhances all these abilities?

Fitness augments a Hero's running speed and jumping height early on, and eventually it allows him to recover lost Hit Points and lost Endurance at an accelerated rate at its upper levels. All of these benefits can have a major impact on any Hero, no matter what other abilities he happens to develop. The added run speed or leaping height can be a huge benefit during the early stages of your career. And since these abilities are passive and need never to be activated, they are always a benefit and take no Endurance to use.

As higher levels of leaping or running are developed, these basic boosts from the Fitness line stack with them, so again the benefit never becomes obsolete. As the pool develops you even increase your healing rate and your Endurance recovery rate, both of which are also passive abilities that never lose their value.

So when you can take four basic powers that enhance abilities all Heroes need throughout their entire career, all of them passive and never turn off, all of them cost absolutely no Endurance, and one of them impacts the most critical statistic in the game (Endurance), it is pretty easy to see the value of this pool.

◆ If you take your movement power pool before selecting this set, carefully consider how your first power selection here will complement the choice. If you can Hover you might consider Swift over the added jumping height Hurdle brings.

◆ Make sure to load up those Enhancements for your healing and Endurance recovery rates as soon as possible. There are few ways in the game to directly impact your overall effectiveness more than having your hit points and Endurance recover faster than normal.

◆ If you work your way to Stamina, you can then spend a lot more of your Enhancements on other powers to increase range, Accuracy, damage or effect. This allows you to not only save Endurance, but also become more effective in each and every power you have.

Power researched by i3ullseye.

Fitness Effects

Swift

Run Speed (Minor)

Hurdle

Leap (Minor)

Health

Regeneration (Minor)

Stamina

Endurance Recovery (Minor)

FITNESS STATS

Name	Type	Attacks (Acc)	Cost	Act	Rech	Range	Target	Enhancements
Swift	Auto		0.0	–	–	–	Self	Run
Hurdle	Auto		0.0	–	–	–	Self	Jump
Health	Auto		0.0	–	–	–	Self	Heal
Stamina	Auto		0.0	–	–	–	Self	Recovery

Type: **Togl** (Toggle); **Clk** (Click)
Attacks: **Le**thal, **Sm**ash, **Fi**re, **En**ergy, **Me**lee, **NgEn** (Negative Energy), **Co**ld, **Psi**onic
Rech: Recharge Time
Enhancements: **Acc**uracy, **Dam**age, **Dmg Resist**, **Defense+** (buff), **Defense–** (Debuff), **End**urance **Drain**, **KB** (Knockback), **REC** (Reduce Endurance Cost), **Rng** (Range), **To Hit+** (buff), **To Hit-** (Debuff), **Int**errupt, and **Rech** (recharge)

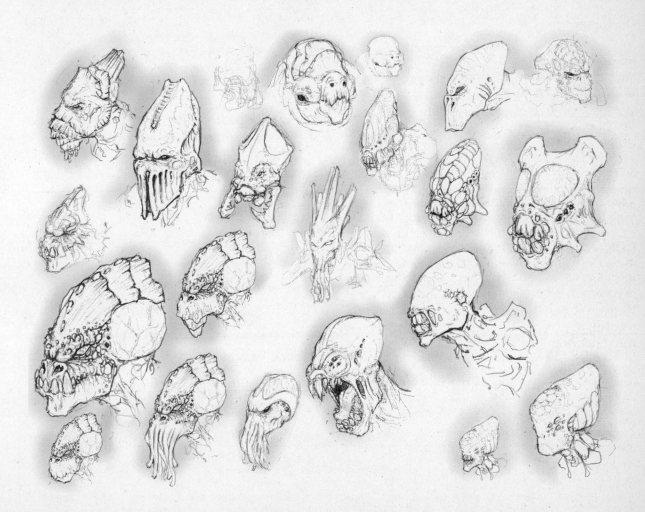

FLIGHT

Hover. For the first experience in flying through the skyscrapers of Paragon City, Hover will be it. However, you will find that the speed of Hover is less then that of a walking Hero. Hover takes very little Endurance, and provides you with a Defense bonus.

Air Superiority. This is the only combat power in this pool. Air Superiority is a mighty, two-handed, overhead Smash that knocks villains down. Not only does it knock them down — it removes them from the air. Flying villains are never safe with this power.

Fly. Finally, you're zooming through the city, flying over the tallest building, and enjoying the world above. Fly is much faster then Hover, but fly does take a toll on your Endurance pool. As you progress through the game, the cost will lower slightly, and the speed of flight will increase. Note that Fly does not provide you with Defense, and it makes your attacks less accurate while airborne.

Team Fly. For those speedy travels across Paragon City, Team Fly will be a good choice. The moment the power is activated, all your team members become weightless, and can fly as if they had just activated the Fly power. However,

this is very draining on the Hero that activates the power. As the number of team members under the Team Fly increase, so does the Endurance cost. Despite the fun in Team Fly, it is the slowest group travel power.

Power researched by Dariuas.

Flight Effects

Hover

> Fly
> Melee Defense (Moderate)
> Ranged Defense (Moderate)
> Fly (Very Slow)

Air Superiority

> Fly (Stopped)
> Smashing Damage (Moderate)
> Knockup (Minor)

Fly

> Fly

Group Fly

> Fly

FLIGHT STATS

Name	Type	Attacks (Acc)	Cost	Act	Rech	Range	Target	Enhancements
Hover	Togl		0.1	–	–	–	Self	REC, Defense, Flying
Air Superiority	Clk	Me, Sm	7.5	1.5	4	5	Foe	Acc, Dam, REC
Fly	Togl		1.0	–	–	–	Self	REC, Flying
Group Fly	Togl		0.5	2.0	–	–	Ally/Self (60' sphere)	REC, Flying

Type: Togl (Toggle); **Clk** (Click)
Attacks: Lethal, **Sm**ash, **Fi**re, **En**ergy, **Me**lee, **NgEn** (Negative Energy), **Co**ld, **Psi**onic
Rech: Recharge Time
Enhancements: Accuracy, **Dam**age, **Dmg Resist**, **Defense+** (buff), **Defense–** (Debuff), **End**urance **Drain**, **KB** (Knockback), **REC** (Reduce Endurance Cost), **Rng** (Range), **To Hit+** (buff), **To Hit–** (Debuff), **Int**errupt, and **Rech** (recharge)

LEADERSHIP

Tactics. Increases your nearby team members' Accuracy with this toggle power. Great for outdoor hunting, where the targets con higher than you, or door hunting with a wide party level spread. If party levels are fairly close and you're doing a door mission, this power's probably not needed. If you solo a lot of door missions, Tactics can be helpful, but it's not as useful as some of the other powers in the set.

Maneuvers. A toggled Point Blank Area of Effect (PBAoE) that raises your nearby team members' Defense, making them harder to hit. Maneuvers is an excellent group and solo skill. Usually, it is more useful than Tactics in both group and solo situations. Maneuvers can be the difference between life and death, as far as damage taken goes.

Assault. Yet another Toggle PBAoE, Assault increases your team's damage potential. Assault is a must out of this power pool. It makes a big difference in damage output even solo. Pair it with a team, and it's devastating. For non-assault Heroes — that is, Controllers and maybe Defenders — it can help add a significant amount of damage to their lower amounts, making them more viable soloing.

Vengeance. Vengeance is a passive skill. If the skill owner dies, it grants party members considerable Accuracy, Defense, recharge and damage bonus. This skill is for those unlucky ones who count on themselves falling a lot.

Power researched by Praxi.

Leadership Effects

Maneuvers
Melee Defense (Moderate)
Ranged Defense (Moderate)

Assault
Add Smash Damage (Moderate)
Add Lethal Damage (Moderate)
Add Fire Damage (Moderate)
Add Cold Damage (Moderate)
Add Energy Damage (Moderate)
Add Neg.Energy Damage (Moderate)
Add Psionic Damage (Moderate)

Tactics
To Hit Buff (Moderate)

Vengeance
Melee Defense (High)
Ranged Defense (High)
To Hit Buff (High)
Add Smash Damage (High)
Add Lethal Damage (Very HIgh)
Add Fire Damage (High)
Add Cold Damage (High)
Add Energy Damage (High)
Add Neg Damage (High)
Add Psionic Damage (High)

LEADERSHIP STATS

Name	Type	Attacks (Acc)	Cost	Act	Rech	Range	Target	Enhancements
Maneuvers	Togl		0.2	3.7	15	–	Ally/Self (60' sphere)	REC, Rech, Defense
Assault	Togl		0.2	3.7	15	–	Ally/Self (60' sphere)	REC, Rech
Tactics	Togl		0.2	3.7	15	–	Ally/Self (60' sphere)	REC, Rech, To Hit+
Vengeance	Clk		0.0	1.2	300	–	Ally (80' sphere)	To Hit+, Defense

Type: Togl (Toggle); **Clk** (Click)
Attacks: Lethal, **Sm**ash, **Fi**re, **En**ergy, **Me**lee, **NgEn** (Negative Energy), **Co**ld, **Psi**onic
Rech: Recharge Time
Enhancements: Accuracy, **Dam**age, **Dmg Resist, Defense+** (buff), **Defense–** (Debuff), **End**urance **Drain, KB** (Knockback), **REC** (Reduce Endurance Cost), **Rng** (Range), **To Hit+** (buff), **To Hit-** (Debuff), **Int**errupt, and **Rech** (recharge)

LEAPING

Jump Kick. Jump Kick is an attack that does decent damage and has a high chance of knocking your opponent over. This is not a standing jump kick, however, but rather a backflip motion. Your opponent may get knocked down, but so will you. You'll get up faster than your target (giving you time for an unanswered quick attack), but if fighting multiple opponents, your own downtime makes this an ineffective method of crowd control. Also, the follow-up attack coming out of this kick is best done with another kick or a punch. If you're a weapons fighter, your weapon will be put away as you perform the Jump Kick, and so you'll have to take the time to draw it again before you can make your next attack.

Combat Jumping. This toggled power has two important uses. Outside of combat, your jumping height and distance will increase noticeably, making travel over fences and walls much easier. During combat, this power provides an increase to your Defense, making you harder to hit, and grants some resistance to Immobilization as well. You'll turn this power on, and quite possibly never turn it off voluntarily again!

Super Jump. Forget jumping over walls — you'll be jumping over whole buildings now! With practice and timing, you can use a series of jumps to find that perfect screenshot moment of your Hero watching over the entire city from atop a skyscraper. The vertical height isn't the whole story, either — the distance you travel while leaping forward is many times faster than anything you'll get out of sprinting. Also, Super Jump has a miniscule Endurance drain compared to other travel powers, which makes it a very easy escape tool for getting away from a fight that isn't working out like you'd hoped. Most enemies won't give chase beyond one or two getaway jumps.

Acrobatics. Activating this power gives you full control over your movement, granting two resist-ances. First, you'll become highly resistant to Knockback effects, and second, enemies with Hold powers will find they have a very hard time keeping you paralyzed. Acrobatics could really save you when up against some powerful bosses — falling victim to Hold effects can take you out in a hurry!

Power researched by Almeric.

Leaping Effects

Jump Kick

Smashing Damage (Moderate)
Knockback (Moderate; 25% chance)

Combat Jumping

Jump (High)
Melee Defense (Moderate)
Ranged Defense (Moderate)

Super Jump

Leap (Moderate)

Acrobatics

Resist Knockback (Moderate)
Resist Knockup (Moderate)
Resist Hold (Minor)

LEAPING STATS

Name	Type	Attacks (Acc)	Cost	Act	Rech	Range	Target	Enhancements
Jump Kick	Clk	Me, Sm	6.3	3.0	3.1	5	Foe	Acc, Dam, REC, Rech, KB
Combat Jumping	Togl		0.0375	–	–	–	Self	REC, Jump, Defense
Super Jump	Togl		0.3	–	–	–	Self	REC, Jump
Acrobatics	Togl		0.3	0.7	10	–	Self	REC, Rech

Type: Togl (Toggle); **Clk** (Click)

Attacks: Lethal, **Sm**ash, **Fi**re, **En**ergy, **Me**lee, **NgEn** (Negative Energy), **Co**ld, **Psi**onic

Rech: Recharge Time

Enhancements: Accuracy, **Dam**age, **Dmg Resist**, **Defense+** (buff), **Defense–** (Debuff), **End**urance **Drain**, **KB** (Knockback), **REC** (Reduce Endurance Cost), **Rng** (Range), **To Hit+** (buff), **To Hit–** (Debuff), **Int**errupt, and **Rech** (recharge)

MEDICINE

A good set for anyone. Be sure to put interrupt Enhancements into all of theses. Then put lots of recharge Enhancements into **Stimulant**, so you can protect your entire team from Sleep, Hold and Immobilize effects.

Medicine Effects

Aid Other

Heal (High)

Stimulant

Resist Stun (Minor)
Resist Sleep (Minor)
Resist Immobilize (Minor)
Resist Hold (Minor)
Resist Confusion (Minor)
Resist Fear (Minor)

Aid Self

Heal (High)

Resuscitate

Heal (Moderate)
Revive
Endurance Recovery (None)

MEDICINE STATS

Name	Type	Attacks (Acc)	Cost	Act	Rech	Range	Target	Enhancements
Aid Other	Clk		7.5	2.9	10	15	Ally	REC, Heal, Rech, Int
Stimulant	Clk		15.0	2.9	10	15	Hero	REC, Heal, Rech, Int
Aid Self	Clk		15.0	3.3	20	–	Self	REC, Heal, Rech, Int
Resuscitate	Clk		37.5	3.3	180	15	Downed Hero	REC, Heal, Rech, Int

Type: Togl (Toggle); **Clk** (Click)
Attacks: Lethal, **Sm**ash, **Fi**re, **En**ergy, **Me**lee, **NgEn** (Negative Energy), **Co**ld, **Psi**onic
Rech: Recharge Time
Enhancements: Accuracy, **Dam**age, **Dmg Resist**, **Defense+** (buff), **Defense–** (Debuff), **End**urance **Drain**, **KB** (Knockback), **REC** (Reduce Endurance Cost), **Rng** (Range), **To Hit+** (buff), **To Hit-** (Debuff), **Int**errupt, and **Rech** (recharge)

PRESENCE

This power set consists of taunts and Fear powers to help you with anger management.

Challenge. Single target taunt. Weaker than the Taunt powers of Scrappers and Tankers, but available to altruistic Defenders or crazed Blasters and Controllers. Like all taunts, Challenge is ranged and can be used to grab running enemies. Given the weaker nature of Challenge, likely you will want to commit a decent amount of taunt Enhancements to bring this power up to the task.

Provoke. This is the first power in the Presence set that Tankers and Scrappers will want to take. Unlike the standard Taunt, Provoke is AoE and grabs the attention of all surrounding villains. With a few taunt enhancers, this can be a very powerful control tool … or a swift trip to the hospital. You definitely should have a healer or buffer in your group, to keep you vertical and continuing to fight the good fight.

Intimidate. Single target Fear. Great for temporarily thinning the numbers of foes. Should you or your companions find themselves surrounded by more enemies than you feel you can handle, Intimidate can force enemies to run away for a time, giving you a few precious moments to regain control of the situation. Adding Fear duration Enhancements will ensure that the fleeing villain will stay away that much longer. Another trick is to use Intimidate for Fear kiting. By forcing an enemy to run from you, you can trail them, getting in a few free shots at their backside.

Invoke Panic. PBAoE Fear. Sometimes things just go horribly wrong. This power is a good panic button. If surrounded, hitting Invoke Panic will cause villains that succumb to run away, giving you time to recover or make your getaway. Adding Fear duration Enhancements is a big plus: the longer the villains are gone, the better your chances to overcome the situation. Fear attacks also act as a To Hit Debuff, so adding a To Hit Debuff Enhancement could help out.

Power researched by Lohengrin.

Presence Effects

Challenge
Taunt (High) Mag 4

Provoke
Taunt (Very High) Mag 4

Intimidate
Fear (High) Mag 3
To Hit Debuff (High)

Invoke Panic
Fear (High) Mag 2
To Hit Debuff (High)

PRESENCE STATS

Name	Type	Attacks (Acc)	Cost	Act	Rech	Range	Target	Enhancements
Challenge	Clk		0.0	2.7	3	60	Foe	REC, Rech, Taunt
Provoke	Clk		0.0	1.7	3	60	Foe (15' sphere)	Rng, Taunt
Intimidate	Clk		15.0	1.7	10	60	Foe	Acc, Rech, REC, To Hit–, Fear, Rng
Invoke Panic	Clk		26.3	2.0	20	–	Foe (15' sphere)	Acc, Rech, REC, To Hit–, Fear

Type: Togl (Toggle); **Clk** (Click)
Attacks: Lethal, **Sm**ash, **Fi**re, **En**ergy, **Me**lee, **NgEn** (Negative Energy), **Co**ld, **Psi**onic
Rech: Recharge Time
Enhancements: Accuracy, **Dam**age, **Dmg Resist, Defense+** (buff), **Defense–** (Debuff), **End**urance **Drain, KB** (Knockback), **REC** (Reduce Endurance Cost), **Rng** (Range), **To Hit+** (buff), **To Hit-** (Debuff), **Int**errupt, and **Rech** (recharge)

SPEED

The Speed power pool is one of the four travel power pools, and contains powers for high-speed overland travel.

Flurry. A series of low-damage blows, all delivered in quick succession with one animation. The damage does not compare to even the low-damage Scrapper or Tanker attacks, but it provides a great filler attack if you're using slow-recharge attacks and need fillers. It's not a great option for ranged Heroes, as it requires them to get into melee range and stay there for the duration of the animation, and does far less damage then their ranged attacks would. It is also an all-or-nothing attack, meaning they all the blows hit or miss based upon one attack roll, so Accuracy Enhancements are a must. Given the low damage of the attacks, damage Enhancements will not show an appreciable affect.

Hasten. Provides an increase to your power recharge speed, meaning that all of your power buttons will recharge faster. The power must be activated, and the Endurance cost hits you at the end of the duration, frequently leaving you exhausted. This power is a must-have for concepts that involve long-recharge powers they wish to use frequently, but for those who either have several powers, or powers with quick recharges, they are frequently waiting on animation speed (which Hasten does not affect) and not recharge, so this power will be of little benefit. Recharge and Endurance Enhancements are needed for this power, if you wish to rely upon it.

Speed. The actual travel power, this allows you to zoom through the streets at speeds in excess of 50 miles per hour. In a flat out race, this power is the second fastest available, with teleport being a bit faster. However, nothing in Paragon is "flat," which means that while the fliers, jumpers and teleporters are taking the crow's path, you are zooming along the streets, looking for ramps, stairs and ledges to hop up on to get across the

city zones. Zones like Faultline also tend to be quite frustrating to the speedster who is unable to jump much further than a normal person. While it is tempting to load this up with running Enhancements, keep in mind that this power is capped out at about 80 mph, so don't waste too many sockets on upping your velocity. One big advantage of Speed is the fact that, while your Accuracy is seriously reduced, your defenses are seriously increased, which helps because you'll frequently be "outrunning" the spawn rate on the streets, and end up running full tilt into it before you see it appear.

Whirlwind. Spin in a circle and throw folks in the air, though it doesn't damage them. Great power for a Tanker or Scrapper who has no other form of damage mitigation, but many targets are very resistant to Knockback, so you might find yourself spinning to no effect, and burning Endurance like mad, as this power sucks it back quickly.

Speed Effects

Flurry

Smashing Damage (Minor)
Stun (Moderate; 20% chance) Mag 2

Hasten

Recharge Increase (Very High)
Endurance Cost (High)

Super Speed

Run Speed (Very High)
Defense (Minor)
To Hit Debuff (High)

Whirlwind

Knockup (Moderate)
Running (Very Slow)
Fly (Very Slow)
Endurance Cost (Moderate)

SPEED STATS

Name	Type	Attacks (Acc)	Cost	Act	Rech	Range	Target	Enhancements
Flurry	Clk	Me, Sm	6.3	3.1	3	5	Foe	Acc, Dam, REC, Rech, Stun
Hasten	Clk		0.0	0.7	300	–	Self	Rech
Super Speed	Togl		0.3	–	–	–	Self	REC, Run
Whirlwind	Togl		1.8	1.2	20	–	Foe (5' sphere)	Rech, REC, KB

Type: **Togl** (Toggle); **Clk** (Click)
Attacks: **Le**thal, **Sm**ash, **Fi**re, **En**ergy, **Me**lee, **NgEn** (Negative Energy), **Co**ld, **Psi**onic
Rech: Recharge Time
Enhancements: **Acc**uracy, **Dam**age, **Dmg Resist**, **Defense+** (buff), **Defense–** (Debuff), **End**urance **Drain**, **KB** (Knockback), **REC** (Reduce Endurance Cost), **Rng** (Range), **To Hit+** (buff), **To Hit-** (Debuff), **Int**errupt, and **Rech** (recharge)

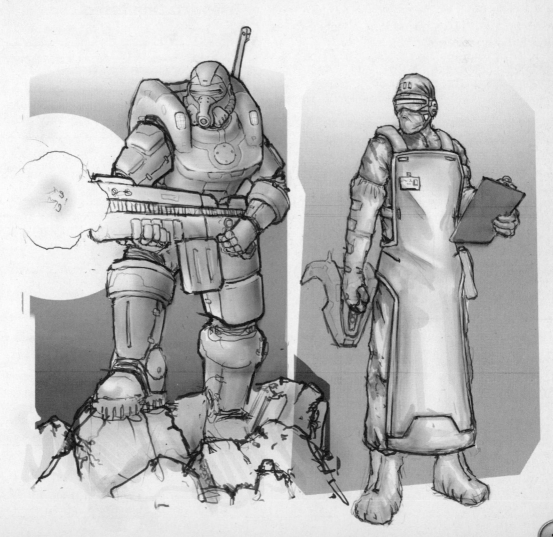

TELEPORTATION

Teleport Friend. You can teleport slow-moving teammates to the next mission entrance. It can also be used to gather up lost teammates inside a door mission. It only works from within the same zone. A word of caution — if you are constantly looking for trouble, then summoning teammates to you to get you out of it is a good way to make people mad. One of the best uses of this power is as a "ripcord," especially in the hands of an empathy healer. The healer is watching the team's hit points, sees one of the Tankers going down, and "yanks" him out with this power to heal him away from the crowd, saving him the death and debt, plus giving him a chance to rest if his Endurance is down as well.

Teleport Foe. Bring the members of a large enemy pack to you one at a time. Even a missed Teleport Foe is very unlikely to pull multiple foes.

Teleport. The quickest travel power around, Teleport is tricky to master. It has a high Endurance cost and a short range by default. Pick your destination, and repeatedly activate the power to travel. Upon use it grants a two-second hover, designed to keep you from falling right away. You travel 100 yards in the direction desired, unless terrain is in your way. The bullseye gives good indicators on where you will end up. For example, if you angle towards the ground from the air, the bullseye will actually conform to the surface it's on, if you have enough range to make the jump.

If you're running low on Endurance, land on a perch somewhere to rest.

Teleport Group. Teleport Group is very similar to Teleport, the main differences being nearby teammates get teleported with you, and it sucks Endurance like a Juicer Freak getting a fix. Often times you'll find it makes more sense to get yourself to your destination, then Teleport Friend the rest of your group in one at a time.

Power researched by Praxi.

Teleportation Effects

Recall Friend

Teleport

Teleport Foe

Teleport

Teleport

Teleport
Fly
Fly (Very Slow)

Team Teleport

Teleport
Endurance Cost (Moderate)
Fly
Fly (Very Slow)

TELEPORTATION STATS

Name	Type	Attacks (Acc)	Cost	Act	Rech	Range	Target	Enhancements
Recall Friend			20	1.9	6	10,000	0	Rech, REC, Rng, Int
Teleport Foe			20	1.9	20	200	0	Rech, REC, Rng, Int, Acc
Teleport			15	1.7	—	300	0	REC, Rng
Team Teleport			15	1.7	—	25	0	Rech, REC, Rng

Type: **Togl** (Toggle); **Clk** (Click)
Attacks: **Le**thal, **Sm**ash, **Fi**re, **En**ergy, **Me**lee, **NgEn** (Negative Energy), **Co**ld, **Psi**onic
Rech: Recharge Time
Enhancements: **Acc**uracy, **Dam**age, **Dmg Resist**, **Defense+** (buff), **Defense–** (Debuff), **End**urance **Drain**, **KB** (Knockback), **REC** (Reduce Endurance Cost), **Rng** (Range), **To Hit+** (buff), **To Hit-** (Debuff), **Int**errupt, and **Rech** (recharge)

ENHANCEMENTS

Enhancements may be received as a reward when you win a battle. They may also be traded with other Heroes, or acquired with Influence. Enhancements increase the effectiveness of your powers. They're not permanent, but they do have the potential to last for several levels before needing to be replaced.

Unless otherwise noted, the name of the Enhancement indicates the kind of power it improves. Note that some Enhancements can be used with a broad range of different powers, while others are highly specific, applying only to a very few powers.

Enhancement	Generic	Dual Origin	Single Origin	Enhancement	Generic	Dual Origin	Single Origin
Accuracy	8.3%	16.7%	33.3%	Interrupt	8.3%	16.7%	33.3%
Cone	5.0%	10.0%	20.0%	Jump	8.3%	16.7%	33.3%
Confuse	8.3%	16.7%	33.3%	Knockback	8.3%	16.7%	33.3%
Damage	8.3%	16.7%	33.3%	Range	5.0%	20.0%	20.0%
Defense Buff	5.0%	10.0%	20.0%	Recharge	8.3%	16.7%	33.3%
Defense Debuff	8.3%	16.7%	33.3%	Recovery	8.3%	16.7%	33.3%
Drain Endurance	8.3%	16.7%	33.3%	Res Damage	5.0%	10.0%	20.0%
Endurance Discount	8.3%	16.7%	33.3%	Run	8.3%	16.7%	33.3%
Fear	8.3%	16.7%	33.3%	Sleep	8.3%	16.7%	33.3%
Fly	8.3%	16.7%	33.3%	Snare	8.3%	16.7%	33.3%
Heal	8.3%	16.7%	33.3%	Stun	8.3%	16.7%	33.3%
Hold	8.3%	16.7%	33.3%	Taunt	8.3%	16.7%	33.3%
Immobilize	8.3%	16.7%	33.3%	To Hit Buff	8.3%	16.7%	33.3%
Intangible	8.3%	16.7%	33.3%	To Hit Debuff	8.3%	16.7%	33.3%

TRAINING (GENERIC)

Name	Enhances	Boost
Training: Accuracy	Accuracy	8.3%
Training: Cone Range Increase	Cone	5.0%
Training: Confusion Duration	Confuse	8.3%
Training: Damage	Damage	8.3%
Training: Defense Buff	Defense Buff	5.0%
Training: Defense Debuff	Defense Debuff	8.3%
Training: Endurance Drain	Drain Endurance	8.3%
Training: Endurance Reduction	End. Discount	8.3%
Training: Fear Duration	Fear	8.3%
Training: Flight Speed	Fly	8.3%
Training: Healing	Heal	8.3%
Training: Hold Duration	Hold	8.3%
Training: Immobilization Duration	Immobilize	8.3%
Training: Intangibility	Intangible	8.3%
Training: Activation Acceleration	Interrupt	8.3%
Training: Jumping	Jump	8.3%
Training: Knockback Distance	Knockback	8.3%
Training: Range Increase	Range	5.0%
Training: Recharge Reduction	Recharge	8.3%
Training: Recovery Increase	Recovery	8.3%
Training: Resist Damage	Res Damage	5.0%
Training: Run Speed Increase	Run	8.3%
Training: Sleep Duration	Sleep	8.3%
Training: Slow	Snare	8.3%
Training: Disorient Duration	Stun	8.3%
Training: Taunt Duration	Taunt	8.3%
Training: To Hit Buff	To Hit Buff	8.3%
Training: Accuracy Debuff	To Hit Debuff	8.3%

FOCUSING DEVICES (MUTATION/MAGIC DUAL ORIGIN)

Name	Enhances	Boost
Visor	Accuracy	16.7%
Collar	Cone	10.0%
Mask	Confuse	16.7%
Gauntlet	Damage	16.7%
Circlet	Defense Buff	10.0%
Chain	Defense Debuff	16.7%
Bracelet	Drain Endurance	16.7%
Torque	End. Discount	16.7%
Lenses	Fear	16.7%
Boots	Fly	16.7%
Headband	Heal	16.7%
Glove	Hold	16.7%
Cuirass	Immobilize	16.7%
Periapt	Intangible	16.7%
Ring	Interrupt	16.7%
Belt	Jump	16.7%
Vambrace	Knockback	16.7%
Helmet	Range	20.0%
Amulet	Recharge	16.7%
Pauldron	Recovery	16.7%
Cord	Res Damage	10.0%
Greaves	Run	16.7%
Helm	Sleep	16.7%
Breastplate	Snare	16.7%
Bracer	Stun	16.7%
Glasses	Taunt	16.7%
Goggles	To Hit Buff	16.7%
Necklace	To Hit Debuff	16.7%

GENETIC ALTERATION (MUTATION/SCIENCE DUAL ORIGIN)

Name	Enhances	Boost
Genome Alteration Reflex Boost	Accuracy	16.7%
DNA Resequencing Cone Range Boost	Cone	10.0%
DNA Resequencing Confuse Boost	Confuse	16.7%
DNA Resequencing Damage Boost	Damage	16.7%
DNA Resequencing Shield Boost	Defense Buff	10.0%
Genome Alteration Shield Drain	Defense Debuff	16.7%
Genome Alteration Endurance Drain	Drain Endurance	16.7%
Molecular Bonding Adrenal Boost	End. Discount	16.7%
Genome Alteration Nightmare Boost	Fear	16.7%
Genome Alteration Flight Boost	Fly	16.7%
Genome Alteration Healing Boost	Heal	16.7%
DNA Resequencing Hold Boost	Hold	16.7%
Molecular Bonding Entangle Boost	Immobilize	16.7%
Genome Alteration Phase Boost	Intangible	16.7%
Molec. Bonding Time Manipulation Boost	Interrupt	16.7%
Molecular Bonding Jump Boost	Jump	16.7%
DNA Resequencing Knockback Boost	Knockback	16.7%
Genome Alteration Range Boost	Range	10.0%
Molecular Bonding Charge Rate Boost	Recharge	16.7%
Genome Alteration Recovery Boost	Recovery	16.7%
Molecular Bonding Resistance Boost	Res Damage	10.0%
Molecular Bonding Run Boost	Run	16.7%
Molecular Bonding Neuro-Paralysis Boost	Sleep	16.7%
Molecular Bonding Deadliness Drain	Snare	16.7%
DNA Resequencing Stun Boost	Stun	16.7%
DNA Resequencing Taunt Boost	Taunt	16.7%
Genome Alteration Accuracy Boost	To Hit Buff	16.7%
Molecular Bonding Accuracy Drain	To Hit Debuff	16.7%

RELICS (NATURAL/MAGIC DUAL ORIGIN)

Name	Enhances	Boost
Crowley's Ring	Accuracy	16.7%
Crowley's Necklace	Cone	10.0%
Li Tieh Kuai's Band	Confuse	16.7%
Li Tieh Kuai's Earring	Damage	16.7%
Nectanebo's Brooch	Defense Buff	10.0%
Nectanebo's Gloves	Defense Debuff	16.7%
Nectanebo's Cup	Drain Endurance	16.7%
Li Tieh Kuai's Shard	End. Discount	16.7%
Crowley's Wand	Fear	16.7%
Li Tieh Kuai's Gem	Fly	16.7%
Li Tieh Kuai's Candle	Heal	16.7%
Li Tieh Kuai's Net	Hold	16.7%
Li Tieh Kuai's Lens	Immobilize	16.7%
Crowley's Gate	Intangible	16.7%
Li Tieh Kuai's Sheath	Interrupt	16.7%
Nectanebo's Phylactery	Jump	16.7%
Li Tieh Kuai's Bottle	Knockback	16.7%
Nectanebo's Stone	Range	10.0%
Crowley's Incense	Recharge	16.7%
Nectanebo's Scroll	Recovery	16.7%
Nectanebo's Gourd	Res Damage	10.0%
Li Tieh Kuai's Goblet	Run	16.7%
Crowley's Jewel	Sleep	16.7%
Crowley's Bracelet	Snare	16.7%
Crowley's Symbol	Stun	16.7%
Nectanebo's Ankh	Taunt	16.7%
Nectanebo's Book	To Hit Buff	16.7%
Crowley's Coin	To Hit Debuff	16.7%

REWARDS

INVENTIONS (SCIENCE/TECHNOLOGY DUAL ORIGIN)

Name	Enhances	Boost
Bioluminescent Filter	Accuracy	16.7%
Micro-Electric Propulsion	Cone	10.0%
Paraxial Modifier	Confuse	16.7%
Quantum Balancer	Damage	16.7%
Interdiffusion Modifier	Defense Buff	10.0%
Epidermal Degenerator	Defense Debuff	16.7%
Cellular Degenerator	Drain Endurance	16.7%
Metastable Capacitor	End. Discount	16.7%
Isotatic Inversion	Fear	16.7%
Micro Adaptive Flow Control	Fly	16.7%
Bioregenerator	Heal	16.7%
Bonding Compound	Hold	16.7%
Kinetic Inhibitor	Immobilize	16.7%
Oscillator Overthruster	Intangible	16.7%
Chronotranstabilizer	Interrupt	16.7%
Centripetal Augmenter	Jump	16.7%
Kinetic Accelerator	Knockback	16.7%
Magnetic Aspirator	Range	10.0%
Mercurial Theorem	Recharge	16.7%
Adrenal Graft	Recovery	16.7%
Composite Epidermal Underlay	Res Damage	10.0%
Transmatrix Bipedal Amplifier	Run	16.7%
Hyperbaric Matrix	Sleep	16.7%
Muscular Atrophier	Snare	16.7%
Dynamic Inhibitor	Stun	16.7%
Photonic Capacitor	Taunt	16.7%
Cardiac Compensator	To Hit Buff	16.7%
Cardio Destabilizer	To Hit Debuff	16.7%

GADGETS (TECHNOLOGY/NATURAL DUAL ORIGIN)

Name	Enhances	Boost
Illumination Grenade	Accuracy	16.7%
Amplifier Device	Cone	10.0%
Cacophony Projector	Confuse	16.7%
High Explosive Grenade	Damage	16.7%
Defender Projector	Defense Buff	10.0%
Adhesive Grenade	Defense Debuff	16.7%
Sap Grenade	Drain Endurance	16.7%
Oxygen Device	End. Discount	16.7%
Dread Grenade	Fear	16.7%
Ascendance Device	Fly	16.7%
Medical Device	Heal	16.7%
Net Projector	Hold	16.7%
Entangle Grenade	Immobilize	16.7%
Phase Device	Intangible	16.7%
Chronoenhancer Device	Interrupt	16.7%
Hydraulic Device	Jump	16.7%
Repulsion Projector	Knockback	16.7%
Reach Device	Range	10.0%
Haste Device	Recharge	16.7%
Protection Device	Recovery	16.7%
Aegis Device	Res Damage	10.0%
Acceleration Device	Run	16.7%
Neuralyzer Grenade	Sleep	16.7%
Nullifier Device	Snare	16.7%
Flashbang Grenade	Stun	16.7%
Agony Grenade	Taunt	16.7%
Targeting Projector	To Hit Buff	16.7%
Blind Grenade	To Hit Debuff	16.7%

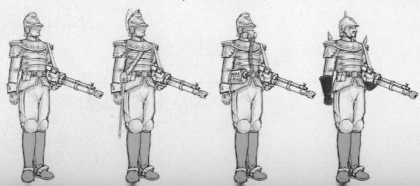

DIMENSIONAL ENTITIES (MAGIC SINGLE ORIGIN)

Name	Enhances	Boost
Insight of Grey	Accuracy	33.3%
Rage of Joule	Cone	20.0%
Perplexity of Hermes	Confuse	33.3%
Fury of Joule	Damage	33.3%
Shield of Joule	Defense Buff	20.0%
Devastation of Joule	Defense Debuff	33.3%
Marathon of Hermes	Drain Endurance	33.3%
Power of Grey	End. Discount	33.3%
Horror of Hermes	Fear	33.3%
Swiftness of Joule	Fly	33.3%
Grace of Joule	Heal	33.3%
Paralyzation of Joule	Hold	33.3%
Bands of Hermes	Immobilize	33.3%
Phasing of Grey	Intangible	33.3%
Skip of Joule	Interrupt	33.3%
Stride of Grey	Jump	33.3%
Smite of Hermes	Knockback	33.3%
Extension of Joule	Range	20.0%
Renewing of Hermes	Recharge	33.3%
Resistance of Grey	Recovery	33.3%
Shield of Hermes	Res Damage	20.0%
Stride of Grey	Run	33.3%
Rest of Hermes	Sleep	33.3%
Pacification of Hermes	Snare	33.3%
Bewildering of Hermes	Stun	33.3%
Voice of Hermes	Taunt	33.3%
Aim of Joule	To Hit Buff	33.3%
Neglect of Joule	To Hit Debuff	33.3%

SECONDARY MUTATIONS (MUTATION SINGLE ORIGIN)

Name	Enhances	Boost
Awakening: Improved Accuracy	Accuracy	33.3%
Catalyst: Cone Extension	Cone	20.0%
Awakening: Increased Confusion	Confuse	33.3%
Catalyst: Improved Damage	Damage	33.3%
Catalyst: Defense Extension	Defense Buff	20.0%
Awakening: Defense Degradation	Defense Debuff	33.3%
Evolution: Endurance Draining	Drain Endurance	33.3%
Awakening: Reduced Endurance	End. Discount	33.3%
Awakening: Increased Fear	Fear	33.3%
Catalyst: Amplified Flying	Fly	33.3%
Catalyst: Amplified Healing	Heal	33.3%
Catalyst: Stasis Amplification	Hold	33.3%
Catalyst: Increased Immobilization	Immobilize	33.3%
Awakening: Phase Extension	Intangible	33.3%
Catalyst: Chronometric Manipulation	Interrupt	33.3%
Evolution: Improved Jump	Jump	33.3%
Awakening: Extended Knockback	Knockback	33.3%
Awakening: Extended Range	Range	20.0%
Evolution: Reduced Recharge	Recharge	33.3%
Awakening: Recovery Acceleration	Recovery	33.3%
Catalyst: Improved Resistance	Res Damage	20.0%
Awakening: Amplified Running	Run	33.3%
Evolution: Neural Paralysis	Sleep	33.3%
Evolution: Damage Degradation	Snare	33.3%
Evolution: Increased Stun	Stun	33.3%
Evolution: Annoyance Factor	Taunt	33.3%
Catalyst: Accuracy Extension	To Hit Buff	33.3%
Evolution: Accuracy Degradation	To Hit Debuff	33.3%

TECHNIQUES (NATURAL SINGLE ORIGIN)

Name	Enhances	Boost
Dragon Strike	Accuracy	33.3%
Military Tactics	Cone	20.0%
Dragon Flurry	Confuse	33.3%
Dragon Rage	Damage	33.3%
Dragon Defense	Defense Buff	20.0%
Back Alley Stunning Hit	Defense Debuff	33.3%
Military Exhaustion	Drain Endurance	33.3%
Military Encouragement	End. Discount	33.3%
Back Alley Intimidation	Fear	33.3%
Dragon Flight	Fly	33.3%
Military Healing	Heal	33.3%
Back Alley Paralyzer	Hold	33.3%
Military Immobilization Technique	Immobilize	33.3%
Dragon Elusiveness	Intangible	33.3%
Back Alley Abbreviation	Interrupt	33.3%
Dragon Leap	Jump	33.3%
Back Alley Bull Rush	Knockback	33.3%
Military Extension	Range	20.0%
Military Speed	Recharge	33.3%
Dragon Recovery	Recovery	33.3%
Dragon Scales	Res Damage	20.0%
Military Sprint	Run	33.3%
Back Alley Nerve Strike	Sleep	33.3%
Back Alley Crippling Blow	Snare	33.3%
Military Daze Strike	Stun	33.3%
Military Insight	Taunt	33.3%
Military Targeting	To Hit Buff	33.3%
Back Alley Blind Strike	To Hit Debuff	33.3%

EXPERIMENTS (SCIENCE SINGLE ORIGIN)

Name	Enhances	Boost
Gamma Particle Irradiation	Accuracy	33.3%
Beta Wave Exposure	Cone	20.0%
Theta Wave Bombardment	Confuse	33.3%
Xenon Exposure	Damage	33.3%
Barium Irradiation	Defense Buff	20.0%
Radon Irradiation	Defense Debuff	33.3%
Uranium Irradiation	Drain Endurance	33.3%
Boron Exposure	End. Discount	33.3%
Cosmic Ray Exposure	Fear	33.3%
Ionic Bombardment	Fly	33.3%
Polonium Irradiation	Heal	33.3%
Thallium Exposure	Hold	33.3%
Auroral Particle Bombardment	Immobilize	33.3%
Hydrazine Exposure	Intangible	33.3%
Thermodynamic Bombardment	Interrupt	33.3%
Butadiene Exposure	Jump	33.3%
Fluorine Research	Knockback	33.3%
Neodymium Irradiation	Range	20.0%
Alpha Particle Exposure	Recharge	33.3%
Astatine Exposure	Recovery	33.3%
Argon Experiment	Res Damage	20.0%
Electromagnetic Wave Bombardment	Run	33.3%
Cesium Exposure	Sleep	33.3%
Hydrogen Exposure	Snare	33.3%
Alpha Wave Bombardment	Stun	33.3%
Positron Bombardment	Taunt	33.3%
Nitrogen Exposure	To Hit Buff	33.3%
Tellurium Bombardment	To Hit Debuff	33.3%

CYBERNETICS (TECHNOLOGY SINGLE ORIGIN)

Name	Enhances	Boost
Benedict Tech Adv. Targeting Eye	Accuracy	33.3%
Portacio Ind Nanoenhancers	Cone	20.0%
WetWare Eng Vocal Mimicker	Confuse	33.3%
Portacio Ind Internal Munitions	Damage	33.3%
Portacio Ind Synapse bridge	Defense Buff	20.0%
Portacio Ind Nanodisintegrators	Defense Debuff	33.3%
Portacio Ind Nano-amp	Drain Endurance	33.3%
WetWare Eng Cyberheart	End. Discount	33.3%
Benedict Tech Facial Reconstruction	Fear	33.3%
WetWare Eng Auxiliary Boosters	Fly	33.3%
Portacio Ind Nanodoctors	Heal	33.3%
Benedict Tech Stasis Regenerator	Hold	33.3%
WetWare Eng Neuralparalyzer	Immobilize	33.3%
Portacio Ind Destabilizer	Intangible	33.3%
WetWare Eng Accelerator	Interrupt	33.3%
Benedict Tech Cyberlegs	Jump	33.3%
Benedict Tech Repulsion Field	Knockback	33.3%
Benedict Tech Telescoping Eye	Range	20.0%
WetWare Eng Adrenal Gland Booster	Recharge	33.3%
WetWare Eng Electroactive Polymers	Recovery	33.3%
Portacio Ind Subdermal Plating	Res Damage	20.0%
Benedict Tech Cyberhips	Run	33.3%
WetWare Eng Neuralyzer	Sleep	33.3%
Portacio Ind Nanodegenerators	Snare	33.3%
Benedict Tech Holey Field Generator	Stun	33.3%
Benedict Tech Agonizer	Taunt	33.3%
Portacio Ind Nanooptics	To Hit Buff	33.3%
Portacio Ind Nanovirus	To Hit Debuff	33.3%

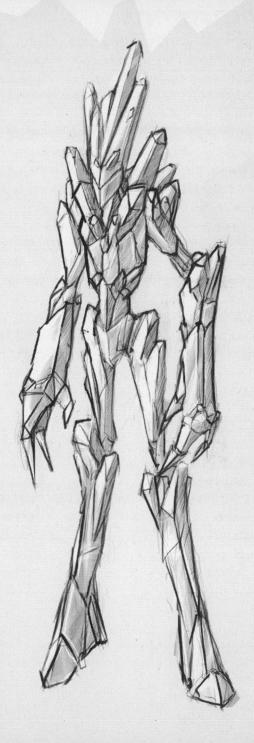

REWARDS

INSPIRATIONS

Inspirations may be received as a reward when you win a battle. They may also be traded with other Heroes, or acquired with Influence. An Inspiration is a one-shot power-up — a little extra boost to help you through a particularly tight situation. Once you use an Inspiration it is gone for good. You can activate an Inspiration by clicking on it in the Inspiration Window. There are seven different types of Inspiration, each of which comes in three power levels. The higher the level of the opponent from whom you won the Inspiration, the more powerful it is likely to be.

Respite Recovers 1/4 of your Hit Points.

Dramatic Improvement Recovers 1/3 of your Hit Points.

Resurgence Recovers 1/2 of your Hit Points.

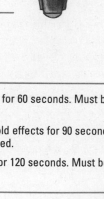

Luck Boosts your Defense by 25% for 60 seconds.

Good Luck Boosts your Defense by 33% for 60 seconds.

Phenomenal Luck Boosts your Defense by 50% for 60 seconds.

Insight Makes your attacks 25% more accurate for 60 seconds.

Keen Insight Makes your attacks 33% more accurate for 60 seconds.

Uncanny Insight Makes your attacks 50% more accurate for 60 seconds.

Enrage Increases all your damage by 25% for 60 seconds.

Focused Rage Increases all your damage by 33% for 60 seconds.

Righteous Rage Increases all your damage by 50% for 60 seconds.

Discipline Slightly boosts your resistance to Immobilization, Sleep, Disorient and Hold effects for 60 seconds. Must be used before you are Slept, Held or Disoriented, but can be used after being Immobilized.

Strength of Will Moderately boosts your resistance to Immobilization, Sleep, Disorient and Hold effects for 90 seconds. Must be used before you are Slept, Held or Disoriented, but can be used after being Immobilized.

Iron Will Greatly boosts your resistance to Immobilization, Sleep, Disorient and Hold effects for 120 seconds. Must be used before you are Slept, Held or Disoriented, but can be used after being Immobilized.

Catch a Breath Recovers 1/4 of your Endurance.

Take a Breather Recovers 1/3 of your Endurance.

Second Wind Recovers 1/2 of your Endurance.

Awaken When you are defeated, you wake up with 1/4 of your Hit Points. However, you will be Disoriented, have no Endurance, and be unable to recover Endurance for 20 seconds.

Bounce Back When you are defeated, you wake up with 1/2 of your Hit Points. However, you will be Disoriented, have no Endurance, and be unable to recover Endurance for 10 seconds.

Restoration When you are defeated, you wake up with 3/4 of your Hit Points. However, you will have no Endurance and be unable to recover Endurance for 10 seconds.

ENHANCEMENTS

Enhancements are the "loot" of **City of Heroes**, and allow you to increase the effectiveness of aspects of your Hero's powers. There are three types of Enhancements and a myriad of effects. The types are Generic, Dual-Origin and Single-Origin. The effects within those types include Damage, Range, Endurance Cost, and many others. Essentially an Enhancement effect exists for every aspect of every power.

Before going into the details of the Enhancements and their effects, it is important to explain exactly how Enhancements work. The degree to which an Enhancement affects a power is dictated by its type, and the color of the number displayed on the Enhancement, not the number itself. For example, a level 40 single-Origin Enhancement is *not* better than a level 20 single-Origin Enhancement. In fact, they are completely identical in all aspects but the number.

So how do Enhancements enhance? A Hero can "socket" (that is, place an Enhancement into an empty slot on one of his powers) any Enhancement that is within 3 levels of his combat level. This means that a Level 20 Hero can socket Enhancements between 17th and 23rd level. The difference between the Hero's combat level and the number on the Enhancement dictates how effective that Enhancement is going to be for the socketed power.

◆ If the Enhancement's level is above that of the Hero, i.e. 21st or higher for a Level 20 Hero, the number on the Enhancement will be green and the Enhancement will be operating above its normal bonus, providing an extra increase to the power or effect. This bonus is approximately +1% for each level difference.

◆ If the Enhancement's level is equal to that of the Hero, the number will be white and the Enhancement operates at its normal bonus.

◆ If the Enhancement's level is less than that of the Hero, the number will be yellow and the Enhancement's bonus is reduced by approximately -1% for each level difference.

◆ If the Hero's level rises to more than 3 over the Enhancement's, or the Enhancement is greater than 3 levels over the Hero, the number on the Enhancement will be red and it offers no bonus at all. Red Enhancements that are socketed on a power need to be destroyed using the trash icon on the Enhancements window.

Note: This is based upon combat level, not security level, so the moment a Hero sees the flash and is told he needs to level up, his Enhancements are affected. This means that holding off training will not delay the reduction in his Enhancement's effectiveness.

THE TACTICS OF ENHANCEMENTS

General Notes on Enhancements

◆ Store-bought Enhancements only come in increments of 5, but Enhancements dropped by foes can be any level.

◆ Their listed effect is modified by their level compared to the Hero's combat level, as described above.

◆ The bonus of a green Generic is less than that of a yellow dual-Origin.

◆ The bonus of a green dual-Origin is less than that of a yellow single-Origin.

◆ The game tracks decimal increments (i.e., it can add a 5% Enhancement to a 5-point damage power), but the interface rounds

REWARDS

down, so socketing an Enhancement may not always give a visible effect.

◆ Right-clicking and selecting "Info" always tells what type an Enhancement is, either in a store or in the Hero's inventory.

◆ Lieutenants and Bosses have a higher chance of dropping Enhancements, and they tend to drop the more valuable ones. The higher level the Boss or Lieutenant, the greater the chance.

Generic or **Training Enhancements** are the first ones you will see. They are available as drops from villains, purchasable from contacts and stores, and exist from 1st level to 40th level. They provide a 5% or 8.3% bonus to a Power effect when they are socketed. These are generally used into the early 20s, due to the prohibitive costs of the more powerful ones. These always look the same, with a silver ring and logo, and the color and name indicating their function.

Dual-Origin Enhancements begin dropping randomly when you approach Level 20, exist from 15th to 40th level, and are purchasable only from certain, Origin-specific stores. These Enhancements provide around a 10% or 16.7% bonus. It is advisable to begin using these as soon as possible, but not at the cost of leaving other powers with empty or red sockets. The best solution is to target the powers that you use most often, or are the most effective, and begin the upgrade process there while maintaining Generics in the other powers, until all powers have been upgraded and maintained. These Enhancements always look different, with a split ring around them, half representing one Origin and the other half the other. They have an icon in the center and use the same color coding as the Generics, but their names are representative of the Origins they are keyed to, be they relics, gadgets, etc.

Single-Origin Enhancements begin dropping very rarely in the late 20s, exist from 20th to 40th level, and are purchasable only from specific stores, based upon Origin. These Enhancements

Now that's a Super Group!

provide a 20% or 33.3% bonus. As the most powerful Enhancements, they are also significantly more expensive. Given that they must be completely refreshed every 6 levels, Heroes must be very careful when deciding to begin investing in these Enhancements, as it is possible to gear up one power and leave all of the others weakened from an inability to afford to maintain their Enhancements. Single-Origin Enhancements have a ring that indicates their Origin, the icon in the center, the color to represent their function, and names commensurate with their Origin and function. Until the very high levels (above 30), the only single-Origin Enhancements that are available in the stores are the "power 5" (Range, Damage, Accuracy, Endurance Reduction and Recharge Increase). All of the others exist, and may drop from villains, but they can be purchased only from specific contacts in the 30th+ zones (Founders, Brickstown and Crey).

Stacking vs. Combining

Stacking multiple Enhancements with the same effect on a single power definitely works, and is better than combining Enhancements in many cases. Here are some examples:

Let's take a power that has a base 10 Hit Points damage.

Adding a single-Origin, same level (white) will provide a 33.3% bonus, adding 3.3 HP damage.

Adding a dual-Origin, same level (white) will provide a 16.7% bonus, adding 1.6 HP damage.

The total damage is now 14.9 HP.

Now, if you find another single-Origin, same level, you have two options:

1. Combine it with the existing one, making it a + lvl (green), and adding ~2% to the 33%, making it 35% and 3.5 HP, total of 15.1hp.

2. If you have an open socket, drop it in there

for another 33% or 3.3 HP bonus, taking the total up to 18.2 HP.

Just remember that many powers have an Enhancement ceiling built in, so myriad identical Enhancements may not provide more benefit than just a couple.

And, of course, multiple Enhancements won't do you any good if they're all red ... but timely combining can keep an Enhancement working for you longer. (See the *City of Heroes Game Manual* for more on combining Enhancements.)

Usage Tips

◆ One of the first Enhancements a melee hero should be socketing is Accuracy, if the power accepts it. Reducing the Endurance or recharge rate or increasing the damage or range are all irrelevant if you can't hit the broad side of a barn. Stepping up the Accuracy first, then stacking the others on top of that, increases your effectiveness overall. Non-melee heroes need to find the most significant Enhancement for their specific power set. If you burn through Endurance fast, perhaps that is it. If your powers take a long time to come back, recharge may be it.

◆ Balance is better than overloading. While it is possible to load 6 damage Enhancements into a power, it is far better to strive for a more balanced approach. 6 damage Enhancements will certainly increase the damage of the attack, but with low Accuracy, you will miss a lot. Poor recharge means you don't swing as often, so misses are even more noticeable. High Endurance cost means you run out of Endurance quickly. Adding a recharge to a power means that it goes off faster, increasing the overall damage per second (D/s). Adding an Accuracy means you hit more often, again increasing D/s. Lowering the Endurance

REWARDS

means you last longer and are less likely to run out of Endurance in a big fight. Balancing the Enhancements provides the highest D/s output for your hero.

◆ Always combine rather than replace whenever possible. At 22, it's possible to buy 25th level Enhancements, but they can't be combined with your existing 22nds because the resulting 25+ is 26th level, and 4 levels above you. However, if you replace the Enhancement instead of combining it, that wastes an entire level of effectiveness. The bonus difference between green and white is not great enough to warrant wasting that extra level, especially given the cost of Enhancements at the higher levels, so every + begins to be worth 100,000s of Influence in the long run across multiple powers.

◆ Be careful in socket selection. Many powers have Enhancement caps (a maximum percentage beyond which Enhancements are not effective) that will not become visible until you begin using single-Origin Enhancements. Consequently, loading six sockets onto a power that only accepts a single Enhancement type in the hopes of using six of the that enhancement, only to find out around Level 30 that the most it will accept is three single-Origin Enhancements, leaves you with three sockets that could have benefited other powers.

◆ Leverage your powers' strengths and enhance them. For example, Storm Kick and Flurry of Blows are small damage powers, so adding damage Enhancements to them will create a negligible return on investment. However, given the long animation time of those powers, and the fact that a miss means that all shots miss and no damage is done, consider using multiple Accuracy Enhancements instead of damage ones, and double up the damage Enhancements on the big-damage powers. Putting a recharge Enhancement on a power whose button comes up in under 10 seconds will also not be all that visible, but putting two or three in a power that takes a minute or more to come back up is extremely effective. Feel out how your powers work, and how you use them, and maintain Enhancements that truly enhance their effectiveness for you, personally.

◆ Always keep your Enhancement inventory clear, so stop and sell or trade your Enhancements between missions. There is little more frustrating than seeing the tab to bring up your Enhancement inventory turn red — meaning your inventory is full — halfway through a mission, and wondering what cool Enhancements you're missing because you don't have room. Or worse, you are forced to delete ones you can not use but could have sold, just to make sure you don't miss any (although deleting Enhancements you can't use is better than running around with a full inventory of useless Enhancements). They don't sell for much — about twice the Influence normally gotten for defeating a even-fight minion — but it is still lost Influence that could be used to upgrade existing Enhancements to better ones.

INSPIRATIONS

Inspirations are very useful and you should always try to have at least a couple on you. Many times seemingly impossible fights are made winnable merely by using a couple Inspirations. *Do **not** hoard them for a rainy day*. They drop frequently and should be used constantly. To save them rather than using them makes life on the streets of Paragon City unnecessarily difficult. Don't hesitate to fire a couple when things look dicey, or merely to be on the safe side. Even if you go through a run of bad luck and few seem to be dropping for you (or perhaps the ones you get aren't the ones you're looking for) you can always return to a contact and spend some Influence to fill out your slots.

When going into a mission, especially solo, it's a good idea to have a full range of Inspirations. Even when you are grouped, things can still go wrong, and having that extra little boost could save you and your friends. Missions where you know a Boss awaits you are made much simpler if you plan ahead and come prepared.

From the very start, Inspirations are useful and helpful to have, but as you level through the game you will find yourself relying on them more and more to overcome villains. Entering into the middle levels, you start to receive better versions of some types. Where Luck added 25% to Defense, Good Luck now adds 33%. Respite recovers 25% of your Hit Points, while Dramatic Improvement recovers 33%. These are base numbers though, and are adjusted by your Security Level. The same Inspiration that healed you for 101 HP in the previous level might heal you for 123 on the next. So don't discount base level Inspirations or feel you will outlevel their usefulness; they grow with you.

Certain archetypes will favor some Inspirations more than others. Tankers can likely get away

with not having a handy Luck on them, as they are more suited to taking punishment anyway. Something like Discipline (resists Hold, Stun, Confusion, Root) is extremely useful for a Tanker in the thick of battle, especially at higher levels where the villains start busting out with powers of their own. There's nothing worse than a Tanker watching himself or his companions being thrashed soundly as he stands helplessly swaying. Blasters might be the lords of hot and fast damage, but none have the staying power of a Tanker or Scrapper. Arming themselves liberally with health and defense inspirations helps to offset this weakness. With that in mind, Inspirations are useful for anyone at most times.

Inspirations stack with other buffs. Any buffs your Hero might have on him from himself or teammates sit nicely next to the additions Inspirations bring. Quickly using Inspirations for Accuracy, damage, defense and discipline makes an orange Boss into a minion with a few extra hit points.

Luck/Good Luck/Phenomenal Luck. Boosts your Defense for a fight or two. Great for when multiple villains take a special interest in you. The Defense add is significant enough to see lots more misses and fewer hits on you. Tankers and Scrappers are more likely to be able to shrug damage off, but a bit more Defense is still good to have. Being surrounded by ten grumpy minions unwilling to accessorize with prison gray can be taxing. Luck can make more of them swing at air.

Respite/Dramatic Improvement/Resurgence. Gives a stack of Hit Points, instantly healing your Hero. At least one is a must. Heroes are shockingly resilient, but even the stoutest of Tankers needs to have one of these in his back pocket.

Catch a Breath/Take a Breather/Second Wind. Returns Endurance instantly to your Hero. A true life saver in a long fight, having a couple is a wise idea if you find you gobble up Endurance fast.

Enrage/Focused Rage/Righteous Rage. Provides additional damage to attacks made by your Hero — a *noticeable* amount of extra damage, giving rise to the quote "a Good Offense is a Larger Offense." When things need to go down now, smoke 'em if you got 'em. Stacks nicely with Build-Up for truly obscene amounts of judicial law enforcement.

Insight/Keen Insight/Uncanny Insight. Improves your Hero's Accuracy. Slower attacking characters might find these invaluable. Missed shots hurt, particularly if you rely on slower, high-damage attacks, and if you find you or your team need to bring tougher villains to justice, Accuracy certainly helps to land hits on higher enemies.

Discipline/Strength of Will/Iron Will. Provides Immunity verses Hold, Sleep, Root, Confusion and Disorient powers. Good to have at least one on you if you are a melee character, especially going into the mid-levels and up. Bosses, lieutenants and even minions will start using these types of powers frequently. At the very least, have one with you going into a Boss mission.

Awaken/Bounce Back/Restoration. Self Resurrect — your Hero returns with a portion of Hit Points, no Endurance, and is Disoriented for a time.

Generally, its a good idea to have at least one of each on your character. More than one Self Rez isn't important unless you have a tendency to make frequent hospital visits. Extras, or Inspirations you don't feel you need can always be traded to your teammates or simply deleted (right-click and select Delete).

Summed up, Inspirations are good. Use them ... a lot.

Researched by Lohengrin

Hoo Boy! I could use a little Inspiration right about now!

TIPS AND TACTICS

THE FIVE GAMES OF COH

From level 1-10, we're just getting our feet wet, feeling invincible, and are very effective compared to enemies our level. We can easily defeat yellow and often orange foes, and attacking a red enemy does not seem like complete insanity.

Levels 11-19 are a wakeup call, where all of a sudden the villains are hitting a lot more often, are starting to use real powers, and 1:1 effectiveness drops quite quickly. If we haven't grouped yet, here is where we start teaming up for survival's sake.

Levels 20-29 are the power game — this is when we truly become Heroes and we're fighting actual villains that use powers and bosses who seem unstoppable (boss damage starts to rise to the mid three-figure range). Things are really rough at this level.

Levels 30-36 is the high-level game, where we're fighting major factions like Crey and the Rikti and taking down real monsters. Soloing at this level is still difficult, but as Heroes start to approach their full potential, it starts to get more manageable.

Levels 37-40 are for the trial levels, where your task forces have moved beyond missions and are fighting major, city-wide threats in the trial zones, like the Hive and the lower sewers. Your Hero is approaching his or her full potential, and you get to really play a champion.

UNEQUAL COMBAT MODIFIERS

When you fight a Villain whose level is higher or lower than yours, the power of your attacks is modified. You attack Villains below your level with greater power; you attack Villains above your level with reduced power.

The modifiers listed to the right affect your chance to hit, as well as the duration of the power (for powers with duration) and the magnitude of the power (for example, for powers that inflict a certain amount of damage with each strike).

5+ levels below you	X1.50
4 levels below you	x1.44
3 levels below you	x1.33
2 levels below you	x1.22
1 level below you	x1.11
Same level as you	x1.00
1 level above you	x.90
2 levels above you	x.81
3 levels above you	x.73
4 levels above you	x.66
5 levels above you	x.60
6 levels above you	x.55
7 levels above you	x.51
8 levels above you	x.48
9 levels above you	x.46
10 levels above you	x.45
11 levels above you	x.44
12 levels above you	x.43
13 levels above you	x.42
14 levels above you	x.41
15 levels above you	x.39
16 levels above you	x.38
17 levels above you	x.37
18 levels above you	x.36
19 levels above you	x.35
20 levels above you	x.34
21 levels above you	x.33

Beyond a 21-level difference, the chance to hit and the magnitude continue to decline, down to about .02%, but the duration never goes below 33%.

TEAM UPS

Forming a team in *City of Heroes* could not be simpler. The lone Hero has two avenues she can take to join a team up. She can either start one herself, or she can advertise herself as available to groups already formed, or currently forming.

To join a team, open up the Group Window and click on Seeking Group. Toggling this will allow members of already formed super teams (and solo players interested in teaming up) in the same zone to see that you are in fact looking for a group to join. They can then send you an invitation from anywhere in the zone, so it's not necessary to actually be in the leader's presence to team up. If you are already the leader of a team up and you'd like to recruit the help of a few more courageous Heroes, simply go to the same Group Window and choose Seeking Members to see the list of available Heroes. Once you find good matches for your group, send them a /tell to ask if they'd like to join you, and then invite away and have them come meet you. (It's considered just a bit rude to send an Invite to a stranger without saying something first, particularly if the other Hero hasn't listed himself as looking for a team.) Once in a group, your team members appear on the map as waypoints, and it's easy to find each other. Your teammates appear on your zone map as little directional arrows, just like you do. Those arrows are color coded to indicate your teammates' health status.

Playing on a super team, the tactics you will deploy are different from any other MOG. There are no "perfect" groups in *City of Heroes*. Each archetype has its obvious benefits, but a group without a healer is not gimped, so worrying too much about that isn't productive. Obviously, a healer is nice to have, but it's not a requirement if you know how to work to each teammate's advantages. If you have a lot of range and no melee, a Defender with good Knockback or Knockdown powers will be as useful as a healer would be to melee Tankers. That same Defender would end up irritating melee Tankers in a different group, since they would have to chase the knocked-back foes around the map. Learning to play to the unique strengths of your group's different powers will make all the difference, and directly influence how many trips to the hospital you make.

Team leaders in *CoH* have some unique abilities that set them apart from the rest of the group, and force them to actually lead. The leader of the super group has the ability to choose which missions the group concentrates on, and set those missions as "Active" in the mission Team Window. Once a mission is active, all the members must do that mission until the leader either cancels it or sets another as active. Also, once missions are active, each group member will have a waypoint set for that mission. The only requirements are that the person who actually has the mission must be in the same zone as the leader in order for the leader to select it, and if a member is currently on a door mission the leader must wait till that group member is finished or leaves the mission. Missions become more difficult while in a group, when compared to solo, since the mission gears itself up to accommodate the bigger group. This is great for the prepared team, but can overwhelm the unprepared team and send everybody to the hospital. Knowing each others' roles, using team tactics, and playing towards your team's advantages is what teamwork is all about.

Take that, you villain!!

Teammates also have a few nice abilities at their disposal. As with many MOGs, the team roster allows you to watch your teammates' hit points and Endurance, and target them easily for buffs and heals, instead of trying to actually click on them while they're in melee. Another important feature in *CoH* is the Assist command. Selecting the party's Tanker (to take the most common example) and hitting an attack button will automatically target whatever he is targeting, and you'll attack that. On that same note, for a healer, if you target the Tanker and attack, you'll attack the foe the Tanker is targeting, but if you activate a heal or buff it will heal or buff your teammate. This makes it extremely easy for the whole team to target the toughest enemies first, as well as giving the frontline fighter full control of the situation, if they know how to handle it.

Don't make Totems angry. You won't like them when they're angry.

Team Composition

Once you have a team, everyone needs to identify their role in it. As mentioned before, *CoH* groups can be made of virtually any combination of archetypes, so there's not necessarily a "healer" or "a mezzer" in every group. A group of 8 Blasters is lethally effective, as is a group of 4 Tankers and 4 Defenders. This means it's possible to group with your friends, regardless of their archetypes, and still have a very viable chance of succeeding.

That said, there are a few configurations that tend to work better.

If possible, try to have an Invulnerable or Stone Tanker, preferably one with the Presence pool. This provides optimal melee crowd control.

Almost any Controller or Defender is good to have, but Force Field Defenders and Empathy Controllers or Defenders increase the survivability of the group significantly.

Something to avoid are Blasters or Scrappers when no crowd control exists — either a true Controller, or Tankers who can manage aggro — as this creates either a group that runs a lot … or

dies a lot due to unmanaged aggro. The only real function that every group needs to agree upon is crowd control, as poor crowd control makes for significant death debt.

Again, these are loose strategic guidelines and in no way means any archetype is a requirement or any archetype is less effective, as all archetypes can find a way to improve any group dynamic.

Team Tactics

Are you going to pull enemies away from their friends, or wade into the middle of them? If you're a Tanker/Scrapper-heavy team, wading may be more efficient. If you're ranged-heavy, pulling is much safer.

How are you pulling? Do you have Teleport Foe available? If not, a taunting Tanker or ranged attack might suffice.

Know the rules of pulling and make sure everyone follows them. Pulling a mob with a ranged attack, then having a Controller Root him before he gets

to the Heroes can aggro the rest of the enemies and completely defeat the purpose of pulling in the first place. Pulling is an art form, and for it to be successful the group must all work in conjunction, otherwise you might as well just wade.

If there is a mix of melee and ranged, make sure the melee Heroes know to keep an eye on the Health Bars of the ranged Heroes, and the location of the foes in relation to the group. All it takes is some Death Mage bum rushing the group and self-detonating for 100s of hit points to wipe out the entire ranged contingent. Let the ranged Heroes deal with runners — do not follow them, as they will only lead you into other groups. Be ready and able to switch targets quickly if a new threat arises.

Lastly, everyone either needs to be in agreement on mob target priority, or a leader (usually the puller) needs to be assigned to call the shots. Spreading out and attacking multiple foes may not be the best solution, if a boss or special-attacking mob is in the mix.

In intense combats there needs to be a team leader calling the shots, and everyone in the group must respect the leader's decisions and follow them to a "T."

Avoid the crazed aggro player, fighting above his head and then scrapping off bad guys on unsuspecting others trying to have their fun. Ranged fighters particularly should be on the lookout for this behavior. Since there is no PvP and there are restraints on language and behavior, you just have to suck it up and deal with the problem within your group if it arises.

PULLING FOES

Pulling, or the art of breaking a group of foes into more manageable pieces, is a complex but necessary skill that many of the Heroes of Paragon need to learn, especially those that have any thoughts of trying a solo career. There are four ways to pull targets from a group: Aggro, Ranged, Taunt and Teleport Foe.

Aggro pulling is the poor-man's taunt and requires no specific powers, but is the least reliable. To aggro pull, simply approach the group slowly,

making sure that the closest enemy is facing in your direction. When the target turns to fully face you and changes posture to a combat-ready stance, perhaps spouting some text to indicate he sees you, stop advancing and stand still. After a few seconds, he will turn aggressive and begin attacking. At this point, back away and get behind something, forcing him to close on you instead of shooting at you from the group. Because you've done no damage to him, the aggro he has for you is tentative — if you back away too fast, he may not follow at all, so multiple attempts may be necessary.

The upside of this pulling is not having to invest in any powers in it at all; any Hero can do this.

The downside is that it's extremely unreliable and stands the greatest chance of pulling more than you desire, frequently the entire group. It also requires line of sight (LoS), and the puller being very close to the group, so the puller needs a very steady hand and must be very patient.

Ranged pulling employs a ranged attack to "snipe" at one of the villains in the group in order to make him aggressive toward you, and retaliate. In most cases, only the targeted mob will come, and the key here is to quickly duck behind something to force him to close instead of fighting from range.

The upside is it uses powers most ranged Heroes have, without requiring a dedicated pool.

The downside is that it requires LoS, though at a much longer range than aggro pulling. Also, only certain attacks can be used for this, as a ranged attack that has an AoE (area of effect), or does a lot of damage, runs the chance of aggroing the entire group.

Taunt pulling uses the melee power of Taunt, which creates an artificial aggression on the target, triggering him turn and rush you (the taunter).

The upside here is that, because the aggression is limited and artificial, it has the least chance to fail and pull the entire group.

The downsides are that it requires LoS, its range is almost as short as aggro pulling, and the aggression is only temporary — which means a ranged target might try to stay with the group and not close, then forget it's aggro and stay.

Teleport Foe is the best form of pulling, using the power Teleport Foe to translocate the target to the place of your choosing.

The upsides here are a very long range that does not require LoS, meaning your Hero does not have to duck, and the target is forced to move and close to the puller. It has the same chance of aggroing the entire group as Taunt.

The downside is that it requires spending one of your pool slots on the Teleport power pool, one that may not fit into your character concept.

General Pulling Guidelines

◆ Never attack a pulled enemy until he's at least 150% of the aggro radius away from its group. Attacking it within that radius will light the other mobs up and bring them to its aid.

◆ Once a group is poorly pulled, they will always be poorly pulled until they despawn. So, if there are 8 mobs, you try to pull 1, and get 8, if you run away, rest, and try to pull again, all 8 will always come, no matter how successful the second and subsequent pull attempts might have been. Your best bet, if it's an option (i.e., not in a mission), is to simply go find another group and let this one despawn.

◆ The higher level the target is over the puller, the greater the chance of a failed pull and/or a cascade pull of many/all of the mobs around the target. Lieutenants and bosses get a bonus to this, and bosses can never be successfully teleported. The teleport may say it was successful, but the boss will make his way on foot to where you are waiting.

◆ Try to aim any Knockback attacks of a pulled mob away from the group and any nearby groups. Damaged mobs have a larger aggro range and will call for help, bringing any group to its defense that it gets near while you actively attack it. This doesn't apply to runners — a runner who runs through a group will not aggro them — but if you blast a runner in the middle of a new group, that *will* aggro the group to the blaster.

B U N G E E E E E E

---

l3ullseye

Joined: 28 Sep 2002
Posts: 74

📄 Posted: 23:19 pm 02 09 2004   Post subject: 💬 quote

Got 24 hour access... and also teleport team mate now. nothing like landing on an 80 story building in Atlas and calling a group mate to the roof with you. I even tested starting the port and having the target jump off the building. With the right timing you bring them back up top before they hit... combine this with a ranged attack and things could get real fun.

_____

i3ullseye

~"You're pretty good. But me? I'm magic!"

Back to top   👤 profile   ✉ pm

MacAllen

Joined: 27 Jan 2004
Posts: 258

📄 Posted: 23:22 pm 02 09 2004   Post subject: 💬 quote

Good lord, what an insane tactic.

First, timing is everything. One lag spike and the guy has 1hp on the ground in front of a mob.

Then there's the chance the mob simply will be gone by the second bounce.

That's an awful lot of work to kill a single mob :p

Back to top   👤 profile   ✉ pm   🌐 www

---

l3ullseye

Joined: 28 Sep 2002
Posts: 74

📄 Posted: 23:32 pm 02 09 2004   Post subject: 💬 quote

It looks wild and is fun as hell.

I was thinking it a good pulling tactic for small groups of flying MOBs. All it really does it let you get farther range effect. T-port allies has unlimted range, where T-port others has a very specific range. You can NTO use it from a tall rooftop... but with a long range blast at extreme range you could do it and hit something on the ground. Of course just porting someone ON the gorund to you after they hit is is much easier and safer, but you don't get near as many cool points for that now do you?

Now I was disappointed by soemthings. I was under the impression Recall Friend would summon a fallen ally. I tried this on a corpse to pull them for a rez and found you can not summon them when fallen. Is this intentional? I could have sworn I saw somewhere it said you can summon fallen allies.

My whole EQ Necro tactic was ruined... and I wept........

_____

i3ullseye

~"You're pretty good. But me? I'm magic!"

Back to top   👤 profile   ✉ pm

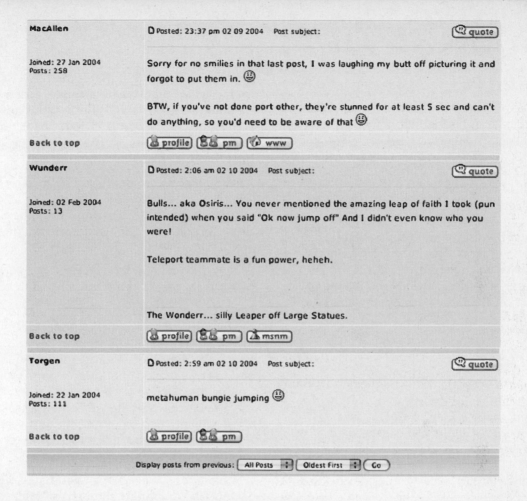

MacAllen

Joined: 27 Jan 2004
Posts: 258

Posted: 23:37 pm 02 09 2004   Post subject: quote

Sorry for no smilies in that last post, I was laughing my butt off picturing it and forgot to put them in. 😊

BTW, if you've not done port other, they're stunned for at least 5 sec and can't do anything, so you'd need to be aware of that 😊

Back to top   profile   pm   www

Wunderr

Joined: 02 Feb 2004
Posts: 13

Posted: 2:06 am 02 10 2004   Post subject: quote

Bulls... aka Osiris... You never mentioned the amazing leap of faith I took (pun intended) when you said "Ok now jump off" And I didn't even know who you were!

Teleport teammate is a fun power, heheh.

The Wonderr... silly Leaper off Large Statues.

Back to top   profile   pm   msnm

Torgen

Joined: 22 Jan 2004
Posts: 111

Posted: 2:59 am 02 10 2004   Post subject: quote

metahuman bungie jumping 😊

Back to top   profile   pm

Display posts from previous: [All Posts] [Oldest First] (Go)

For those of you who wonder how our playtester panel works together, here's an example of how crazy things can get while we're researching a game. The tactic described above does work ... try it at your own risk, if you wish. However, this discussion dates from a relatively early point in beta testing, and there have been some relevant changes to the game since then. Specifically, the Recall Friend power now does work to call fallen allies out of danger areas.

All the folks involved in putting a MOG together, especially the dev team, but also the beta testers and even the strategy guide writers, are constantly exploring the game in ways like this to make sure that the final product is the most enjoyable game possible. This is just one of the more extreme examples.

GENERAL TIPS

ETIQUETTE

If you see another Hero in trouble, if possible try to freeze or stun his foe, rather than just running in and taking it out. That way, he gets to finish the battle he started, and you are not accused of kill-stealing. "Kill-stealing" is the abusive habit of running up to characters in combat who are not having trouble with their foes, and jumping in to the fight uninvited in the hopes of quickly and safely grabbing some of the experience and perhaps a useful drop. This behavior is extremely uncool, and will quickly turn your "Hero" into a pariah among other players. Even in the most "massive" of MOGs, a bad reputation is hard to hide from.

RUNNERS

Unlike some other games, where monsters rather illogically turn to flee when they're at their most wounded, many villains in **CoH** will run away at the sight of you. Once you've played long enough, you'll begin to see the pattern and know who will run and who won't. For example, the guy taking the purse always runs, unless he's powered (for example, a Shocker). In a drug deal or some type of sale, it's almost always the one that is standing opposite the others with his hands crossed across his chest. Sometimes he is one from a different gang. When it's a fight between members of different gangs, it's usually one of the guys who's actually fighting. The more guys there are, the less likely any will run away, and so on.

Unless you have a Root power, you may want to let the runner go, because once the game determines a mob is a runner, it will always run, even if you wait and it comes back to the scene of the crime (which it will always try to do).

Keep in mind, though, that if the runner comes from a group that was harassing a citizen — a mugging or shakedown — letting the runner go means the citizen won't come to thank you after the fight, and you'll lose the Influence bonus you get when that happens.

Because our attacks don't go off while moving, if you give pursuit you'll be chasing him all over the place, and he will try to scrape you off on other groups. Let it go — it won't aggro anyone else, and it will come back eventually.

However, if you absolutely must make sure it dies, here's some tactics you might find useful.

Leap is, by far, the melee Hero's friend for apprehending runners. Target the runner, press autofollow, turn on Leap, hit your jump key and, while in the air, queue your attack. You'll turn in the air and follow, land right in front of him, and always get the attack off, even if he never stops. Try to use a Knockdown or Stun/Disorient attack so he stops running, and remember to turn Leap off, as it sucks back Endurance like there's no tomorrow in a fight.

If you don't have Leap, then you have to use Sprint. Turn on Sprint, and take off after the guy on manual, queuing your attack up. He is running from you, not in a pattern, so you need to get really good at navigating. Zip in front of him and stop. When he comes close, your power will go off and you'll nail him. However, remember that he's trying to scrape you off on other mobs and get away, and don't follow him if he makes a foolish leap (for example, over a cliff).

Which brings us full circle to ... just ignore him. It's far easier and less stressful, and in the time it takes you to hunt him down, you could've found three other mobs ... two of which will inevitably run away.

One thing to note; a ranged-heavy mob will run just far enough to be out of your reach and still use his ranged attack. This is much harder to ignore and more than a trifle annoying. However, chasing after him has the same problems as above, as he will frequently run into groups of his friends to shoot at you. Now, he won't aggro his friends by doing that, but if you either shoot back or run in to hit him, you will most definitely aggro them. As above, if you have no way to prevent him from running, it may still be your wisest choice just to ignore him and move on to another group.

NAMING

If you're really stuck for a name, here's one way to do it …

Take any superheroic type name — add *one* letter, and *voila!*

Examples:

Crusher => Crushter!
Deathray => Deathgray!
Armageddon => Armageddron!
Doom => Droom!

Laugh if you want, but comic book writers have been doing it for decades …

THE INTERFACE

Auto-Fire. Holding Ctrl+left-click on a power makes that power go off automatically every time it recharges. You can still queue up other powers between auto-fires, and you can only auto-fire one attack at a time. Yes, it's in the manual, but it bears repeating.

Assist. You can Assist your teammate by keeping *her* targeted in combat instead of your enemies. You attack whatever she has targeted at the moment, but a buff or heal from you goes directly to her. (This is useful for healers, letting them attack and still monitor a key teammate's health.)

ENHANCEMENT MANAGEMENT

Influence is everything. Influence leads to the best Enhancements, and top-quality Enhancements are the real secret to a really effective Hero. Try not to buy what you don't need, and don't be afraid to sell what you're carrying around without much reason to use it. Inspirations and Enhancements drop quite frequently and should be sold, or even trashed to keep from cluttering up your empty slots (and possibly keeping you from getting that one good thing for your level).

Don't update your Enhancements until you hit the x3 or x8 levels, then combine them with your existing ones. Buying Enhancements, which come in increments of 5 at the store, at x2 (like buying level 15s at Level 12) means you have to replace instead of combine, and lose an entire level of usefulness.

Even your basic abilities (Sprint, Brawl, Rest) can be more useful when you add Enhancement slots to them, and they will serve you from level 1 through 40. Accuracy is at least as important as damage when considering Enhancements, so focus more on balance and the big picture instead of loading up on any given type.

Be creative in your use of Enhancements. Sure, maintain a good balance, but some great tactics are possible with the unusual usage of Enhancements. For example, loading a sniper attack with ranged enhancers if you have Fly or Hover may allow you to stay out of harm's way while sniping at foes on the ground, especially ones with little to no ranged attacks (see below, under **Hover Blasting**). Loading a stun attack with several stun extensions can keep foes wandering dazed for long periods of time, reducing the overall damage you do. Granted, in both of those cases, you'll miss a lot due to the lack of Accuracy enhancers, but you get the idea. Experiment to find the optimum configuration for your powers and tactics.

GAMEPLAY

HUNTING

Try Rooftops …

While they are not always easy to get to, rooftops often have higher-level encounters on them.

Watch out, though. If you accidentally stumble off one of the high buildings, you'll take quite a bit of damage from the fall itself. Of course if you have Hover/Fly, that falling issue is a moot point. (You can't die from a fall, but you can be reduced as low as 1 hit point. So fall all you want, as long as you don't fall into a group of bad guys.)

Hover Blasting

This tactic involves hovering over a group of villains and hammering them from above with ranged attacks. With some bad guys (particularly at lower levels) it's possible to do this for a long time, while taking virtually no significant damage. From a flying Blaster point of view, Perez Park is the primo spot to level, particularly when you're in your early teens. As you rise in level it becomes increasingly hard to find villains to hover blast that are completely safe for you.

Even if the villain does have a ranged counterattack, though, you have to look at the big picture. First, Hover does increase your defense, so you're hit less often. Most importantly, if you target can hit you for, say, 45 ranged and 190 melee, that fact alone means you've reduced the damage you take by almost 80% over what you'd take if you fought on the ground.

Port 'n' Bump. Another useful application of Teleport Foe … teleport a bad guy up to a perch spot (for example, a building ledge), then use a Knockback power, knocking it off the perch. Repeat as necessary. This is another good way to do lots of damage without taking so much.

ADVENTURING AT THE STARTING LEVELS

At this point in your career, your only goal is advancement. One advantage you have is that, for the first four levels you do not accumulate experience debt upon defeat. Also, for this entire range of levels, you're more effective vs. yellow (and higher) mobs than you will be for the rest of your career. take advantage of this.

Do not be afraid to push the envelope and attack a foe that is red. If you win, the rewards are significant. If you lose, you have a quick run back to the action. The more risks you take, especially at Level 4 and below, the faster you get through these levels. Once you hit Level 5, tone the risks down a bit and don't be afraid to run, as you want to avoid debt. *CoH*'s "death" penalty system is the most lenient of almost any MOG, but it still reduces your advancement efficiency, and you want to avoid that.

Grouping is useful at this level, but not strictly necessary, as advancement grouped or solo is pretty much equal. So group only for social reasons, or just for practice.

Maintain your Contacts and make sure you push through your missions and raise your relationship with them. They are your gateway to later contacts and better missions down the road.

Make absolute *sure* you pick up your travel power pool between Levels 6 and 12. This is the fastest you'll be advancing in the game, and Level 14 (when you can take your primary travel power) is a long way away. You must already have the first or second power in your travel pool before you can take a primary travel power at Level 14.

In fact, it's a good idea to have already planned the pools you want up front, and start them off at Levels 6, 8, 10 and 12 (though there is no requirement to take all four, and for some character concepts taking that many pools can be a serious mistake). Taking all four pools means you skipped four chances to get new primary or secondary powers, but it gives you many more choices down the road. You probably will want to take at least two or three pools, depending upon your concept.

(On a side note, the Teleport pool brings with it two very choice powers that have little to do with power and are available immediately: Teleport Foe and Teleport Friend, both *very* useful in groups.)

Having all these pools open now means you'll be able to acquire the higher-level pool powers much more quickly when you want them in your 20s or 30s.

You'll begin your career in Atlas Park or Galaxy City, and probably want to graduate to Kings Row at around Level 5 or so, and Perez Park by 8.

Use the civilians as "thug radar." If you see some running down the sidewalk in a panic, head back to where they came from. They have run into some thugs and are fleeing in panic.

The first two Inspirations you get in the game will most likely be the best you are going to see for quite a while. They're a +75 damage and +75 health inspiration. Try to buy a few of these from other Heroes if you can — they just help so much in early boss fights.

Use this time to get familiar with the controls. Learn how to kite foes, Jump, Fight, and so forth.

Look around. Enjoy the scenery. This isn't a race to become the first to do this or that ... unless you want it to be.

Be Selfish!

Yup, to heck with others. What this means is, your first 10 levels or so will be done mostly solo, or maybe in small groups. You need to work on what *you* need to survive alone, first and foremost. This can impact you most when choosing a group aid power over that first pool power. If you

take Resurrection at Level 6 in the Empathy set, you'll be ready to heal and help the world ... but then you'll have to wait until Level 8 to get Hover. The number of times you'll actually *use* that Res between Level 6 and 8 will probably be negligible. In fact, you could probably easily wait until Level 12 or so before it really becomes a power you need in your arsenal.

Let's look at another example from Empathy: Heal Other. When you're starting out the *only* power you can use to help yourself in the Empathy line is Healing Aura. Healing others for a higher amount is great in a group, but better to pick up another damage dealing power in your secondary line first. You will not see the impact of *not* having single target heals till you are in larger groups ... and this occurs most in your teens.

So even if you plan to be a group-oriented support character, build as selfishly as possible at least through Level 10.

ADVENTURING IN YOUR TEENS

The game changes at this level, and your playstyle needs to adapt or you'll get to tour all the zone hospitals ... and let me save you the trouble — they all look absolutely identical from the inside.

This is when villains with powers begin to become common, but more importantly, this is when they start hitting *hard*. Tactics that some melee and ranged PBAoE Heroes use — pulling in a lot of mobs around them so they can do damage to several foes at once — begin to backfire as the bad guys are now hitting for up to 100hp per strike, which can drop a Hero like laundry in a hamper.

While villain melee damage is almost always greater than their ranged, the difference in this level range is quite startling — a differential of 3 to 5 times or more. They also start using Hold,

PRIMA'S OFFICIAL STRATEGY GUIDE

Spelled my name wrong … again.

Stun and Disorient effects, though they are still quite rare, so avoiding unwanted melee becomes more important to survival.

In other words, all of the tactics that were useful in the prior range go out the window, and new ones need to be formed.

Pulling becomes more a requirement at this level, as the mobs are now able to destroy a ranged Hero in as little as 2 to 3 hits, so uncontrolled aggro is significantly less desirable.

There are a *lot* of foes at this level, in zones like Perez Park, Skyway City, Steel Canyon, Boomtown and Faultline, so finding viable targets is not difficult.

Grouping and running missions becomes the fastest way to advance through this range, so making sure you managed your contacts properly from the prior range is very helpful, and you should continue that through this one.

Enhancements begin becoming a significant factor, because your powers are now doing real damage, so make sure you keep them green and optimize how you combine them to get the most

out of them. Trade with friends and barter for them before you sell and buy, because the buy-back value at the store is 1:4, meaning you need to sell 4 at a given level to buy one at the same level that you might want or need. Use your super group's vault to store unneeded ones instead of selling them, as the Influence gained from capturing villains is far more than any you'd get from selling them. Also, dual-Origin Enhancements will start falling at the higher end of this range, so use any usable ones you find and begin your transition to dual-Origins for all your powers at that point.

At Level 10, you can start to undertake Task Force missions, beginning with Positron in Steel Canyon. These are tremendous experience and reward boosts, and they're highly recommended, though they do take a significant time investment for the entire group — do not enter into them lightly.

Level 10 also opens up the option to build a super group, making the vault and other group-specific benefits available to your team.

If you made the right selections in the prior range, your travel powers will become available and you're moving around the map *much* faster than you were before.

Also, and this is *important* … you may still be able to solo orange on a minion, or yellow on a lieutenant. But bosses will quickly start to eat you alive unless …

- You have range and they do not (rare)
- You have a good number of Inspirations to burn
- You have a power set particularly suited to take them (like Fire Resistance against a flame-based boss)
- Your tactics are impeccable

But unless you are 100% confident here, call for help. This is where bosses really start to boss you around.

ADVENTURING IN YOUR 20S

This level is where you need to start realizing you are *not* invincible. If you could routinely solo a few yellows before, here is where they will start really laying the smackdown on you.

Your missions start taking you to higher-end zones, and getting *through* Dark Astoria is often more challenging than actually killing those Sky Raiders behind the door, depending on your character build. But there's certainly an amazing view along the way!

Endurance conservation really starts to have more of an impact here also. You are facing tougher foes, your fights last longer, and you tend to get tuckered out a bit more often. Now, of course by now you have *many* Enhancement slots to try to rectify it, but if you want your damage to keep good pace, your Endurance drain will suffer, since you still have the same amount of Endurance you had from Day One.

Big tip … the higher-end tram stations have trainers stationed there. No need to run back to AP or Galaxy, and if you know this early it can save you a lot of travel time when you start hunting more in Steel Canyon and the like.

Level 20 opens up a whole new series of zones, a new group of enemy factions, and a new type of fighting. Trial zones also begin to come available — large-scale fights with great rewards for the groups who are brave enough to face them.

Stun, mez, Sleep, Disorient, and Psionic attacks become commonplace, and villains with powers are the norm. As with the prior range, this range brings in yet another rethinking of your tactics, because now a melee Hero is facing foes that can and will hit for a third of your hit points — which means *all* of a Blaster's — in a single hit. Mobs begin self-reviving, healing themselves and each other, and in general making combat much more complex.

Soloing at this level is much harder and grouping becomes the fastest way to advance by far. Solo play is still quite viable, it just requires a great deal of creativity.

Missions are also still the best way to advance, as they provide a guaranteed line-up of targets at your level, in just the right size for your group, with nowhere for them to run, and without you having to hunt all over the place and risk aggroing more than you can handle.

In this level, you will start replacing your Generic enhancers with dual-Origin ones, and single-Origin ones will start dropping. While the single-Origins do provide a greater bonus than the dual-Origin ones, they also cost a great deal more, and put you on the track of having to pay that much to maintain them. Investing in them is not recommended until you are completely green on all your duals and are higher up in this range. Otherwise, you may find yourself at one point with red singles or duals, and not enough Influence to upgrade them.

The fights at this level become larger and more volatile, as the villains are using AoE attacks, mezzes and Stuns, so solo Heroes must pick their targets very carefully (for example, just because that Consigliere is alone does not make him a choice target for a solo Hero) and groups must take care to properly order their targets to make sure the correct ones are eliminated first, before they can wreak great havoc upon the team.

SIDEKICKS

If you are doing a two-man run, take a sidekick that can do what you can not. Even at a significantly lower level, this versatility is a godsend.

For example:

A low-level sidekick with Invisibility and Recall Friend can get you to *any* hard mission objective, even if she has to walk there slowly. This can be attained by Level 8.

If you are a Tanker or Scrapper, a Level 6 will heal you almost as well as an equal level peer, once sidekicked to you.

If you have no range, a low-level Controller can stop those runners.

The list is near endless … if you are a high-level Defender with Empathy, and feel you can not solo effectively, grab a Level 6 Tanker and really make his day. You can keep him alive for hours, and he will not normally go low on Endurance, as he has fewer attacks/powers, and tends not to overburn like the higher-level Tankers might.

Also, effects do matter. If you are going up against a boss with a name like Torch, maybe bringing along a partner with higher Fire Resistance would be a good plan. Fighting Clockwork? A Scrapper or Tanker who can run with no Endurance on their basic Brawl attack will not be nearly as impacted by the incessant Endurance drain those little mechanical monstrosities assail you with.

Most Heroes, even into their high 20s, are probably relying upon their first three powers for the largest part of their effectiveness. Consequently, that Level 8 Scrapper can be extremely effective sidekicked with a Level 25 Controller or Defender, because she assumes the hit points and damage, and is simply missing some of the other attacks that aren't absolutely necessary.

However, there is a downside to sidekicking that must be noted, when the two Heroes in question are relatively close together in level. If you are Level 14 and you're adventuring with a 20, and you group without sidekicking, you are not likely to be terribly effective, but you will get a *lot* of experience points for fighting against mobs that are 6 levels over your head — a high-level Scrapper or Tanker picking up a low-level Empathy Defender or Controller and power leveling him this way is very effective. Once you are sidekicked and the mobs turn yellow or white, the amount of experience you get from each kill is drastically lowered, to the point where you're getting just as much as if you were fighting even-con targets your own level.

Things to be careful of while sidekicking … watch the range to your sidekick. Get too far away and she drops in level quickly. If the Scrapper or Tanker is the one sidekicked and this happens in a fight, she dies almost instantly. If you die, do *not* hit OK to go to the hospital until you know your sidekick is safe.

Sidekicks can not go into hazard zones unless their real security level is high enough, regardless of the mentor's level. (Yes, the SWAT guys do card.)

Look at all the pretty lights!

YOU CAN'T SPELL "ORIGINAL" WITHOUT "ORIGIN"!

By Kwip

Look, let's get one thing straight: I'm not the greatest Hero. In fact, if we were to rank all the Heroes out there, I'd fall somewhere in between "Clogged Septic Tank Man" and Mary Kate and Ashley Olsen. However, in my defense, I will state that even if I do nothing superb or extraordinary, I can at least be slightly original.

I was lucky enough to be in the Beta for *City of Heroes* from a pretty early point. I saw the servers when barely anyone was on. I saw some of the biggest names in the Beta grow from average players to legends. I've read some really fantastic origin stories, and I've seen some amazing costume designs. And that is why, when I run into 5P|D3RM@N, I want very badly to become a villain.

I understand wanting to be like your favorite Hero or video game character. There's nothing wrong with that. *City of Heroes* will even allow you to take many of the same powers as your favorite Hero. But really, that's where it should end. Hero worship is one thing; Hero copycatting is something else. And if I were in charge, in addition to the CoC (Code of Conduct), I'd introduce another set of rules: the CoCC — Code of CopyCatting.

The CoCC would include rules about naming your Hero after comic book characters, movie characters, cartoon characters and characters from video games (yes, that includes the ENTIRE NES era!). The rules would be, in summation: don't do it. There would be an additional rule that would include making your character look like an existing character. So you're fine to pick a blue, skin-tight body suit. You can even add red underwear and red boots. But the second you add a red "S" on your chest, you're fried.

Violations of the CoCC wouldn't result in bans or anything so harsh. No, what would happen is this: if you're in violation of the CoCC, the moment you attack an enemy, no matter what his level, power set or affiliation, the first thing he'd do is cast a spell on you that would turn you into a small, pink bunny. You wouldn't be able to resist this spell, and it would last for 24 hours. In addition, the spell would strip every power from you, leaving you solely with the "Nibble Their Bum" attack, which would only do 1 point of damage.

I'm not trying to advocate power roleplaying or anything of that sort; frankly, I could care less if you choose to roleplay or not. You could name your Hero "Bob" and wear jeans and a t-shirt for all I care. In fact, that's a pretty creative setup (and it's MINE, don't go stealing it!). What I'm trying to tell you is that the absolute worst original character concept is one MILLION times better than the best copied character concept.

If you're having trouble coming up with an original concept, don't worry, I'm here to help! I'll take what the game tells you and break it down into bite-sized, understandable concepts that will make it easy to come up with your own original Hero!

GAMEPLAY

PART ONE: ORIGINS

First off, let's look at your Origin type. From the list below, pick a description that best suits you. Uh, I mean, your *Hero*.

* MUTANT

Mutants are created when one (or both) of your parents spent too much time eating microwaved food.

* SCIENCE

A Science Origin is usually the result of getting a "Kids' Chemistry Set" as a birthday present on your birthday and drinking all the contents.

* TECHNOLOGY

Technology Heroes are the kind of people who not only stick forks into toasters, they proceed to figure out ways to make the toaster launch those forks out at super-high velocities, turning them into deadly weapons.

* NATURAL

Going "Natural" means your Hero doesn't care for the feeling of clothing against his skin. These sorts tend to wear very minimalist costumes, and they don't eat any foods containing dangerous MSGs.

* MAGIC

Your average Magician and Sorceress spent their childhood telling their friends to tie them up as best they could so they could escape, just like Houdini. Their parents could be relied upon to untie them when they didn't show up for dinner.

PART TWO: ARCHETYPES

Your Archetype will depend upon what sort of fighting you like to do.

* BLASTER

Blasters were the kids in school that could launch a spitwad all the way from the back of the classroom and still have it smash into the chalkboard with enough force to actually leave cracks in the slate.

ART: JUSTIN PARKS   STORY: SHAWN "KWIP" WILLIAMS

NOTE: Just for the record, attempting to duplicate a trademarked character in *City of Heroes* is a violation of terms of service, and the GMs will not have a sense of humor about it.

* CONTROLLER

Controllers are the good-looking people that can use just a smile and flick of their eyelids to make you think that selling body organs to buy them jewelry is a wise investment.

* DEFENDER

Defenders are the people that got outraged when they saw a nerd being bullied and stood up for him. They can commonly be distinguished by their underwear having been 'wedgied' to somewhere around their shoulders.

* SCRAPPER

Scrappers were the bullies that did the previously mentioned 'wedgieing' of underwear to shoulder level.

* TANKER

Tankers are the people who put mugs of beer on their heads and dare their friends to punch them in the stomach as hard as they can, insisting they won't spill a drop. They're also the people most often admitted to the Emergency Room with ruptured spleens.

PART THREE: BODY TYPE

Male, Female or Huge. This should have been covered in your Elementary School Phys Ed. class. If you're confused, I recommend Huge.

PART FOUR: COSTUMES

After you've picked your Origin and Archetype, you get to design your costume. Designing a costume is fairly easy, provided you adhere to Kwip's Rules of Costuming:

Stare at your costume for thirty seconds, and then look away. If you're still able to see and you don't have flashes of magenta bursting before your vision, it's a good costume.

Look through your comic books, your video games, your movies and your cartoon collection. If you don't see your costume in any of these, it's a good costume.

Show your costume to your significant other/pet. If he don't threaten to leave you (in case of your pet) or hiss and claw your face (in case of your significant other), it's a good costume. Er, wait, strike that; reverse it.

PART FIVE: NAMES

See rule #2 of Costumes. The same theory applies here, only with the additional prohibition against using numbers or characters in place of letters.

Finished! Now you've got a completely unique, *original* Hero, and you're ready to go out and fight crime.

Excelsi … er … I mean … Up and at … Er …

Oh, never mind. Just go have fun!

— *Shawn "Kwip" Williams' and Justin "Kaigon" Parks' unique views of this and other games can be found on the web at neenerneener.net.*

GAMEPLAY

EMOTES

Whether it is standing idly by reading a newspaper, waving to a friend from afar, or even giving a big thumbs up for justice, nothing can help you express your Heroes' moods like well-placed emotes. The emote system activates various animations for your Hero to act out.

Some emotes are triggered animations with associated dialogs attached, while others are motions only. Some of the associated text may even be colored to allow it to stand out during the chaos of combat (**Stop!** is red, **Go!** is green and **Attack!** is orange).

Emotes can be called in one of two ways. The first is to use the emote slash command. This will display any text typed in as a "thought bubble" for your Hero, or (if it is a recognized name of an animated emote) it will trigger that animation. There are four basic commands for using emotes from your chat window. Typing **/e**, **/em** or **/emote** allows you to then type the emote name (or text string) immediately following it, or you can just hit the semicolon (;) and the chat window will be ready for you to type the name or text of the emote immediately.

> **/e** hi `Enter`
>
> **/em** bow `Enter`
>
> **;cheer** `Enter`
>
> **/e** I wonder if her mama knows she wears that costume? `Enter`

The first three above are correct ways to trigger an animated emote from the chat window. The fourth would produce a "thought bubble" with the indicated text inside.

The second way to navigate through the emote system is through the word balloon icon at the bottom right of your chat menu. This opens the Emote Menu. Most of the animated emotes in the game are listed in this menu, which can then be navigated by clicking on the name of the section or emote you want, or by typing the highlighted letter in its name once the menu on which it appears is open.

EMOTES BY NAME

Wave	Paper	Kata
Hi	Scissors	Laugh
BigWave	Dice	Lecture
OverHere	CoinToss	Lotus
Whistle	Bow	Newspaper
Attack	Burp	Point
Point	Cheer	Praise
RaiseHand	Clap	Roar
Stop	Disagree	Salute
ThumbsUp	Explain	Shrug
Yes	Flex	Tarzan
No	Flex1	Taunt1
DontAttack	Flex2	Taunt2
CrossArms	Flex3	WaveFist
Rock	Jumping Jacks	Yoga

MAIN EMOTE MENU

- **G** Greetings
- **V** Converse
- **D** Decide
- **T** Travel
- **C** Combat
- **E** Other Emotes

EMOTE SUB MENUS

GREETINGS

- **H** Hi (waves hand)
- **I** Introduce Self (waves hand)
- **L** Looking for Team (no animation)
- **O** Hello <target> (waves hand)

CONVERSE

- **A** Arrrgggh! (no animation)
- **E** Excellent (thumbs up)
- **G** Grrrrr! (no animation)
- **H** Huh? (shrugs)
- **J** Good job (left thumb up)
- **L** <laughs> (throw head back and laugh)
- **M** Mua ha ha ha! (throw head back and laugh)
- **N** No (arms folded across chest)
- **O** Sorry (bow)
- **P** No problem (no animation)

- **S** Yes Sir (salute)
- **T** Thank you (no animation)
- **W** You're welcome (no animation)
- **Y** Yes (thumbs up)

DECIDE

These Emotes have no dialog, only animation, as indicated by the name of the emote.

- **C** Coin Toss (after the animation, a coin will appear showing either heads or tales)
- **D** Dice (after the animation, a single die will appear showing the result of the throw, 1-6)
- **E** Explain
- **I** Disagree
- **L** Lecture
- **N** No (as under Converse, but animation only)
- **P** Paper
- **R** Rock
- **S** Scissors
- **Y** Yes (as under Converse, but animation only)

TRAVEL

- **D** Onward! (throws arm forward)
- **F** Follow me! (throws arm forward)
- **G** Let's go! (no animation)
- **H** Over here! (long wave overhead with arm)
- **L** Lead on! (thumbs up)
- **M** Get a mission? (no animation)
- **O** On my way (no animation)
- **R** Ready? (no animation)
- **S** Stop! (holds up hand)
- **T** Where to? (no animation)
- **W** Wait here (holds up hand)
- **Y** Yoo hoo! (whistles with fingers)

COMBAT

- **A** Attack! (throws arm forward)
- **C** Come get some! (point, then pound fist until interrupted)
- **D** Don't attack (waves both hands "NO" in front of chest)
- **E** Need health (no animation)
- **G** Go! (throws arm forward)
- **H** Help! (no animation)

- **I** Incoming! (no animation)
- **L** Look out! (no animation)
- **N** Now! (throws arm forward)
- **O** On my mark (holds up hand)
- **R** Run! (no animation)
- **S** Stop! (holds up hand)
- **W** Wait (holds up hand)

OTHER

These Emotes have no dialog, only animation, as indicated by the name of the emote.

- **B** Bow
- **C** Clap
- **F** Wave Fist
- **H** Cheer
- **J** Jumping Jacks
- **L** Laugh
- **N** Point
- **O** Over here
- **P** Praise
- **R** Roar
- **T** Taunt
- **U** Salute
- **W** Warm Up
- **Y** Yoga
- **Z** Tarzan
- **1** Flex 1
- **2** Flex 2
- **3** Flex 3

GAMEPLAY

SLASH COMMANDS

Many functions of the game can be accessed directly in the chat menu by utilizing a slash command. These are commands where the name of the command is typed after a slash (/), and then any parameters necessary for that command are given. Some of these commands have quite a few variables to deal with, like the emote command discussed above, while others are basically an on/off switch.

GENERAL COMMANDS

bind	Binds a key to any command in the list of Slash Commands.
camdist	Sets the distance between you and camera. You must specify the distance in feet.
camdistadjust	When bound to the mouse wheel, moves the camera forward or back.
camreset	Resets the camera behind you.
follow	Sets follow mode. 1 = follow selected target; 0 = stop following.
fullscreen	Sets game to fullscreen mode.
quit	Quits game.
stuck	Tries to get you unstuck.
whoall	Requests a list of players on the current map.
screenshot	Saves a.tga format screenshot.
screenshotui	Saves a.tga format screenshot.
showfps	Show current frame rate.
toggle_enemy	Cycles through targetable enemies.
toggle_enemy_prev	Cycles through targetable enemies in reverse.
unselect	Clears current target.

MENU AND WINDOW COMMANDS

contextmenu	Activates a slot in the current context menu.Menu/Window
hide	Forces the specified window to be hidden.
manage	Takes you to Enhancement management screen.
map	Toggles the Map Window.
maximize	Maximizes window.
menu	Toggles the Menu.
nav	Toggles the Navigation Window.
target	Toggles the Target Window.
toggle	Shows a specified window if hidden, or hides it if shown.
window_color	Changes the window colors.
window_hide	Forces the specified window to be hidden.
window_resetall	Resets all window locations, sizes, and visibility to their defaults.

window_show	Forces the specified window to be shown.
window_toggle	Shows a specified window if hidden, or hides it if shown.
windowcolor	Changes the window colors.

COMMUNICATION AND CHAT COMMANDS

afk	Indicates that you're away from your keyboard and displays a specified message.
auction	Starts chatting in the Request Channel.
autoreply	Replies to the last player to send a private message. Note: this command works when bound to key, but does not work when typed in the Chat Window.
beginchat	Starts chatting in currently selected Chat Channel.
b or broadcast	Starts chatting in the Broadcast Channel.
chat	Toggles the Chat Window.
copychat_b	Copies a specified number of lines from the bottom Chat Window to the clipboard.
copychat_t	Copies a specified number of lines from the top Chat Window to the clipboard.
e or em or emote	Emotes a specified text string.
ignore	Ignores a specified user.
ignorelist	Displays a list of ignored users.
l or local	Starts chatting in the Local Channel.
me	Emotes a specified text string.
p or private	Sends a message to the specified player.
quickchat	Pops up the Quickchat Menu.
req or request	Starts chatting in the Request Channel.
s or say	Starts chatting in the current Chat Channel.
sell	Starts chatting in the Request Channel.
slashchat	Starts Chat Entry mode with a slash.
startchat	Starts chatting in currently selected Chat Channel.
t or tell	Sends a message to the specified player.
trade	Invites a specified player to trade.
trade_accept	Accepts an invitation to trade.
trade_decline	Declines an invitation to trade.
unignore	Removes a specified player from Ignore list.

whisper	Sends a message to the specified player.
y or yell	Starts chatting in the Broadcast Channel.

SOCIAL AND GROUPING COMMANDS

demote	Demotes a specified Supergroup member by one rank.
estrange	Removes a specified player from Friends list.
f	Starts chatting it the Friends Channel.
findmember	Displays the list of players currently looking for a team.
fl	Displays Friends list.
friend	Adds a specified player to Friends list.
friendlist	Displays Friends list.
g or group	Starts chatting in the Team Channel.
i or invite	Invites a specified player to join a team.
k or kick	Kicks a specified player from team.
leaveteam	Causes you to leave your current team.
namecaptain	Renames the captain rank of a Supergroup.
nameleader	Renames the leader rank of a Supergroup.
namemember	Renames the member rank of a Supergroup.
promote	Promotes a specified Supergroup member by one rank.
sg	Starts chatting in the Supergroup Channel.
sg_accept	Accepts an invitation to a Supergroup.
sg_decline	Declines an invitation to a Supergroup.
sgi or sginvite	Invites a specified player to join a Supergroup.
sgk or sgkick	Kicks a specified player from a Supergroup.
sgleave	Causes you to leave your current Supergroup.
sgsetmotd	Sets Supergroup "Message of the Day".
sgsetmotto	Sets Supergroup motto.
sgstats	Displays Supergroup info in chat window.
sk or sidekick	Invites a specified player to be your Sidekick.
sidekick_accept	Accepts an invitation to be a Sidekick.
sidekick_decline	Declines an invitation to be a Sidekick.
supergroup	Starts chatting in the Supergroup Channel.
team	Starts chatting in the Supergroup Channel.
team_accept	Accepts an invitation to a team.
team_decline	Declines an invitation to a team.
team_select	Targets a team member specified by number.
unfriend	Removes a specified player from Friend list.
unsk or unsidekick	Ends the Sidekick/Mentor relationship.

POWER AND INSPIRATION COMMANDS

inspexec_name	Activates an Inspiration specified by name.
inspexec_slot	Activates the lowest Inspiration in a specified Inspiration slot.
inspexec_tray	Activates an Inspiration slot in a specified row and column.
inspirationslot	Activates the lowest Inspiration in a specified Inspiration slot.
powexec_abort	Cancels the auto-attack power and the queued power.
powexec_altslot	Executes the specified power slot from the alternate Power Tray.
powexec_auto	Sets a specified power to auto-attack. If the specified power is already set to auto-attack, this command removes the setting. You can also remove the auto-attack setting by specifying no power.
powexec_name	Executes a power specified by name.
powexec_slot	Executes the specified power slot from the current Power Tray.
powexec_tray	Executes a power in the specified Power Tray and slot.

TRAY COMMANDS

alttray	Toggles the secondary Power Tray as long as you hold down the key.
alttraysticky	Toggles the secondary Power Tray.
goto_tray	Goes to a Power Tray. You must specify the Tray by number.
macro	Adds a macro to the first empty slot.
macroslot	Adds a macro to the specified slot.
next_tray	Goes to the next Power Tray.
next_tray_alt	Goes to the next secondary Power Tray.
prev_tray	Goes to previous Power Tray.
prev_tray_alt	Goes to previous secondary Power Tray.
tray	Toggles the Power Tray Window.

EMAIL COMMANDS

emaildelete	Deletes a message. You must specify the message by number.
emailheaders	Requests email headers.
emailread	Requests a message. You must specify the message by number.
emailsend	Sends an e-mail. You must specify the recipient's name, the subject and the message. These fields must be separated by commas; if a field contains spaces, it must be bracketed by quotation marks.

GAMEPLAY

PUTTING IT ALL TOGETHER: MACROS AND BINDING!

Of all the slash commands listed, two deserve special attention, and allow for a much greater control of your Hero's actions. First is the Macro command. The syntax for the macro (and macroslot) command is:

/macro <string1> "<string 2>"

This creates a button in the first open spot on your current hotbar. The name of this button is defined by the text in string 1. The text of string 2, which must appear in "quotes," is the actual function of your macro button. If you were to type this …

/macro Hi "emote wave"

You will create a button named Hi. When you click this button your character would use the wave animated emote.

Note: when using slash commands within macros, they do not require that the slash actually be typed. You can expand upon this and add further commands to your macros like this …

/macro Hi "local hello citizen!$$emote wave"

Notice that you separate the multiple commands with $$. It is usually best to use full slash command names in macros, like using **emote** instead of **em**.

The macros are very powerful, but all commands within a macro trigger at basically the same time. Always ensure there are no spaces on either side of the $$ characters so that the macros know where to begin and end each command properly. Since they trigger simultaneously, you can't set up action/response type macros (macros to do something only if something else occurs first), nor can you set any delays into the macros themselves. Macros can not be used to call other macros, and only one action of each similar item

in a macro (i.e., 1 of 2 chat elements speeches, 1 of 2 powers executed) will execute, and by default it will be the last one encountered. Macros allow you to be very creative, but not to program little Hero XP drones.

You can further personalize your macros by using replaceable variables to represent commonly used phrases and words, like your target's name. Adding further to our example macro we can come up with this …

/macro Hi "local Hello $target. How are you today?$$emote wave"

This will then say hello, specifically naming the target you currently have selected, as your current target's name replaces the $target variable. Immediately below is the current list of replaceable parameters, but none will likely see nearly as much use as $target. All the other variables refer to the Hero executing the macro, except $target.

$target
$archetype
$origin
$name
$level

BINDING

If the thought of clicking on macros from the Tray doesn't appeal, you have an alternative. The **/bind** command lets you assign macros directly to your keyboard. The syntax is very similar to the **/macro** command, but this replaces the need for a macro name with the actual name of the key to be used. We can continue with our previous example and assign our greeting macro to the Ⓖ key.

/bind g "local Hello $target. How are you today?$$emote wave"

Now when you hit G this macro will execute. The rules for using **/bind** are identical to those for using **/macro**, the only difference being how the actual macro is going to be triggered.

Many of the keys already have default bindings applied to them, like hitting the W key to move forward. On the next page is the default listing of key bindings the game starts with, and each of the actual commands listed are in the exact same format you would keep them in to use in your own macros. For example, the default bind for W is …

> /bind w "+forward"

This means that if you were to add +forward to a macro of your own, the forward movement would be part of that macro.

SAVING AND LOADING BIND SETS

Now that you have your binds ready to go, what happens when you want to play a new character? Or maybe you are joining friends on a new server — what happens to all the hard work you put into your macros and binds? Fortunately, it is possible to export them out to a text file so they can then be loaded under any character you want, on any server. This is done with **/bind_save** and **/bind_load**.

Using **/bind_save** will save a text file in **c:\keybinds.txt** with all of your current keybinds. This file can then be edited by hand for future use. To load this exact file you use **/bind_load**. This way that individual file can be loaded under each character you play. A bind set is stored for each character, so adding a single bind to load this file at launch saves you the hassle of typing out every bind and macro on each and every character.

But you can rename this file once it is created, or create text files by hand to add to it directly also. How would you load those? Use **/bind_load_file**

[name] where the name is the name of the text file you want to load. This is an additive load, in that it *only* changes those items in that particular bind file, nothing else. So you can create a file named forcefieldbind.txt and have it set up your keys for characters with force field. Then when a character is created with force field you can type a few initial bind commands to load up all the keys you may have set up for a previous character with force field.

Type …

> /bind_Load and then /bind_Load_File Forcefield.txt

… and you are done!

The **/bind_Load_file** will also take a path name to the file to be loaded, so it can be placed anywhere on your system you like. The default location if no path is given is still the root of the **C:** drive. Now if you wanted to be very aggressive about this you could have a set of communication binds, and a set of combat binds, and then a set of support binds for when your character is in a group … and then hotkey each one to load them on the fly depending on what you are doing. There really is no limit.

FINAL TIPS

There are a few very powerful commands that you will want to become familiar with if you want to utilize your own bindings and macros, but none will serve you more than the **Powexec_name** command. This command allows you to execute *any* power in the game (as long as your Hero has it) by name. Here is one great example of how this command can save you a few keystrokes of time.

> /bind f12 "local Get over here $target!$$powexec_name teleport foe"

Now, when you hit your F12 key, whatever dastardly villain you have targeted will soon be sum-

DEFAULT KEY BINDINGS

MOVEMENT

W	+forward
A	+left
S	+backward
D	+right
Q	+turnleft
E	+turnright
R	++autorun
F	follow
Spacebar	+up
X	+down

VIEW

🖱	+mouse_look
Page Up	+camrotate
🖱	+camrotate
Page Down	camreset
B	++third
mousewheel	+camdistadjust

CHAT

Enter	"show chat$$startchat"
/	"show chat$$slashchat"
;	"show chat$$slashchat"
Backspace	autoreply
,	"show chat$$beginchat /tell $target, " (Starts /tell to target)
'	quickchat

POWERS

Z	powexec_abort
1	"powexec_slot 1"
2	"powexec_slot 2"
3	"powexec_slot 3"
4	"powexec_slot 4"
5	"powexec_slot 5"
6	"powexec_slot 6"
7	"powexec_slot 7"
8	"powexec_slot 8"
9	"powexec_slot 9"
0	"powexec_slot 10"
left Alt 1	"powexec_altslot 1"
left Alt 2	"powexec_altslot 2"
left Alt 3	"powexec_altslot 3"
left Alt 4	"powexec_altslot 4"
left Alt 5	"powexec_altslot 5"
left Alt 6	"powexec_altslot 6"
left Alt 7	"powexec_altslot 7"
left Alt 8	"powexec_altslot 8"
left Alt 9	"powexec_altslot 9"
left Alt 0	"powexec_altslot 10"
F1	"inspexec_slot 1"
F2	"inspexec_slot 2"
F3	"inspexec_slot 3"
F4	"inspexec_slot 4"
F5	"inspexec_slot 5"
Home	"powexec_name Sprint"
End	"powexec_name Rest"

TRAY

left Alt	+alttray
right Alt	alttraysticky
=	next_tray
−	prev_tray
left Alt =	next_tray_alt
left Alt −	prev_tray_alt
left Ctrl 1	"goto_tray 1"
left Ctrl 2	"goto_tray 2"
left Ctrl 3	"goto_tray 3"
left Ctrl 4	"goto_tray 4"
left Ctrl 5	"goto_tray 5"
left Ctrl 6	"goto_tray 6"
left Ctrl 7	"goto_tray 7"
left Ctrl 8	"goto_tray 8"
left Ctrl 9	"goto_tray 9"
left Ctrl 0	"goto_tray 10"

TEAM

left Shift 1	"team_select 1"
left Shift 2	"team_select 2"
left Shift 3	"team_select 3"
left Shift 4	"team_select 4"
left Shift 5	"team_select 5"
left Shift 6	"team_select 6"
left Shift 7	"team_select 7"
left Shift 8	"team_select 8"

WINDOWS

M	"map"
N	"nav"
P	"powers"
\	"menu"
T	"target"
C	"chat"

MISC

Tab	toggle_enemy
lft Shift Tab	toggle_enemy_prev
rt Shift Tab	toggle_enemy_prev
Esc	unselect
Sys Req	screenshot
F6	"local RUN!"
F7	"say $$ emote thumbsup"
F8	"local HELP! $$ emote whistle"
F9	"local level $level $archetype$$local Looking for team"
F10	"say ATTACK! $$ emote attack"
F11	"emote hi$$local Hi, My name is $name, and I'm a $origin $archetype and a Libra. I believe in justice and long evening walks on rooftops."

moned to you by your Teleport Foe power. Your Hero will also say "Get over here" and the target's name, so your group will know which villain is headed their way. Now no matter which hotbar you are on, the F12 key calls an enemy to you.

Some ideas may require you to move some of the default binding to other keys, or you can even make a macro for that command to click if it is used less than a typical power you always use. A good example of this is the follow command (macro command "follow"). Once you can Fly you will certainly find yourself Flying or Hovering far more than following another player, so we can correct this.

Step 1. Move follow to a macro button with this ...

/macro Follow "follow"

Now move that button to a hotbar you can switch to when you actually need to follow someone. This now frees up the F key for our other uses.

Step 2. Create the macro to activate your flight.

/bind F "powexec_name fly"

Now when you hit the F key you will fly, and when you hit it again you will stop flying. Easy enough. But when you want to fight in the air or save Endurance, then you need to hover.

Step 3. Create the macro to activate Hover.

/bind H "powexec_name hover"

Voila! You now hit the F key to Fly, and the H key to Hover. No more will you have to activate these two often used powers by clicking in the button bars. And while you're at it, you will certainly want to relocate that pesky 'target' that is bound by default to your T key if you are a teleporter.

Macros researched by i3ullseye

GAMEPLAY

Eden, huh? Lots of serpents and no apple trees in sight.

CONTACTS

Contacts are the people who tell you, as a Hero, what is going on in Paragon City. They have inside information on certain factions and access to certain Enhancements and Inspirations to assist you, of course for a small Influence cost.

Your very first contact is based off of your Origin and is found inside either the City Hall in Atlas Park or Freedom Corps HQ in Galaxy City, depending on where you decided to start. You gain this first contact at Level 2, and he or she will give you a mission when you wish it.

Mission content is broken down into Stature levels. These are invisible level ranges that determine your usable contacts and missions. The break down is as follows:

◆ SL1 is levels 1 to 4

◆ SL2 is levels 5 to 14

◆ SL3 is levels 15 to 19

◆ SL4 is levels 20 to 24

◆ SL5 is levels 25 to 29

◆ SL6 is levels 30 to 34

◆ SL7 is levels 35 to 39

◆ SL8 is levels 40 to 44

◆ SL9 is levels 45 and up

You start off with one contact at SL1. As you perform missions for that contact, you increase your relationship until your contact eventually introduces you to one contact at SL2.

The SL2 contact will introduce you to another SL2 contact and then to an SL3 contact.

This other SL2 contact will introduce you to other SL2 contacts and then to SL3 contacts. You can have up to five SL2 contacts (which lead to five

SL3 contacts if you complete every one of the SL2 contact's missions).

If you don't complete all the SL2 contacts, don't worry — eventually your SL3 contacts will introduce you to more SL3 contacts. You can get up to five of these as well.

This works up the chain of Stature levels as you advance, and advance your relationship with each contact. Your Stature eventually grows higher than your lower Stature level contacts, and they will not have any more missions for you, instead directing you to move on to your higher SL contacts. Also, as your Stature level contacts increase, the general Enhancements and Inspirations they are able to provide to you increase as well. The Enhancements are grouped much like the Stature levels, as follows:

◆ Contact SL1 provides Enhancement levels 1, 5, 10

◆ Contact SL2 provides Enhancement levels 5, 10, 15

◆ Contact SL3 provides Enhancement levels 10, 15, 20

◆ Contact SL4 provides Enhancement levels 15, 20, 25

◆ Contact SL5 provides Enhancement levels 20, 25, 30

◆ Contact SL6 provides Enhancement levels 25, 30, 35

◆ Contact SL7 provides Enhancement levels 30, 35, 40

◆ Contact SL8 provides Enhancement levels 35, 40, 45

◆ Contact SL9 provides Enhancement levels 40, 45, 50

When you perform missions for your contacts, they warm up to you, and will eventually give you their cell phone number to just call them for missions. This happens at the third tier mission, about halfway up the relationship scale. When the contact gives you a cell phone number, a "Call" button appears on the contact information. From that point forward, you no longer need to run to that contact. You may, instead, contact him from any outdoor zone to report in, using the "Call" button to get new missions. Once you have won him over with your performance, by gain in Stature level, he will give you the option to introduce you to one of two other contacts.

You will eventually outgrow your initial contact and have to go to your newer contacts for missions. Contacts will only give you missions suitable for your level. If you reach a point where your contact is not giving you missions, but is not saying that she is finished with you, that means the next missions she has for you are higher level than you are. Return to that contact after you have achieved the next security level. You have to attain certain security levels before the Hazard Zones become available. Police are standing outside the entrance to these districts, and will tell you what security level you need to be to gain entrance.

Watch that first step! It's a doozey!

Read the descriptions of your potential contacts carefully. Each contact specializes in certain factions of villains. Your contacts will give you missions based off the factions they specialize in. The greater the variety of enemies your contacts are aware of, the greater the variety of missions and enemies you have to face. Also, your contacts are in different geographical areas of the city. In the beginning, it is easier to group your contacts in the same areas to ease the travel times back to each contact. This is not as important once you get your contact's cell phone number. But be careful that you do not gain a contact in an area that will be very difficult to get to. As you advance out to the higher security level zones, you will gain contacts further out from where you started, and have little choice but to gain contacts out further from the City centers.

CONTACTS AND MISSIONS

If the contact says, "there is trouble in so-and-so zone, but any zone in the city would be welcome," that is a General Patrol mission — defeating that faction anywhere in the city, including within a Door mission zone, counts towards that mission.

If the contact says "there is trouble in so-and-so neighborhoods, but any neighborhood in the zone would be welcome," that is a Specific Patrol mission and only that faction, outdoors in that specific zone, will count toward the mission accomplishment.

Additionally, if the contact uses the words "Hurry," or "as soon as possible," or "there is not much time," chances are it's a timed mission. A timed mission's clock starts the moment you accept the mission, and you have that much time to get to the mission and complete it before it counts as a failure. Failures do not advance your relationship with your contact, and do not give any rewards, even if the mission was

99 percent complete. After the mission is completed, the countdown may still be going down, but this is OK — you are not required to return to the contact within this time limit, just complete the mission.

Missions frequently have multiple objectives, some of which are secondary and not always clearly defined. For example, a mission to remove the bombs from a building may reward you for doing that, and then reward you again if you stay and eliminate all other threats from the building. For that reason, even if the mission notifies you that you've completed it, if there are sections of the map that are unexplored, or enemies you know are still on the mission map, do not "click out," but eliminate all foes before leaving the mission area on the chance that the mission has a secondary objective to complete.

Periodically, your contact will give you a temporary power to use for a mission. These powers show up on your Powers tab, can be dragged to your powers bar and used like any other power. Some have charges associated with them, others do not, but all stop working and vanish from your character when you complete the mission and talk to that contact again. You can not have more than two temporary powers at a time.

Once you complete your mission, you return to the contact who gave you the mission to finish it. At that point you may take on another mission from that person, or he may direct you to another contact.

The different selections you make as you advance through Paragon City will cause completely different and unique contact trees. Not all contacts will be the same for everyone. Each Hero will have his own unique contacts as he develops his superheroic career.

VILLAINS

5TH COLUMN

Locations: The 5th Column has a presence in Steel Canyon, Independence Port, Boomtown, Founders' Falls and Brickstown.

Types: There are four basic types of units in the ranks of the 5th Column: soldiers, robots, wolves and vampyr.

The soldiers are the bulk of the units and the majority of what you'll face, especially before the mid-20s. They are broken up into ranks and weapon-types. The ranks change as you advance, starting at Nebel (Fog Soldiers), then Nacht (Night Soldiers), and lastly the Raserei (Fury Soldiers). As for weapons, they run the full gamut of assault weapons, including flamethrowers, machine guns, chain guns, grenade launchers, missile launchers and more.

The Mek Men, the Steel Valkyrie and the Wolfpack robots fill the robot ranks. The Mek Men use the Energy Punch suite of powers, with an Energy Blast ranged attack, while the Wolfpacks use a wide range of assault weapons — they're the equivalent of walking weapons platforms. The Steel Valkyrie fly and carry a small subset of the Wolfpack robot armament.

The Lycans are large, lethal claw-wielding tanks with a lot of hit points and the ability to dish out a plenty of damage through melee. They have no ranged powers at all, but are able to super leap to get to a flying opponent if they need to. Many of the wolves, especially the Champions, are able to return to human form, so you may be fighting an officer in the higher ranks, nearly defeat him, and then watch him transform before your eyes into a whole new, tougher foe to fight.

The Vampyr are the mutated children of Nosferatu, and wield the full range of Dark ranged and Dark melee attacks. Equally effective ranged and melee, these are the roughest of the 5th Column soldiers, able to suck the life from a Hero to sustain their own.

Tactics: As with most other factions, always take down the bosses first. When selecting targets, focus on the highest-powered ones first, so Vampyr over wolves, wolves over robots, and so forth. The Vampyr will lock you down and leave you vulnerable. The wolves will cut you to ribbons if they are not kept off their feet. Otherwise, general tactics apply.

NEBEL
Minion   **Levels 1-4**

It doesn't take much training or expertise to join the 5th Column. Members who have neither receive basic weapons and are immediately put into service in the ranks of the Nebel, the 5th Column's front-line ranks. After all, the 5th Column believes in survival of the fittest.

Nebel Rifle

Brawl. Minor Smashing
Incend Assault Rifle. Moderate Lethal & Fire, long range
Cryonic Assault Rifle. Moderate Lethal & Cold, Slow, long range

Nebel Rocket, Nebel Grenade, Nebel Fire, Nebel Force

Brawl. Minor Smashing
Missile Launcher. Moderate Smashing, Lethal, & Knockback, moderate range
Flamethrower. Minor Fire damage, short range
Chain Gun. Moderate Lethal, short range
Grenade launcher. Moderate Smashing, Lethal, & Knockback, moderate range

Nebel Fist

As far as the 5th Column's concerned, the best way to prove one's worthiness is to survive and blossom in the crucible of combat. The 5th Column Martial Artists are good at doing just that. They are the best soldiers in their squads, and they're not above pointing this out to their comrades.

Thunder Kick. Moderate Smashing & Stun
Crane Kick. High Smashing & Knockback
Crippling Axe Kick. Minor Smashing, Slow, and Immobilize
Autopistol. Minor Lethal, med range

NEBEL UNTEROFFIZIERE

Lieutenant	Levels 1-4

Only those Nebel Soldiers who have proven both resilient and trustworthy achieve the rank of Unteroffiziere, or 'underofficer.' Through their skill in combat and their dedication to the 5th Column's cause, they have begun to earn real respect from their masters. In return, they receive better equipment and training, and are trusted with some low-level secrets.

Brawl. Minor Smashing
12 Gauge. Moderate Lethal & Knockback, short range

NEBEL OBERST

Boss	Levels 1-4

To be commissioned an Oberst, or Colonel, a Nebel soldier must prove himself over the course of many battles. Many of them resent having to continue working with raw recruits, but this indignity is more than compensated for by their first taste of super soldier serums and body enhancements. Combined with their combat experience, these enhancements make them formidable foes.

Brawl. Minor Smashing
12 Gauge. Moderate Lethal & Knockback, short range

NEBEL (HIGHER LEVELS)

Minion	Levels 5-19

Once a soldier has proven his total commitment to the cause, he is transferred into the ranks of the Elite. Only one in five soldiers survives long enough to achieve this promotion. Nebel Elites receive first stage super soldier serum that improves their physical prowess to the level of Olympic athletes. They also go through training courses before being put back into the battle lines. After all, the 5th Column has made an investment in their success.

Nebel Elite Rifle

Brawl. Minor Smashing
Incend Assault Rifle. Moderate Lethal & Fire, long range
Cryonic Assault Rifle. Moderate Lethal & Cold, Slow, long range

Nebel Rocket, Grenade, Fire, Force

Brawl. Minor Smashing
Missile Launcher. Moderate Smashing, Lethal, & Knockback, moderate range
Flamethrower. Minor Fire damage, short range
Chain Gun. Moderate Lethal, short range
Grenade launcher. Moderate Smashing, Lethal, & Knockback, moderate range

Nebel Fist

Thunder Kick. Moderate Smashing & Stun
Crane Kick. High Smashing & Knockback
Crippling Axe Kick. Minor Smashing, Slow, and Immobilize
Autopistol. Minor Lethal, med range

NEBEL ELITE UNTEROFFIZIERE

Lieutenant	Levels 5-19

A high-ranking Nebel Elite Unteroffiziere is a force to be reckoned with. His increased physical prowess is now matched by improved tactical skills and the steely resolve of a combat veteran. The super soldier serum and attendant propaganda have left the soldier utterly devoted to the 5th Column's cause. He is willing to follow any order, and he seldom worries about the messy consequences.

Brawl. Minor Smashing
12 Gauge. Moderate Lethal & Knockback, short range

NEBEL ELITE OBERST

Boss	Levels 5-19

The leaders of the Nebel Elite are near perfect soldierly specimens. In addition to the normal super soldier serum, they receive a special formula that enhances intellect and problem-solving skills. An Elite Oberst is utterly devoted to the 5th Column's cause, and he can finally be trusted to lead his soldiers without direction from above.

Brawl. Minor Smashing

12 Gauge. Moderate Lethal & Knockback, short range

NEBEL UBERMENSCHEN

Minion	Levels 20-24

An Ubermensch, or 'Over Man,' is a 5th Column soldier who has undergone a long and painful regimen of super soldier treatments. The Nebel Ubermenschen are the most numerous of these medical marvels, but that doesn't mean they're common. They've had extensive training and thousands of dollars worth of drugs pumped into them. It's an investment that usually pays off, since a first rank Ubermensch is stronger than five normal men.

Nebel Ubermenschen Rifle

Brawl. Minor Smashing

Incend Assault Rifle. Moderate Lethal & Fire, long range

Cryonic Assault Rifle. Moderate Lethal & Cold, Slow, long range

Nebel Ubermenschen Rocket, Grenade, Fire, Force

Brawl. Minor Smashing

Missile Launcher. Moderate Smashing, Lethal, & Knockback, moderate range

Flamethrower. Minor Fire damage, short range

Chain Gun. Moderate Lethal, short range

Grenade launcher. Moderate Smashing, Lethal, & Knockback, moderate range

Nebel Ubermenschen Fist

Thunder Kick. Moderate Smashing & Stun

Crane Kick. High Smashing & Knockback

Crippling Axe Kick. Minor Smashing, Slow, and Immobilize

Autopistol. Minor Lethal, med range

NEBEL UBERMENSCHEN UNTEROFFIZIERE

Lieutenant	Levels 20-24

The pinnacle of frontline soldiers, the Ubermenschen Unteroffiziere are nearly unstoppable fighting machines. It often takes an anti-tank weapon just to faze one of these juggernauts. Fortunately, their numbers are small, though the 5th Column keeps making more of them as their soldiers become more experienced.

Brawl. Minor Smashing

12 Gauge. Moderate Lethal & Knockback, short range

NEBEL UBERMENSCHEN OBERST

Boss	Levels 20-24

The highest ranking soldiers among the Nebel, the Nebel Ubermenschen Obersts are strikingly capable field officers, able to formulate and execute grand military campaigns. Unlike most modern officers, these Ubermenschen are not afraid to personally lead their soldiers into battle. After all, their own abilities far surpass those of all normal men and many superpowered Heroes.

Brawl. Minor Smashing

12 Gauge. Moderate Lethal & Knockback, short range

NACHT

Minion	Levels 5-19

The Nacht is the 5th Column's special operations division, tasked with covert ops, assassinations and espionage. Even the lowest-level recruits receive some special training, particularly in stealth and evasion techniques. New recruits must have some military or law enforcement experience before being accepted into the Nacht.

Nacht Rifle

Brawl. Minor Smashing

Incend Assault Rifle. Moderate Lethal & Fire, long range

Cryonic Assault Rifle. Moderate Lethal & Cold, Slow, long range

Nacht Rocket, Grenade, Fire, Force

Brawl. Minor Smashing

Missile Launcher. Moderate Smashing, Lethal, & Knockback, moderate range

Flamethrower. Minor Fire damage, short range

Chain Gun. Moderate Lethal, short range

Grenade launcher. Moderate Smashing, Lethal, & Knockback, moderate range

Nacht Fist

Thunder Kick. Moderate Smashing & Stun

Crane Kick. High Smashing & Knockback

Crippling Axe Kick. Minor Smashing, Slow, and Immobilize

Autopistol. Minor Lethal, med range

NACHT UNTEROFFIZIERE

Lieutenant	Levels 5-19

The Nacht Unteroffiziere have completed their covert ops training and are on the verge of being promoted to Elite status. They have yet to benefit from a course of super soldier serum, but they have honed their stealth and physique to a near perfect level. Unteroffiziere are often tasked with leading squads of Nacht soldiers on raids to raise funds for the 5th Column.

Brawl. Minor Smashing

12 Gauge. Moderate Lethal & Knockback, short range

VILLAINS

NACHT OBERST

Boss   **Levels 5-19**

A Nacht Oberst is responsible for overseeing squads of covert operatives. Since covert ops need to be precise and perfectly executed, a Nacht Oberst is valued chiefly for his ability to follow orders precisely and make sure his troops do the same. In return for loyalty and good service, Obersts receive their first taste of super soldier serum, making them stronger and quicker than any normal human could be.

Brawl. Minor Smashing
12 Gauge. Moderate Lethal & Knockback, short range

NACHT ELITE

Minion   **Levels 20-24**

The Nacht Elites are world-class special forces operatives, as well trained as any Navy SEAL. They're expert insurgents, capable of infiltrating a target swiftly and silently, then taking it down. Elites undergo a basic super soldier regimen designed to heighten their stealth, Accuracy, and concentration. These enhancements make them incredibly dangerous, especially when encountered in force.

Nacht Elite Rifle

Brawl. Minor Smashing
Incend Assault Rifle. Moderate Lethal & Fire, long range
Cryonic Assault Rifle. Moderate Lethal & Cold, Slow, long range

Nacht Elite Rocket, Grenade, Fire, Force

Brawl. Minor Smashing

Missile Launcher. Moderate Smashing, Lethal, & Knockback, moderate range
Flamethrower. Minor Fire damage, short range
Chain Gun. Moderate Lethal, short range
Grenade launcher. Moderate Smashing, Lethal, & Knockback, moderate range

Nacht Elite Fist

Thunder Kick. Moderate Smashing & Stun
Crane Kick. High Smashing & Knockback
Crippling Axe Kick. Minor Smashing, Slow, and Immobilize
Autopistol. Minor Lethal, med range

NACHT ELITE UNTEROFFIZIERE

Lieutenant   **Levels 20-24**

A Nacht Elite at the peak of his game may earn the rank of Unteroffiziere, and with it a large upgrade in super soldier serum. He is on the verge of Ubermensch status, and his mind has become focused with laser-like intensity. High ranking Elites are some of the best shots and most dedicated insurgents in the world. They can, and have, assassinated heads of state as well as world famous Heroes.

Brawl. Minor Smashing
12 Gauge. Moderate Lethal & Knockback, short range

NACHT ELITE SHARPSHOOTER

Sniper   **Levels 1-50**

Those gifted with incredible accuracy are quickly transferred into the Nacht division, where they undergo lengthy treatments to refine their abilities. The Sharpshooters are natural loners and disdain associating with the rank and file. The only praise they seek is the satisfaction of a silent kill.

Brawl. Minor Smashing
Sniper Rifle. High Lethal & Knockback, very long range

NACHT ELITE OBERST

Boss   **Levels 20-24**

While most Elites concentrate on learning the basic skills required for special ops, the Obersts receive additional training in tactics. They're also trained in technological skills, such as wiretapping and circumventing security systems. Combined with their prodigious super soldier enhancements, these skills make Elite Obersts well-prepared to plan and carry out small covert ops.

Brawl. Minor Smashing
12 Gauge. Moderate Lethal & Knockback, short range
Lycanthropy (some have it)

NACHT UBERMENSCHEN

Minion   **Levels 25-29**

The Ubermenschen of the Nacht have transcended mere special ops status. They are each unto themselves a powerful covert force, capable of taking on operations that would normally require an entire team of commandos. In addition to their enhanced physical and mental attributes, they receive training in security systems, computer infiltration, and surveillance equipment. In many ways, they are the perfect spies.

NACHT UBERMENSCHEN UNTEROFFIZIERE

Lieutenant   Levels 25-29

Unlike their counterparts in the other branches of the 5th Column hierarchy, the Nacht Ubermenschen Unteroffiziere have considerable autonomy. The 5th Column feels that the subversive activities that fall within the Nacht's purview require a certain amount of independence. This makes the Nacht Ubermenschen quite unpredictable at times — and thus, quite deadly.

Brawl. Minor Smashing

12 Gauge. Moderate Lethal & Knockback, short range

Lycanthropy (some have it)

NACHT UBERMENSCHEN OBERST

Boss   Levels 25-29

The Nacht Ubermenschen Obersts author their own plans to sow terror and fear across Paragon City. Many are in command of small military cells, completely cut off from their compatriots — both for the sake of security, and to encourage independent thinking.

Brawl. Minor Smashing

12 Gauge. Moderate Lethal & Knockback, short range

RASEREI

Minion   Levels 15-19

The Raserei are the pride and joy of the 5th Column's army. They represent the ideal to which all other followers of the cause should aspire. Not only are they disciplined, well-trained soldiers; they're also perfect students of the fascist beliefs that form the core of the 5th Column's ideology. Only those who have proven both their ability and loyalty are permitted to join the ranks of the Raserei.

Raserei Rifle

Brawl. Minor Smashing

Incend Assault Rifle. Moderate Lethal & Fire, long range

Cryonic Assault Rifle. Moderate Lethal & Cold, Slow, long range

Raserei Rocket, Grenade, Fire, Force

Brawl. Minor Smashing

Missile Launcher. Moderate Smashing, Lethal, & Knockback, moderate range

Flamethrower. Minor Fire damage, short range

Chain Gun. Moderate Lethal, short range

Grenade launcher. Moderate Smashing, Lethal, & Knockback, moderate range

Raserei Fist

Thunder Kick. Moderate Smashing & Stun

Crane Kick. High Smashing & Knockback

Crippling Axe Kick. Minor Smashing, Slow, and Immobilize

Autopistol. Minor Lethal, med range

RASEREI UNTEROFFIZIERE

Lieutenant   Levels 15-19

Raserei Unteroffiziere are zealots in every sense of the word. They believe in the 5th Column creed so fiercely that they have become experts at recruiting new members from the disaffected elements of society. Raserei Unteroffiziere are in equal parts soldier and proselytizer.

Brawl. Minor Smashing

12 Gauge. Moderate Lethal & Knockback, short range

Nacht Ubermenschen Rifle

Brawl. Minor Smashing

Incend Assault Rifle. Moderate Lethal & Fire, long range

Cryonic Assault Rifle. Moderate Lethal & Cold, Slow, long range

Nacht Ubermenschen Rocket, Grenade, Fire, Force

Brawl. Minor Smashing

Missile Launcher. Moderate Smashing, Lethal, & Knockback, moderate range

Flamethrower. Minor Fire damage, short range

Chain Gun. Moderate Lethal, short range

Grenade launcher. Moderate Smashing, Lethal, & Knockback, moderate range

Nacht Ubermenschen Fist

Thunder Kick. Moderate Smashing & Stun

Crane Kick. High Smashing & Knockback

Crippling Axe Kick. Minor Smashing, Slow, and Immobilize

Autopistol. Minor Lethal, med range

VILLAINS

RASEREI OBERST

Boss
Levels 15-19

The Raserei Obersts are the living essence of the 5th Column beliefs. While the Unteroffiziere brim with enthusiasm, the Oberst radiate a palpable aura of danger. The Raserei carefully foster this mystique in order to keep order within the ranks of the 5th Column.

Brawl. Minor Smashing

12 Gauge. Moderate Lethal & Knockback, short range

RASEREI ELITE

Minion **Levels 20-24**

Elite members of the Raserei have not only proven their loyalty to the cause, they've also shown themselves capable of bringing new members into the fold. Only those who have achieved Elite status are allowed to interact directly with potential recruits.

Raserei Elite Rifle

Brawl. Minor Smashing

Incend Assault Rifle. Moderate Lethal & Fire, long range

Cryonic Assault Rifle. Moderate Lethal & Cold, Slow, long range

Raserei Elite Rocket, Grenade, Fire, Force

Minion

Brawl. Minor Smashing

Missile Launcher. Moderate Smashing, Lethal, & Knockback, moderate range

Flamethrower. Minor Fire damage, short range

Chain Gun. Moderate Lethal, short range

Grenade launcher. Moderate Smashing, Lethal, & Knockback, moderate range

Raserei Elite Fist

Minion

Thunder Kick. Moderate Smashing & Stun

Crane Kick. High Smashing & Knockback

Crippling Axe Kick. Minor Smashing, Slow, and Immobilize

Autopistol. Minor Lethal, med range

RASEREI ELITE UNTEROFFIZIERE

Lieutenant **Levels 20-24**

The Elite Raserei Unteroffiziere are those destined for positions of authority in the 5th Column hierarchy. Their authority supercedes nearly every other rank. These Unteroffiziere reward the 5th Column with fanatical devotion to the cause. By the time these soldiers have reached this lofty level, they have given up any semblance of a normal life. They belong to the Column, body and soul.

Brawl. Minor Smashing

12 Gauge. Moderate Lethal & Knockback, short range

RASEREI ELITE OBERST

Boss **Levels 20-24**

The Raserei Elite Obersts are among the few soldiers permitted to express their opinions to the 5th Column's leaders, though most wisely avoid doing so. They control almost all the internal operations of the 5th Column organization.

Brawl. Minor Smashing

12 Gauge. Moderate Lethal & Knockback, short range

RASEREI UBERMENSCHEN

Minion **Levels 25-40**

Every member of the 5th Column aspires to become one of the Raserei Ubermenschen, but few of them achieve this lofty goal. They are the spiritual and philosophical leaders of the 5th Column, totally devoted to its beliefs and goals. Like any good soldier, they lead by example. Their intense training and physical enhancements make them perfect soldiers and perfect models of behavior. In battle, they serve as an inspiration to all who fight at their side.

Raserei Ubermenschen Rifle

Brawl. Minor Smashing

Incend Assault Rifle. Moderate Lethal & Fire, long range

Cryonic Assault Rifle. Moderate Lethal & Cold, Slow, long range

Raserei Ubermenschen Rocket, Grenade, Fire, Force

Brawl. Minor Smashing

Missile Launcher. Moderate Smashing, Lethal, & Knockback, moderate range

Flamethrower. Minor Fire damage, short range

Chain Gun. Moderate Lethal, short range

Grenade launcher. Moderate Smashing, Lethal, & Knockback, moderate range

Raserei Ubermenschen Fist
Minion   Levels 25-40

Every member of the 5th Column aspires to become one of the Raserei Ubermenschen, but few of them achieve this lofty goal. They are the spiritual and philosophical leaders of the 5th Column — totally devoted to its beliefs and goals. Like any good soldier, they lead by example. Their intense training and physical enhancements make them perfect soldiers and perfect models of behavior. In battle, they serve as an inspiration to all who fight at their side.

Thunder Kick. Moderate Smashing & Stun

Crane Kick. High Smashing & Knockback

Crippling Axe Kick. Minor Smashing, Slow, and Immobilize

Autopistol. Minor Lethal, med range

RASEREI UBERMENSCHEN UNTEROFFIZIERE
Lieutenant   Levels 25-40

Raserei Ubermenschen Unteroffiziere have the responsibility of leading large numbers of troops. They are concerned with training their men into peak fighting form — and recruiting new members to the cause. Until recently, none have ever been taken alive by the authorities.

Brawl. Minor Smashing

12 Gauge. Moderate Lethal & Knockback, short range

RASEREI UBERMENSCHEN OBERST
Boss   Levels 25-40

The Raserei Ubermenschen Obersts make up the inner circle that surrounds the 5th Column leadership. They are charged with the grand stratagems that further the ultimate goal of the 5th Column: the eventual domination of the world. The leaders of the Column foster competitiveness between these high ranking officers in order to prevent any single one of them from acquiring too much power and becoming a threat.

Brawl. Minor Smashing

12 Gauge. Moderate Lethal & Knockback, short range

MEK MAN
Minion   Levels 25-34

Vandal, the genius behind the 5th Column's technology, created the first Mek Men during World War II. He's been improving on them ever since. The tough and deadly versions in operation today are 100 times more dangerous than their predecessors of 60 years ago. Modern Mek Men have tough, thick armor, redundant systems that resist damage, and a powerful onboard AI that makes them faster and smarter than most human soldiers.

Energy Punch. Moderate Smashing, Energy, & Stun

Barrage. Minor Smashing, Energy, & Stun

Whirling Hands. Moderate Smashing, Energy, & Stun

Stun. Minor Smashing, Energy, & Stun

Blast. Moderate Smashing, Energy, & Knockback, moderate range

High resist. Lethal, Energy, Psionic

Low resist. Smashing

Immune. Sleep, Fear

STEEL VALKYRIE
Minion   Levels 30-42

The Steel Valkyrie class Hoverbot is one of the 5th Column's more ingenious inventions. Rumor has it that Vandal was inspired by the Rikti attack drones, but there have been versions of the Valkyrie in service since WWII. Mounted with omni-directional jets and banks of armor piercing rockets, the Steel Valkyries are quite maneuverable and pack a deadly punch. They can make the skies a very dangerous place.

Missile Launcher. High Smashing, moderate Lethal & Knockback

High resist. Lethal, Energy, Psionic

Low resist. Smashing

Immune. Sleep, Fear

Flight

NIGHTWOLF (35-39), DARKWOLF (40-50)
Minion   Levels 35-50

The nature of the Nightwolves remains a terrifying mystery. These monstrous, werewolf-like creatures were once human beings, but they have since been warped beyond all recognition. Unlike the Vampyri, these beasts are not the result of any known super serum treatment. Many suspect that some kind of magic is involved in their transformation.

Claws. High Lethal & Knockback

Superleap

Moderate resist. Immobilize

NIGHTWOLF CHAMPION, WARWOLF

Lieutenant (Nightwolf Champion)
Levels 1-50
Boss (Warwolf)   **Levels 1-50**

The Nightwolf Champions and Warwolves have lost all of their humanity to whatever force transformed them into monstrous killing machines. Unlike the more sedate Nightwolf warriors, the Champions and Warwolves are in a wild state and can barely be controlled. They are berserkers, unwilling to obey any orders when their enemy is in sight. They are, however, nearly impossible to kill, which makes up for their disobedient nature.

Some Nightwolves have mastered the ability to temporarily transform back into their human body. This allows these soldiers to infiltrate targeted facilities before revealing their monstrous nature. The authorities have little time to react once they realize what they're dealing with.

Claws. High Lethal & Knockback
Superleap
Moderate resist. Immobilize
Lycanthropy (some have it)

VAMPYR PARASITE, MESMERIST

Minion   **Levels 35-50**

The Vampyri are not true vampires at all. They are instead the ultimate result of the 5th Column's super soldier program. It takes a full year of chemical treatments and surgical enhancements to create a single Vampyr, but the result is one of the most deadly killing

machines in the world. All Vampyri have incredible strength, speed, and resilience. The Vampyr Mesmerist has potent hypnotic abilities that entrance enemies and render them helpless.

Vampyr Parasite

Pummel. Moderate Smashing & Knockback
Shadow punch. Minor Smashing, Negative, & Accuracy debuff
Gloom. Minor Negative Energy, & Accuracy debuff
Siphon Life. Moderate Negative Energy, heal self, & Accuracy debuff
Life Drain. Moderate Negative Energy, heal self, & Accuracy debuff, short range
Fast Healing. Moderate regeneration

Vampyr Mesmerist

Pummel. Moderate Smashing & Knockback
Shadow punch. Minor Smashing, Negative, & Accuracy debuff
Gloom. Minor Negative Energy, & Accuracy debuff
Mesmerize. Sleep & minor Psionic
Dominate. Hold
Reconstruction. Moderate heal self
Fast Healing. Moderate regeneration

VAMPYR ADJUTANT

Lieutenant   **Levels 35-50**

The Vampyri Adjutants are soldiers who have been promoted from the Ubermenschen ranks and given the singular honor of becoming a Vampyr. This honor is one the masters of the 5th Column are loathe to give, since it means a year of inactive duty for the Ubermensch. The result, however, is a Vampyr who has both the power and the experience to lead his monstrous soldiers into battle.

Pummel. Moderate Smashing & Knockback
Shadow punch. Minor Smashing, Negative, & Accuracy debuff
Gloom. Minor Negative Energy, & Accuracy debuff
Siphon Life. Moderate Negative Energy, heal self, & Accuracy debuff
Life Drain. Moderate Negative Energy, heal self, & Accuracy debuff, short range
Mesmerize. Sleep & minor Psionic
Dominate. Hold
Reconstruction. Moderate heal self
Fast Healing. Moderate regeneration

VAMPYR COMMANDANT

Boss   **Levels 35-50**

The Vampyri Commandants are the assistants to Nosferatu, the man responsible for the 5th Column's super soldier program. Commandants are scientists as well as super soldiers, and have a hand in the creation of other Vampyri. They often personalize their own transformation process, giving themselves special abilities and powers that lesser beings can only dream of.

Pummel. Moderate Smashing & Knockback
Shadow punch. Minor Smashing, Negative, & Accuracy debuff
Gloom. Minor Negative Energy, & Accuracy debuff
Siphon Life. Moderate Negative Energy, heal self, & Accuracy debuff
Life Drain. Moderate Negative Energy, heal self, & Accuracy debuff, short range
Mesmerize. Sleep & minor Psionic
Dominate. Hold
Reconstruction. Moderate heal self
Fast Healing. Moderate regeneration

DARK VAMPYR

Boss   **Levels 35-50**

The Dark Vampyri are the assistants to Nosferatu, the man responsible for the 5th Column's super soldier program. Commandants are scientists as well as super soldiers, and have a hand in the creation of other Vampyri. They often personalize their own transformation process, giving themselves special abilities and powers that lesser beings can only dream of.

Pummel. Moderate Smashing & Knockback
Shadow punch. Minor Smashing, Negative, & Accuracy debuff
Gloom. Minor Negative Energy, & Accuracy debuff
Siphon Life. Moderate Negative Energy, heal self, & Accuracy debuff
Life Drain. Moderate Negative Energy, heal self, & Accuracy debuff, short range
Mesmerize. Sleep & minor Psionic
Dominate. Hold
Reconstruction. Moderate heal self
Fast Healing. Moderate regeneration
Lycanthropy

MK I WOLFPACK ROBOT

Lieutenant   **Levels 40-50**

The Mk I Wolfpack robot has been favorably compared to a battle tank when it comes to both firepower and resilience. The big difference is that the Mk I is controlled by an ingenious artificial intelligence that can capably command troops in the field. It carries enough firepower to take out heavily armored targets, and its own armor stands up to anything

less than an anti-tank weapon.

Pummel. High Smashing, Knockback
Power Blast. Moderate Smashing, Energy & Knockback
Missile launcher. High Smashing, Lethal, & Knockback
High resist. Knockback, Knockup
High resist. Lethal, Energy, Psionic
Low resist. Smashing
Immune. Sleep, Fear

MK II WOLFPACK ROBOT

Boss   **Levels 30-39**

The ultimate in automated fighting systems, the Mk II Wolfpack robot is fearsome in combat, capable of taking on whole armored companies by itself. The robots' unerring aim and large caliber weaponry make them a threat to any Hero they come across. Their enhanced AI allows them to coordinate with the 5th Column's human troops, making them the perfect battlefield commanders.

Pummel. High Smashing, Knockback
Power Blast. Moderate Smashing, Energy & Knockback
Missile launcher. High Smashing, Lethal, & Knockback
High resist. Knockback, Knockup
High resist. Lethal, Energy, Psionic
Low resist. Smashing
Immune. Sleep, Fear

REQUIEM

ArchVillain   **Levels 48-50**

Ridolfo Uzzano has come a long way from his humble beginning as one of Mussolini's lapdogs. The primary cause of his success was his fusion with a Nictus, a being of utter darkness. The

Nictus gave Ridolfo the ability to scorch his foes with an infernal fire. Though he is now over 100 years old, Requiem remains a fearsome foe in battle.

High resist. Knockup, Knockback
Resist. Fire, Hold, Stun, Fear, Sleep, Confusion
Vulnerable. Cold
Healing Flames. Moderate self heal
Blazing Aura. Minor Fire PBAoE
Scorch. Moderate Fire cone, very short range
Fireball. Moderate Fire & Smashing, very long range
Fireblast. High Fire damage, moderate range

VANDAL

ArchVillain   Levels 28-30

The fiend known as Vandal was once a humble tinkerer named Othman Doul. In the late 1930's, the villain Requiem recognized Doul's usefulness and recruited him to the nascent 5th Column. Othman was happy to oblige, since it meant he could indulge his scientific curiosity without restraint. Over the years, Vandal has mechanically augmented himself to prolong his lifespan. Now, he seeks to advance his own position within the 5th Column and perhaps even challenge Requiem for supremacy.

High Resist. Knockup, Knockback
Moderate Resist. Smashing, Hold, Stun, Fear, Sleep, Confusion
Vulnerable. Psionic

Energy Punch. Moderate Smashing, Energy, & Stun
Bone Smasher. Moderate Smashing, Energy, & Stun
Power Blast. High Smashing, Energy, & Knockback, very long range
Missile Launch. Moderate Smashing, Fire, Knockback, long range

NOSFERATU

ArchVillain   Levels 38-40

Few truly appreciate the genius of Nosferatu's super soldier program, and none more so than himself. Nosferatu was so entranced by his ability to create the super strong Vampyri that he became one of them. He has since improved upon his original design by granting himself several new abilities. He can mesmerize his opponents, leav-

ing them helpless. Some say he can even siphon off the life force of his foes.

High Resist. Knockup, Knockback
Moderate resist. Negative Energy, Hold, Fear, Stun, Sleep, Confusion
Chill of the Night. Moderate Negative Energy, & Accuracy debuff
Fast Healing. Moderate regeneration
Reconstruction. Moderate self-healing
Dull Pain. High self-healing
Siphon Life. High Negative Energy, self-heal, & Accuracy debuff
Smite. Moderate Smashing, Negative Energy, & Accuracy debuff
Mesmerize. Moderate Psionic, & Sleep
Total Domination. High Hold
Dark Consumption. High Negative Energy & Endurance drain
Life Drain. Moderate Negative Energy, self heal, & Accuracy debuff
Gloom. Minor Negative Energy & Accuracy debuff

MEK MAN

Minion   Levels 29-35

These former 5th Column robots have achieved sentience and no longer obey their programming. They now seek to further only their own inhuman goals.

Energy Punch. Moderate Smashing, Energy, & Stun
Barrage. Minor Smashing, Energy, & Stun
Whirling Hands. Moderate Smashing, Energy, & Stun
Stun. Minor Smashing, Energy, & Stun
Blast. Moderate Smashing, Energy, & Knockback, moderate range
High resist. Lethal, Energy, Psionic
Low resist. Smashing
Immune. Sleep, Fear

HOVERBOT

Minion   Levels 29-35

These former 5th Column robots have achieved sentience and no longer obey their programming. They now seek to further only their own inhuman goals.

Missile Launcher. High Smashing, moderate Lethal & Knockback
High resist. Lethal, Energy, Psionic
Low resist. Smashing
Immune. Sleep, Fear
Flight

MK I WOLFPACK ROBOT

Lieutenant   Levels 29-35
Boss   Levels 29-35

These former 5th Column robots have achieved sentience and no longer obey their programming. They now seek to further only their own inhuman goals.

Pummel. High Smashing, Knockback
Power Blast. Moderate Smashing, Energy & Knockback
Missile launcher. High Smashing, Lethal, & Knockback
High resist. Knockback, Knockup
High resist. Lethal, Energy, Psionic
Low resist. Smashing
Immune. Sleep, Fear

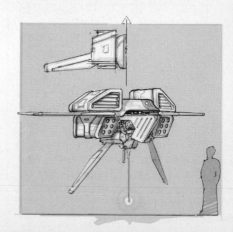

BANISHED PANTHEON

Locations: Dark Astoria is their primary zone, with some appearing on Talos Island. Mission doors for them can be generated anywhere.

Types: There are three basic types of Banished: Soldiers, Shaman and Masks.

Soldiers are the corpses and husks, the slow, lumbering infantry. They use brawling for melee and rifles for ranged damage, and typically do more damage in melee than at range.

Shaman are powered villains who use storm or earth control, or darkness powers. Their melee and ranged damage are secondary to their Knockdown and Disorienting abilities, which can render a Hero effectively defenseless.

Masks come in two forms, either a floating Tiki mask or a full-blown walking Totem. Masks have a wide range of powers, from Disorienting, Stunning and Sleeping, to direct damage blasts. Totem have some ranged abilities, but rely upon their massive melee attacks most of the time.

Tactics: In any engagement with the Banished Pantheon, it is imperative to eliminate the Shaman before they incapacitate your Heroes and leave them as fodder for the Soldiers. The earth and storm control power sets have a large number of effects that can have Heroes bouncing up and down and unable to use any powers, either offensive or defensive.

Beyond that, Soldiers run very slowly and are easy to evade, and do more melee damage than ranged, so kiting or keeping them at range is an option.

Masks fly very quickly and once they become aggressive, are very difficult to shake. They also have a very diverse set of powers, so they are a wild card in any engagement. In general, they should be taken out quickly. The Totems are slow-moving and vulnerable to Smashing damage.

DESICCATED HUSK (20-22), DRY HUSK (23-25), ROTTING HUSK (26-29)
Minion　　　　　**Levels 20-29**

The Banished Pantheon's powers reach from the spirit world to raise the bodies of long dead soldiers armed with the weapons of our forefathers. These dried out Husks of men provide the backbone of the Pantheon's armies — a never ending supply of undead warriors.

Musket. Moderate Lethal, moderate range
Lee-Enfield Rifle. Moderate Lethal & Knockback, moderate range
Brawl. Moderate Smashing
Tomahawk. High Lethal, Defense debuff
Wooden club. High Smashing
Low resist. Sleep, Fear, Cold, Psionic, Negative Energy, Stun
Vulnerable. Fire, Lethal, Energy

DESICCATED CHAMBER (21-23), DRY CHAMBER (24-26), ROTTING CHAMBER (27-29)
Minion　　　　　**Levels 21-29**

Their hatred for humanity and utter disdain for life have left the Banished Pantheon with few allies. Thus they must make their own, by raising the dead to create armies of zombie-like servants totally devoted to their devilish agenda.

Musket. Moderate Lethal, moderate range
Lee-Enfield Rifle. Moderate Lethal & Knockback, moderate range
Brawl. Moderate Smashing
Tomahawk. High Lethal, Defense debuff
Wooden club. High Smashing
Low resist. Sleep, Fear, Cold, Psionic, Negative Energy, Stun
Vulnerable. Fire, Lethal, Energy

STORM SHAMAN
Lieutenant　　　　　**Levels 21-29**

The Storm Shaman have mastered the power of the tempest. Their summoned thunderstorms assail their foes with fiery bolts of lightning, while their windstorms make it difficult for their enemies to fight back.

Knife. Moderate Lethal
Thunderclap. PBAoE, minor Stun
Hurricane. PBAoE, minor Accuracy debuff & Knockback
Lightning Storm. Summon storm

DEATH SHAMAN
Lieutenant　　　　　**Levels 21-29**

Death Shaman have done what few have dared. They have descended into the Underworld,

and returned. After such an experience, these Shaman have power over life and death. They can drain the life from their victims or summon zombies to fight by their side.

Knife. Moderate Lethal
Life Drain. High Negative Energy, self heal, & Accuracy debuff
Summon Husk. Raise a husk soldier

AVALANCHE SHAMAN
Lieutenant   **Levels 21-29**

To become an Avalanche Shaman, one must climb the highest mountains in the world to commune with the Pantheon's dread gods. Once these labors are completed, Avalanche Shaman can command the Earth itself. Their favorite trick is to trap their foes in deadly prisons of stone. They delight in hearing the cries of their victims as the stones grind together mercilessly.

Knife. Moderate Lethal
Snow Storm. Moderate Slow
Tremor. Moderate Smashing, Knockback
Earthquake. Summon earthquake
Stone Prison. High Immobilize

SPIRIT OF SORROW
Boss   **Levels 20-22**

One of the four types of Corrupt Spirits, the Spirits of Sorrow thrive on sadness and depression. These spirits project blasts of pure sorrow that explode in life-sapping bursts, seeping the will and life force from anyone caught in the explosion.

Flight
Neutron Bomb. Moderate Energy, & Defense debuff
Low resist. Defense debuffs
Vulnerable. Psionic

SPIRIT OF PAIN
Boss   **Levels 20-22**

One of the four types of Corrupt Spirits, the Spirits of Pain delight in agony and misery. They particularly delight in the pain that they dish out by projecting blasts of pure destruction at their enemies.

Flight
Power Blast. Moderate Smashing, & Energy
Immune. Taunt
Low resist. Defense debuffs
Vulnerable. Psionic

SPIRIT OF DESIRE
Boss   **Levels 23-25**

One of the four types of Corrupt Spirits, the Spirits of Desire feed upon greed, avarice, and the loss of control that comes with overwhelming need. They like to flood an area with telepathic imagery, confusing and even damaging opponents with visions of their greatest desires.

Flight
Mental Blast. High Psionic
Low resist. Defense debuffs
Vulnerable. Psionic

SPIRIT OF DEATH
Boss   **Levels 23-25**

One of the four types of Corrupt Spirits, the Spirits of Death take joy in anyone's demise, be they friend or foe. Once they've become focused on a victim, they become single-minded in their attacks and cannot be distracted. They will even destroy themselves if it means defeating their opponent of choice.

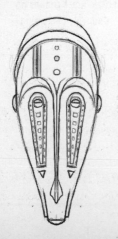

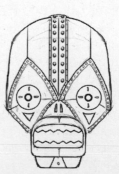

Flight
Dark Blast. High Negative Energy & Accuracy debuff
Immune. Taunt
Suicide. Massive Negative Energy
Low resist. Defense debuffs
Vulnerable. Psionic

TOTEM

Boss   **Levels 26–29**

The Totems are avatars of the ancient gods of the Banished Pantheon. They are powerful, deadly foes who relish tearing Heroes apart with their bare hands. They enjoy it so much that they ignore any attempts to Disorient, dissuade, or divert their focus.

Pummel. Moderate Smashing & Knockback
High Resist. Sleep, Immobilize, Knockup, Knockback, Fear, Stun
Vulnerable. Psionic
Very vulnerable. Smashing

ADAMASTOR

Monster   **Levels 29**

For centuries, Adamastor caused havoc and destruction to sailors off the coast of Africa. According to legend, he attacked the sea goddess Thetis and was banished from the ocean forever. Miserable and bereft, Adamastor wandered the Dark Continent seeking mortal prey — until the Banished Pantheon found a use for him in Paragon City.

Dry Heave. AoE, moderate Negative Energy, moderate range, resist debuff for Smashing/Lethal/Fire/Cold/Energy/Negative Energy/Psionic
Foot Stomp. PBAoE, Moderate Smashing & Knockback
Foot Stomp. PBAoE moderate Smashing & Knockback
High Resist. Knockup, Knockback, Fear, Immobilize, Stun, Hold, Sleep
Resist. Negative Energy, Psionic, Cold
Vulnerable. Lethal, Energy, Fire

CONTAMINATED

Locations: Only in the tutorial mission.

Types: Basic thugs.

Tactics: At this point in your career you don't have many options, and the Contaminated certainly don't offer any huge surprises. Hit 'em with whatever you've got until they fall down.

Minion   **Level 1**

These thugs have gotten their hands on a mysterious drug that drives them mad. The source of this drug remains a mystery, but without help these Contaminated brutes will tear the city apart.

CONTAMINATED BRAWLER

Brawl. Moderate Smashing
Rock. Moderate Smashing

CONTAMINATED SCAVENGER

Pipe. Moderate Smashing
Rock. Moderate Smashing

CONTAMINATED SLICER

Knife. Moderate Lethal
Rock. Moderate Smashing

CONTAMINATED THUG

Revolver. High Lethal, short range

CIRCLE OF THORNS

Locations: The Circle of Thorns make their home in Perez Park. They are also found in the crevasses of Faultline, Talos Island, Founders' Falls and Dark Astoria.

Types: There are four types of Circle of Thorns: Guards, Daemons, Casters and Behemoths.

Guards are simple, balanced thugs with crossbows for range and a variety of edged weapons for Lethal damage.

Daemons are summoned, floating, disembodied spirits that use the dark ranged and dark melee power pools.

Casters are the lieutenants and bosses, equipped with themed power suites. Earth casters use stone mastery, Fire casters use fire mastery, and so forth. They essentially are elemental Controllers.

Behemoth are massive flame Tankers that also use fire manipulation.

Tactics: Take the targets in the reverse order listed above, focusing on Behemoth over Casters, over Daemons, over Guards. Behemoths use both ranged and area of effect attacks and dish out a lot of damage. When engaging Casters, only have one person in direct melee contact with them at a time. If more than one person is meleeing them, or they are the last enemy left, they will self-detonate for a LOT of hit points, frequently taking out ranged Heroes who were unprepared. Always leave a Guard or Daemon around until the casters are down or not only will they blow up and hurt you, you also lose all the experience points they waste by exploding.

Many who have lost hope go looking in dark places for the answers to life's questions. The Followers are those whose search has taken them to the Circle of Thorns. Now they must prove their true devotion by serving the Circle's evil will.

GUARD
Minion   Levels 5-12

Dagger. Minor Lethal
Falchion. Moderate Lethal & Negative Energy
Sword. High Lethal and Defense debuff
Scimitar. High Lethal & Negative Energy
Thorn Sword. Moderate Lethal, Negative Energy, & Slow
Hand Crossbow. Minor Lethal & Negative Energy, short range
Crossbow. Moderate Lethal, Negative Energy & Knockback, moderate range

ARCHER
Minion   Levels 13-22

Dagger. Minor Lethal
Falchion. Moderate Lethal & Negative Energy
Sword. High Lethal and Defense debuff
Scimitar. High Lethal & Negative Energy
Thorn Sword. Moderate Lethal, Negative Energy, & Slow
Hand Crossbow. Minor Lethal & Negative Energy, short range
Crossbow. Moderate Lethal, Negative Energy & Knockback, moderate range

DEFENDER
Minion   Levels 23-30

Dagger. Minor Lethal
Falchion. Moderate Lethal & Negative Energy
Sword. High Lethal and Defense debuff
Scimitar. High Lethal & Negative Energy
Thorn Sword. Moderate Lethal, Negative Energy, & Slow
Hand Crossbow. Minor Lethal & Negative Energy, short range
Crossbow. Moderate Lethal, Negative Energy & Knockback, moderate range

GUIDE
Minion   **Levels 31-38**

Dagger. Minor Lethal
Falchion. Moderate Lethal & Negative Energy
Sword. High Lethal and Defense debuff
Scimitar. High Lethal & Negative Energy
Thorn Sword. Moderate Lethal, Negative Energy, & Slow
Hand Crossbow. Minor Lethal & Negative Energy, short range
Crossbow. Moderate Lethal, Negative Energy & Knockback, moderate range

THORN WIELDER
Minion   **Levels 5-13**

The mighty Thorn Wielders are the elite guardians of the Circle of Thorns. They wield the sacred Thorn Blades, enchanted weapons that leave a taint of foul magic on anyone they strike.

Greater Thorn Sword. High Lethal, Negative Energy & Slow
Throwing Dagger. Minor Lethal & Negative Energy, short range

SPECTRAL FOLLOWER (14-18), SPECTRAL KNIGHT (19-23), SPECTRAL DAEMON (24-29)
Minion   **Levels 14-29**

The Circle's sunken city of Oranbega is rumored to be filled with the ancient ghosts of its original inhabitants. Some of these spirits become malevolent Specters, angry and incorporeal beings immune to physical attacks but capable of causing tremendous damage to living beings.

Smite. Minor Smashing, Negative Energy, Accuracy debuff
Siphon Life. Moderate Negative Energy, Psionic, Accuracy debuff, & self-heal

Midnight Grasp. High Negative Energy, Accuracy debuff, and Immobilize
Chill of the Night. Minor Negative Energy & Accuracy debuff
Moderate Resist. Smashing, Lethal, Negative Energy
Vulnerable. Energy, Psionic
Ethereal. Invulnerable
Flight

SPECTRAL DAEMON LORD
Lieutenant   **Levels 14-29**

Smite. Minor Smashing, Negative Energy, Accuracy debuff
Siphon Life. Moderate Negative Energy, Psionic, Accuracy debuff, & self-heal
Midnight Grasp. High Negative Energy, Accuracy debuff, and Immobilize
Chill of the Night. Minor Negative Energy & Accuracy debuff
Moderate Resist. Smashing, Lethal, Negative Energy
Vulnerable. Energy, Psionic
Ethereal. Invulnerable
Flight

FIRE THORN CASTER
Minion   **Levels 30-34**

Weaving magical effects from fire can be dangerous for the novice mage, but Fire Casters have perfected the art. They can conjure up fires to immolate or distract their enemies, and some can even draw on their foes' body heat to restore their own power.

Dagger. Minor Lethal
Falchion. Moderate Lethal & Negative Energy
Sword. High Lethal and Defense debuff
Scimitar. High Lethal & Negative Energy
Thorn Sword. Moderate Lethal, Negative Energy, & Slow
Flares. Minor Fire, moderate range
Fire Ball. Moderate Fire & Smashing, moderate range

Ring of Fire. Minor Fire, Immobilize, moderate range
Char. Hold, moderate range
Consume. PBAoE, minor Fire, Endurance recharge

EARTH THORN CASTER
Minion   **Levels 35-39**

The Earth Casters' mastery over stone and sand makes them quite valuable in the underground city that the Circle of Thorns inhabits. But they can use their magic for more than digging tunnels and repairing walls. Under their control, the very ground beneath a Hero's feet can become a deadly weapon.

Dagger. Minor Lethal
Falchion. Moderate Lethal & Negative Energy
Sword. High Lethal and Defense debuff
Scimitar. High Lethal & Negative Energy
Thorn Sword. Moderate Lethal, Negative Energy, & Slow
Stone Prison. Minor Smashing, Immobilize
Stone Spears. Moderate Lethal
Quicksand. Summon quicksand
Rock Armor. Adds high Smashing & Lethal Defense

AIR THORN CASTER
Minion   **Levels 40-44**

Air Casters can harness the winds to give themselves the power of flight. They can also conjure up meteorological menaces from lightning bolts to snow storms.

Dagger. Minor Lethal
Falchion. Moderate Lethal & Negative Energy
Sword. High Lethal and Defense debuff
Scimitar. High Lethal & Negative Energy

VILLAINS

Thorn Sword. Moderate Lethal, Negative Energy, & Slow

Lightning Bolt. High Energy and Endurance drain, moderate range

Thunder Clap. Pale Stun

Snow Storm. AoE Slow, moderate range

Flight

ICE THORN CASTER

Minion   **Levels 45-49**

The frigid magics of the Ice Casters take careful study to master. In the hands of these mages, ice becomes a deadly weapon, either shredding enemies with jagged blasts or freezing them in place and chilling them to their bones.

Dagger. Minor Lethal

Falchion. Moderate Lethal & Negative Energy

Sword. High Lethal and Defense debuff

Scimitar. High Lethal & Negative Energy

Thorn Sword. Moderate Lethal, Negative Energy, & Slow

Ice Blast. Moderate Smashing, Cold, & Slow, moderate range

Block of Ice. Hold, moderate range

Chilblain. Minor Cold, Immobilize, moderate range

Freeze Ray. Moderate Cold & Sleep, moderate range

Hoarfrost. Adds high resist to Smashing, Lethal, Fire & Cold

BEHEMOTH

Minion   **Levels 46-50**

Summoned from the hellish pits of some other dimension, the Behemoths are fiery demons that inspire nightmares in all who see them. They can summon flaming swords to strike down their enemies, or breath fire from their mouths to incinerate all who stand before them.

Fire Smash. Moderate Smashing, Fire, & Knockback

Fire Sword. Moderate Lethal & Fire damage

Scorch. Moderate Fire damage

Flares. Moderate Fire, short range

Superleap

High Defense. All damage

Moderate resist. Fire

Vulnerability. Cold

LIFE MAGE

Lieutenant   **Levels 5-10**

Magical mastery over life can be a powerful tool for good, but in the hands of the Life Mages it is a deadly weapon. They can suck the very life force out of their foes, weakening and eventually killing them.

Brawl. Moderate Smashing

Poison Staff. Moderate Negative Energy, self heal

Kamikaze. PBAoE, high Energy

ENERGY MAGE

Lieutenant   **Levels 11-16**

Within their fabled lost city, the High Mages of Energy provide light, heat, and energy for their brethren. In battle they unleash their power in blasts of utter destruction, capable of ripping apart flesh, stone, and steel.

Brawl. Moderate Smashing

Thorn Staff. Minor Energy, Endurance reduction

Kamikaze. PBAoE, high Energy

FORCE MAGE

Lieutenant   **Levels 17-22**

The High Mages of Force deal with the primal forces that move the universe. In their sunken city, they are responsible for preventing cave -ins by siphoning off the Earth's seismic energy into useful pursuits. In battle, they can sap the very strength from a foe's limbs and add it to their own.

Brawl. Moderate Smashing

Crystal staff. High Smashing, Knockback, reduce resist on all damage

Kamikaze. PBAoE, high Energy

BEHEMOTHS

Summoned from the hellish pits of some other dimension, the Behemoths are fiery demons that inspire nightmares in all who see them. They can summon flaming swords to strike down their enemies, or breath fire from their mouths to incinerate all who stand before them.

The Behemoth Lords are — fortunately — very rare. Likewise they are very deadly. Their mastery of fire allows them to immolate multiple foes simultaneously, and they can quickly heal their own wounds by basking in the heat of their infernal fire.

Behemoth Master
Boss
Levels 26-30

Fire Smash. Moderate Smashing, Fire, & Knockback
Fire Sword. Moderate Lethal & Fire damage
Scorch. Moderate Fire damage
Flares. Moderate Fire, short range
Superleap
High Defense. All damage
Moderate resist. Fire
Vulnerability. Cold

Behemoth Overlord
Boss
Levels 31-35

Fire Breath. AoECone, moderate Fire, short range
Flares. moderate Fire, moderate range
Fire Blast. Moderate Fire, moderate range

Fire Sword. Moderate Fire, moderate Lethal
Swipe. High Lethal, Fire, & Knockback
Healing Flames. Self heal
Moderate resists. Fire, Stun
Vulnerability. Cold

Behemoth
Lieutenant   **Levels 29-35**

Fire Smash. Moderate Smashing, Fire, & Knockback
Fire Sword. Moderate Lethal & Fire damage
Scorch. Moderate Fire damage
Flares. Moderate Fire, short range
Superleap
    High Defense. All damage
    Moderate resist. Fire
    Vulnerability. Cold

    Behemoth Lord
    Lieutenant Levels 36-40

    Fire Breath. AoECone, moderate Fire, short range
    Flares. moderate Fire, moderate range
    Fire Blast. Moderate Fire, moderate range
    Fire Sword. Moderate Fire, moderate Lethal
    Swipe. High Lethal, Fire, & Knockback
    Healing Flames. Self heal
    Moderate resists. Fire, Stun
    Vulnerability. Cold

ENVOY OF SHADOW
Boss Levels 34-40

Unbound and unnamed, it has crossed the gulf of worlds on a bridge of greed and pain. The Envoy of Shadow is the ambassador of the Prince of Demons, here to offer the Circle of Thorns great power and dark alliances. Its consuming flames and cloak of darkness are manifestations of its endless evil.

Fire Breath. AoECone, moderate Fire, short range
Flares. moderate Fire, moderate range
Fire Blast. Moderate Fire, moderate range
Fire Sword. Moderate Fire, moderate Lethal
Swipe. High Lethal, Fire, & Knockback
Healing Flames. Self heal
Moderate resists. Fire, Stun
Vulnerability. Cold
Shadow. Minor Negative Energy, Accuracy debuff
Moderate resist. Negative Energy
Vulnerability. Energy

BAPHOMET
Monster   **Levels 40**

The Baphomet is the oldest and most feared of the Behemoth Lords. The ground beneath its cloven feet burns with its own infernal fire.

Fire Blast. Moderate Fire, very long range
Fire Ball. AoE, moderate Fire & Smashing, moderate range
Flash Stomp. PBAoE, moderate Fire & Knockback
Fire Breath. Cone, moderate Fire, short range
Greater Fire Sword. Moderate Fire & Lethal
Swipe. High Lethal & Knockback
High resist. Knockup, Knockback, Fire, Fear, Stun, Confusion
Vulnerability. Cold
Healing Flames. Self-heal

SOUL MAGE

Lieutenant   **Levels 23-28**

The High Mages of the Soul delve into the deepest reaches of the human spirit. They are largely responsible for the gathering and training of specters and other spirits. When forced into combat, they petrify their foes in a wave of inescapable self-contemplation that leaves them incapable of any action.

Brawl. Moderate Smashing
Darkness Staff. Hold
Darkness Staff Gloom. Minor Negative Energy, Accuracy debuff
Kamikaze. PBAoE, high Energy

MADNESS MAGE

Boss   **Levels 5-14**

The Masters of Madness can control every aspect of the psyche. For their friends, they provide a constant aura of mental fortitude that helps them in all endeavors. In battle, their enemies suffer complete mental domination that leaves them incapable of any action at all.

Falchion. Moderate Lethal & Negative Energy
Dominate. Hold
Mesmerize. Moderate Psionic, Sleep
Dummy. Taunt
Fortitude. Buff all damage, to hit, all defenses
Kamikaze. PBAoE, high Energy

RUIN MAGE

Boss   **Levels 15-24**

In ancient times, the Masters of Ruin could level whole cities with their powerful earthquake magic. Today these masters of mayhem are still deadly foes, capable of summoning localized tremors that cause great devastation in a short time.

Falchion. Moderate Lethal & Negative Energy
Tremor. PBAoE, Moderate Smashing & Knockback
Earthquake. Summon Earthquake
Dummy. Taunt
Siphon Power. Reduce all dmg target, buff all dmg self
Dispersion Bubble. Buff all Defense, resist Hold, Stun, & Immobilize
Kamikaze. PBAoE, high Energy

AGONY MAGE

Boss   **Levels 25-34**

There is not greater distraction than pain and suffering. The Masters of Agony often help relieve their friends of such distractions in times of peace. But when it comes to battle, they are adept at harming their foes through powerful and disruptive enchantments.

Falchion. Moderate Lethal & Negative Energy
Tar Patch. Summon Tarpatch
Dummy. Taunt
Absorb Pain. Heal self
Kamikaze. PBAoE, high Energy

DEATH MAGE

Boss   **Levels 35-44**

The most powerful of all the Circle's mages, the Masters of Death are lords of the afterlife. They help to wrangle and control the Behemoths and other beasts the Circle summons, but their most fearsome power is the ability to create a pervasive zone of death that sucks the life out of any foes in the vicinity.

Falchion. Moderate Lethal & Negative Energy
Chill of the Night. Minor Negative Energy, Accuracy debuff
Twilight Grasp. Accuracy and all damage debuff, moderate range
Kamikaze. PBAoE, high Energy

CLOCKWORK

Locations: Atlas Park, Galaxy City, Kings Row, Steel Canyon, Skyway City, Perez Park, Boomtown, Faultline

Types: The basic grunts are the Sprockets and the higher-level Cogs. Cogs are noticeably bigger than Sprockets. Oscillators are hovering grunts with rotors. For all these Clockwork, their biggest danger is their short-range Endurance drain capability. If you let them surround you, a group of Clockwork can quickly leave you drained and virtually helpless.

Knights are the Clockwork lieutenants, and they come in two types: the Cannon Knights, whose most dangerous attack is a long-range ball-lightning blast, and the Tesla Knights, with their more advanced draining and rooting attacks.

The bosses are either Dukes (at low levels) or Princes (at higher levels). They come in Cannon and Tesla flavors as well, plus a new treat … the Assembler, with the ability to assemble new minions, seemingly out of thin air.

The Clockwork also boast both a monster (Babbage, who wanders around in Boomtown) and an Archvillain (the Clockwork King, naturally).

Tactics. Clockwork tend to spawn in largish groups, particularly in the Hazard zones. Try not to let them surround you, or otherwise even a few grunts can leave you quickly sucked dry of Endurance. Try to either pull them off one or two at a time, or have some kind of crowd control option available.

In a mixed group, take out Assemblers first, then Teslas. Cannons tend to be more of a threat at long range, so they can wait until last, as long as you're out of their line of sight. Then you can mop up the minions. When the bosses are defeated, they break down into smaller Gears, annoying little guys that get in the way, disrupt interruptible attacks, and have to be dealt with eventually.

SPROCKET (1-10), COG (11-20)
Minion   Levels 1-20

These pint-sized junkyard hellions have become a real plague on the streets of certain neighborhoods. Their exact workings are mysterious, but there's no mystery about the deadly bolts of electricity they hurl at anyone who gets in their way.

Moderate Resists. Stun & Lethal
Vulnerability. Psionic, Sleep, Knockback, Knockup, Repel
Charged Brawl. Minor Smashing & Energy
Charged Bolts. Moderate Energy & Endurance drain, moderate range

GEAR
Small   Levels 1-20

Gears emerge from the remnants of destroyed Clockwork Princes. Though tiny, they can still pack quite a punch.

Vulnerability. Psionic, Smashing, Fire, Cold, Energy & Negative Energy
High Vulnerability. Sleep, Knockback, Knockup, & Repel
Charged Brawl. Minor Smashing & Energy
Charged Bolts. Minor Smashing & Energy, moderate range

OSCILLATORS· PROTOTYPE (6-11), LINE (12-14), ADVANCED (15-17), PERFECTED (18-20)
Minion   Levels 6-20

The airborne Clockwork Oscillators are a new and deadly threat to Paragon City's skies. Like their grounded counterparts, the Sprockets, these highly flying mechanical men attack using bolts of electricity. They are immune to any psychological attacks.

Moderate Resists. Stun & Lethal
Vulnerability. Psionic, Sleep, Knockback, Knockup, Repel
Charged Brawl. Minor Smashing & Energy
Charged Bolts. Moderate Energy & Endurance drain, moderate range
Flight

VILLAINS

KNIGHTS

Lieutenant   **Levels 1-20**

The Knights make up the bulk of the leadership class within the twisted court of the Clockwork King. The Tesla Knights are especially dangerous because they enclose foes in deadly electrical cages.

Cannon Knight

Moderate Resists. Stun & Lethal
Vulnerability. Psionic & Sleep
Charged Brawl. Minor Smashing & Energy

Charged Bolts. Moderate Energy & Endurance drain, moderate range
Lightning Bolt. High Energy & Endurance drain, moderate range
Ball Lighting. AoE, minor Energy and Endurance drain, moderate range

Tesla Knight

Moderate Resists. Stun & Lethal
Vulnerability. Psionic & Sleep
Charged Brawl. Minor Smashing & Energy
Charged Bolts. Moderate Energy & Endurance drain, moderate range
Tesla Cage. Minor Energy, Sleep, & Endurance drain, moderate range.

Lightning Field. PBAoE, minor Energy & Endurance drain

DUKES

Boss   **Levels 1-10**

Like any monarch, the Clockwork King has his own court, although in his case it's composed of mechanical nobles called Dukes. These oversized robots are dangerous foes, possessing powerful long range electrical attacks.

Cannon Duke

Moderate Resists. Stun & Lethal
Vulnerability. Psionic & Sleep
Charged Brawl. Minor Smashing & Energy
Charged Bolts. Moderate Energy & Endurance drain, moderate range
Lightning Bolt. High Energy & Endurance drain, moderate range
Ball Lighting. AoE, minor Energy and Endurance drain, moderate range

Tesla Duke

Moderate Resists. Stun & Lethal
Vulnerability. Psionic & Sleep
Charged Brawl. Minor Smashing & Energy
Charged Bolts. Moderate Energy & Endurance drain, moderate range
Tesla Cage. Minor Energy, Sleep, & Endurance drain, moderate range.
Lightning Field. PBAoE, minor Energy & Endurance drain

Assembler Duke

Moderate Resists. Stun & Lethal
Vulnerability. Psionic & Sleep
Charged Brawl. Minor Smashing & Energy
Charged Bolts. Moderate Energy & Endurance drain, moderate range
Summon Clockwork

PRINCES

Boss   **Levels 11-20**

The heirs apparent to the Clockwork King's throne, the Princes represent the pinnacle of the mad genius's creations.

Cannon Prince

Although Cannon Princes sometimes seem almost human because of their advanced robotic brains, they're still immune to mental attacks and can deal out massive electrical blasts.

High Resist. Knockup, Knockback
Moderate Resist. Stun & Lethal
Vulnerability. Psionic & Sleep
Summon Gears
Charged Bolts. Moderate Energy, Endurance drain, moderate range
Charged Brawl. Minor Smashing & Energy
Pummel. Moderate Energy, Smashing, & Knockback
Lightning Bolt. High Energy & Endurance drain, moderate range
Ball Lighting. AoE, minor Energy and Endurance drain, moderate range

Tesla Prince

Although Tesla Princes sometimes seem almost human because of their advanced robotic brains, they possess the decidedly inhuman ability to imprison their foes in cages of electricity.

High Resist. Knockup, Knockback
Moderate Resist. Stun & Lethal
Vulnerability. Psionic & Sleep
Summon Gears
Charged Bolts. Moderate Energy, Endurance drain, moderate range
Charged Brawl. Minor Smashing & Energy
Pummel. Moderate Energy, Smashing, & Knockback

Tesla Cage. Minor Energy, Sleep, & Endurance drain, moderate range.
Lightning Field. PBAoE, minor Energy & Endurance drain

Assembler Prince

Assembler Princes' powerful electric attacks can blanket an area with painful lightning blasts. But it's their ability to rapidly produce more Clockwork soldiers that makes them truly insidious.

High Resist. Knockup, Knockback
Moderate Resist. Stun & Lethal
Vulnerability. Psionic & Sleep
Summon Gears
Charged Bolts. Moderate Energy, Endurance drain, moderate range
Charged Brawl. Minor Smashing & Energy
Pummel. Moderate Energy, Smashing, & Knockback
Summon Clockwork

CLOCKWORK KING

ArchVillain   **Level 20**

The mad Clockwork King imagines himself the center of a mechanical court. His powerful mind continually creates more subjects to his insane rule. The true horror is that his massive steel chassis holds a human brain.

High Resist. Knockup, Knockback, Fear, Stun, Sleep, & Confuse
Resist. Psionic, Lethal
Vulnerability. Smashing
Pummel. High Smashing & Knockback
Telekinetic blast. Moderate Smashing, Psionic, & Knockback, very long range
Psychic Scream. Moderate Psionic, moderate range
Subdue. High Psionic & Immobilize, moderate range
Will Domination. High Psionic & Sleep, moderate range

BABBAGE

Monster   **Levels 19**

For reasons unknown, the Clockwork King created this giant automaton and loosed it upon Boomtown. Babbage seems chiefly interested in collecting metal scrap for its King, though it also fervently defends its territory from any incursions.

Lightning Bolt. High Energy & Endurance drain, very long range
Tesla Cage. Minor Energy & Endurance drain, Sleep, moderate range
Summon Clockwork
Lightning Field. PBAoE, minor Energy & Endurance drain

Ball Lightning. AoE, minor Energy & Endurance drain, moderate range
High Resist. Knockup, Knockback, Lethal, Fear, Stun
Vulnerability. Psionic

CREY

Locations: Founders' Falls, Crey's Folly and Eden. Mission doors for them can be generated anywhere.

Types: There are four types of Crey: Support, Snipers, Tanks and Protectors.

There are over two dozen different types of Support personnel, ranging from Medics who can heal allies, to Riot Specialists who have a wide range of melee and range attacks. Almost all of them have some form of Disorient, Hold or Knockdown attack.

Crey Snipers perch on rooftops and — with amazingly long range weapons and uncanny accuracy — dish out significant damage to the faction's enemies. They are also frequently found in support of groups on the ground, so always look to the rooftops when approaching a group of Crey.

Tanks are heavily armored, are very damage resistant, and have a number of different power sets. Voltaic use electricity, Cryo use Cold, Power use energy melee and Protectors use force field to protect allies. All have attacks to Knockdown or Disorient Heroes.

Paragon Protectors are the elite Crey forces and all use invulnerability powers to drastically reduce the damage they take

from attacks. They use Quills, Energy Melee, or Claws, along with a number of Crey-specific attacks, all with devastating effect. They also fly, will fly away when Stunned or Disoriented to avoid damage, and will pursue through the air if you flee from them.

Tactics: With such a complex array of potential powers to face, there is no single tactic that will work vs. any group of them. The greatest obvious thread is the Paragon Protectors, and they must be engaged first as they will wreak untold havoc upon the rest of the team if unengaged. The Medics only heal using the healing power set, so they are not as much a threat as they might be, so the next priority should be the Tanks, due to their Disorienting and lockdown power sets. The Snipers are a wild card, especially if they engage from a distance and are not even noticed until then, so it's imperative to at least identify if a Sniper will be involved in the combat.

GUARD

Minion	Levels 30-39

Crey's Security Agents have become an almost ubiquitous sight in Paragon City, especially in any Crey owned facility. They're armed with standard law enforcement weapons, from riot batons to assault weapons.

Riot Guard

Brawl. Moderate Smashing
Riot Baton. Moderate Smashing & Stun
Automatic Pistol. Moderate Lethal, moderate range
Moderate Resistance. Lethal, Confusion

Patrol Guard

Brawl. Moderate Smashing
Assault Rifle. Moderate Lethal, Defense debuff, long range
Moderate Resistance. Lethal, Confusion

Mob Specialist

Boxing. Moderate Smashing & Stun
Brawl. Moderate Smashing
Kick. Moderate Smashing & Knockback
Submachine Gun. Moderate Lethal, Defense debuff, moderate range
Moderate Resistance. Lethal, Confusion

SCIENTISTS & RESEARCHERS
Minion   **Levels 32-41**

Crey Industries believes firmly in hands on, frontline research, and they demand more from their scientists than most companies. Indeed, Crey Scientists often venture into the field, armed with Cryo weapons to help them collect samples — and do serious damage to anyone who get in their way.

Research Assistant

Brawl. Moderate Smashing
Cryo Pistol. Minor Cold, Slow, & Sleep, moderate range

Scientist

Brawl. Moderate Smashing
Cryo Rifle. Moderate Cold, Slow, Sleep, moderate range

Researcher

Brawl. Moderate Smashing
N2 Cannon. AoE, minor Cold & Slow, short range

Medic

Brawl. Moderate Smashing
Hypo. Heal Other
Minor Resist. Stun, Hold, Sleep, Immobilize, Confusion, Fear

Geneticist

Brawl. Moderate Smashing
Raise dead ally

Radiologist

Brawl. Moderate Smashing
Radiation Infection. Accuracy & Defense debuff, moderate range

AGENTS
Minion   **Levels 35-45**

The stone-faced, suit clad Field Agents are Crey's main investigative branch. They can be found carrying out a variety of missions, from espionage to assassination ops. They carry the latest weapons and receive intense close combat training.

Field Agent

Adv SMG. Minor Lethal, Defense debuff, long range
Brawl. Moderate Smashing

Vigilant

Automatic Pistol. Moderate Lethal, moderate range
Barrage. Minor Smashing, Energy, & Stun
Energy Punch. Moderate Smashing, Energy & Stun
Bone Smasher. High Energy, Smashing, & Stun

Infiltrator

Automatic Pistol. Moderate Lethal, moderate range
Thunderkick. Moderate Smashing & Stun
Storm Kick. Minor Smashing
Crane Kick. High Smashing & Knockback

CHIEF SCIENTISTS
Lieutenant   **Levels 30-31**

The leaders of every Crey research team receive special training in leadership, tactics, and combat techniques. They also have access to the latest advanced weaponry, making them especially dangerous.

Chief Cryo Scientist

Brawl. Moderate Smashing
Heavy Cryo Rifle. Minor Cold, Slow, & Hold, moderate range

Chief Plasma Scientist

Brawl. Moderate Smashing
Flamethrower. Minor Fire, short range

ELITE SECURITY AGENT
Lieutenant   **Levels 32-34**

The leaders of Crey's security teams are experts at identifying threats and picking them off from a distance. With the latest in advanced assault weaponry at their disposal, these agents are a force to be reckoned with.

Adv Assault Rifle. High Lethal, Knockback, very long range
Brawl. Moderate Smashing
Focus. Defense buff vs ranged & melee

SPECIAL AGENTS
Lieutenant   **Levels 32-34**

The Special Agents are the best of Crey's field operatives. They have superb training, the best weapons, and a seemingly preternatural focus on the task at hand. They often carry heavy weapons, since Crey trusts them enough to use them discreetly and appropriately.

Special Agent Vigilant

Automatic Pistol. Moderate Lethal, moderate range
Barrage. Minor Smashing, Energy, & Stun
Energy Punch. Moderate Smashing, Energy & Stun
Bone Smasher. High Energy, Smashing, & Stun
Focus. Defense buff vs ranged & melee

Special Agent Infiltrator

Automatic Pistol. Moderate Lethal, moderate range
Thunderkick. Moderate Smashing & Stun
Storm Kick. Minor Smashing
Crane Kick. High Smashing & Knockback
Focus. Defense buff vs ranged & melee

VILLAINS

SPECIAL AGENT SHARPSHOOTER

Sniper   **Levels 30-50**

These are the best of Crey's field operatives. They have superb training, the best weapons, and a seemingly preternatural focus on the task at hand. They often carry heavy weapons, since Crey trusts them enough to use them discreetly and appropriately.

Sniper Rifle. High Lethal, Knockback, long range

Brawl. Moderate Smashing

Focus. Defense buff vs ranged & melee

CREY ELIMINATOR

Lieutenant   **Levels 35-39**

With their heavy chain guns and advanced training, these armor clad leaders carry enough firepower to stop a tank. They're also almost as hard to hurt, though they are vulnerable to mental assaults.

Chain Gun. Minor Lethal, moderate range

Brawl. Moderate Smashing

Boxing. Moderate Smashing, Stun

Moderate resist. Lethal, Smashing, Energy, Fire, Cold

Vulnerable. Confusion

CREY CRISIS UNIT

Lieutenant   **Levels 35-39**

Crey sends these specialized units to handle big problems. Their grenade launchers can fire a variety of munitions, making them well-equipped to handle any situation. These armor clad leaders carry enough firepower to stop a tank. They're also almost as hard to hurt, though they are vulnerable to mental assaults.

Grenade Launcher. Moderate Lethal,

Smashing & Knockback, moderate range

Sleep Gas. Sleep, moderate range

Brawl. Moderate Smashing

Boxing. Moderate Smashing, Stun

Moderate resist. Lethal, Smashing, Energy, Fire, Cold

Vulnerable. Confusion

CREY JUGGERNAUT

Lieutenant   **Levels 35-39**

With their powerful personal force fields, missile launchers, and advanced training, these armor clad leaders carry enough firepower to stop a tank. They're also almost as hard to hurt, though they are vulnerable to mental assaults.

Missile Launcher. Moderate Smashing, Lethal & Knockback, long range

Brawl. Moderate Smashing

Boxing. Moderate Smashing, Stun

Moderate resist. Lethal, Smashing, Energy, Fire, Cold

Vulnerable. Confusion

Personal Force Field. Invulnerable

TIME BOMB

Small   **Levels 1-50**

10...9...8...7...6...5...

CREY PROTECTOR

Boss   **Levels 30-34**

With their powerful force fields, heavy weapons, and advanced training, these armor clad leaders carry enough firepower to stop a tank. They're also almost as hard to hurt, though they are vulnerable to mental assaults.

Cryo Rifle. Moderate Cold, Slow, & Sleep, moderate range

Brawl. Moderate Smashing

Boxing. Moderate Smashing, Stun

Moderate resist. Lethal, Smashing, Energy, Fire, Cold

Vulnerable. Confusion

Dispersion Bubble. Buff to all defenses

CREY VOLTAIC TANK

Lieutenant   **Levels 32-37**

Crey's perfected Voltaic Armor can turn any soldier into the proverbial irresistible force. Voltaic Tanks can generate almost limitless electrical current, which they can hurl at great distances.

Charged Bolts. Moderate Energy, Endurance drain, moderate range

Lightning Bolt. High Energy, Endurance drain, moderate range

Ball Lightning. AoE, minor Energy, Endurance drain, moderate range

Charged Brawl. Moderate Smashing, Energy, Endurance drain

Havoc Punch. High Smashing ,Energy, Knockback, & Endurance drain

Thunder Strike. High Smashing, Stun, & Knockback

Resistance. Lethal, Smashing, Energy, Fire, Cold

Superleap

CREY CRYO TANK

Lieutenant   **Levels 32-37**

Crey's perfected Cryo Armor can turn any soldier into the proverbial irresistible force. Cooled with liquid nitrogen, the Cryo Tanks can absorb almost limitless heat and hurl great chunks of ice at their foes.

Frost. Cone minor Cold, Slow, short range

Frozen Fists. Minor Cold, Smashing, Slow

Ice Bolt. Minor Smashing, Cold, Slow, moderate range

Ice Blast. Moderate Smashing, Cold, Slow, moderate range

Freeze Ray. Moderate Cold, Sleep, moderate range

Resistance. Lethal, Smashing, Energy, Fire, Cold

Superleap

CREY POWER TANK

Boss   **Levels 32-37**

Crey's perfected Power Armor can turn any soldier into the proverbial irresistible force. Power Tanks can generate almost limitless power, which they can hurl at great distances.

Barrage. Minor Smashing, Energy, Stun
Energy Punch. Moderate Smashing, Energy, Stun
Whirling Hands. Moderate Energy, Smashing, Stun
Bone Smasher. Moderate Smashing, Energy, Stun
Power Bolt. Moderate Smashing, Energy, Stun, moderate range

Explosive Blast. Moderate Smashing, Energy, Knockback, moderate range
Resistance. Lethal, Smashing, Energy, Fire, Cold
Superleap

PARAGON PROTECTOR

Boss   **Levels 35-40**

Crey denies the rumors that the Paragon Protectors are corporate pawns, but no one outside the company knows the truth for sure. The Claw Pattern Hero is a master of melee combat, using both claws and enhanced physical attributes to make mincemeat of his or her opponents.

Swipe. Moderate Lethal
Strike. High Lethal
Slash. High Lethal & Defense debuff
Spin. Sphere high Lethal
Eviscerate. Very high Lethal
Focus. High Lethal, Knockback
Focused Fighting. Melee and ranged Defense buff
Unstoppable. Very high resist to all attacks but Psionic
Flight

PARAGON PROTECTOR

Boss   **Levels 35-40**

No one knows who these helmet clad Heroes are, or where they come from. The only thing that's certain is their loyalty to Crey. The Power Paragon Protectors can generate powerful blasts of Energy in both melee and ranged combat situations.

Energy Punch. Moderate Smashing, Energy, Stun
Whirling Hands. Moderate Energy, Smashing, Stun
Bone Smasher. Moderate Smashing, Energy, Stun
Foot Stomp. PBAoE moderate Smashing & Knockback
Power Bolt. Moderate Smashing, Energy, Stun, moderate range
Power Blast. Moderate Smashing, Energy, Knockback, moderate range
Energy Torrent. AoE minor Energy, Smashing, Knockback, short range
Explosive Blast. Moderate Smashing, Energy, Knockback, moderate range
Dull Pain. Self-heal
Moment of Glory. Self-heal, recovery, resist all attacks but Psionic
Flight

PARAGON PROTECTOR

Boss   **Levels 35-40**

The Paragon Protectors keep their names and faces a secret. That way, their good deeds all get credited to Crey, while their less virtuous activities can be plausibly denied in court. The Quill Pattern Heroes use a variety of deadly ranged and melee attacks to fill their enemies with holes.

Barb Swipe. Minor Lethal, Slow, Immobilize
Lunge. Moderate Lethal, Slow, Immobilize
Impale. Moderate Lethal, Immobilize, Slow, very short range
Spine throwing. Moderate Lethal, Slow, Immobilize, short range
Ripper. High Lethal, Knockback, Immobilize
Temp Invulnerability. High resist Smashing & Lethal
Invincibility. High Defense buff to all attacks but Psionic
Flight

HOPKINS

ArchVillain   **Levels 32-34**

Hopkins is the devoted servant and bodyguard of the mysterious Countess Crey. Since the day he was hired, he's been at her side constantly, rarely venturing outside the range of her voice. Hopkins is clearly the second in command in the Crey hierarchy.

Energy Punch. Moderate Smashing, Energy, Stun
Whirling Hands. Moderate Smashing, Energy, Stun
Bone Smasher. Moderate Smashing, Energy, Stun
Foot Stomp. AoE moderate Smashing, Knockback
Cryo Rifle. High Cold, Sleep, Slow, very long range
N2 Cannon. Minor Cold, Slow
Resists. Knockup, Knockback, Fear, Hold, Stun, Sleep, Confusion, Smashing

COUNTESS CREY

ArchVillain   **Levels 48-50**

Countess Crey runs her corporation with an iron fist. Though others Hold the lofty title of president and CEO, everyone understands that this is just a legal fiction. The countess is the one holding the strings behind the vast corporation — and woe to anyone who gets in her way.

Telekinetic blast. High Smashing, Psionic
Brawl. Moderate Smashing
Boxing. Moderate Smashing, Stun
Mass Hypnosis. large sphere, Sleep, moderate range
Psychic Scream. Cone, moderate Psionic, Slow, long range
Mental Blast. Moderate Psionic, Slow, long range
Resists. Knockup, Knockback, Fear, Hold, Stun, Sleep, Confusion

7TH GENERATION PARAGON PROTECTOR

Lieutenant

Crey denies the rumors that the Paragon Protectors are corporate pawns, but no one outside the company knows the truth for sure. The Claw Pattern Hero is a master of melee combat, using both claws and enhanced physical attributes to make mincemeat of his or her opponents.

Swipe. Moderate Lethal
Strike. High Lethal
Slash. High Lethal & Defense debuff
Spin. Sphere high Lethal
Eviscerate. Very high Lethal
Focus. High Lethal, Knockback
Focused Fighting. Melee and ranged Defense buff
Unstoppable. Very high resist to all attacks but Psionic
Flight

7TH GENERATION PARAGON PROTECTOR

Lieutenant   **Levels 35-40**

No one knows who these helmet clad Heroes are, or where they come from. The only thing that's certain is their loyalty to Crey. The Power Paragon Protectors can generate powerful blasts of Energy in both melee and ranged combat situations.

Energy Punch. Moderate Smashing, Energy, Stun
Whirling Hands. Moderate Energy, Smashing, Stun
Bone Smasher. Moderate Smashing, Energy, Stun
Foot Stomp. PBAoE moderate Smashing & Knockback
Power Bolt. Moderate Smashing, Energy, Stun, moderate range
Power Blast. Moderate Smashing, Energy, Knockback, moderate range
Energy Torrent. AoE minor Energy, Smashing, Knockback, short range
Explosive Blast. Moderate Smashing, Energy, Knockback, moderate range
Dull Pain. Self-heal
Moment of Glory. Self-heal, recovery, resist all attacks but Psionic
Flight

7TH GENERATION PARAGON PROTECTOR

Lieutenant   **Levels 35-40**

Paragon Protectors keep their names and faces a secret. That way, their good deeds all get credited to Crey, while their less virtuous activities can be plausibly denied in court. The Quill Pattern Heroes use a variety of deadly ranged and melee attacks to fill their enemies with holes.

Barb Swipe. Minor Lethal, Slow, Immobilize
Lunge. Moderate Lethal, Slow, Immobilize
Impale. Moderate Lethal, Immobilize, Slow, very short range
Spine throwing. Moderate Lethal, Slow, Immobilize, short range
Ripper. High Lethal, Knockback, Immobilize
Temp Invulnerability. High resist Smashing & Lethal
Invincibility. High Defense buff to all attacks but Psionic
Flight

PARAGON PROTECTOR

Boss   **Levels 35-40**

Crey denies the rumors that the Paragon Protectors are corporate pawns, but no one outside the company knows the truth for sure. The Claw Pattern Hero is a master of melee combat, using both claws and enhanced physical attributes to make mincemeat of his or her opponents.

Swipe. Moderate Lethal

Strike. High Lethal

Slash. High Lethal & Defense debuff

Spin. Sphere high Lethal

Eviscerate. Very high Lethal

Focus. High Lethal, Knockback

Focused Fighting. Melee and ranged Defense buff

Unstoppable. Very high resist to all attacks but Psionic

Flight

PARAGON PROTECTOR

Boss   **Levels 35-40**

No one knows who these helmet clad Heroes are, or where they come from. The only thing that's certain is their loyalty to Crey. The Power Paragon Protectors can generate powerful blasts of Energy in both melee and ranged combat situations.

Energy Punch. Moderate Smashing, Energy, Stun

Whirling Hands. Moderate Energy, Smashing, Stun

Bone Smasher. Moderate Smashing, Energy, Stun

Foot Stomp. PBAoE moderate Smashing & Knockback

Power Bolt. Moderate Smashing, Energy, Stun, moderate range

Power Blast. Moderate Smashing, Energy, Knockback, moderate range

Energy Torrent. AoE minor Energy, Smashing, Knockback, short range

Explosive Blast. Moderate Smashing, Energy, Knockback, moderate range

Dull Pain. Self-heal

Moment of Glory. Self-heal, recovery, resist all attacks but Psionic

Flight

PARAGON PROTECTOR

Boss   **Levels 35-40**

The Paragon Protectors keep their names and faces a secret. That way, their good deeds all get credited to Crey, while their less virtuous activities can be plausibly denied in court. The Quill Pattern Heroes use a variety of deadly ranged and melee attacks to fill their enemies with holes.

Barb Swipe. Minor Lethal, Slow, Immobilize

Lunge. Moderate Lethal, Slow, Immobilize

Impale. Moderate Lethal, Immobilize, Slow, very short range

Spine throwing. Moderate Lethal, Slow, Immobilize, short range

Ripper. High Lethal, Knockback, Immobilize

Temp Invulnerability. High resist Smashing & Lethal

Invincibility. High Defense buff to all attacks but Psionic

Flight

VILLAINS

203

DEVOURING EARTH

Locations: The home of the Devouring Earth is Eden, though they can be found on Power Island in Independence Port, as well as scattered through Founders' Falls, Talos Island, Crey's Folly and Terra Volta.

Types: The Devouring Earth (DE) are one of the most complex foes in *City of Heroes*, with each type possessing at least one ranged attack, one melee attack and one special. The DE come in six varieties: Creepers, Mushrooms, Rocks, Geodes, Devoured and pets.

Creepers look like big trees, have simple brawling/pummeling attacks, use thorns/spurs for their ranged attacks, which can Knockdown, and are resistant to Smashing damage. They drop a pet called the Tree of Life which increases regeneration for all DE in the radius, but is immobile, and Swarms, which have a DoT and flit about obnoxiously. The regenerative effect of the Tree is negligible, but the Swarms' damage adds up quickly, especially to ranged Heroes in the "backfield."

Mushrooms are resistant to Smashing damage, use pummel/brawl for melee, and spore burst attacks which can Hold, choke and put to Sleep anyone in the affected area. They also drop a Fungi pet that provides

significant resistance vs. Sleep, Disorient, Hold, Immobilize, Fear, confuse and taunt to all DE in the radius. Mushrooms are rarely alone and usually are interspersed with Creepers and Rocks, making their incapacitating attacks more effective in conjunction with the more damaging attacks of their cohorts.

Rocks are essentially Stone Tankers, resistant to Lethal damage, using pummel/brawl for melee, and hurling boulders for a ranged attack with serious damage and Knockback. When defeated, they frequently break down into Rubble, smaller versions of themselves, much like Clockwork bosses. (The ability of a big Bedrock to turn into a much smaller Rubble has earned these monsters the nickname "Fredanbarnies.") On rare occasions, they can plant a Cairin pet that enhances the damage resistance of all DE in the radius.

Geodes are resistant to Energy, vulnerable to Smashing, use pummel/brawl for melee, and hurl shards for severe damage at range. When defeated, they break down into Shards, which are smaller versions of them-

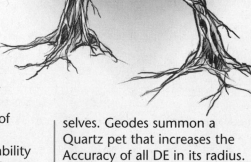

selves. Geodes summon a Quartz pet that increases the Accuracy of all DE in its radius.

Devoured are resistant to Knockback, Smashing, and Energy damage, use claws for Lethal melee, and spit a poison spray that has a DoT effect at range, as well as summoning Swarms as pets (see in Creepers, above). Devoured do massive amounts of damage, and like the Mushrooms above, are rarely alone, coordinating their attacks and pets with their cohorts.

Tactics: There are no "canned" tactics for fighting the Devouring Earth, because each group of them requires a different approach. Typically speaking, the bosses are the highest priority, followed by the lieutenants and minions. The pets are generally targets of opportunity, but they must never be dismissed, for a couple of reasons. First, the pet effects stack, so three Trees of Life mean the DE are regenerating at thrice their normal rate. This can completely counteract small-damage AoE and DoT attacks. In addition, meet enough of the smaller pets, like Swarms, Rubble and Shards, and ranged Heroes can easily be overrun by harassing damage that completely disrupts the support structure of most well organized teams. Lastly, each DE can summon multiple pets, so seeing a single Devoured does not mean there can only be a single Swarm.

Care must be taken in any engagement with the Devouring Earth to ensure all targets are accounted for and everyone in the group is aware of all of the additional targets that will appear once combat is engaged.

BLADEGRASS (25-30), RAZORVINE (31-36), BLACKROSE (37-42), DEATHBLOSSOM (43-47)

Minion Levels 25-47

These horrid perversions of normal flora have become one of the most identifiable monsters in the Devouring Earth's maniacal menagerie. In addition to their astonishing mobility, they can fire swarms of thorns at their enemies, tearing flesh to shreds in an instant.

Pummel. High Smashing & Knockback
Thorn Blast. Cone, moderate Lethal, Knockback, moderate range
Spur. High Lethal, Immobilize, moderate range
Moderate Resist. Smashing
Vulnerability. Negative Energy & Lethal

HERDER
Lieutenant | **Levels 25-34**

The older, more mature plant creatures serve as leaders for their deadly cousins. They're stronger, tougher, and more deadly than the lesser plant creatures. They also have the ability to summon forth Swarms to further trouble their enemies.

Pummel. High Smashing & Knockback
Thorn Blast. Cone, moderate Lethal, Knockback, moderate range
Spur. High Lethal, Immobilize, moderate range
Moderate Resist. Smashing
Vulnerability. Negative Energy & Lethal
Summon Swarm
Summon Tree of Life

HERDER
Lieutenant | **Levels 38-42**

The older, more mature plant creatures serve as leaders for their deadly cousins. They're stronger, tougher, and more deadly than the lesser plant creatures. They also have the ability to summon forth Swarms to further trouble their enemies.

Pummel. High Smashing & Knockback
Thorn Blast. Cone, moderate Lethal, Knockback, moderate range
Spur. High Lethal, Immobilize, moderate range
Moderate Resist. Smashing
Vulnerability. Negative Energy & Lethal
Summon Swarm
Summon Tree of Life

FUNGOID (26-30), DEATHSPORE (31-35), DEATHCAP (36-40)
Minion | **Levels 26-40**

Fungus run amok' is probably the best way to describe these loathsome creatures. Like their inanimate ancestors, mushroom men prefer dark, dank places. In combat they can release clouds of deadly spores that choke and disable nearby enemies.

Pummel. High Smashing & Knockback
Spores. AoE sphere, Hold, moderate range
Spore Burst. PBAoe sphere, Sleep
Moderate Resist. Smashing
Vulnerability. Negative Energy & Lethal

FUNGOID
Lieutenant | **Levels 26-42**

These horrid parodies of men lead the fungi armies of the Devouring Earth. Their pummeling attack can shatter bones while their spore clouds disable their victims. Meanwhile, their summoned Swarms hold other foes at bay.

Pummel. High Smashing & Knockback
Spores. AoE sphere, Hold, moderate range
Spore Burst. PBAoe sphere, Sleep
Moderate Resist. Smashing
Vulnerability. Negative Energy & Lethal
Summon Swarm
Summon Fungi

BEDROCK (27-42), BOULDER (43-49)

Minion   **Levels 27-49**

Made from assemblages of rocks that are somehow given form and consciousness, the Rock Troops are tough, resilient creatures who can either pound their opponents in close combat or hurl rocks from a distance.

Pummel. High Smashing & Knockback
Hurl Boulder. High Smashing, Knockback, moderate range
Summon Rubble
Resists. Lethal
Vulnerability. Negative Energy & Smashing

SENTRY (46-48), GRANITE (49-50)

Lieutenant   **Levels 46-50**

The leaders of the Rock Troops are tougher, smarter, and better equipped to take on whatever foes the Devouring Earth sets them against. In addition to the rock wielding skills of their subordinates, they have the ability to summon forth deadly Swarms of insects.

Pummel. High Smashing & Knockback
Hurl Boulder. High Smashing, Knockback, moderate range
Summon Rubble
Resists. Lethal
Vulnerability. Negative Energy & Smashing
Summon Cairin

GRANITE (38-42)

Lieutenant   **Levels 38-42**

The leaders of the Rock Troops are tougher, smarter, and better equipped to take on whatever foes the Devouring Earth sets

them against. In addition to the rock wielding skills of their subordinates, they have the ability to summon forth deadly Swarms of insects.

Pummel. High Smashing & Knockback
Hurl Boulder. High Smashing, Knockback, moderate range
Summon Rubble
Resists. Lethal
Vulnerability. Negative Energy & Smashing
Summon Cairin

GEODE (31-35), QUARTZ (36-40), SARDONYX (41-46)

Minion   **Levels 31-46**

Devouring Earth grows these crystalline warriors in special caves deep beneath the Earth. Their blasts of shards can cut deeply into a target's flesh and bone, and Energy attacks have a diminished effect against their crystalline forms. Luckily, they're susceptible to Smashing attacks.

Pummel. High Smashing & Knockback
Crystal Shards. Moderate Smashing, Lethal, moderate range
Shatter
Resists. Energy & Negative Energy
Vulnerability. Smashing

GUARDIAN

Lieutenant   **Levels 35-45**

These Crystal leaders command their sparkling soldiers in combat, chattering amongst one another with voices like breaking glass. In combat they rain down shards of razor sharp crystal and pummel their opponents mercilessly. Like their followers, these creatures fear Smashing attacks.

Pummel. High Smashing & Knockback
Crystal Shards. Moderate Smashing, Lethal, moderate range
Shatter
Resists. Energy & Negative Energy
Vulnerability. Smashing
Summon Quartz

THE SWARM

Small   **Levels 25-49**

These nettlesome Swarms are sometimes encountered in groups, though they can also be summoned by other Devouring Earth creatures. They are immune to Smashing and Lethal attacks, but theses flying hordes don't fare well when confronted with Fire or Energy based assaults.

Sting. Minor special, Slow
Swarm. Speed
Flight
Resists. Smashing, Lethal, Stun
Vulnerability. Energy, Negative Energy, Fire, Knockback, Knockup, Repel

LESSER DEVOURED

Boss   **Levels 25-39**

The Devoured were once normal human beings, but they have since been transformed into horrifying creatures. Their bodies have been mutated grotesquely, and even their brains have been perverted into believing the radical environmental precepts of the Devouring Earth. In combat they show their hatred for the world of men by spitting poison at their foes.

Pummel. High Lethal & Knockback
Spit. High special, moderate range
Resists. Knockup, Knockback, Smashing, Energy

Vulnerability. Negative Energy
Summon Swarm

GREATER DEVOURED
Boss   **Levels 40-49**

The ultimate eco-warriors, the Greater Devoured incorporate the biomass of fallen Heroes into their monstrous forms. They rend foes with their slashing talons, spitting poison on those they can't reach. A Greater Devoured is a formidable foe, resistant to most kinds of attacks.

Pummel. High Lethal & Knockback
Spit. High special, moderate range
Hurl Boulder. High Smashing, short range

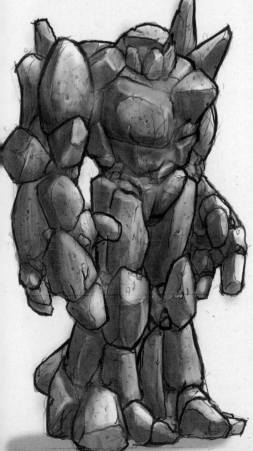

Foot Stomp. PBAoE sphere, moderate Smashing & Knockback
Resists. Knockup, Knockback, Smashing, Energy, Sleep, Stun, Fear
Vulnerability. Negative Energy, Hold
Summon Swarm

TERRA
ArchVillain   **Levels 35-40**

Transformed by a Devouring Earth drug, this raging beast was once the woman Tanya Tyler. Now capable of breeding Devouring Earth creatures, Terra is the monsters' greatest offensive weapon in their war against humanity.

Pummel. High Lethal & Knockback
Hurl Boulder. High Smashing, short range
Foot Stomp. PBAoE sphere, moderate Smashing & Knockback
Spit. High special, moderate range
Resists. Knockup, Knockback, Smashing, Energy, Sleep, Stun, Fear
Vulnerability. Negative Energy, Hold
Summon Swarm

THORN
Monster   **Levels 38-42**

No one knows exactly how Hamidon breathed life into this colossal tree. What is certain is that the tree is grateful. Thorn defends Hamidon's Eden with a fearsome vigor, and seems to have no sympathy for anything that walks on two legs.

Resistant to all dmg types
Summon Swarm
Foot Stomp. PBAoE sphere, High Smashing, Knockback
Thorn Blast. AoE cone, high Lethal, Knockback, moderate range
Thorn. High Lethal, Immobilize, long range

STROPHARIA
Monster   **Levels 38-42**

Catch it unawares, and you may find this giant mushroom blissfully content, drinking in the atmosphere of Hamidon's strange Eden. If it sees you, though, watch out! Stropharia seems intent on exacting revenge for all its cousins that met their fate in a buttery saucepan.

Resistant to all dmg types
Summon Swarm
Foot Stomp. PBAoE sphere, High Smashing, Knockback
Spores. AoE sphere, Sleep, long range
Spore Burst. PBAoE, minor special

QUARRY
Monster   **Levels 38-42**

The greatest of Hamidon's rock beasts, Lattice roams Eden with a single purpose — to destroy any humans who stray inside. It may not be the smartest of Hamidon's followers, but it's certainly among the strongest. More than one Hero has met his fate beneath Lattice's stony foot.

Resistant to all dmg types but Smashing
Summon Rubble
Fault. AoE sphere, high Smashing, Knockup, Stun, very short range
Hurl Boulder. AoE sphere, high Smashing, Knockback, long range

LATTICE
Monster   **Levels 38-42**

This giant crystal monster may be the most beautiful of Hamidon's strange creations. It is also one of the deadliest. Quarry will happily slaughter any human being who sets foot within Hamidon's bizarre paradise.

Resistant to all dmg types but Smashing
Crystal Shards. AoE sphere, moderate Smashing, Lethal, long range
Summon Shards
Foot Stomp. PBAoE sphere, High Smashing, Knockback

JURASSIK

Monster	Levels 35-40

The giant monster was dubbed Jurassik by a Hero some time ago, and the name has stuck (though the Hero has regrettably disappeared). It appears that Jurassik has been mutated by the many pollutants and chemicals in Crey's Folly. Now, it is a creature of pure violence.

Fault. AoE sphere, moderate Smashing, Knockup, Stun, very short range
Jurassik Club. High Smashing, Stun, & Knockback
Hurl Boulder. AoE, high Smashing, Knockback, very long range
Resists. Knockup, Knockback, Fear, Immobilize, Hold, Stun, Sleep, Confusion, Lethal
Vulnerability. Smashing, Negative Energy
Summon Rubble

JURASSIK RUBBLE

Minion	Level 40

Jurassik has fallen, but from the rubble a smaller creature has arisen to vex Heroes!

Pummel. High Smashing & Knockback
Hurl Boulder. High Smashing, Knockback, moderate range
Summon Rubble
Resists. Lethal
Vulnerability. Negative Energy & Smashing

RUBBLE

Small	Levels 27-50

Large Rock Beasts might fall, but from rubble smaller creatures arise to plague Heroes!

Brawl. Moderate Smashing
Hurl Boulder. High Smashing, short range
Resists. Lethal
Vulnerability. Negative Energy & Smashing

SHARDS: GEODE (31-35), QUARTZ (36-40), SARDONYX (41-46), GUARDIAN (35-45)

Small	Levels 31-46

Even Shards from a fallen crystalline creature can prove deadly.

Brawl. Moderate Smashing
Crystal Shards. Moderate Smashing, Lethal, moderate range
Resists. Energy & Negative Energy
Vulnerability. Smashing

PETS

Pet	Levels 1-50

Tree of Life

These tiny trees don't do much to Heroes, but their aura boosts the healing rate of all Devouring Earth creatures nearby.

Fungi

The Fungi emit spores that strengthen the immunity of Devouring Earth creatures. As a result, nearby creatures become resistant to many effects, including Knockback, Sleep, Disorient, and Stun.

Cairn

These tiny Cairns channel the Earth's energies, making nearby Devouring Earth creatures more resistant to damage.

Quartz

These small quartz shrines focus the Earth's energies, boosting the Accuracy of all Devouring Earth attacks.

HAMIDON

ArchVillain	Levels 40-50

Hamidon is nucleus of a giant single celled organism, spawned from some twisted primordial soup. Its has one instinct, to Devour the Earth and all that infests it.

Immune. Knockup, Knockback, Repel, Fear, Immobilize
Resists. Hold, Stun, Sleep, Confusion
Vulnerability. All damage types
Protoplasm. PBAoE Slow
Electrolytic Blast:. Moderate Energy, Knockback, extreme range

MITOCHONDRIA ANTIBODIES

ArchVillain	Levels 40-50

These creatures seem to be the organelles of the giant single cell organism that is devouring the land around you. These Mitochondria are definitely the cells' main defense mechanism.

Immune. Knockup, Knockback, Repel, Fear, Immobilize, Hold, Stun, Sleep, Confusion
Cytoplasmic Blast. High special, extreme range
Mitosis. Duplicate self
Flight

MENDING MITOCHONDRIA
ArchVillain   **Levels 40-50**

These creatures seem to be the organelles of the giant single cell organism that is devouring the land around you. These Mitochondria seem to function as repair units for the cell.

Immune. Knockup, Knockback, Repel, Fear, Immobilize, Hold, Stun, Sleep, Confusion
Heal Other
Mitosis. Duplicate self
Flight

MITOCHONDRIA ELECTROLYTES
ArchVillain   **Levels 40-50**

These creatures seem to be the organelles of the giant single cell organism that is devouring the land around you. These Mitochondria are definitely the cells Defense mechanism.

Immune. Knockup, Knockback, Repel, Fear, Immobilize, Hold, Stun, Sleep, Confusion
Paralytic Blast. Hold, Slow, very long range
Mitosis. Duplicate self
Flight

CYTOPLASM
Pet   **Levels 40-50**

Cytoplasm. Create Cytoplasm, Knockback
Self Destruct
Untouchable

HAMIDON BUD
Hamidon   **Levels 40-50**

Although defeated, it seems the pieces of the Hamidon are still a threat. Left uncheck, it is likely that each piece could one day grow to become as big a menace as the original. It must be stopped.

Electrolytic Bolt. Minor Energy, short range

DEVOURING SWARM
Minion   **Levels 40-50**

These nettlesome Swarms are encountered either in groups or are summoned forth by members of the Devouring Earth. They are immune to Smashing and Lethal attacks but theses flying hordes do not fare well when confronted with Fire or Energy based assaults.

Sting. Minor special, disrupts flight & teleport
Flight
Resists. Smashing, Lethal, Stun
Vulnerability. Energy, Negative Energy, Fire, Knockup, Knockback, Repel

EXPLOSION
Pet   **Levels 1-50**

Electrolytic Blast. PBAoE, moderate Energy, Knockback, & Stun

ROCK WALL
Boss   **Levels 40-44**

The power of the Devouring Earth seems to have no bound. The very rock face itself has come alive to consume the Earth.

Hurl Rubble. High Smashing, Knockback, very long range
Resists. Resists to all attacks
Immunity. Immobilize, Fear, teleport, Knockup, Knockback, & Repel

MOLD WALL
Boss   **Levels 40-44**

The power of the Devouring Earth seems to have no bound. The very mold that grows on the rock face itself has come

alive to consume the Earth.

Hurl Rubble. High Smashing, Knockback, very long range
Resists. Resists to all attacks
Immunity. Immobilize, Fear, teleport, Knockup, Knockback, & Repel

LICHEN COLONY
Boss   **Levels 40-44**

The power of the Devouring Earth seems to have no bound. This Lichen Colony seems to generating some sort of spores.

Summon Lichen
Resists. Resists to all attacks
Immunity. Immobilize, Fear, teleport, Knockup, Knockback, Repel

LICHEN
Minion   **Levels 40-44**

The power of the Devouring Earth seems to have no bound. These Lichens are not to be trifled with.

Lichen Spore. Moderate special, moderate range
Resists. Smashing
Vulnerability. Negative Energy

TITAN
Monster   **Levels 38-42**

This giant crystal monster may be the most beautiful of Hamidon's strange creations. It is also one of the deadliest. Quarry will happily slaughter any human being who sets foot within Hamidon's bizarre paradise.

Resistant to all dmg types but Smashing
Crystal Shards. AoE sphere, moderate Smashing, Lethal, long range
Summon Shards
Foot Stomp. PBAoE sphere, High Smashing, Knockback

VILLAINS

THE FAMILY

Locations: The Family is found primarily in Independence Port, though they have spread their influence into Steel Canyon. Heros will get mission doors for them in most of the other non-hazard zones.

Types: All of the villains in The Family have both ranged and melee attacks, and can be broken into three basic types: Controllers, Tankers and Blasters. Overall, melee damage is vastly greater than ranged.

Controllers are the Consigliere bosses who use their control powers to paralyze Heroes, then use telekinesis to beat them down. While paralyzed, all active powers are turned off, making the Hero vulnerable.

Tankers are the Muscle (Capo Muscle and Button Man Muscle) and the Underboss bosses who use super strength to deliver a lot of damage as well as Knockback and Disorient attacks, which turns off the Heroes' active powers. The Muscles also use pistols at range, and the Underboss has a machine gun.

Blasters are the Gunners (Capo Gunner and Button Man Gunner) that use machine guns and prefer to stay at range, though they also have brawling available if the Hero closes on them, and they typically do not run to remain at range.

Named bosses will use Underboss or Consigliere powers.

Tactics: The suggested order of engagement for Family targets: Consigliere, other bosses, Capo Muscle, the rest. The Consiglieres can neutralize Heroes, so they need to be removed. The other bosses and the Capo Muscle inflict lots of damage as well as Knockback and Disorientation, so they need to be removed before the rest of the targets.

BUTTON MEN

Minion	Levels 20-29

Organized crime has always had plenty of competition in Paragon City, but that doesn't stop young street toughs from wanting to swear allegiance to their Don and live like a wise guy. It helps to be a stone Cold killer with a gun, like these guys.

Button Man Muscle

Brawl. Moderate Smashing
Boxing. Moderate Smashing, Stun
Automatic Pistol. Moderate Lethal, short range

Button Man Buckshot

Shotgun. Cone moderate Lethal & Knockback, short range

Button Man Gunner

Submachine Gun. Minor Lethal, Defense debuff, moderate range

CAPOS

Lieutenant	Levels 20-29

Each Capo controls his own crew of Button Men. It's a kind of authority you don't earn unless you've proven yourself both ruthless and lucky. Capos save the best weapons and women for themselves and are inevitably smart, tough fighters.

Capo Muscle

Jab. Moderate Smashing & Stun
Punch. Moderate Smashing & Knockback
Haymaker. High Smashing & Knockback
Automatic Pistol. Moderate Lethal, short range

Capo Gunner

Assault Rifle. Minor Lethal, Defense debuff, long range

UNDERBOSS

Boss	Levels 20-29

The Underbosses report directly to the Don, and each has control over a number of Capos. In Paragon City, you don't rise to the top without a little super-powered help, and many Underbosses have heightened abilities or access to specialized gear that helps them stay on top in their cutthroat business.

Jab. Moderate Smashing & Stun
Punch. Moderate Smashing & Knockback
Haymaker. High Smashing & Knockback
Assault Rifle. Minor Lethal, Defense debuff, long range
Focus. Buffs to melee and ranged attacks

CONSIGLIERE

Boss   **Levels 20-29**

In Paragon City, you don't become one of the Don's trusted advisors without a little super-powered expertise.

Consiglieres have far more subtle powers than their Underboss counterparts, which match their more subtle responsibilities within the Family.

Crush. Minor Smashing, Immobilize, Slow, moderate range

Gravity Distortion. Hold, Slow, moderate range

Propel. High Smashing & Knockback, short range

FREAKSHOW

Locations: Freakshow are found primarily in Terra Volta, Talos Island and Crey's Folly, with a few strays in Independence Port. Mission doors for them can be generated anywhere.

Types: Most all Freakshow are Tankers of some sort, though some will have pistols and shotguns when forced to engage at range. At higher levels, Juicers and Stunners use ranged attacks that will Disorient Heroes, dropping their active powers and making them vulnerable. When they are down to less than 1/3 health, all Freakshow will use Dull Pain to heal back up to almost half, and many Lieutenants and Bosses (and higher-level minions) will use Revive to get back up after being taken down, with near full Hit Points and little Endurance.

Melee Freaks typically use either giant hammers (Smashing damage), or huge scythes or blades (Lethal damage). A few will have shotguns or machine guns, and the Tank bosses will hurl massive blades for significant damage. On the whole, their melee damage is vastly greater than their ranged.

Tactics: The bulk of Freakshow foes can be fought like most other villain groups, with a few exceptions. Stunners and Juicers need to be taken down quickly due to their ability to lock Heroes down and make them vulnerable.

Most Freakshow, however, either do not have ranged, or their ranged damage is insignificant compared to their melee, so fighting them at range is typically safer. Juicers and Stunners are the only exception, which not only use ranged electrical attacks, but also fly, making them the primary target for Heroes who wish to engage at range.

Tanker bosses have a great deal more hit points, a very large amount of Smashing damage resistance, and almost always revive, so never turn away from a fallen one as it will very likely get back up. The best way to defeat them is to use non-Smashing damage while melee Heroes keep them engaged, as they do a great deal of damage when they hit, melee or ranged.

FREAKS

Minion   **20-26**

The dregs of Freakshow society, the Freaks are newbies who haven't earned their metal yet. They have to prove themselves by using axes, bats, guns and anything else they can get their hands on to cause as much damage as possible.

Freak Chopper

Fireman Axe. High Lethal & Defense debuff

Heavy Revolver. High Lethal, Knockback, moderate range

Dull Pain. Self-heal

Freak Slammer

Sledgehammer. High Smashing & Knockback

Heavy Revolver. High Lethal, Knockback, moderate range

Dull Pain. Self-heal

Freak Buckshot

Shotgun. AoE cone, moderate Lethal, Knockback
Dull Pain. Self-heal

Freak Gunner

Submachine Gun. Minor Lethal, Defense debuff, moderate range
Dull Pain. Self-heal

MAD FREAKS

Minion   **Levels 21-33**

Mad Freaks have earned their Excelsior Feeder, a device that pumps the drug directly into their bloodstream. That makes them stronger and tougher than humanly possible, as well as more than a little bit crazy.

Mad Freak Chopper

Fireman Axe. High Lethal & Defense debuff
Heavy Revolver. High Lethal, Knockback, moderate range
Dull Pain. Self-heal

Mad Freak Slammer

Sledgehammer. High Smashing & Knockback
Heavy Revolver. High Lethal, Knockback, moderate range
Dull Pain. Self-heal

Mad Freak Buckshot

Shotgun. AoE cone, moderate Lethal, Knockback
Dull Pain. Self-heal

Mad Freak Gunner

Submachine Gun. Minor Lethal, Defense debuff, moderate range
Dull Pain. Self-heal

ENFORCERS

Minion   **Levels 22-32**

The Enforcers are what every-
one thinks of when they hear the word Freakshow — dangerous punks with over-sized mechanical arms ending in nasty looking weapons. They are the true heart of the Freakshow, deadly in combat but not yet totally insane.

Enforcer Swiper

Cybernetic Blade. Moderate Lethal
Heavy Revolver. High Lethal & Knockback, moderate range
Dull Pain. Self-heal
Revive. Self-resurrect
Resists. Cold
Vulnerability. Energy

Enforcer Smasher

Cybernetic Hammer. Moderate Smashing & Stun
Heavy Revolver. High Lethal & Knockback, moderate range
Dull Pain. Self-heal
Revive. Self-resurrect
Resists. Cold
Vulnerability. Energy

JUICER FREAK

Minion   **Levels 27-39**

Juicers undergo a very specific and unusual cybernetic enhancement, one that sets them apart from all other Freaks and does strange things to their brains. A network of electrical wiring and emitters allows the Juicers to shoot forth great gouts of electrical Energy that can devastate their foes.

Shock Punch. Minor Smashing & Energy
Lightning Bolt. High Energy & Endurance drain, moderate range
Ball Lightning. AoE sphere minor Energy & Endurance drain, moderate range
Flight

Dull Pain. Self-heal
Revive. Self-resurrect
Resists. Cold
Vulnerability. Energy

STUNNER FREAK

Minion   **Levels 27-39**

Stunners undergo a specific and unusual cybernetic enhancement, one that sets them apart from all other Freaks and does strange things to their brains. A network of electrical wiring and emitters allows these Stunners to Immobilize even the strongest Heroes for a short period of time.

Shock Punch. Minor Smashing & Energy
Charged Bolts. Moderate Energy & Endurance drain, moderate range
Tesla Cage. Minor Energy, Endurance drain, & Sleep, moderate range
Flight
Dull Pain. Self-heal
Revive. Self-resurrect
Resists. Cold
Vulnerability. Energy

METAL FREAKS

Minion   **Levels 28-39**

A Metal Freak's devotion to the cause is obvious — both arms are replaced with robotic contraptions good only for destruction. He must rely on other Freaks to feed him, but in combat he is a whirling nightmare.

Metal Swiper

Cybernetic Blade. Moderate Lethal
Cybernetic Blades. High Lethal
Sawblade. Moderate Lethal, Knockback, moderate range
Dull Pain. Self-heal
Revive. Self-resurrect
Resists. Cold
Vulnerability. Energy

Metal Smasher

Cybernetic Hammer. Moderate Smashing & Stun

Cybernetic Hammers. High Smashing & Stun

Hammer Clap. PBAoE sphere, Stun & Knockback

Dull Pain. Self-heal

Revive. Self-resurrect

Resists. Cold

Vulnerability. Energy

CHIEFS
Lieutenant	22-26

A combination of revolutionary fervor and massive doses of Excelsior allows the leaders of the Enforcers to completely ignore the effects of pain. This trait lets them keep on fighting when by all rights they should have dropped dead.

Chief Swiper

Cybernetic Blade. Moderate Lethal

Heavy Revolver. High Lethal & Knockback, moderate range

Dull Pain. Self-heal

Revive. Self-resurrect

Resists. Cold

Vulnerability. Energy

Chief Smasher

Cybernetic Hammer. Moderate Smashing & Stun

Heavy Revolver. High Lethal & Knockback, moderate range

Dull Pain. Self-heal

Revive. Self-resurrect

Resists. Cold

Vulnerability. Energy

CHAMPIONS
Lieutenant	Levels 32-39

These are the Heroes of the Freakshow, devoted utterly to Smashing the state and having a great time while they're doing it. They're totally without care or mercy; point them in the right direction (or even the wrong one) and mayhem ensues.

Champion Swiper

Cybernetic Blade. Moderate Lethal

Cybernetic Blades. High Lethal

Sawblade. Moderate Lethal, Knockback, moderate range

Dull Pain. Self-heal

Revive. Self-resurrect

Resists. Cold

Vulnerability. Energy

Champion Smasher

Cybernetic Hammer. Moderate Smashing & Stun

Cybernetic Hammers. High Smashing & Stun

Hammer Clap. PBAoE sphere, Stun & Knockback

Dull Pain. Self-heal

Revive. Self-resurrect

Resists. Cold

Vulnerability. Energy

TANKS
Boss	Levels 20-29

The fully armored, incredibly tough Tank Freaks are a rare breed indeed. As their name suggests, they're almost unstoppable in combat. The one ray of hope when confronting a Tank Freak is that their electronics are not always top of the line, leaving them vulnerable to Energy attacks.

Tank Swiper

Cybernetic Blades. High Lethal

Sawblade. Moderate Lethal, Knockback, moderate range

Tank Grenade. AoE sphere moderate Lethal, Smashing, & Knockback, moderate range

Dull Pain. Self-heal

Revive. Self-resurrect

Resists. Cold

Vulnerability. Energy

Resists. Smashing, Lethal, Knockup, Knockback, Stun

Tank Smasher

Cybernetic Hammers. High Smashing & Stun

Hammer Clap. PBAoE sphere, Stun & Knockback

Tank Grenade. AoE sphere moderate Lethal, Smashing, & Knockback, moderate range

Dull Pain. Self-heal

Revive. Self-resurrect

Resists. Cold

Vulnerability. Energy

Resists. Smashing, Lethal, Knockup, Knockback, Stun

CHIEFS
Lieutenant	Levels 27-31

It takes some skill to control death dealing levels of electricity as they course through your nervous system, and Juicer leaders have that control. They can use their implants to generate massive balls of lightning. They're no fun in close combat either, as their punch packs a heck of an electrical wallop.

Juicer Chief

Shock Punch. Minor Smashing & Energy

Lightning Bolt. High Energy & Endurance drain, moderate range

Ball Lightning. AoE sphere minor Energy & Endurance drain, moderate range

Flight

Dull Pain. Self-heal

Revive. Self-resurrect

Resists. Cold

Vulnerability. Energy

VILLAINS

213

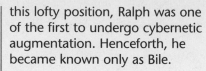

Stunner Chief

Shock Punch. Minor Smashing & Energy
Charged Bolts. Moderate Energy & Endurance drain, moderate range
Tesla Cage. Minor Energy, Endurance drain, & Sleep, moderate range
Flight
Dull Pain. Self-heal
Revive. Self-resurrect
Resists. Cold
Vulnerability. Energy

CLAMOR

ArchVillain
Level 25

Eve van Dorn's had a hard time finding friends as dedicated to violence as herself. For a while she found a home in the 5th Column, but she could only make it so far in that organization. So she turned to the Freakshow. Under the name Clamor, Eve's had no trouble rallying other Freaks to her banner.

Resists. Knockup, Knockback, Fear, Stun, Sleep, Confusion, Cold
Vulnerability. Energy
Cybernetic Claw. High Lethal
Neutron Bomb. AoE sphere moderate Energy & Defense debuff, moderate range
Electron Haze. AoE cone moderate Energy, Knockback, & Defense debuff, moderate range
Neutrino Bolt. Moderate Energy, Defense debuff, very long range

BILE

ArchVillain   **Level 30**

Ralph Francesco was an early members of the nihilistic group that would later become the

Freakshow. his experience as an army veteran made it inevitable that he'd become one the organization's top men. Because of

this lofty position, Ralph was one of the first to undergo cybernetic augmentation. Henceforth, he became known only as Bile.

Resists. Knockup, Knockback, Fear, Stun, Sleep, Confusion, Cold
Vulnerability. Energy
Cybernetic Claw. High Lethal, Knockback
Neutron Bomb. AoE sphere moderate Energy & Defense debuff, moderate range
Electron Haze. AoE cone moderate Energy, Knockback, & Defense debuff, moderate range
Neutrino Bolt. Moderate Energy, Defense debuff, very long range

DRECK

ArchVillain   **Level 34**

Born Daniel Watson, Dreck is the glue that holds the militantly independent Freakshow together. Freaks may chafe at his orders, they may laugh at his haircut, but they all respect Dreck's absolute lust for violence.

Resists. Knockup, Knockback, Fear, Stun, Sleep, Confusion, Cold
Vulnerability. Energy
Cybernetic Claw. High Smashing, Stun
Neutron Bomb. AoE sphere moderate Energy & Defense debuff, moderate range
Electron Haze. AoE cone moderate Energy, Knockback, & Defense debuff, moderate range
Neutrino Bolt. Moderate Energy, Defense debuff, very long range

HELLIONS

Locations: Atlas Park, Galaxy City, Perez Park.

Types: Minions are called Blood Brothers, and they come in all the usual armament varieties (Brawler, Slugger, Slicer, Slammer, Chopper).

Lieutenants are called the Fallen, and they can be distinguished from minions by the fact that they use firearms — either the shotgun-using Buckshots or the Gunners, who wield an SMG.

Bosses are called The Damned (natu-rally), and they have quite dangerous Fire Blast Powers.

A few unique Hellion bosses appear in door missions.

Tactics: Hellions pretty much exist in the game so you can learn basic street fighting tactics. Always take out the Damned first, and if you're solo try not to engage them except one-on-one, particularly if they con yellow. Follow them up by taking out any Buckshot, then Slammers (to avoid inconvenient Knockdowns), then Gunners and finally all other grunts.

Any time you attack a group of lieutenants and minions you'll probably get at least one or two runners. Good, let 'em run. Don't try to catch up to them until you've disposed of the whole main body. Do watch out, however, for Buckshot who only run far enough to get you within blasting range from behind.

BLOOD BROTHERS
Minion   **Levels 1-14**

The Hellions have found their special edge by using the power of mystical artifacts to increase their strength and skill. Only the highest ranked gang members know where these artifacts really come from. The gang values secrecy and solidarity; only those who have undergone the initiation ritual and ceremonially cut themselves can be called Blood Brothers.

Blood Brother Brawler

Brawl. Moderate Smashing
Revolver. High Lethal, short range
Resists. Fire
Vulnerability. Cold

Blood Brother Slicer

Knife. Moderate Lethal
Revolver. High Lethal, short range
Resists. Fire
Vulnerability. Cold

Blood Brother Slugger

Baseball Bat. High Smashing
Revolver. High Lethal, short range
Resists. Fire
Vulnerability. Cold

Blood Brother Slammer

Sledgehammer. High Smashing & Knockback
Revolver. High Lethal, short range
Resists. Fire
Vulnerability. Cold

Blood Brother Chopper

Fireman Axe. High Lethal & Defense debuff
Revolver. High Lethal, short range
Resists. Fire
Vulnerability. Cold

FALLEN
Lieutenant   **Levels 1-14**

In the satanic worldview of the Hellions, falling is a good thing. The Fallen have proven their willingness to take on any

VILLAINS

215

power the gang's mystic artifacts can give them, no matter how twisted or base. The hellfire that burns within them protects them from Fire but leaves them susceptible to Cold.

Fallen Buckshot

Shotgun. AoE cone moderate Lethal & Knockback, short range
Resists. Fire
Vulnerability. Cold

Fallen Gunner
Lieutenant

In the satanic worldview of the Hellions, falling is a good thing. The Fallen have proven their willingness to take on any

power the gang's mystic artifacts can give them, no matter how twisted or base. The hellfire that burns within them protects them from Fire but leaves them susceptible to Cold.

Submachine Gun. Minor Lethal & Defense debuff, moderate range
Resists. Fire
Vulnerability. Cold

DAMNED

Boss	Levels 1–14

The hellfire burns bright inside the leaders of the Hellions. So bright, in fact, that they can call it forth to incinerate their enemies. This inner fire keeps them

safe from Fire damage, but leaves them quite susceptible to Cold.

Scorch. Moderate Fire
Combustion. Pale sphere minor Fire
Incinerate. Minor Fire
Flares. Moderate Fire, short range
Fire Breath. AoE cone moderate Fire, short range
Fire Blast. Moderate Fire, moderate range
Fire Ball. AoE sphere moderate Smashing, Fire, & Knockback, moderate range
Resists. Fire
Vulnerability. Cold

HYDRA

The Hydra gang can be found in large concentrations in the Everett Lake section of Perez Park. They are bipedal piles of sludge that tend to congregate in groups of three to nine. Their hierarchy is broken down into Spawn minions, Protean lieutenants and the Man O' War bosses, and their level range is thirteen to fourteen. They also appear in the Sewers, at far higher levels.

The Hydra's main ranged attack is an acidic spit that has a Damage Over Time effect. Just because you manage to escape a barrage of attacks from them

doesn't mean you'll live to tell about it.

While this might seem quite deadly, the Hydra do not have exceptional range to their attacks. This makes them very easy opponents for anyone who can fly or hover above the water and hit them with long ranged attacks. And because of their large concentrations in a fairly wide open area, they are very easy targets for Area of Effect attacks.

The Hydra in Perez Park make great targets for players and groups from levels 11 to 15. After that, the experience

gained tends to taper off enough that you should considering finding new hunting grounds.

There's just one final word of caution about hunting the Hydra … and that's beware of the Kraken, the Hydra Monster that lurks in Everett Lake.

Villains researched by Skoriksis.

TENTACLE
Minion   **Levels 35-40**

For years, rumors have persisted about a giant monster living in the depths of the sewers. This strange tentacle stretches down into the mulch. Who knows what it's connected to?

Tentacle Smash. High Smashing

or

Tentacle Spray. Moderate special
Resists. Knockup, Knockback, teleport, Repel, fly, Fear
Vulnerability. Lethal, Negative Energy

TENTACLE
Lieutenant   **Levels 35-40**

Tentacle Smash. High Smashing

or

Tentacle Spray. Moderate special
Resists. Knockup, Knockback, teleport, Repel, fly, Fear
Vulnerability. Lethal, Negative Energy
Duplicate self (perhaps)

SPAWN
Minion   **Levels 1-40**

These formless creatures appear to be controlled by some other entity. Studies of their remains have revealed that they lack any sort of brain. Nevertheless, their actions demonstrate a fearsome cunning and a total hatred of mankind.

Pummel. High Smashing
Spit. Moderate special
Resists. Smashing
Vulnerability. Lethal

PROTEAN
Lieutenant   **Levels 1-40**

Some of the creatures found in the sewers are endowed with greater power than their fellows. They don't, however, seem to have any control over the weaker spawn. One thing has been shown; the genetic material of these creatures is unlike anything on this planet.

Pummel. High Smashing
Spit. Moderate special
Resists. Smashing
Vulnerability. Lethal

MAN O' WAR
Boss   **Levels 1-40**

The Men O' War are the strongest of the strange amoeba-like men that dwell within the sewers. Recently, scientists examined some DNA from a captured Man O' War. Strangely, it contained the genetic code of viruses and plants that are common on Earth.

Pummel. High Smashing
Spit. Moderate special
Resists. Smashing
Vulnerability. Lethal

HYDRA
ArchVillain   **Levels 35-40**

The alien Rikti created the Hydra to guard their secret bases beneath the city. It seems programmed to attack anything that isn't Rikti. Heroes must stop this creature from growing any larger and threatening the city as a whole.

Immune. Knockback, Knockup

KRAKEN
Monster   **Level 14**

The Kraken appears to be a mutation of the strange Hydra Spawn that live in the sewers. For unknown reasons, it stalks the streets of Perez Park. The Kraken is quite powerful and can destroy full teams of Heroes without effort.

FORCE FIELD GENERATOR POD
Pet   **Levels 35-40**

This generator seems to serve two purposes. It not only keeps the Hydra safe from all attacks, but also appears to keep the fearsome creature under Rikti control.

HYDRA
Pet   **Levels 1-50**

The alien Rikti created the Hydra to guard their secret bases beneath the city. It seems programmed to attack anything that isn't Rikti. Heroes must stop this creature from growing any larger and threatening the city as a whole.

NEMESIS

Locations: Founders' Falls, Crey's Folly and Eden.

Types: There are four types of Nemesis you will face: Soldiers, Support, Elite and Jaeger. Each type comes with its own medic role, labeled a surgeon.

Soldiers (Chasseur, Armiger, & Lance) are just that, grunts: line soldiers who do most of the fighting. They use assault rifles with axe-bayonets and do Fire damage at range and Lethal in melee. Surgeons at this rank do single-target healing.

Support ranks (Carabineir, Fusilier, and Grenadier) are filled with heavy-weapon specialists who use heavy machine guns, assault rifles and cluster cannons, capable of doing massive amounts of Fire and Lethal damage at range. Nemesis

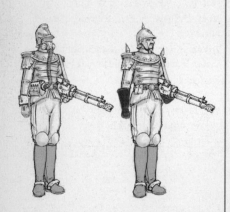

Snipers fall into this category and are frequently distanced from the group, on a nearby rooftop, providing covering fire with deadly accuracy. The Surgeons in this rank have an area-of-effect heal.

The Elite ranks (Cuirasseur, Hussar, Dragoon) are enhanced Support ranks. They are very resistant to Lethal and Smashing damage, move very quickly, have faster attack rates, and do massive amounts of damage at range and in melee. The Dragoons use no weapons as they project blasts of Energy from their hands and fly. The Surgeons here not only do area-of-effect heal, but also have an area-of-effect Fortitude that significantly increases the entire group's defensive and offensive capabilities.

Tactics: When engaging any group of Nemesis, it is imperative to properly identify every single target in the group, including scanning the rooftops for Snipers. Wading into a group of Nemesis is an extremely deadly proposition, as the initial volley on the Hero that draws aggro can be in multiples of thousands of hit points in damage taunting, pulling and crowd control must be used. Surgeons should be removed first, then the group should be attacked from the top down, so Lance over Armiger,

Fusilier over Carabineir, etc. No villain faction is capable of delivering more damage, in a short time, as a group, than Nemesis. Groups that exercise poor crowd control vs. Nemesis will soon be making a team visit to the hospital.

CHASSEUR (30-32), ARMIGER (33-35), LANCER (36-38)

Minion   **Levels 30-38**

Although Nemesis likes to dress his soldiers in 19th century style, their weaponry is decidedly modern. Most infantrymen attach their bayonets to special assault rifles that outperform all modern equivalents.

Bayonet. High Lethal
Nemesis Rifle. Moderate Lethal, moderate range
Resists. Fear, Confusion

SURGEONS-CHASSEUR (30-32), ARMIGER (33-35), LANCER (36-38)

Minion   **Levels 30-38**

The Battle Surgeons are charged with the vital duty of getting wounded soldiers back into the fight as quickly as possible. Most Nemesis officers frown upon those who refuse to fight again; courage in the face of danger is highly valued in the Nemesis army ranks.

Bayonet. High Lethal

Nemesis Rifle. Moderate Lethal, moderate range

Triage. Heal other + resists to Stun, Hold, Sleep, Immobilize, Confusion, & Fear

Resists. Fear, Confusion

CARABINEIR (30·32), FUSILIER (33·35), GRENADIER (36·38)

Minion	Levels 30-38

The Nemesis army's main support weapon is the storm rifle, a long barreled weapon with a bayonet affixed to the end. It fires compact shells that carry a tremendous punch, exploding with the force of a heavy grenade or rocket shell.

Bayonet. High Lethal

Storm Rifle. AoE sphere minor Smashing, Lethal, & Knockback

Resists. Fear, Confusion

COMETS·

LANCE CORPORAL (30·32), SUBALTERN (33·35), LANCE SGT (36·38), SERGEANT MAJOR (39·41), LIEUTENANT (42·44), CAPTAIN (45·47), COLONEL (48·50)

Sniper	Levels 30-50

At first glance, the Nemesis lance looks much like the spear from which it takes its name. Though it can be used as a spear, it's also a very powerful, accurate rifle. The Nemesis lance fires explosive rounds over long distances and requires great skill to use effectively.

Lance. Moderate Lethal

Lace Rifle. AoE sphere moderate Fire, Lethal, & Knockback, long range

Vengeance. PBAoE on death, ally buff

Resists. Fear, Confusion

LANCE CORPORAL (30·32), SUBALTERN (33·35), LANCE SGT (36·38), SERGEANT MAJOR (39·41), LIEUTENANT (42·44), CAPTAIN (45·47), COLONEL (48·50)

Lieutenant	Levels 30-50

Nemesis' officers are some of the best trained soldiers in the world, and they show amazing discipline and devotion to their master. They're armed with the Nemesis lance, a long rifle that can also operate effectively as a spear. Their skill with this weapon makes them deadly at any distance.

Lance. Moderate Lethal

Lace Rifle. AoE sphere moderate Fire, Lethal, & Knockback, long range

Vengeance. PBAoE sphere on death, ally buff

Resists. Fear, Confusion

CUIRASSEUR (42·44), HUSSAR (45·47), DRAGOON (48·50)

Minion	Levels 42-50

The elite troops of Nemesis' army have tremendous discipline and skill that allows them to stand fast in the face of danger. They carry a deadly weapon that melds a scorching flamethrower with a powerful Gatling gun, giving them all the firepower they need for any foe.

Knife. Moderate Lethal

Gatling Gun. Minor Lethal, moderate range

Flamethrower. AoE cone minor Fire, short range

Resists. Fear, Confusion

CHASSEUR (33·35), ARMIGER (36·38), LANCER (39·41)

Minion	Levels 33-41

Although Nemesis likes to dress his soldiers in 19th century style, their weaponry is decidedly modern. Most infantrymen attach their bayonets to special assault rifles that outperform all modern equivalents.

Bayonet. High Lethal

Nemesis Rifle. Moderate Lethal, moderate range

Resists. Fear, Confusion

SURGEONS·CHASSEUR (33·35), ARMIGER (36·38), LANCER (39·41)

Minion	Levels 33-41

The Battle Surgeons are charged with the vital duty of getting wounded soldiers back into the fight as quickly as possible. Most Nemesis officers frown upon those who refuse to fight again; courage in the face of danger is highly valued in the Nemesis army ranks.

Bayonet. High Lethal

Nemesis Rifle. Moderate Lethal, moderate range

Triage. Heal other + resists to Stun, Hold, Sleep, Immobilize, Confusion, & Fear

Resists. Fear, Confusion

CARABINEIR (33·35), FUSILIER (36·38), GRENADIER (39·41)

Minion	Levels 33-41

The Nemesis army's main support weapon is the storm rifle, a long barreled weapon with a bayonet affixed to the end. It fires compact shells that carry a

tremendous punch, exploding with the force of a heavy grenade or rocket shell.

Bayonet. High Lethal

Storm Rifle. AoE sphere minor Smashing, Lethal, & Knockback

Resists. Fear, Confusion

TIRAILLEUR SUBALTERN (33-35), LANCE SGT (39-41), SERGEANT MAJOR (39-41), LIEUTENANT (42-44), CAPTAIN (45-47), COLONEL (48-50)

Sniper   **Levels 33-50**

The main support weapon is the storm rifle, a long barreled weapon with a bayonet affixed to the end. This seemingly simple weapon is actually quite versatile. The Tiraailleurs have modified their weapons to fire poison gas grenades.

Bayonet. High Lethal

Gas Grenade. Create gas cloud

Storm Rifle. AoE sphere minor Smashing, Lethal, & Knockback

Resists. Fear, Confusion

SUBALTERN (33-35), LANCE SGT (39-41), SERGEANT MAJOR (39-41), LIEUTENANT (42-44), CAPTAIN (45-47), COLONEL (48-50)

Lieutenant   **Levels 33-50**

Nemesis' officers are some of the best trained soldiers in the world, and they show amazing discipline and devotion to their master. They're armed with the Nemesis lance, a long rifle that can also operate effectively as a spear. Their skill with this weapon makes them deadly at any distance.

Lance. Moderate Lethal

Lace Rifle. AoE sphere moderate Fire, Lethal, & Knockback, long range

Vengeance. PBAoE sphere on death, ally buff

Resists. Fear, Confusion

CUIRASSEUR (42-44), HUSSAR (45-47), DRAGOON (48-50)

Minion   **Levels 42-50**

The elite troops of Nemesis' army have tremendous discipline and skill that allows them to stand fast in the face of danger. They carry a deadly weapon that melds a scorching flamethrower with a powerful Gatling gun, giving them all the firepower they need for any foe.

Knife. Moderate Lethal

Gatling Gun. Minor Lethal, moderate range

Flamethrower. AoE cone minor Fire, short range

Resists. Fear, Confusion

JAEGER (39-50), GEWEHR JAEGER (41-50), WERFER JAEGER (43-50)

Minion   **Levels 39-50**

Jaegers take their name from the German word for 'hunter'. They're some of the strangest and most advanced combat robots to ever stalk the streets of Paragon City. Nemesis seems to have a limitless supply of these steam-powered killers, each armed with powerful ranged or melee weaponry.

Jaeger Gun. Minor Lethal, moderate range

Jaeger Cannon. AoE sphere moderate Smashing, Lethal, & Knockback, moderate range

Gas Grenade. Summon gas cloud, long range

Jaeger Saw. Minor Lethal

Jaeger Mace. Moderate Smashing & Stun

Resists. Sleep, Confusion, Fear, Stun, Psionic

Explode. PBAoE sphere moderate Lethal, Fire, & Knockback

WARHULK

Boss   **Levels 30-39**

The War Hulk is the largest and most powerful killing machine built by the Prussian Prince of Automatons. It's a veritable walking tank, armed with flamethrowers, storm cannons, and an impressively brutal power claw.

Pummel. High Lethal & Knockback

Storm Cannon. AoE sphere moderate Lethal, Smashing, & Knockback, moderate range

Flamethrower. AoE cone moderate Fire, short range

Resists. Confusion, Fear, Stun, Knockup, Knockback, Immobilize

Explode. PBAoE sphere moderate Lethal, Fire, Knockback

FAKE NEMESIS

Boss   **Levels 40-50**

No one alive has ever seen Nemesis' true face. He hides within his finely wrought armor, safe behind personal force fields and a variety of armaments. He has many such suits of armor, each of which is a robot in its own right, capable of acting — and killing — independently.

Fake Nemesis

Nemesis Staff. High Smashing & Stun

Staff Bolt. High Smashing, Knockback, Stun, very long range

Personal Force Field. Untouchable

Dispersion Bubble. Defense buff, all attacks

Protection Shield. Defense buff, all attacks

Resists. Fear, Confusion

Fake Nemesis

Nemesis Staff. High Smashing & Stun

Staff Bolt. High Smashing, Knockback, Stun, very long range

Personal Force Field. Untouchable

Dispersion Bubble. Defense buff, all attacks

Protection Shield. Defense buff, all attacks

Resists. Fear, Confusion

Resists Psionic, Sleep, Fear, Confusion Vulnerability. Cold

NEMESIS

ArchVillain   **Level 50**

Nemesis has had over 100 years to perfect his armor and his combat skills. He is a formidable, and wily, opponent.

Nemesis Staff. High Smashing & Stun

Staff Bolt. High Smashing, Knockback, Stun, very long range

Personal Force Field. Untouchable

Dispersion Bubble. Defense buff, all attacks

Protection Shield. Defense buff, all attacks

Resists. Fear, Confusion

Resists. Knockup, Knockback

NEMESIS GAS

Pet   **Levels**
1-50

This poisonous gas was once a part of Nemesis' plot to conquer America. Though his plan to poison several major cities was thwarted, he still keeps large quantities of the gas around to help tip battles in his favor.

AUTOMATONS

Minion   **Levels 33-42**

Perhaps it's the careful precision of every movement, or the way they perform the same tasks over and over, but something about this seemingly normal citizen doesn't look quite right. In fact, they seem almost mechanical.

Soldier Automaton

Bayonet. High Lethal

Nemesis Rifle. Moderate Lethal, moderate range

Resists. Fear, Confusion

Support Automaton

Bayonet. High Lethal

Storm Rifle. AoE sphere minor Smashing, Lethal, & Knockback

Resists. Fear, Confusion

Elite Automaton

Knife. Moderate Lethal

Gatling Gun. Minor Lethal, moderate range

Flamethrower. AoE cone minor Fire, short range

Resists. Fear, Confusion

Lieutenant Automaton

Lieutenant   **Levels 33-42**

Lance. Moderate Lethal

Lace Rifle. AoE sphere moderate Fire, Lethal, & Knockback, long range

Vengeance. PBAoE sphere on death, ally buff

Resists. Fear, Confusion

WARHULK

Boss   **Levels 33-42**

The War Hulk is the largest and most powerful killing machine built by the Prussian Prince of Automatons. It's a veritable walking tank, armed with flamethrowers, storm cannons, and an impressively brutal power claw.

Pummel. High Lethal & Knockback

Storm Cannon. AoE sphere moderate Lethal, Smashing, & Knockback, moderate range

Flamethrower. AoE cone moderate Fire, short range

Resists. Confusion, Fear, Stun, Knockup, Knockback, Immobilize

Explode. PBAoE sphere moderate Lethal, Fire, Knockback

VILLAINS

221

OUTCASTS

Locations: Outcasts area in Steel Canyon and Boomtown. Mission doors for them can be generated anywhere.

Types: There are only two types of Outcasts, Thugs and Powered villains.

The typical Outcasts are exactly like the Skulls or Hellions, wielding bats, hammers, knives, pistols, shotguns, or machine guns, and do significantly more melee damage than ranged. The exact same tactics used to fight those other groups can be used against them.

The Powered Outcasts are the Shockers, the Infernos, and the Bricks. As the names imply, Shockers use electric blast powers and fly, Infernos use Fire blast powers, and Bricks use stone powers. The Shockers do equal ranged and melee damage and are extremely difficult to shake once they decide to pursue. The Inferno do not fly, but their damage is similar to the Shockers. The Bricks do *major* melee damage, combined with Stun and Knockback, and reasonable ranged.

Outcast bosses are simply more powerful powered villains with the name "Lead" stuck at the beginning of their name: Lead Shocker, Lead Inferno, Lead Brick. As would be expected, their damage and abilities are

significantly increased over their non-boss counterparts.

Tactics: Outcast bosses are by far the greatest threat, with the Bricks being the most important target, as they are capable of doing as much damage as any two other Outcasts combined. Slugging toe-to-toe with a Lead Brick is generally not advised, and the best tactics to use involve keeping the target off its feet and/or Disoriented to prevent it from quickly dispatching any Hero engaged with it. Beyond that, the powered villains are the next target and the minions are last, with no special tactics needed.

OUTCAST MINIONS
Minion   **Levels 11-20**

Unlike the higher ranked members of the Outcasts, these thugs seldom have elemental powers strong enough to warm their morning coffee. They're limited to hand weapons and firearms, like any other common gangster.

Outcast Bruiser

Brawl. Moderate Smashing
Boxing. Moderate Smashing & Stun
Heavy Revolver. High Lethal & Knockback, moderate range

Outcast Slugger

Baseball Bat. High Smashing
Heavy Revolver. High Lethal & Knockback, moderate range

Outcast Slammer

Sledgehammer. High Smashing & Knockback
Heavy Revolver. High Lethal & Knockback, moderate range

Outcast Buckshot
Minion

Shotgun. AoE cone moderate Lethal & Knockback, short range

Outcast Gunner

Submachine Gun. Moderate Lethal & Defense debuff, moderate range

SHOCKER
Lieutenant   **Levels 11-13**

Masters of the air, the Shockers can fly and call forth blasts of lightning. They are without a doubt the flashiest of the Outcasts, and enjoy flamboyant displays of their power.

Boxing. Moderate Smashing & Stun
Knife. Moderate Lethal
Lightning Bolt. High Energy & Endurance drain
O2 Boost. Self heal, resist Stun, Immobilize, Confusion, Sleep
Hurricane. PBAoE sphere, Accuracy debuff, Knockback
Flight

LEAD SHOCKER
Boss   **Levels 11-13**

Experienced Shockers are masters of their chosen element. They soar with the expertise of veteran flyers and can make electricity dance at their commands. They're especially fond of entrapping their rivals in fields of lightning.

Boxing. Moderate Smashing & Stun
Knife. Moderate Lethal
Lightning Bolt. High Energy & Endurance drain
Lightning Field. PBAoE sphere minor Energy & Endurance drain
Lightning Storm. Summon lightning storm
Flight

SCORCHER

Lieutenant   **Levels 19-20**

Rivals to the title of the city's premiere arsonists, these Outcasts can conjure up a variety of flame-based attacks to scorch their enemies. Manipulating fire requires concentration and determination, two traits common in all Scorchers.

Scorch. Moderate Fire
Incinerate. Minor Fire
Flares. Moderate Fire, moderate range
Fireball. AoE sphere, moderate Fire & Smashing, moderate range
Fire Blast. Minor Fire, moderate range

LEAD SCORCHER

Boss   **Levels 19-20**

These are the pinnacle pyros of the Outcasts, masters of the element of Fire. They can perform a myriad of fiery marvels, one of the flashiest of which is the creation of Fire Imps — malevolent humanoids of pure Fire who pounce upon the Scorchers' foes.

Scorch. Moderate Fire
Incinerate. Minor Fire
Ring of Fire. Immobilize, minor Fire, moderate range
Flashfire. AoE sphere minor Fire & Stun, moderate range
Fire Imps. Summon Imps
Resists. Fire, Cold
Fire Shield. Resists Smashing, Lethal, Fire, Cold
Blazing Aura. PBAoE minor Fire

FREEZER

Lieutenant   **Levels 17-18**

Not just an appliance anymore, the Freezers have mastery over Cold and ice. As their name suggests, they're cool as ice and calm under pressure, even as they cast bolts of jagged ice that pierce flesh and bone alike.

Frost. AoE cone, minor Cold, very short range
Frozen Fists. moderate Cold, Smashing, & Slow
Ice Bolt. Moderate Cold, Smashing, & Slow
Frost Breath. AoE cone, moderate Cold & Slow, short range
Ice Armor. Defense buff Smashing & Lethal, resist Cold

LEAD FREEZER

Boss   **Levels 17-18**

The top-dog Freezers are constantly surrounded by an area of Cold, even on the hottest summer's day. They can create a host of different Cold-based effects, from frost armor for themselves to freezing prisons for their foes.

Shiver. AoE cone, Slow, moderate range
Ice Blast. Moderate Smashing, Cold, & Slow, moderate range
Freezing Touch. Hold, minor Cold
Hoarfrost. Resist Cold, Smashing, Lethal & Fire
Chilling Embrace. PBAoE sphere Slow
Levels   17,18

BRICK

Lieutenant   **Levels 14-16**

The Bricks are one with the Earth, although not in a hippie kind of way. Instead they use stone and rock to Smash their rivals, hurling boulders or conjuring up mallets with which to maul anyone who gets in their way.

Stone Fist. Moderate Smashing & Stun
Rock Armor. Defense buff Smashing & Lethal
Fault. AoE sphere Knockup & Stun, short range
Hurl Boulder. High Smashing, Knockback, short range

LEAD BRICK

Boss   **Levels 14-16**

The biggest, baddest, Bricks on the block have complete control over the earth beneath their feet. They can turn soil into quicksand, cause stalagmites to erupt at the snap of a finger and generally make life miserable for anyone they don't like who happens to be standing on the ground.

Stone Prison. Immobilize, Defense debuff, moderate range
Stone Mallet. High Smashing & Knockback
Stalagmites. Minor Lethal & Stun, moderate range
Quicksand. Summon Quicksand
Earth's Embrace. Self-heal
Mud Pots. Immobilize

PRISONERS

Locations: Brickstown.

Types: The Prisoners of the Zig have their powers suppressed, so while they might be formidably tough, they have to rely on brute strength in combat. Occasionally a lieutenant or boss prisoner will show up, but there's not much difference between them and the grunts, the main thing being that the higher-ranking prisoners get to carry guns, giving them some ranged combat potential.

Tactics: Basic street-fight tactics are all you need for these bruisers. Just remember to con significant groups of Prisoners before wading in, to make sure that there's not a boss in there waiting to give you an unpleasant surprise.

PRISONER
Minion   **Levels 30-38**

The Zigursky Prison, or 'Zig' as it's known on the street, houses the most dangerous criminals in Paragon City. Despite the Zig's advanced security systems, a few hardened criminals occasionally escape. With nothing but time on their hands, these cons stop at nothing to win their freedom.

Brawl. Moderate Smashing
 or
Knife. Moderate Lethal
or
Pipe. Moderate Smashing
Rock. Moderate Smashing

JOHNNY
Lieutenant   **Levels 30-38**

Even prisoners have their hierarchies. Some convicts rise to leadership positions because of their ruthlessness and ferocity.

Revolver. High Lethal, short range

TRASH
Boss   **Levels 30-38**

In some jailbreaks, the toughest of the prisoners manage to overpower the Zig's security guards and grab their weapons.

Shotgun. Moderate Lethal & Knockback, short range
or
Submachine Gun. Minor Lethal & Defense debuff, moderate range

THE LOST

Locations: The Lost can be found in significant numbers in Perez Park and Skyway City, as well as in the recesses of Terra Volta and Kings Row.

Types: The Lost get less human as they get more powerful. There's no real tactical difference between the low-level Minion Scavengers and the more bizarre-looking mutates, you'll just meet them at different security levels.

Headsmen Lieutenants are given access to Rikti technology, so they do formidable hand-to-hand damage with their enormous Rikti blades, as well as having some Stun and Knockback capability with their Energy weapons.

The Lost become a much more significant threat, however, when you start dealing with the Aberrants (low-level bosses) and Anathema (high-level lieutenants). These Lost have significant Psionic powers (you know, the kind virtually no Hero has any significant resistance to), and can easily leave you dazed or asleep at a crucial moment.

Aberrants and Anathema are only the warm-up act, however, for the high-level Pariah bosses. These offer the same sort of Psionic threat as the previous threats, but at a much more dangerous level.

Tactics: Take out Pariahs, Anathema or Aberrants first. Try to keep them too off-balance to use their powers and give them as little time as possible to make you into a stationary target for the grunts. Try to avoid taking on multiple Psionic bosses, especially when solo, even if they con out favorably. Once the Psionic villains are out, take out the Headsmen (with their superior damage potential), then the grunts.

Even at low level, Lost tend to spawn in large groups, almost always with a boss present. Anything you can do for crowd control will be a sorely needed edge, from taunting stragglers away from the group to advanced mez and root powers.

SCROUNGERS
Minion   **Levels 5-19**

Despite their bedraggled appearance, Scroungers are actually very dangerous opponents. The Lost are organized much like a street gang or organized crime syndicate, though their weapons are often of surprisingly good quality.

Scrounger Brawler

Brawl. Moderate Smashing
Revolver. High Lethal, short range

Scrounger Slicer

Knife. Moderate Lethal
Revolver. High Lethal, short range

Scrounger Chopper

Fireman Axe. High Lethal & Defense debuff
Revolver. High Lethal, short range

Scrounger Slugger

Baseball Bat. High Smashing
Revolver. High Lethal, short range

Scrounger Slammer

Sledgehammer. High Smashing & Knockback
Revolver. High Lethal, short range

Scrounger Buckshot

Shotgun. AoE cone, moderate Lethal & Knockback, short range

Scrounger Gunner

Submachine Gun. Minor Lethal & Defense debuff, moderate range

MUTATIONS
Minion   **Levels 20-29**

After a few months in the service of the Lost, members begin to mutate, becoming distorted, grotesque looking men. Although they still use the same weapons as the Scroungers, their mutations give them increased strength and resilience, making them much more dangerous.

Mutate Brawler

Brawl. Moderate Smashing
Revolver. High Lethal, short range+C2087

Mutate Slicer

Knife. Moderate Lethal
Revolver. High Lethal, short range+C2087

Mutate Slugger

Baseball Bat. High Smashing
Revolver. High Lethal, short range+C2087

Mutate Slammer

Sledgehammer. High Smashing & Knockback
Revolver. High Lethal, short range+C2087

Mutate Chopper

Fireman Axe. High Lethal & Defense debuff

Revolver. High Lethal, short range+C2087

Mutate Buckshot

Shotgun. AoE cone, moderate Lethal & Knockback, short range

Mutate Gunner

Submachine Gun. Minor Lethal & Defense debuff, moderate range

HEADSMEN

| Lieutenant | Levels 5-19 |

Mutates are fearsome, dedicated fighters, and their leaders, the Headmen, prefer to by in the thick of the fighting. Headmen have more advanced mutations than their followers, and they're not afraid to charge into combat with anyone who stands in their path.

Headman Swordsman

Rikti Sword. High Lethal & Stun
Revolver. High Lethal, short range+C2087

Headman Blaster

Rikti Pistol. Moderate Energy & Stun, moderate range

Headman Rifleman

Rikti Rifle. High Energy, Knockback & Stun, moderate range

ANATHEMA

| Lieutenant | Levels 20-29 |

The Anathema are members of the Lost who have undergone substantial mutation, becoming huge creatures that are barely recognizable as humans. They engage their foes with an unnatural brutality, using what-

ever weaponry they can find.

Brawl. Moderate Smashing
Rikti Sword. High Lethal & Stun
Mental Blast. Moderate Psionic & Slow, long range
Psychic Scream. AoE cone moderate Psionic & Slow, moderate range
Telekinetic blast. Moderate Smashing, Psionic, & Knockback, long range
Subdue. High Psionic & Immobilize, long range
Will Domination. High Psionic & Sleep, long range
Resists. Sleep, Hold, Stun, Knockup, Knockback

ABERRANTS

| Boss | Levels 5-19 |

The leaders of the Anathema have fully mutated minds that allow them to project their indomitable will onto others. They can use these powers to Immobilize, hypnotize, or even dominate lesser wills.

Aberrant Rector

The Rectors are the masters of one-on-one conversions; their persuasive abilities work best on a single target.

Brawl. Moderate Smashing
Rikti Sword. High Lethal & Stun
Mental Blast. Moderate Psionic & Slow, long range
Mesmerize. Moderate Psionic & Sleep, long range
Dominate. Hold, moderate range
Resists. Sleep, Hold, Stun, Knockup, Knockback

Aberrant Eremite

The Eremites are the preachers of the Lost. Their psychic abilities allow them to entrance crowds of possible converts.

Brawl. Moderate Smashing
Rikti Sword. High Lethal & Stun
Mental Blast. Moderate Psionic & Slow, long range
Mass Hypnosis. AoE sphere, Sleep, moderate range
Total Domination. AoE sphere, Immobilize, moderate range
Resists. Sleep, Hold, Stun, Knockup, Knockback

PARIAHS

| Boss | Levels 20-29 |

The most fully mutated Lost, the Pariahs no longer bear any resemblance to the humans they once were. They've become true monsters, although it's not their claws you should Fear — it's their prodigious psychic powers, which can rend an opponent's mind faster than any claw can tear flesh.

Pariah Prelate

Brawl. Moderate Smashing
Rikti Sword. High Lethal & Stun
Mental Blast. Moderate Psionic & Slow, long range
Mesmerize. Moderate Psionic & Sleep, long range
Dominate. Hold, moderate range
Resists. Sleep, Hold, Stun, Knockup, Knockback

Pariah Anchorite

Brawl. Moderate Smashing
Rikti Sword. High Lethal & Stun
Mental Blast. Moderate Psionic & Slow, long range
Mass Hypnosis. AoE sphere, Sleep, moderate range
Total Domination. AoE sphere, Immobilize, moderate range
Resists. Sleep, Hold, Stun, Knockup, Knockback

RIKTI

Locations: True Rikti can be found in Founders' Falls and Crey's Folly.

Types: The four types of Rikti are Monkeys, Drones, Soldiers and Mentalists.

Monkeys are annoying little thugs that run in packs and can quickly over-run a careful who is not being careful. They have no ranged capability and are strictly melee, but very fast.

Drones are flying robots with ranged energy attacks and massive defenses, making them extremely difficult to hit, but once you connect they are rather fragile.

Soldiers are the line infantry of the Rikti forces and wield large Rikti blades and stun rifles for ranged attacks.

Mentalists use a wide range of Psionic powers to mesmerize,

Sleep, Stun, Hold, Disorient and seriously damage their foes.

Tactics:
Mentalists must always be the primary target, both because few Heroes are resistant to the large amount of Psionic damage they are capable of delivering, but also because they can and will lock down Heroes, leaving the defenseless (active defenses down), and at the mercy of the rest of the Rikti forces. After that, go down the ranks, removing the greater threats in the standard manner.

RIKTI MONKEY (30-33), WILD RIKTI MONKEY (34-37), VICIOUS RIKTI MONKEY (38-50)
Small   **Levels 30-50**

Often referred to as ruin monkeys, these horrible creatures were created by the Rikti, then let loose in the city to wreak

havoc. They roam in packs and pounce with tremendous speed and ferocity. Unfortunately, the Rikti seem to have a never-ending supply of them.

Superleap
Monkey Brawl. Moderate Smashing
Gas. Summon Monkey Gas

DRONE (30-33), IMPROVED DRONE (34-37), ADVANCED DRONE (38-50)
Minion   **Levels 30-50**

During the Rikti War these flying Drones swarmed all over the city's skies. Today these machines still sweep through the air with some frequency. Their quick evasive maneuvering and powerful Energy cannon make them a constant menace.

Drone Blast. High Energy, Knockback, moderate range
Flight
Immune. Sleep, Fear
Resist. Psionic
Defense Buff vs All melee and ranged
Vulnerability. Smashing, Lethal, Fire, Cold, Energy, Negative Energy

HEADMAN
Lieutenant   **Levels 31-40**

Rikti Sword. High Lethal & Stun
Rikti Rifle. High Energy, Knockback, & Stun, moderate range

VILLAINS

RIKTI MINIONS

The Rikti have come to stand for everything humans hate and fear in the universe. Their unprovoked invasion of Earth has left much of the planet traumatized and angry. Even out of their battle armor, their high-tech weaponry makes Rikti dangerous opponents.

Infantry
Minion   **Levels 30-39**

Rikti Sword. High Lethal & Stun
Rikti Pistol. High Energy & Stun, moderate range

Conscript
Minion   **Levels 40-50**

Rikti Sword. High Lethal & Stun
Rikti Rifle. High Energy, Knockback, & Stun, moderate range

Guardian
Minion   **Levels 30-50**

Rikti Pistol. High Energy & Stun, moderate range
Radiation Emission. Self-heal
Accelerate Metabolism. PBAoE sphere, buff all damage, resist Hold, Stun, Sleep, Immobilize
Protection Shield. Buff Defense all attacks

Communications Officer
Minion   **Levels 30-50**

Rikti Pistol. High Energy & Stun, moderate range
Transponder

RIKTI CHIEFS

The Rikti battle armor is more advanced than any armor found on Earth. It offers the alien invaders protection from most normal kinds of physical attack. Armed with powerful Energy weapons, these armored soldiers continue to pose a deadly threat to humans everywhere.

Headman Gunman
Lieutenant   **Levels 30-39**

Rikti Rifle. High Energy, Knockback, Stun, moderate range
Resist. Sleep, Smashing, Lethal, Energy
Teleport
Superleap

Chief Soldier
Boss   **Levels 30-50**

Greater Rikti Sword. High Lethal & Stun
Rikti Rifle. High Energy, Knockback, & Stun, moderate range
Resist. Sleep, Smashing, Lethal, Energy

Chief Mentalist
Boss   **Levels 30-39**

Greater Rikti Sword. High Lethal & Stun
Mental Blast. Moderate Psionic & Slow, long range
Mesmerize. Moderate Psionic, Sleep, long range
Dominate. Hold, moderate range
Resist. Sleep & Confusion

Chief Mentalist
Lieutenant   **Levels 40-50**

Greater Rikti Sword. High Lethal & Stun
Mental Blast. Moderate Psionic & Slow, long range
Mesmerize. Moderate Psionic, Sleep, long range
Dominate. Hold, moderate range
Resist. Sleep & Confusion

Chief Mesmerist
Boss   **Levels 40-50**

Rikti Sword. High Lethal & Stun
Mental Blast. Moderate Psionic, Slow, long range
Mass Hypnosis. AoE sphere Sleep, moderate range
Total Domination. AoE sphere Hold, moderate range
Resist. Sleep & Confusion

PORTAL
Pet   **Levels 1-50**

This Rikti Communications Officer can open a portal to bring more Rikti soldiers to Earth. It must be destroyed!

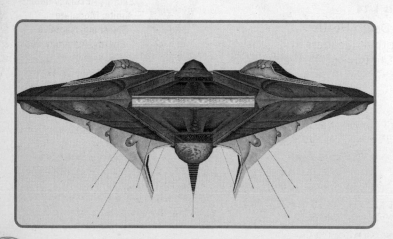

SKULLS

Locations: Kings Row, Perez Park.

Types: Minions are Gravediggers, and they come in all the usual armament varieties (Brawler, Slugger, Slicer, Slammer, Chopper).

Lieutenants are Death's Heads, and they can be distinguished from the minions by the fact that they use firearms — either the shotgun-using Buckshots, or the Gunners, who wield an SMG.

Bosses are Bone Daddies, and they fight with a wide variety of negative energy attacks.

A few unique Skull bosses appear in door missions.

Tactics: The tactics for taking on Skulls are pretty much the same as those for Hellions (see p. 215).

GRAVEDIGGERS
Minion   **Levels 1-14**

The Skulls worship death in a very personal, creepy way. The Gravediggers are the gang's foot soldiers — wannabes who must prove their skill with knives and guns before they (literally) earn their bones.

Gravedigger Brawler

Brawl. Moderate Smashing
Revolver. High Lethal, short range
Resists. Negative Energy
Vulnerable. Energy

Gravedigger Slicer

Knife. Moderate Lethal
Revolver. High Lethal, short range
Resists. Negative Energy
Vulnerable. Energy

Gravedigger Slugger

Baseball Bat. High Smashing
Revolver. High Lethal, short range
Resists. Negative Energy
Vulnerable. Energy

Gravedigger Slammer

Sledgehammer. High Smashing & Knockback
Revolver. High Lethal, short range
Resists. Negative Energy
Vulnerable. Energy

Gravedigger Chopper

Fireman Axe. High Lethal & Defense debuff
Revolver. High Lethal, short range
Resists. Negative Energy
Vulnerable. Energy

DEATH HEADS
Lieutenant
Levels 1-14

The Death Heads are proven leaders in the Skulls — utter nihilists who worship death in the hopes of eventually defying it. These bloodthirsty, Cold-blooded killers are armed to the teeth and resistant to any kind of Negative Energy attacks.

Death Head Buckshot

Shotgun. AoE cone moderate Lethal & Knockback, short range
Resists. Negative Energy
Vulnerable. Energy

Death Head Gunner

Submachine Gun. Minor Lethal & Defense debuff, moderate range
Resists. Negative Energy
Vulnerable. Energy

BONE DADDY
Boss   **Levels 1-14**

The Skulls' leaders, the Bone Daddies, have become living embodiments of the power of death. They can literally suck the life out of a foe to feed their own spirits. They can also focus the pure darkness of the netherworld into physical attacks that cause massive damage.

Brawl. Moderate Smashing
Revolver. High Lethal, short range
Resists. Negative Energy
Vulnerable. Energy
Shadow Punch. Moderate Smashing, Negative Energy, Accuracy debuff
Smite. Moderate Smashing, Negative Energy, Accuracy debuff
Shadow Maul. Moderate Negative Energy, Smashing, Accuracy debuff
Siphon Life. Moderate Negative Energy & self heal
Gloom. Moderate Negative Energy & Accuracy debuff, moderate range
Dark Blast. Moderate Negative Energy & Accuracy debuff, long range

VILLAINS

SKY RAIDERS

Locations: Terra Volta, with some showing up in Independence Port. Mission doors for them can be generated anywhere.

Types: The Sky Raiders are a varied group, with many different types of units.

Raiders are the bulk of the force, and use a variety of weapons — from machine guns and assault rifles to flamethrowers and missile launchers — for ranged attacks, and brawling for melee. Porters are raiders that can teleport. Engineers can place a shield generator that puts up a dispersion field to add to the defense of every Raider within it. Additionally, the Lieutenants (Captains) use a vicious machete that delivers a great deal of Lethal damage.

Wing Raiders are as above, but also have the ability to hover and fly as needed.

Sky Skiffs are Raider bosses sitting in large flying machines equipped with rocket launchers.

Jump Bot Incinerators are bosses that use flamethrowers and brawling.

On the whole, Sky Raiders have a balance between ranged and melee damage, with most minions doing more ranged than melee, and the Lieutenants doing more melee than ranged.

Tactics: Sky Raiders prefer to engage at range, but are not limited to range-only attacks and are fully capable of delivering melee damage, as well. The best tactic to use against them is to eliminate the Incinerators first, as they deliver damage in a cone and deliver the most damage overall against you. After that, the typical strategy of removing Bosses and Lieutenants first is appropriate.

JUMP BOTS

Boss   **Levels 20-29**

Jump Bots are a recent addition to the mercenary Sky Raiders' arsenal. Their effectiveness in combat has allowed the Raiders to greatly expand operations. Well armed and armored, the Jump Bots earned their name from their leaping ability, which allows them tremendous maneuverability.

Jump Bot Incinerator

Brawl. Moderate Smashing
Flamethrower. AoE cone minor Fire
Superleap
Resists. Stun, Psionic
Immune. Sleep & Fear
Vulnerability. Energy
Explode. PBAoE moderate Fire, Lethal, & Knockback

Assault Jump Bot

Brawl. Moderate Smashing
Adv Submachine Gun. Minor Lethal, Defense debuff, very long range
Superleap

Resists. Stun, Psionic
Immune. Sleep & Fear
Vulnerability. Energy
Explode. PBAoE moderate Fire, Lethal, & Knockback

RAIDERS

Minion   **Levels 20-25**

The basic Sky Raider infantrymen, Assault Raiders are usually found inside buildings where flight packs wouldn't be an asset. They are typically armed with submachine guns, flamethrowers, or other weapons suitable for fighting in confined spaces.

Assault Raider

Brawl. Moderate Smashing
Machete. High Lethal & Slow
Adv Submachine Gun. Minor Lethal, Defense debuff, very long range

Inferno Raider

Brawl. Moderate Smashing
Machete. High Lethal & Slow
Flamethrower. AoE cone minor Fire

RAIDER ENGINEER

Minion   **Levels 20-29**

Sky Raider Engineers can deploy a hovering force field generator to protect nearby troops. They are typically armed with submachine guns, flamethrowers, or other weapons suitable for fighting in confined spaces.

Brawl. Moderate Smashing
Machete. High Lethal & Slow
Adv Submachine Gun. Minor Lethal, Defense debuff, very long range
Summon Generator

WING RAIDER

Minion   **Levels 23-29**

The iconic soldiers of this mercenary outfit, the Wing Raiders wear advanced flight packs that allow them to soar through the air with the speed and grace of a fighter plane. They're armed with advanced infantry weapons and know how to use them with a professional soldier's effectiveness.

Brawl. Moderate Smashing
Machete. High Lethal & Slow
Adv Assault Rifle. High Lethal & Knockback, very long range
Flight

PORTER

Minion   **Levels 23-29**

Because they have a relatively small number of men, the Sky Raiders rely on speed and maneuverability to win battles. No one is faster than the Porters, special forces who can teleport directly into or out of battle, allowing them to strike where the enemy's weakest and retreat from dire situations.

Brawl. Moderate Smashing
Machete. High Lethal & Slow
Adv Submachine Gun. Minor Lethal, Defense debuff, very long range
  or
Adv Assault Rifle. High Lethal & Knockback, very long range
Teleport

OFFICERS

Lieutenant   **Levels 20-29**

The Sky Raiders officer corps consists of combat veterans who fought both before and during the Rikti War. They've become disenchanted with the government and its current reliance on super-powered Heroes, but they haven't lost any of their military ability or discipline.

Captain

Brawl. Moderate Smashing
Machete. High Lethal & Slow
Adv Assault Rifle. High Lethal & Knockback, very long range
Summon Generator

Wing Raider Officer

Brawl. Moderate Smashing
Machete. High Lethal & Slow
Flamethrower. AoE cone minor Fire
Flight

SKY SKIFF

Boss   **Levels 20-29**

The Sky Skiffs are light aircraft whose small size belies their impact on the battlefield. Among the most advanced flying machines ever made, these vehicles are armed with banks of powerful missiles that allow the Sky Raiders to maintain air superiority from a great distance.

Missile Launcher. AoE sphere moderate Smashing, Lethal, Knockback, long range
Flight

DURAY

ArchVillain   **Level 25**

Colonel Virgil Duray has had a long time to culture his hatred for the Heroes he holds responsible for the Rikti War. In combat with Heroes, he won't give an inch.

Resists. Knockback, Knockup, Fear, Stun, Sleep, confused
Personal Force Field. Untouchable

Flamethrower. AoE cone Moderate Fire, moderate range
Punch. Moderate Smashing & Knockback
Flight

FORCE FIELD GENERATOR

Pet   **Levels 1-50**

The Sky Raiders have created effective force field generators to protect their fast moving troops.

Buff Defenses. Smashing, Lethal, Fire, Cold, Energy, Negative Energy, Stun, Immobilize
Resists. Sleep, Fear, taunt
Flight
Resists. Stun, Psionic
Immune. Sleep & Fear
Vulnerability. Energy
Explode. PBAoE moderate Fire, Lethal, & Knockback

VILLAINS

TROLLS

Locations: The Trolls' home is the alleys and street corners of the Skyway, though they can be found in Boomtown, Steel Canyon and Kings Row.

Types: There's only one type of Troll, the thug.

All Trolls carry the standard thug weapons, like pistols, shot guns and machine guns. The lieutenants, the Gardvord, also have a superstrength power set and are quite a frightening change from the standard thug, as they slam haymakers on unsuspecting Heroes. Bosses are Ogres and Calibans, who have the same power sets as the Gardvord.

Tactics: Take out the bosses, then the lieutenants, or they will put most of your Heroes on the pavement with their Knockdown attacks. Then clean up the rest.

TROLLKIN
Minion   **Levels 8-20**

The Trolls have abused their bodies with a particularly dangerous drug called Superadine. It has begun to literally turn them into monsters. These low ranking gang members aren't showing many signs of changing, but that doesn't stop them from acting like beasts.

Trollkin Bruiser

Boxing. Moderate Smashing & Stun
Kick. Moderate Smashing & Knockback
Brawl. Moderate Smashing
Heavy Revolver. High Lethal & Knockback, moderate range

Trollkin Buckshot

Shotgun. AoE cone moderate Lethal & Knockback, short range

Trollkin Gunner

Submachine Gun. Minor Lethal & Defense debuff, moderate range

GARDVORD
Lieutenant   **Levels 8-20**

Veteran Trolls have been around long enough to feel some positive effects from their body-changing drugs. Like the trolls of legend, they have become exceptionally fast healers, making them very difficult to kill.

Punch. Moderate Smashing & Knockback
Haymaker. High Smashing & Knockback
Assault Rifle. Minor Lethal, Defense debuff, long range
Regeneration
Integration. Resist Knockback, Knockup, Stun, Hold, Immobilize, Sleep

OGRE AND CALIBAN
Boss   **Levels 8-20**

The leaders of the Trolls have developed truly superhuman abilities. Not only do they heal fast and resist a variety of damage types, they're also capable of feats of tremendous strength.

As a result, they have no need for weapons of any kind.

Ogre

Tremor. PBAoE moderate Smashing & Knockback
Fault. AoE sphere moderate Knockup & Stun, short range
Hurl Boulder. High Smashing & Knockback, moderate range
Regeneration
Integration. Resist Knockback, Knockup, Stun, Hold, Immobilize, Sleep

Caliban

Punch. Moderate Smashing & Knockback
Haymaker. High Smashing & Knockback
Invincibility. Defense buff Smashing, Lethal, Fire, Cold, Energy, Negative Energy
Regeneration
Integration. Resist Knockback, Knockup, Stun, Hold, Immobilize, Sleep

TSOO

Locations: The Tsoo are located primarily on Talos Island and in Independence Port, with a small presence in Dark Astoria and Steel Canyon. Mission doors for them may be generated anywhere.

Types: There are five basic types of Tsoo: Enforcers, Sorcerers, Ink Men, Ancestor Spirits and Bosses.

Enforcers are katana- or bow-wielding Scrappers with a ranged shiruken attack that is much smaller than their melee.

Sorcerers use teleportation to stay out of range, pop back to heal their allies, use maelstrom and paralyze to knock back or freeze Heroes, and have an effective melee attack. These need to be the highest priority, even over the bosses, because two or more Sorcerers can fully heal their allies, then paralyze the Heroes before teleporting away, prolonging the combat unnecessarily.

Ink Men (Yellow, Green and Red) have minimal ranged damage capabilities, but all can mez, Sleep and Disorient both at range and via melee. Yellow Ink Men use Kama and brawling, while Green and Red Ink Men use energy melee, all for significant damage on top of the debilitating effects. In addition, Red Ink Men use enhanced speed and leaping and will pursue a fleeing Hero for great distances.

Ancestor Spirits are flying, super-strength-using Tankers, who regularly employ haymaker and hand-clap to knock down and Stun Heroes, as well as delivering significant amounts of melee damage. They have no known ranged attack, but their ability to fly makes them difficult to keep at range and pursue when they flee.

Tsoo bosses are wild cards with a variety of powers and capabilities from pretty much every possible power se, including storm control, fire control, lightning melee and a plethora of Disorienting and Stunning powers and massive melee attacks. Their ranged damage is always far less than their melee, though many use ranged energy attacks of some form. Some have Stun effects attached, so any Tsoo boss should be approached warily.

Tactics: When engaging the Tsoo, it is imperative to properly identify every target in the group, because many of the bosses look like sorcerers or enforcers, and failing to properly identify them before engaging a group can lead to a rude awakening in the local hospital. Sorcerers should be the primary target, but don't pursue them when they teleport. Attempt to Disorient and defeat them as fast as possible, but if one teleports away simply switch targets to any other opponent,

damage it, and the Sorcerer will instantly return to heal it. Failure to remove the Sorcerers from the equation can unnecessarily lengthen the combat and put you or your team at greater risk.

After that, the bosses and Ink Men need to be dealt with, usually with about equal priority, because of their combined melee damage and incapacitating attacks. Once they are removed, the rest of the opponents are simple melee and can be dispatched in no particular order.

PHA

Minion	Levels 15-22

The Pha, or Enforcers, are the foot soldiers of the Tsoo. They have yet to receive magical tattoos, and so must rely on their own strength and their weaponry. They train constantly and are especially deadly in close combat situations.

Eagle Enforcer, Tiger Enforcer, Serpent Enforcer, Dragon Enforcer, Crane Enforcer

Kama. Moderate Lethal & Accuracy debuff
Claws. Moderate Lethal
Sai. Moderate Lethal & Accuracy debuff
Katana. High Lethal & Defense debuff
Brawl. Moderate Smashing
Shuriken. Moderate Lethal, short range
Caltrops
Bow. High Lethal, moderate range
Superleap

VILLAINS

EAGLE, SERPENT, TIGER AND DRAGON YELLOW INK MEN

Minion	Levels 19-22

The enchanted inks used in Tsoo tattoos grant these soldiers special powers. The yellow ink enhances the Tsoo's agility and dexterity, allowing him to strike with superhuman Accuracy and Speed. Yellow Ink Men are formidable martial artists.

Kama. Moderate Lethal & Accuracy debuff
Claws. Moderate Lethal
Sai. Moderate Lethal & Accuracy debuff
Katana. High Lethal & Defense debuff
Brawl. Moderate Smashing
Mesmerize. Moderate Psionic, Sleep, long range
Dominate. Hold, moderate range
Superleap

GREEN INK MAN, GREEN INK MAN GUNNER, GREEN INK MAN BUCKSHOT

Minion	Levels 23-26

The enchanted inks used in Tsoo tattoos grant these soldiers special powers. The green ink enhances a Tsoo's mental powers, giving him the ability to dominate and entrance his opponents. Green Ink Men can easily render their victims vulnerable to attack.

Energy Punch. Moderate Smashing, Energy, & Stun
Barrage. Moderate Smashing, Energy, & Stun
Whirling Hands. Moderate Smashing, Energy, & Stun
Stun. Minor Smashing, Energy, & Stun
Automatic Pistol. Moderate Lethal, moderate range
Submachine Gun. Minor Lethal & Defense buff, moderate range
Shotgun. AoE cone moderate Lethal & Knockback, short range
Superleap

EAGLE, SERPENT, TIGER AND DRAGON RED INK MEN

Minion   **Levels 27-29**

The enchanted inks used in Tsoo tattoos grant these soldiers special powers. The green ink enhances a Tsoo's mental powers, giving him the ability to dominate and entrance his opponents. Green Ink Men can easily render their victims vulnerable to attack.

Kama. Moderate Lethal & Accuracy debuff
Claws. Moderate Lethal
Sai. Moderate Lethal & Accuracy debuff
Katana. High Lethal & Defense debuff
Brawl. Moderate Smashing
Automatic Pistol. Moderate Lethal, moderate range
Submachine Gun. Minor Lethal & Defense buff, moderate range
Shotgun. AoE cone moderate Lethal & Knockback, short range
Siphon Power. Damage debuff, all types
Siphon Speed. Slow target, Speed self
Superleap

SORCERER

Lieutenant   **Levels 15-29**

The Tsoo sorcerers are the most in touch with the Ancestor Spirits that provide the Tsoo their magic and power. They have a wide variety of powers that allow them to either attack whole groups of enemies or aid large numbers of friends, making them potent support players in any fight.

Brawl. Moderate Smashing
Self-heal
Resist. Stun, Immobilize, confused, Sleep
Hurricane. PBAoE Accuracy debuff & Knockback
Petrifying Gaze. Hold, moderate range
Chill of the Night. PBAoE minor Negative Energy & Accuracy debuff
Teleport

ANCESTOR SPIRIT

Lieutenant   **Levels 15-29**

The monstrous Ancestor Spirits are physical manifestations of the long-dead Tsoo progenitors. They're incredibly strong and tough in combat, but they're also wily. They have the ability to become intangible at will, making them slippery opponents to pin down in a fight.

Handclap. PBAoE Stun & Knockback
Haymaker. High Smashing & Knockback
Foot Stomp. PBAoE sphere moderate Smashing & Knockback
Intangible
Untouchable
Flight

DRAGON FLY

Boss   **Levels 15-19**

The Dragonfly Order concentrates on the power of a few key hand to hand techniques, and on extending their inner power to control the forces of wind and rain.

Thunder Kick. Moderate Smashing & Stun
Storm kick. Minor Smashing
Hurricane. PBAoE Accuracy debuff & minor Negative Energy
Superleap

IRON HANDS

Boss   **Levels 15-19**

Masters of the Iron Hand technique have trained their fists to break metal. They have detailed knowledge of human pressure points, which they use to drain the life from a foe and replace their own energies.

Hand Clap. PBAoE Stun & Knockback
Haymaker. High Smashing & Knockback
Cobra Strike. Minor Smashing & Stun
Shuriken. Moderate Lethal, moderate range
Superleap

BRONZE LEOPARD

Boss   **Levels 15-19**

Bronze Leopard Masters use claw-like weapons to deadly effect. They disdain the more spectacular uses of Tsoo power, preferring to concentrate on physical techniques.

Swipe. Moderate Lethal
Strike. Moderate Lethal
Slash. High Lethal, Defense debuff
Shuriken. Moderate Lethal, moderate range
Superleap

VILLAINS

SWIFT STEEL

Boss   **Levels 18-22**

The Swift Steel school emphasizes speed of body and of blade. Masters of the school's techniques can extend their inner power to alter the speed and rhythms of combat, slowing and limiting the power of their foes.

Sai. Moderate Lethal, Defense buff
Katana. High Lethal, Defense debuff
Shuriken. Moderate Lethal, moderate range
Siphon Power. Debuff dmg target, buff dmg self
Siphon Speed. Slow target, Speed self
Quick. Speed self
Superleap

ICE WIND

Boss   **Levels 18-22**

Through special alchemies and meditations, masters of the Ice Wind technique have taken on the powers of winter's fiercest storms. Their chilling techniques can leave a foe frozen and helpless beneath an onslaught of ice.

Frost Breath. AoE cone moderate Cold & Slow, moderate range
Frost. AoE cone moderate Cold & Slow
Snow Storm. AoE Slow, moderate range
Storm Kick. Moderate Smashing
Frozen Fists. Moderate Smashing & Cold, Slow
Superleap

MIDNIGHT

Boss   **Levels 18-22**

The Midnight Order draws its fearsome might from the darkest places within the spirit, amplifying and focusing this darkness into a number of devastating attacks.

Superleap

DEATH MOON

Boss   **Levels 21-25**

Masters of the Death Moon school have learned to tap into the powers of life and death. They can draw out an enemy's life, or concentrate the negative energies of the spirit to grant themselves power.

Shadow Punch. Moderate Smashing, Negative Energy, Accuracy debuff
Smite. Moderate Smashing, Negative Energy, Accuracy debuff
Siphon Life. Moderate Negative Energy, heal self, Accuracy debuff
Gloom. Moderate Negative Energy, Accuracy debuff
Life Drain. Moderate Negative Energy, heal self, Accuracy debuff
Superleap

LIGHTNING BLADE

Boss   **Levels 21-25**

Lightning Blade techniques concentrate on mastering the chaotic powers of electricity and matching it with fearsome sword skills. A disciple of the Lightning Blade school can channel the power of lightning into every attack.

Lightning Katana. High Lethal, Energy, Endurance drain
Charged Brawl. Moderate Smashing, Energy, Endurance drain
Lightning Bolt. High Energy, Endurance drain, moderate range
Superleap

FIRE DAGGER

Boss   **Levels 21-25**

Masters of the art of the Fire Dagger have suffused their internal energies with the power of flame. Fire comes to their fingertips at a whim, allowing them to devastate their foes.

Fire Smash. Moderate Smashing & Fire
Fire Sword. Moderate Lethal & Fire
Scorch. Moderate Fire
Flares. Moderate Fire, moderate range
Superleap

LOST SON

Boss   **Levels 24-28**

The powerful strikes of the Lost Son technique are used in conjunction with deadly knowledge of human pressure points. Masters of this technique can easily cripple and incapacitate their foes.

Crane Kick. High Smashing & Knockback
Crippling Axe Kick. Moderate Smashing, Immobilize, Slow
Eagles Claw. High Smashing, Lethal, Stun
Shuriken. Moderate Lethal
Blind. Immobilize, Stun
Superleap

DEATH'S HEAD

Boss   **Levels 24-28**

The Death's Head Order has mastered and fused techniques

from both the Midnight and Death Moon schools. The order's disciples are masters of a devastating martial art based around control of darkness and shadow. It is said they can kill without even striking.

Gloom. Minor Negative Energy, Accuracy debuff
Life Drain. Moderate Negative Energy, Accuracy debuff, self heal
Dark Katana. Moderate Lethal, Negative Energy, Accuracy debuff
Shadow Maul. Moderate Negative Energy, Smashing, Accuracy debuff
Chill of the Night. PBAoE minor Negative Energy, Accuracy debuff
Superleap

VIRIDIAN FEAR
Boss — Levels 24-28

The Viridian Fear techniques are based around amplifying and controlling the power of Fear itself. A Viridian Fear master can use shadow techniques to manifest the very fears of his enemies.

Petrifying Gaze. Hold, moderate range
Tenebrous Tentacles. AoE cone, moderate Smashing, Negative Energy, Immobilize, Accuracy debuff, short range
Shadow Punch. Moderate Smashing, Negative Energy, Accuracy debuff
Smite. Moderate Smashing, Negative Energy, Accuracy debuff
Superleap

COPPER SERPENT
Boss — Levels 26-29

Members of the Copper Serpent Order suffuse their bodies with toxins to utilize their deadly poison-based martial art. Masters of the style gain the dreaded Body Fang ability, and can create poison thorns on their skin at will.

Barb Swipe. Moderate Lethal, Slow, Immobilize
Lunge. Moderate Lethal, Slow, Immobilize
Impale. Moderate Lethal, Slow, Immobilize, short range
Spine Throwing. AoE cone, moderate Lethal, Slow, Immobilize, short range
Superleap

FAR FIRE
Boss — Levels 26-29

The Far Fire style utilizes the Tsoo's internal energy to burn the very air. Far Fire masters can hurl flame at enemies to burn, blind, or entrap them.

Flares. Moderate Fire, moderate range
Ring of Fire. Minor Fire, Immobilize, moderate range
Flashfire. AoE minor Fire, Stun, moderate range
Katana. High Lethal, Defense debuff
Superleap

CRESCENT
Boss — Levels 26-29

Masters of the Crescent style have learned to tap into the very power of the universe itself and focus it through their own bodies. This power enhances their strength and allows them to alter reality around their foes.

Crush. Moderate Smashing, Immobilize, Slow, moderate range
Gravity Distortion. Hold, moderate range
Propel. High Smashing, Knockback, moderate range
Eagles Claw. High Smashing, Stun, Lethal
Cobra Strike. Minor Smashing, Stun
Crane Kick. High Smashing, Knockback
Superleap

HERALD
Boss — Levels 26-29

The masters called Heralds have sharpened their mental focus to a deadly weapon. They can use the power of their will to render their enemies helpless before their weapons.

Mesmerize. Moderate Psionic, Sleep, long range
Dominate. Hold, moderate range
Kama. Moderate Lethal, Accuracy debuff
Sai. Moderate Lethal, buff Defense
Superleap

SKY FALL
Boss — Levels 26-29

The Sky Fall technique requires incredible internal power to master. Those who have attained it become elemental forces empowered with the might of the storm.

Lightning Storm. Summon storm
Thunder Clap. PBAoE sphere Stun
Hurricane. PBAoE Accuracy debuff, Knockback
Snow Storm. AoE Slow, moderate range
Katana. High Lethal, Defense debuff
Bow. High Lethal, moderate ranged
Lightning Clap. PBAoE, Stun, Knockback
Thunder Strike. Very high Smashing, Stun
Superleap

VILLAINS

VAHZILOK

Dr. Vahzilok and his crazed minions are a minor organization, but you will become intimate with their nefarious plots well before they stop plaguing you (no pun intended). You stop hearing about Doc V and his shambling brood around 19th, but by that time you've picked up a couple of souvenirs from thwarted schemes along the way. Following the story arcs through your contacts, eventually you can come face to face with the good doctor, putting a final chapter to this organization. Here are some notes and tactics to bear in mind when going up against Dr. Vahzilok's cult.

Target Embalmed Cadavers and Abominations first. These minions will hunch down and — if left uninterrupted — explode, consuming themselves and damaging enemies (that's you) in a large radius. Keep them on the ground or keep interrupting them constantly with quick attacks, and pour on the firepower to take them out first. This is especially true in groups, where one can go unnoticed and suicide bomb your group. For a Tanker, that's not a huge concern. For a Controller or Blaster, it's definitely something you want to avoid. Hit points disappear fast if Embalmed aren't kept off guard. More importantly than the potential fireball is the fact that they are

effectively kill-stealing themselves. Experience is awarded for damage done, so you must fully defeat them to gain full experience. Of course, the opposite tactic can be used; hitting them once and running away when you see them prepare for ignition. The experience value is low, but can result in thinning out a pack of Vahzilok for easier or faster wins. (Unfortunately, they don't damage allies when they go boom.) This tactic is handy in a timed mission where you might be down to the wire. Aside from their tendancy to explode in a hellish blast, that act exactly like other Cadavers and Abominations.

Cadavers and Abominations are the rank and file minions. They hit hard, have ranged shots (which can DoT you), and Tanker-esque defenses. All in all though, they are fairly straight-forward brawlers.

Reapers are the first lieutenants you meet. With crazed glee, they torment and stalk the citizens of Paragon City, looking for parts for their creations. They use crossbows for range, with a secondary effect of slowing your foot speed. One hit isn't a concern, but like all debuffs, the effect stacks. Being targeted by several Reapers can turn you into a slow-moving pincushion. If you're then surrounded and

slapped down by Abominations, it will quickly result in laying you out flat. Melee isn't a much better option. Switching from the crossbow, they draw large bonesaws. Bonesaws hurt a lot if you're a Tanker or Scrapper; as a Controller or Blaster you will want to keep track of where your arm flew for later.

Mortificators are generally one level above Reapers when you encounter them together or in missions. They're basically the same as Reapers, only slightly tougher. Oh, and one more thing ...they can resurrect their friends. Morts should be taken out immediately after the Embalmed ... because they can rez Embalmed too, even after they have seemingly exploded to smithereens. Talented fellows; don't let them show off. When they crouch down over a body, they aren't looking for loose change — stop them! Hitting them is sufficient to interrupt their rezzes. Again, you can use this to do the reverse if you like and let them rez their buddies over and over. Full experience is awarded all over again when you take out the newly repaired Vahzilok. In a pinch, you could keep smacking around the same villains for experience all day.

Murk and Mire eidolons are the boss class members of Doc V's crowd. In melee they use dark melee type powers, at range they throw dark miasma bolts. Up close they can use Midnight Grasp (DoT Root) and Siphons to heal themselves. They have a PBAoE effect that is a total shut down. All active powers turn off, you are extremely Slowed and you can do nothing but listen to the ringing in your ears and the echo-y time distorted sounds of getting your righteous self beaten. The Inspiration Discipline is extremely useful here. Use one going into the fight to keep yourself from Rooting and Slowing effects. Even 30 seconds of immunity could mean victory rather than humiliating failure. Knockbacks are really handy here too. This is true for any villain, but not allowing a Eidolon to get their claws in you is a very, very good thing. Once they start their villainous beat down, it's hard to get out of it.

Mission named bosses are patterned after Eldolons — plan accordingly.

Dr. Vahzilok is a unique model and one crazy boy. Like most archvillains, at even level he is still grapetastic. He is a Tanker with the assault blaster power set and a huge battle ax. His ax will easily hit in the triple digits on Tankers. SInce he also possesses a truckload of hit points and a regeneration beyond compare, you *will* need teammates for this one. Other than that, it's standard operating procedure … it just takes a long time.

Vahzilok researched by Lohengrin

CADAVER
Minion Levels 1-10

These reanimated corpses give off a powerful stench that's a mixture of chemicals and rotting flesh. The odor becomes a hundred times worse when they use their favorite attack — vomiting a stream of corrosive acid on their nearby opponents.

Brawl. High Smashing
Vomit. High special, very short range
Resists. Sleep, Fear, Smashing, Immobilize
Vulnerability. Lethal
Vomit. High special, short range

EMBALMED CADAVER
Minion Levels 5-10

These zombie-like constructs have numerous pieces of technological equipment protruding from their dead flesh. The purpose of all this machinery is to turn these creatures into walking bombs. When near a target, they explode to cause maximum damage.

Self-detonate
Resists. Sleep, Fear, Smashing, Immobilize
Vulnerability. Lethal

REAPER
Minion Levels 5-20

The Reapers seem to be the only normal humans among the ranks of Dr. Vahzilok's reanimated legions. They are trained surgeons who collect body parts with the help of poison darts and industrial strength hacksaws.

BoneSaw. Moderate Lethal
Cleaver. High Lethal
DartGun. High Negative Energy, Slow, short range

ABOMINATION
Minion Levels 11-20

In reanimation, as in cooking, better ingredients yield better results. Dr. Vahzilok constructs his Abominations out of the very best ingredients he can find — the organs of fallen Heroes. The Abominations are stronger, tougher, and faster than their Cadaver kin. Unfortunately, they don't smell any better.

Brawl. High Smashing
Vomit. High special, very short range
Resists. Sleep, Fear, Smashing, Immobilize
Vulnerability. Lethal
Vomit. High special, short range

EMBALMED ABOMINATION
Minion Levels 11-20

When an experiment doesn't work out the way he expected, Dr. Vahzilok doesn't complain. Instead, he makes the best of a bad situation, by converting the subject to a lethal weapon. The Embalmed Abominations are faster and tougher than their Cadaver counterparts, and they explode just as violently.

Self-detonate
Brawl. High Smashing
Vomit. High special, very short range
Resists. Sleep, Fear, Smashing, Immobilize
Vulnerability. Lethal

VILLAINS

239

MORTIFICATOR

Lieutenant   **Levels 1-20**

The Reapers seem to be the only normal humans among the ranks of Dr. Vahzilok's reanimated legions. They are trained surgeons who collect body parts with the help of poison darts and industrial strength hacksaws.

BoneSaw. Moderate Lethal
Cleaver. High Lethal
DartGun. High Negative Energy, Slow, short range
Resurrect Zombie

EIDOLONS

Boss   **Levels 1-20**

In Dr. Vahzilok's mind, the Eidolons are mankind's next great evolutionary leap. Unlike the cadavers, they retain all of their memories and personality. The lucky few who can pay to become a Eidolon are augmented with the remains of Heroes, so they often have super powers. Mire Eidolons have mastered the ability to control darkness itself. They tend to root their foes with tendrils of darkness and then launch into an attack.

Mire Eidolon

Brawl. Minor Smashing
Dark Blast. Moderate Negative Energy, Accuracy debuff
Night Fall. AoE cone minor Negative Energy, Accuracy debuff, moderate range
Dark Regeneration. Minor Negative Energy, self heal
Tenebrous Tentacles. Minor Smashing, minor Negative Energy, Immobilize, Accuracy debuff, short range

Murk Eidolon

Shadow Punch. Moderate Smashing, Negative Energy, Accuracy debuff
Dark Embrace. Resists to Smashing, Lethal, Negative Energy
Dark Blast. Moderate Negative Energy, Accuracy debuff, moderate range
Midnight Grasp. High Negative Energy, Immobilize, Accuracy debuff
Oppressive Gloom. PBAoE sphere Stun

Luminous Eidolon

Brawl. Minor Smashing
Neutrino Bolt. Moderate Energy, Defense debuff, moderate range
Focus. Defense buff vs melee and ranged
X-Ray Beam. Moderate Energy, Defense debuff, moderate range
Neutron Bomb. AoE sphere, minor damage, Defense debuff, moderate range
Irradiate. PBAoE Minor Energy, Defense debuff
Electron Haze. AoE moderate Energy, Knockback, Defense debuff, short range

DR. VAHZILOK

ArchVillain
Levels 15-22

The insane leader of the Vahzilok comes across more like a religious zealot than an arch-fiend. Dr. Vahzilok continually proclaims his intention of

overcoming death itself. In his twisted mind, the horrid reanimated corpses he creates are only stepping stones toward greater medical miracles.

Assault Rifle. Moderate Lethal, Defense debuff, long range
Grenade Launcher. AoE moderate Smashing, Lethal, Knockback, very long range
Blade. High Lethal, Knockback
Resists. Knockup, Knockback

WARRIORS

Locations: Talos Island. Mission doors for them can be generated anywhere.

Types: Warriors are either Blasters, Scrappers or Tankers. Blasters will be Buckshot or Gunners, using a shotgun or machine gun. Scrappers are Slashers, using the broadsword power set. Tankers are Hewers, Smashers and Crushers, using the battle axe and war mace power sets.

All Warrior bosses are melee fighters and will close to engage, rather than standing or running to range. Most of the rest will also close to melee range, though some will use ranged powers before closing. On the whole, their melee damage is vastly greater than their ranged.

Tactics: Warrior minions are like most other street gangs (Skulls, Family, Hellions) — mostly melee, with some ranged. Using general tactics will suffice here.

Lieutenants and Bosses deliver a lot of damage in a short amount of time, and rarely have significant ranged attacks, so either engage them at range or use attacks that Disorient or have Knockdown to prevent them from dishing out their damage.

WARRIOR MINIONS

Minion   **Levels 20-29**

A little education can be a dangerous thing. The members of the gang known as the Warriors take their inspiration from ancient Greek Heroes and soldiers. They seem to favor the old school weapons over democracy, literature, and art.

Warrior Bruiser

Boxing. Moderate Smashing, Stun
Kick. Moderate Smashing, Knockback
Brawl. Moderate Smashing
Heavy Revolver. High Lethal, Knockback, moderate range

Warrior Slicer

Knife. Moderate Lethal
Heavy Revolver. High Lethal, Knockback, moderate range

Warrior Slammer

Sledgehammer. High Smashing, Knockback
Heavy Revolver. High Lethal, Knockback, moderate range

Warrior Buckshot

Shotgun. AoE cone, moderate Lethal, Knockback, short range

Warrior Gunner

Submachine Gun. Minor Lethal, Defense debuff, moderate range

CRUSHER

Lieutenant   **Levels 21-29**

The Crushers are experienced Warriors who specialize in the use of maces. Although they prefer to get up close and personal with their enemies, Crushers also carry guns in case they need to take down a faraway foe.

Shotgun. AoE cone, moderate Lethal, Knockback, short range
Bash. Moderate Smashing, Stun
Pulverize. High Smashing, Stun
Clobber. Moderate Smashing, Stun
Shatter. High Smashing, Knockback
Resists. Smashing, Lethal

SLASHER

Lieutenant   **Levels 21-29**

Although they prefer to be called Swordsmen, everyone refers to these Warriors as the Slashers. They're experts at swordplay, and can swing with both finesse and ferocity, making them very dangerous in close combat.

Submachine Gun. Minor Lethal, Defense debuff, moderate range
Hack. Moderate Lethal, Defense debuff
Slash. High Lethal, Defense debuff
Parry. Moderate Lethal, self Defense buff
Whirling Sword. PBAoE moderate Lethal
Resists. Smashing, Lethal

HEWER

Lieutenant   **Levels 21-29**

The age-old axe has always been a popular weapon, especially for those looking to quickly cause great amounts of gruesome damage with both speed and finesse. That descriptions sums up the Choppers perfectly.

Shotgun. AoE cone, moderate Lethal, Knockback, short range

Gash. High Lethal, Knockback

Chop. High Smashing, Knockback

Beheader. Very high Smashing, Knockback

Pendulum. PBAoE cone, high Lethal, Knockback

Resists. Smashing, Lethal

SMASHER ELITE

Boss   **Levels 21-29**

These Warriors have been around long enough that they can not only dish out pain, they can take it as well. On the streets of Paragon City, one doesn't survive long as a mace wielder without building up a resistance to Smashing attacks.

Assault Rifle. Moderate Lethal, Defense debuff, long range

Bash. Moderate Smashing, Stun

Pulverize. High Smashing, Stun

Clobber. Moderate Smashing, Stun

Shatter. High Smashing, Knockback

Resists. Smashing, Lethal

SLASHER ELITE

Boss   **Levels 21-29**

Some of the finest modern swordsmen on the streets, the Slasher Elite are experts at using their blades for both offense and defense. They're very tough and resilient fighters, resistant to Smashing and Lethal damage.

Assault Rifle. Moderate Lethal, Defense debuff, long range

Hack. Moderate Lethal, Defense debuff

Slash. High Lethal, Defense debuff

Parry. Moderate Lethal, self Defense buff

Whirling Sword. PBAoE moderate Lethal

Resists. Smashing, Lethal

HEWER ELITE

Boss   **Levels 21-29**

Those Warriors most experienced with the axe can work themselves into a wild frenzy as they heedlessly chop through the opposition. The more damage they do, the more confident and resilient they become, shaking off damage in their berserker blood lust.

Assault Rifle. Moderate Lethal, Defense debuff, long range

Gash. High Lethal, Knockback

Chop. High Smashing, Knockback

Beheader. Very high Smashing, Knockback

Pendulum. PBAoE cone, high Lethal, Knockback

Resists. Smashing, Lethal

PARAGON CITY ZONES

This is a breakdown of every zone in the city, in the following format:

Name. Name of the zone.

Levels. The Combat Levels of the enemies therein, and the minimum Security Level you need to enter, if it is a hazard or trial zone.

Mission Doors. How many doors of each type exist in the zone. These doors are always locked until activated for a Hero by a "door" mission from a contact. The types of mission doors are:

◆ *Office.* General office layout, can be multi-floored with elevators.

◆ *Abandoned Office (Abn Off).* Same type of map as Office, but dirtier, with broken furniture, overturned desks and so forth.

◆ *Warehouse (Ware).* Large, split-level, sprawling area with catwalks, crates, etc.

◆ *Abandoned Warehouse (Abn Ware).* Same as Warehouse, but neglected and broken down.

◆ *Tech.* Futuristic textures, flashing lights and devices, multi-leveled with elevators.

◆ *Sewers.* Tunnels, pipes spewing green fluid, virtually flat but sloping tunnels give the illusion of multi-level.

◆ *Caves.* Similar to Sewers, except caves, moss and broken mining equipment strewn about.

◆ *5th Column Bunker (5CB).* Futuristic underground bunker, twisting and turning, with lots of stairs, consoles and technological equipment.

◆ *Circle of Thorns Lair (CoT).* Home of the Circle of Thorns, a massive ancient-looking city in an underground cave complex. Lots of stairs, bridges, chasms and massive open areas.

Physical Description. Brief description of how the zone appears.

Background History. Brief synopsis of the zone's history.

Hunting Tips. General tips about the zone.

Resources. A list of the mission contacts, delivery contacts (PNPCs), stores and zone exits in the zone. NPCs are listed by name, Stature Level (StL), origin affiliation and general location. Stature Level tracks the range of combat levels for which the contact provides missions (see **Contacts**, p. 174).

Neighborhoods & Mission Groups. Breaks down the sections of the zone with the types and levels of enemies that can be found there. Names in **bold** spawn only at night. This list is not exclusive and only represents what is "normally" found, as certain missions will create unusual spawns in any zone in the city.

CITY ZONES

City zones are the "civilized" areas of the city, with unrestricted access (no level requirement to enter) and at least some helpful police presence in the form of Police Drones scattered about the zone to neutralize victims that come to close to a defended area. These zones contain the majority of your Contacts and Stores, as well as the Hospitals where you revive when you're defeated. City zone spawn encounters tend to be smaller, geared for teams of 1 to 3 Heroes, though occasionally larger spawns occur.

ATLAS PARK

Levels

Security Levels 1 to 6

Physical Description

Mixed-use urban center. Features a large civic center in the middle of the map, and an industrial park in the west.

- **T** Monorail Station
- ✚ Hospital
- ⑤ Store
- ✖ Trainer
- ▼ Safe Zone Entrance
- ▼ Hazard Zone / Trial

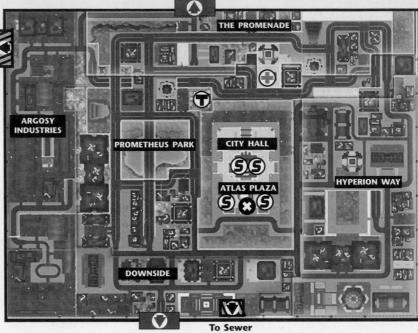

To Steel Canyon

THE PROMENADE

To Perez Park

ARGOSY INDUSTRIES

PROMETHEUS PARK

CITY HALL

ATLAS PLAZA

HYPERION WAY

DOWNSIDE

To Skyway City

To Sewer Network

Mission Doors

Office	Abn Off	Ware	Abn Ware	Tech	Sewers	Caves	5CB	CoT
20	0	0	0	20	13	5	0	0

Background Story

Atlas Park is the city zone at the heart of Paragon City. No landmark exemplifies the heroic nature of the City of Heroes more than the statue of the fallen Hero, Atlas, which stands in front of City Hall. Atlas was one of the first Heroes to respond to the Nazi sneak attack against Paragon City on December 7th, 1941. Almost single-handedly, Atlas kept the German attackers from gaining a foothold past Independence Port. It cost him his life, but he held his ground until the Freedom Phalanx arrived.

Hunting Tips

This is one of the two "newbie" zones where all Heroes first enter the city (after the tutorial). While every Hero's first task is leveling out of this zone, it is important that you not just run out and defeat enemies until you're the right level and neglect your contacts. Move through the contacts and use missions for advancement. At this level, it's faster than hunting the streets and helps you avoid the crowds and potential kill-stealing (but be aware that as your level increases it will become more and more important that you balance missions with street hunting). Missions at this level are particularly important, so that you can get started on the "story arcs" that will teach you the histories of your foes, and lead to confrontations with archvillains at higher levels.

Resources

Name	StL	Origin	Location
Jonathan Smythe	1	Science	In City Hall S.E.R.A.P.H. Room
Rick Davies	1	Tech	In City Hall D.A.T.A. Room
Susan Davies	1	Natural	In City Hall E.L.I.T.E Room
Antonio Nash	1	Mutant	In City Hall G.I.F.T. Room
Azuria	1	Magic	In City Hall M.A.G.I. Room
Laurence Mansfield	2	Magic	In front of Chiron Medical Cntr
Jose Brogan	2	Natural	Between Prometheus Park and Downside, SW area of zone
Tony Kord	2	Tech	In Promenade on overpass near Steel Canyon exit
Henry Peter Wong	2	Science	NW corner of Atlas Plaza
Sarah Peters		PNPC	In Hyperion Way, in park
Sarah Juarez		PNPC	Between Prometheus Park and Downside, SW area of zone
Charlie		PNPC	Between Prometheus Park and Downside, SW area of zone
Iris Parker		PNPC	In Hyperion Way, E side of zone
Security Chief_01		PNPC	In Promenade, across from Steel Canyon exit
Security Chief_04		PNPC	At Perez Park exit
Trainer: Ms. Liberty		Trainer	In front of Atlas statue
4 Freedom Corps		Store	Two at base of Atlas Statue, inside City Hall
Exit to Perez Park			West
Exit to Skyway City			South
Exit to Steel Canyon			North
Exit to the Sewer Network			South
Yellow Line Monorail			Central

Neighborhoods & Villain Groups

Neighborhood	Levels	Villain Group
Atlas Plaza	none	Hellions, **Clockwork**
The Promenade	3 – 4	Hellions, **Clockwork**
Downside	3 – 6	Hellions, **Clockwork**
Hyperion Way	3 – 4	Hellions, **Clockwork**
Prometheus Park	1 – 4	Hellions, **Clockwork**
Argosy Industrial Park	4 – 6	Hellions, **Clockwork**

GALAXY CITY

Levels

Security Levels 1 to 6

Physical Description

Galaxy City is a densely populated region with a business sector to the North, a warehouse district to the South, and a park with a small lake to the Southeast. The Freedom Corp building is in the Northwest sector.

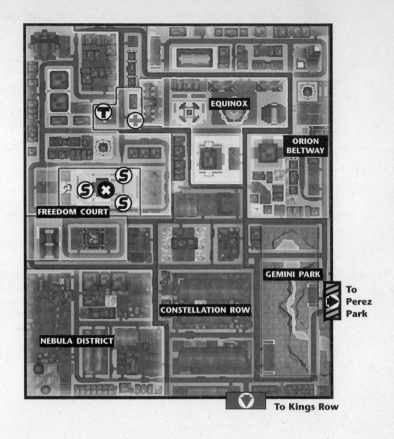

T	Monorail Station
+	Hospital
S	Store
X	Trainer
▼	Safe Zone Entrance
▼	Hazard Zone / Trial

Mission Doors

Office	Abn Off	Ware	Abn Ware	Tech	Sewers	Caves	5CB	CoT
21	0	15	8	10	10	10	0	0

Background Story

The "sister" zone to Atlas Park, Freedom Corps has a significant installation here to provide support to Paragon's Hero population.

Hunting Tips

This is one of the two "newbie" zones where all Heroes first enter the city (after the tutorial).

While every Hero's first task is leveling out of this zone, it is important that you not just run out and defeat enemies until you're the right level and neglect your contacts. Move through the contacts and use missions for advancement. At this level, it's faster than hunting the streets and helps you avoid the crowds and potential kill-stealing (but be aware that as your level increases it will become more and more important that you balance missions with street hunting). Missions at this level are particularly important, so that you can get started on the "story arcs" that will teach you the histories of your foes, and lead to confrontations with archvillains at higher levels.

Resources

Name	StL	Origin	Location
Rebecca Brinell	1	Science	Inside Freedom Corp Building (S.E.R.A.P.H. Room)
Gregor Richardson	1	Magic	Inside Freedom Corp Building (M.A.G.I. Room)
Prince Kiros Nandelu	1	Mutant	Inside Freedom Corp Building (G.I.F.T. Room)
Caitlin Murray	1	Tech	Inside Freedom Corp Building (D.A.T.A. Room)
Derek Ambrose	1	Natural	Inside Freedom Corp Building (E.L.I.T.E. Room)
Paco Sanchez	2	Magic	Left side Cygnus Medical Cntr
Rachel Torres	2	Natural	Orion Beltway North in front of the movie theatre
Maurice Feldon	2	Tech	Orion Beltway Southeast
Kip Cantorum	2	Science	Orion Beltway, back of plaza that's behind a statue
Charlie Sparks			Delivery target only
Clarence Jackson			Delivery target only
Security Chief		PNPC	In courtyard of Freedom Corp building
Super Group Registrar		PNPC	Inside Freedom Corp building at Super Group Registration desk
Back Alley Brawler		Trainer	Freedom Corps Building
3 Freedom Corps		Store	Freedom Corps Building (1 inside, 2 outside in courtyard)
Exit to Perez Park			East
Exit to Kings Row			South
Yellow Line Monorail			Northwest

Neighborhoods & Villain Groups

Neighborhood	Levels	Villain Group
Gemini Park	5 – 6	Hellions, Vahzilok
Freedom Court	1 – 2	Hellions, Vahzilok
Orion Beltway	3 – 4	Hellions, Vahzilok
Equinox	1 – 2	Hellions
Nebula District	3 – 4	Clockwork, Hellions, Vahzilok
Constellation Row	5 – 6	Clockwork, Hellions

ZONES

247

KINGS ROW

Levels

Security Levels 5 to 10

Physical Description

A neglected urban area. Kings Row is an industrial and civic area that has seen better days, a mixture of housing developments, light industrial, industrial and office buildings.

T	Monorail Station
✚	Hospital
S	Store
✖	Trainer
▼	Safe Zone Entrance
▼	Hazard Zone / Trial

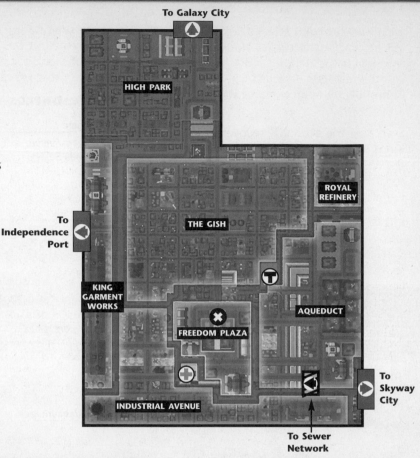

Mission Doors

Office	Abn Off	Ware	Abn Ware	Tech	Sewers	Caves	5CB	CoT
10	11	18	13	10	14	4	0	0

Background Story

In the early days of Paragon City, the area known as Kings Row was a shiny, bustling place filled with hope and promise. Factories manufacturing goods and generating power created a feeling of strong, blue-collar values. At that time, the area was called Kings Row after one the most productive factories to set up shop there, King Garment Works.

Unfortunately, the prosperity didn't last long. When the Depression hit Paragon City, no area

was affected more. Factories shut down, many workers were laid off, and a great deal of the crime sweeping through the city was centered in the row of closed-down factories. The crime bosses who set themselves up there took on the name of the zone. They became known throughout the city as The Kings.

For a time, Kings Row was a place to avoid. It was dark, dirty, and struck fear into the hearts of upright Paragon citizens. When the Statesman began his "war on crime" and formed the Freedom Phalanx, he focused a great deal of his efforts on bringing down the Kings. Eventually, the Freedom Phalanx triumphed over the Kings, but the cost was high. There was some damage to the physical area, but of greater effect was the long-term damage done to the reputation of Kings Row.

Even after the economy recovered, the stigma of Kings Row remained. The Kings are long gone but the name has remained and to this day, the area is regarded as a grimy neighborhood with a reputation for seediness.

Although the area is still generally run-down, it has seen much more activity lately — and not all of it bad. Part of that comes from the fact that the area has become a popular location for raves, drawing in more of Paragon City's white-collar crowd.

Yet the primary reason for the surge of activity in Kings Row is due to the arrival of a gang called the Skulls. The Skulls have been in Paragon City for some time, but they have only recently set up shop in the Row, going so far as to clean up the streets a bit by attacking Vahzilok Cadavers whenever they see them. The Skulls' first order of business seems to be waging war on the Hellions, a gang from Atlas Park. Nearby Perez Park has become the battleground for this gang war n which both sides seem to have backing from more powerful organizations. By using it as a home base of sorts, the Skulls appear to be taking Kings Row back in time and threaten to turn it into crime central once again.

Hunting Tips

This zone is a great spot for hunting from levels 6 to 10. You will face more powerful foes than those in Galaxy City and Atlas Park. There are lots of fences, fire escapes, towers and walls that you can use to keep enemies at range and avoid melee damage, which begins to be a factor in this level range. This zone offers a number of hazards to navigation, particularly if you're trying to move through the back allies, but the street layout is pret-

ty straightforward once you get used to it. The best part about this zone is that it's easy to find things to fight, and the Trolls provide an excellent ramp to the more powerful enemies in the next zones.

Resources

Name	StL	Origin	Location
Juan Jimenez	2	Mutant	Rooftop, S part of The Gish
Linda Summers	2	Mutant	NE of High Park
Ron Hughes	2	Mutant	N entrance to massive building causeway, Aqueduct
Genevieve Sanders	2	Magic	By Crowne Memorial HOSPITAL
Samuel Pierce	2	Science	Orion Beltway W
Paula Dempsey	2	Science	SE area of High Park
Vic Johansson	2	Natural	W section of The Gish
Blue Steel		Trainer	Freedom Plaza, in front of coin
Security Chief			Outside Paragon Police Department
Exit to Skyway City			Southeast
Exit to Galaxy City			North
Exit to Independence Port			West
Exit to the Sewer Network			SE
Yellow Line Monorail			Central

Neighborhoods & Villain Groups

Neighborhood	Levels	Villain Group
High Park	5 – 9	Skulls, Clockwork, COT, Vahzilok, The Lost, Trolls
King Garment Works	6 – 8	Skulls, Clockwork, **COT**, Vahzilok, The Lost, Trolls
The Gish	5 – 9	Skulls, Clockwork, **COT**, Vahzilok, The Lost
Royal Refinery	6 – 9	Skulls, Clockwork, Vahzilok, The Lost
Aqueduct	5 – 9	Skulls, Clockwork, Vahzilok
Freedom Plaza	5 – 9	Skulls, Clockwork, Vahzilok
Industrial Avenue	5 – 9	Skulls, Clockwork, **COT**, Vahzilok, The Lost, Trolls

STEEL CANYON

Levels

Security Levels 10 to 16

Physical Description

Metropolitan financial district. Many large skyscrapers, one park, two lakes and a huge central statue.

Stores

(S1) Orion Labs (*Science*)

(S2) Cooke's Electronics (*Tech*)

(S3) Image, Inc. (*Natural*)

(S4) Pandora's Box (*Magic*)

(S5) Subgenetics (*Mutant*)

(S6) Freedom Corps Basic Training (*Generic*)

(T) Monorail Station

(+) Hospital

(S) Store

(X) Trainer

(▼) Safe Zone Entrance

(NNN) Hazard Zone / Trial

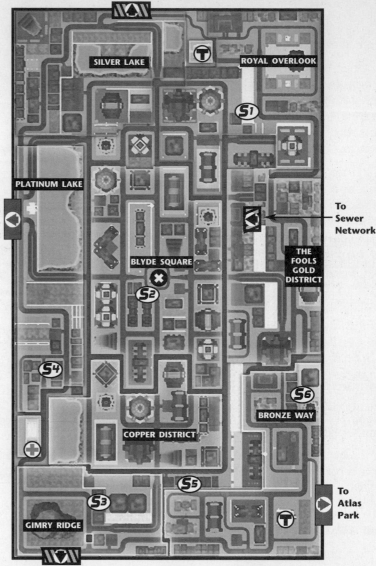

To "Boomtown"

SILVER LAKE

ROYAL OVERLOOK

PLATINUM LAKE

To Independence Port

To Sewer Network

THE FOOLS GOLD DISTRICT

BLYDE SQUARE

COPPER DISTRICT

BRONZE WAY

To Atlas Park

GIMRY RIDGE

To Perez Park

Mission Doors

Office	Abn Off	Ware	Abn Ware	Tech	Sewers	Caves	5CB	CoT
27	4	4	2	32	8	8	0	0

Background Story

Once a prosperous jewelers' district in 19th-century Paragon City, many of Steel Canyon's neighborhoods still possess names dating back to that era. The once prolific mercantile district transformed overnight as brokerage houses, insurance companies and law firms began taking over real estate. By the 1920s, most companies had erected towering skyscrapers to flaunt their success to the rest of the city. Because these huge buildings loomed over city streets like manmade mountains, the newspapers dubbed the area "Steel Canyon."

Today, Steel Canyon remains primarily a financial district, though many jewelers still have their stores in the area. No single villain group has gained preeminence in Steel Canyon, though many compete for control of this wealthy district. The elemental-based Outcasts, the misshapen Trolls and the Tsoo mystics and martial artists all wage fierce battles amongst each other for dominance of Steel Canyon. So far, the conflict has resulted in bloody stalemate, though the businesses and residents of the area hope that the influx of new Heroes will destroy this threat forever.

Hunting Tips

While the Villain Groups section lists many different factions, this zone is filled with Outcasts. The other groups appear here and there, but the vast majority of the enemies in this zone are Outcast thugs and Shockers. When hunting here, begin at 10th level near the Atlas Park zone entrance or the southern train station and work your way north as you advance in level. When moving through the zone to get to a mission door, be wary of passing too close to a Shocker — once they become aggressive, they take flight and are very hard to shake.

Resources

Name	StL	Origin	Location
Hugo Redding	2	Magic	S area of Gimry Ridge near park
Dr. Trevor Seaborn	2	Magic	W side of St Can Med Center
Willy Starbuck	2	Natural	W of monorail station
Wes Schnabel	2	Natural	Near Atlas Park tunnel

Athena Currie	2	Tech	Bronze Way, side of monorail
Kyle Peck	2	Science	Above & S of Subgenics store
Alfonse Rubel	2	Mutant	SW Bronze Way border
Wilson Zucco	2	Mutant	SW area of Bronze Way
Fareed Abdullah	3	Tech	In Bronze Way, SE area
Tom Bowden	3	Tech	In Blyde Square, center
Guy Denson	3	Tech	In Platinum Lake, SW area
Colleen Saramago	3	Science	In Platinum Lake, SW area
Wyatt Anderson	3	Science	In Fool's Gold District, east side central
Olivia Chung	3	Mutant	In Silver Lake, N central area
Virginia Hoffman	3	Magic	In Gimry Ridge, SW area
Shelly Knowles	PNPC		In Platinum Lake, west side
Carlos Herrera	PNPC		In Gimry Ridge, SE area
Security Chief_05	PNPC		At foot of statue in center
Security Chief_06	PNPC		At Boomtown exit
Security Chief_17	PNPC		At sewer entrance
Positron	Task For		In Blyde Square, foot of statue
Valkyrie	Trainer		In Blyde Square, foot of statue
Orion Labs (Science)	Store		In Royal Overlook, N area
Cooke's Electr. (Tech)	Store		In Blyde Square, center
Image, Inc. (Natural)	Store		In Gimry Ridge, SW area
Pandora's Box (Magic)	Store		In Platinum Lake, SW area
Subgenetics (Mutant)	Store		Between Copper District and Gimry Ridge
Freedom Corps BasicTr.	Store		In Bronze Way, east side
Exit to Atlas Park			Southeast
Exit to Boomtown			North
Exit to Perez Park			Southwest
Exit to Independence Port			West
Exit to the Sewer Network			East Central
Yellow Line Monorail			Southeast
Green Line Monorail			North

Neighborhoods & Villain Groups

Neighborhood	Levels	Villain Group
Silver Lake	10 – 16	Outcasts, Clockwork, COT, 5th Column, Vahzilok, Family, Tsoo
Royal Overlook	15 – 16	Outcasts, Clockwork, COT, 5th Column, Vahzilok, Trolls, Family, Tsoo
Fools Gold District	12 – 16	Outcasts, Clockwork, COT, 5th Column, Vahzilok, Trolls, Family, Tsoo
Blyde Square	12 – 16	Outcasts, Clockwork, COT, 5th Column, Vahzilok, Trolls, Tsoo
Bronze Way	10 – 16	Outcasts, Clockwork, COT, 5th Column, Vahzilok, Trolls, Tsoo
Copper District	10 – 16	Outcasts, Clockwork, 5th Column, Vahzilok, Trolls
Gimry Ridge	10 – 13	Outcasts, Clockwork, COT, Vahzilok, Trolls

SKYWAY CITY

Levels

Security Levels 13 to 19

Physical Description

A spaghetti bowl of raised highways over residential and commercial buildings.

Stores

- **S1** Orion Labs (*Science*)
- **S2** Cooke's Electronics (*Tech*)
- **S3** Image, Inc. (*Natural*)
- **S4** Pandora's Box (*Magic*)
- **S5** [Back alley] Subgenetics (*Mutant*)
- **S6** Freedom Corps Basic Training (*Generic*)

- **T** Monorail Station
- **+** Hospital
- **S** Store
- **X** Trainer
- **▼** Safe Zone Entrance
- **⚠** Hazard Zone / Trial

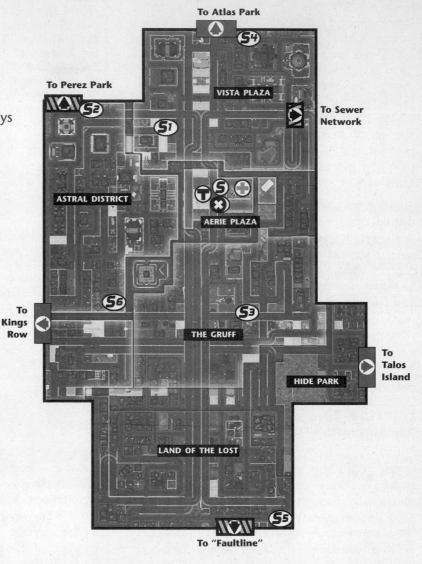

Mission Doors

Office	Abn Off	Ware	Abn Ware	Tech	Sewers	Caves	5CB	CoT
10	17	12	0	14	10	10	0	0

Resources

Name	StL	Origin	Location
Haley Philips	2	Magic	Front of Atlas Park tunnel, by bus stop
Lorenzo DiCosta	2	Natural	Aerie Plaza, E and down from monorail
Carla Brunelli	2	Tech	Vista Plaza, 3 blocks N from Trainer and Hospital
Everett Daniels	2	Tech	SE from Perez Park entrance
Tristan Caine	2	Science	Vista Plaza, on road SE of Atlas Park tunnel
Jill Pastor	2	Science	S of Perez Park entrance
Sanjay Chandra	2	Mutant	Aerie Plaza, front of monorail
Mark Freeman	3	Tech	In Vista Plaza — North
Maggie Greene	3	Science	In Astral District — East
Jake Montoya	3	Science	In The Gruff — SW
Ann-Marie Engles	3	Mutant	In Vista Plaza — NW
Juliana Nehring	3	Mutant	In Vista Plaza — North
Pavel Garnier	3	Mutant	In Land of the Lost — NW
Vitaly Cherenko	3	Magic	In Land of the Lost — SW
Thao Ku	3	Magic	In Astral District — Central
Kong Bao	3	Magic	In Astral District — NE
Cho Ge	3	Natural	In Aerie Plaza in the monorail underground parking
Karen Parker	3	Natural	In The Gruff — West
Suzanne Bernhard	3	Natural	In Land of the Lost — NW
Warren Trudeau	3	Natural	At the building plaza between The Gruff and Astral District
Synapse		Task For	In Aerie Plaza — East
Mynx		Trainer	In Aerie Plaza — East
Hiro Takashi		PNPC	In LaGrange Medical Center
Yolanda Baker		PNPC	In Vista Plaza — NW
Andre Jimenez		PNPC	In Vista Plaza — SW
The Can Man		PNPC	In Vista Plaza — Central
Kira Lange		PNPC	In Astral District — South
Yancy Rhymes		PNPC	In Astral District — SE
Corey McCann		PNPC	In The Gruff — NE
Jerry Kazatsky		PNPC	In Land of the Lost — West
John Townsend		PNPC	Inside LaGrange Medical Cntr
Security Chief			Sewer Entrance (Vista Plaza)
Security Chief			Aerie Plaza
Security Chief			Entrance to Faultline (Land of the Lost)
Orion Labs (Science)		Store	Vista Plaza — West
Cooke's Electr. (Tech)		Store	Astral District — North
Image, Inc. (Natural)		Store	The Gruff — East
Pandora's Box (Magic)		Store	Vista Plaza — North
SubGenetics (Mutant)		Store	Land of the Lost — Southeast
Freedom Corps Basic		Store	Astral District — Southeast
Freedom Corps Basic Tr		Trainer	Aerie Plaza (in the park)
Exit to Atlas Park			North
Exit to Perez Park			Northwest
Exit to Kings Row			West
Exit to Faultline			South
Exit to Talos Island			East
Exit to the Sewer Network			Northeast
Yellow Line Monorail			Central

Neighborhoods & Villain Groups

Neighborhood	Levels	Villains
Land of the Lost	17 – 19	Clockwork, The Lost, Trolls
Hide Park	17 – 19	Clockwork, Trolls
Gruff, The	13 – 16	Clockwork, The Lost, Trolls
Astral District	10 – 12	Clockwork, Trolls
Vista Plaza	13 – 16	Clockwork, Trolls
Aerie Plaza	10 – 12	Trolls

Background Story

Back in the 1970s, with traffic congestion in Paragon City reaching major headache levels, the solution seemed obvious: build upwards! Create graceful sweeping highways! Take the pressure off surface streets by moving traffic above the city on high-spanning bridges. As a result, Skyway City — the big highway in the sky — was born.

The epitome of modern efficiency, Skyway City seemed to be a model for the future. Instead, it became a model of cold concrete and steel — a soulless passage on the way to more interesting destinations. Soon, the original plans for extending the Skyway bridges throughout the city fell by the wayside. Today, Skyway City is the only remnant of this grand but misguided ideal in Paragon City.

With an abundance of salvageable materials on hand, Skyway City is a haven for the deadly Clockwork. Visitors should keep a sharp eye out for these mechanical, scavenging menaces.

More recently, Skyway City has become home to a street gang known as the Trolls. Found camped

ZONES

253

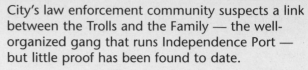

out under the many bridges in the area, the Trolls have made the unstable and dangerous street drug Superadine an integral part of gang membership. This widely popular drug has become a mainstay in their initiation rites and their tests of strength and will, and an increasingly important factor in a member's rise through the ranks. With the ingestion of massive doses, many of the senior Trolls have experienced physical and mental mutations of a monstrous nature, including inhuman strength and resistance. To make matters even worse, Paragon

City's law enforcement community suspects a link between the Trolls and the Family — the well-organized gang that runs Independence Port — but little proof has been found to date.

With Superadine pumping through their bodies and occasionally short-circuiting their brains, the Trolls have become one of the most dangerous and frightening threats to Paragon City. Drug-induced rampages have become the norm; unprovoked, senseless and violent, these acts spare no one in the vicinity.

Skyway City once stood as the bright, soaring promise of a new age. Sadly, it's become the spawning ground of drug-crazed monsters. Something must be done to curb this advancing tide of blood and madness. Without the timely intervention of a new generation of Heroes, the future of this part of Paragon City looks grim indeed.

Hunting Tips

This is the best zone if you love hunting the streets, and the most challenging non-hazard zone when it comes to navigation, particularly if you don't yet have a primary travel power. With Trolls and Clockwork everywhere, all up and down the range of levels for the zone, you'll have no problem finding things to fight. In fact, as densely populated as some of these spawn areas are, you run into the problem of having too much to fight, especially toward the center of the zone, under the bridges, as the Trolls spawn quite close together, making it essential to control crowds and not chase runners. If you're fighting in an elevated area, don't chase after enemies that fall or jump to a lower level. They're not worth the effort it will take you to get back where you started from — just let them go and continue hunting.

TALOS ISLAND

Levels

Security Levels 20 to 27

Physical Description

Talos Island is a scenic area where all the neighborhoods overlook the water. There are several small islands scattered throughout the zone and many citizens of Paragon City have chosen this area to live in, and spend their leisure time.

Background Story

Talos Island is named after the heroic titan, Talos, who sacrificed himself to protect the city. Talos was a giant Hero who defended the city from various giant monster threats throughout the '50s and early '60s. Despite the fact that Talos stood several hundred feet in height, the titan mysteriously disappeared after each battle. Newspaper reporters and scholars alike strove to find the secret of the Talos' identity, but they were left grasping at the enigmatic utterances of the giant himself. Talos claimed to be a protector of humanity who had been around for thousands of years. Beyond that, Talos said very little. The only certain thing about Talos was his close relationship with the young boy Michael McVey. The "terrific titan" (as the headlines dubbed him) strangely appeared whenever the youth was imperiled. In a climactic battle against his arch foe, the Chimera, Talos and the serpentine beast sank into the waters of the bay. Their tremendous underwater struggle shook the city to its foundations. During the battle, the two tore a rift in the ocean's floor and lava erupted from it. An island formed and encased both in its stony embrace.

Decades later, Talos' heroism faded into urban legend. Despite countless articles, photographs and movie clips, most citizens dismiss Talos as a folktale. During the 1980s, developers couldn't pass up the opportunity of an island so close to Paragon City and quickly built it up. Within a matter of months, the once barren island was abuzz with construction sites. As a publicity stunt, the real estate moguls agreed to name the island after the city's mythic giant. An anonymous benefactor donated the huge statue which now sits several hundred yards from the island.

Today, Talos Island is home to many high-tech and venture capital firms. It is considered even now prime real estate; during the Rikti War, the aliens oddly avoided attacking that area. Consequently, many superstitious people believe that the Talos statue gives the place good luck, and this has only driven the real estate prices higher.

Currently, the once peaceful Talos Island is a battleground between two rival gangs. The Warriors, who claim the island as their own private playground, have found themselves embroiled in a bloody turf war with a recently arrived gang known as the Tsoo. What's at stake is more than real estate, as the Warriors have been the controlling force behind the Import of a large number of minor mystical relics and the Tsoo, a gang with arcane leanings, would very much like the lion's share of the action. Out of this dangerously escalating conflict comes a major threat to not only Talos Island but Paragon City as a whole. Heroes are desperately needed to stem this rising tide of blood and destruction ... Talos is watching. Can you measure up?

TALOS ISLAND (CONT.)

Stores

S1 Deimos Innovations (*Science*)

S2 Exarch Industries (*Tech*)

S3 Future Dynamics (*Natural*)

S4 Tabitha Fabish (*Magic*)

S5 BiotechniX (*Mutant*)

S6 Freedom Corps Special Forces Training (*Generic*)

T Monorail Station

✚ Hospital

S Store

✖ Trainer

▼ Safe Zone Entrance

▨ Hazard Zone / Trial

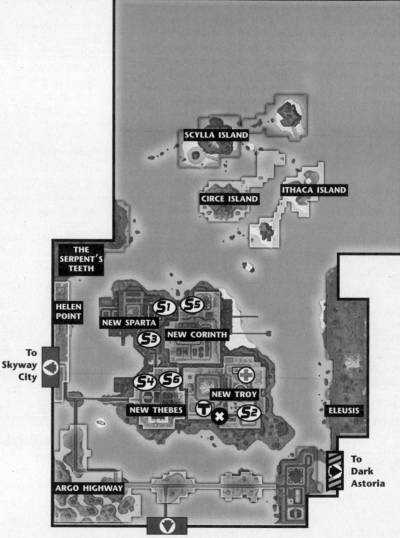

Mission Doors

Office	Abn Off	Ware	Abn Ware	Tech	Sewers	Caves	5CB	CoT
27	0	6	2	18	8	16	14	10

Hunting Tips

Another street hunter-friendly zone, Talos offers a never-ending supply of Freakshow, Tsoo and Warriors for you to challenge. Since the Tsoo near the Skyway entrance can be a bit rough in the beginning, the best starting spot for you is just west of the train station, around Tabitha Fabish's magic shop. You must be careful, however, as Talos spawns are almost as close together as the ones in Skyway, and you can very quickly find yourself in over your head (especially when dealing with Tsoo Sorcerers, who like to teleport atop buildings to get away from you). If they port away, just ignore them, stay on the melee targets, and they'll teleport back to heal the damage you've done. Running after one of these menaces is a surefire way to get more targets angry at you than you can handle.

This zone also offers the first introduction to two of the higher-level gangs, the Devouring Earth and the Banished Pantheon. Approach these with care, even if they con only yellow or less, because this level range is where enemy damage really starts ramping up. What you might be used to dealing with as a yellow or white con will begin to evolve into greater damage. Exercising caution during this period will save you many trips to the hospital — and tens of thousands in debt.

Resources

Name	StL	Origin	Location
Andrew Fiore	4	Tech	In New Thebes — West
Hugh McDougal	4	Tech	In New Sparta — Southeast
Claire Childress	4	Tech	In Argo Highway — Central
Vic Garland	4	Tech	In New Corinth — North
Polly Cooper	4	Science	The bridge between New Thebes and New Sparta
Hinckley Rasmussen	4	Mutant	In Helen Point — Southeast
Lt. Manuel Ruiz	4	Mutant	In New Thebes — Central
Jim Bell	4	Mutant	In New Corinth — South
Tyler French	4	Mutant	In Helen Point E — Beachside
Piper Irving	4	Magic	In New Troy — Central
Andrea Mitchell	4	Magic	Wharf in New Thebes — NW
Oliver Haak	4	Magic	In New Corinth — Northeast

Joesef Keller	4	Magic	In Argo Highway
Cain Royce	4	Magic	In New Troy — West
Barry Gosford	4	Natural	In New Troy monorail station
John Strobel	4	Natural	In New Troy — North
Miriam Bloechl	5	Magic	In New Corinth — Southeast
Marvin Weintraub	5	Tech	In New Corinth — South
Eliza Thorpe	5	Science	In Argo Highway — East
Alexander Pavlidis	5	Other	Pier in New Corinth — East
Bastion		Task For	In New Troy, monorail station
Luminary		Trainer	In New Troy, monorail station
Security Chief			In New Corinth — SouthEast
Security Chief			SWAT entrance to Dark Astoria
Annie Coults		PNPC	In New Corinth — Northwest
Robert Koslowski		PNPC	At Phoenix Medical Center
Betty Abbot		PNPC	Monorail station in New Troy
Janelle Irving		PNPC	In New Thebes — Southeast
Wendy Klein		PNPC	In New Corinth — South
Joshua Stutz		PNPC	On the sidewalk between Argo Highway and Helen Point
Evan DiTimasso		PNPC	Pier in New Corinth — East
Jesse Hobart		PNPC	W Wharf district, New Sparta
BiotechniX (Mutant)		Store	New Sparta — East
Freedom Corps SF		Store	New Thebes — North
Deimos Innov. (Science)		Store	New Sparta — East
Exarch Indus. (Tech)		Store	New Troy — SE
Future Dynamics (Nat.)		Store	New Sparta — South
Tabitha Fabish (Magic)		Store	New Thebes — North
Exit to Skyway City			West
Exit to Founders' Falls			South
Exit to Dark Astoria			Southeast
Green Line Monorail			Central

Neighborhoods & Villain Groups

Neighborhood	Levels	Villain Groups
Helen Point	20 – 22	Tsoo
Serpent's Teeth, The	25 – 27	Devouring Earth
Argo Highway	23 – 24	**Banished Pantheon**, Freakshow, Circle of Thorns, Warriors
New Thebes	20 – 22	Freakshow, Warriors, Tsoo
New Sparta	20 – 27	Freakshow, Tsoo
New Troy	23 – 26	Circle of Thorns, Freakshow, Tsoo, Warriors
Eleusis	25 – 27	Devouring Earth, **Banished Pantheon**
Ithaca Island	20 – 22	Circle of Thorns
Circe Island	23 – 24	Circle of Thorns
Scylla Island	25 – 27	Circle of Thorns, Devouring Earth
New Corinth	20 – 27	Tsoo, Circle of Thorns, Warriors

ZONES

INDEPENDENCE PORT

Levels

Security Levels 22 to 29

Physical Description

Independence Port is a sprawling harbor with the Terra Volta power station at its heart. This critical area is balanced on the edge of a knife and could fall to complete ruin if something is not done to stem the tide of darkness.

Background Story

Port of industry, port of corruption ...

The roots of Independence Port go all the way back to the founding of Paragon City. As Paragon City continued to grow, Independence Port stood proudly as the premiere point of commerce on the eastern coast of the United States.

In the middle of the zone lies Valor Bridge, once a symbol of sacrifice, now a ravaged memory. Sadly since Terra Volta has been overrun, Valor Bridge has become a no man's land filled with abandoned vehicles, transport containers and constant battles between the Tsoo, the 5th Column and the Family.

The battle to keep the peace in this once-prosperous area is ongoing and will certainly require the attention of many Heroes to prevent Independence Port from becoming the latest part of Paragon City to fall to the forces of villainy.

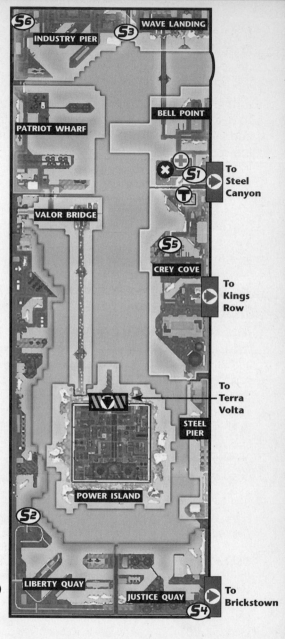

- **T** Monorail Station
- **+** Hospital
- **S** Store
- **X** Trainer
- **▼** Safe Zone Entrance
- **Hazard Zone / Trial**

Stores

S1 Deimos Innovations (*Science*)

S2 Exarch Industries (*Tech*)

S3 Future Dynamics (*Natural*)

S4 Tabitha Fabish (*Magic*)

S5 BiotechniX (*Mutant*)

S6 Freedom Corps Special Forces Training (*Generic*)

Mission Doors

Office	Abn Off	Ware	Abn Ware	Tech	Sewers	Caves	5CB	CoT
0	3	23	21	5	13	0	6	0

Hunting Tips

Independence Port is yet another street hunter-friendly zone, with plenty of enemies across the zone's level range available. The spawns tend to be further apart than in Talos, giving you lots of room to deal with them. Just beneath the train station and within a one-block radius of it is a great starting spot for breaking into this zone. As you advance in level, you work your way south or north toward the end of the zone, where the mobs come closer to the upper level range. Once you hit 25th or so, you can "walk the bridge," meaning you can begin at the entrance to Valor Bridge and fight your way to Power Island, which can give you as many enemies as your typical door mission.

Resources

Name	StL	Origin	Location
Wilma Peterson	4	Tech	In Justice Quay
Jake Kim	4	Tech	In Crey Cove across the street from the East wall
Kirsten Woods	4	Science	In Industry Pier next to the Freedom Corps building
Justine Kelly	4	Science	In Bell Point
Georgia Fields	4	Science	In front of the Future Dynamics building (no neighborhood)
Melanie Peebles	4	Science	In Crey Cove near Kings Row tunnel entrance
Kevin Cordell	4	Science	In Crey Cove
Amanda Loomis	4	Mutant	Roundabout between Justice & Liberty Quay (no neighborhood)
Dennis Ewell	4	Mutant	In Crey Cove at rest stop across from Kings Row tunnel
Dr. Cheng	4	Magic	Bell Point in beach/park area across from Bell Medical Cntr
Wilson Eziquerra	4	Natural	In Industry Pier
Rondel Jackson	4	Natural	In Crey Cove across the street from Deimos Innovations
Oswald Cuthbert	4	Natural	Inside the Monorail Station (no neighborhood)
Justin Greene	4	Natural	In Industry Pier across the street from the north wall
Ashwin Lannister	5	Mutant	Inside Bell Medical Center
Laurie Pennington	5	Mutant	In the Monorail station (no neighborhood)
Laura Brunetti	5	Magic	In Crey Cove across the street from Bell Medical Center
Christine Lansdale	5	Natural	In Crey Cove near Bell Medical Center
Colin Larson	5	Tech	In Crey Cove near Bell Medical Center on the water
Lorenzo Tate	5	Science	Across the street from the west wall (no neighborhood)
Malaise		Trainer	In the side of Bell Medical Center
Sister Psyche		Task For	Side of Bell Medical Center
Wanda Travis		PNPC	In Crey Cove outside the Monorail station
Karl Bolger		PNPC	In the east wall roundabout (no neighborhood)
Future Dynamics (Nat.)		Store	Wave Landing, NE
Deimos Innovations (Sc)		Store	Crey Cove, NE
Exarch Industries (Tech)		Store	Facing the West Warwall in the southern part of the Zone
Freedom Corp SF Tr		Store	Industry Pier, NW corner
Tabitha Fabish (Magic)		Store	Justice Quay, SE corner
BiotechniX (Mutant)		Store	Crey Cove, NE side
Exit to Steel Canyon			Northeast
Exit to Kings Row			East
Exit to Brickstown			Southeast
Exit to Terra Volta			Center, Valor Bridge to Power Island
Green Line Monorail			Northeast

Neighborhoods & Villain Groups

Neighborhood	Levels	Villains
Industry Pier	25 – 26	5th Column, Family, Tsoo
Wave Landing	22 – 24	Family, Tsoo
Patriot Wharf	25 – 26	5th Column, Family
Bell Point	22 – 24	5th Column, Family, Tsoo
Valor Bridge	25 – 26	5th Column, Family, Freakshow, Tsoo, Devouring Earth
Crey Cove	22 – 24	5th Column, Family, Tsoo
Power Island	25 – 26	5th Column, Devouring Earth, Family, Tsoo
Liberty Quay	27 – 29	5th Column, Family, Tsoo
Justice Quay	27 – 29	Family, Tsoo
Steel Pier	25 – 26	Tsoo, 5th Column, Family, Freakshow

ZONES

259

FOUNDERS' FALLS

Levels

Security Levels 31 to 39

Physical Description

Founders' Falls is one of the more exotic locales in Paragon City. Similar to Venice, Founders' Falls is renowned for its waterways, piers and catwalks. On the west side, huge skyscrapers and high rises cover the area. On the east side, tall apartments and condominiums create a sufficient living environment. Surrounding the City portion is a large stretch of land broken into three neighborhoods: Louis Forest, Hutchinson Park and Blackstone Hills.

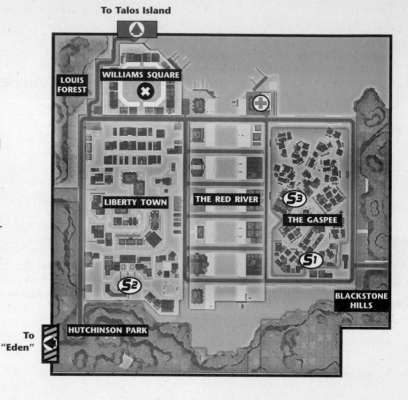

Stores

 Mark IV (*Tech*)

 Penny Preston (*Mutant*)

(S3) [waterway tunnel under building] Agent Six (*Natural*)

(T)	Monorail Station
(+)	Hospital
(S)	Store
(X)	Trainer
(▼)	Safe Zone Entrance
(hazard)	Hazard Zone / Trial

Mission Doors

Office	Abn Off	Ware	Abn Ware	Tech	Sewers	Caves	5CB	CoT
6	0	0	0	8	5	10	9	11

Background Story

When Paragon City began to grow from a small group of colonial townships, the heart of the coalition was Smithtown. Founder's Falls encompasses the area from which that seed began to grow, eventually developing into the sprawling metropolis that is Paragon City. The more modern structures of this zone were built out onto the water to avoid harming many of the historic sites that lie in the area. Amazing architecture blends with sites of significance to make this city zone an important area to keep safe. It is in some ways the spirit of Paragon City, and she needs her Heroes to keep it from being overrun.

Hunting Tips

The highest level city zone, Founders' is not an area to explore casually. This is also the first city zone to contain Rikti, Nemesis and Crey, all extremely powerful factions, out on the street. Navigating around this zone without aggroing villains can be a challenge, due to the fact that many of the enemies are standing on or near the bridges over the canals. However, the spawns are far enough apart that it's relatively easy to take any given group without fear of making another group angry with you. The park areas around the city contain a *lot* of Devouring Earth, in reasonably good-sized groups. This is also a great spot to find 5th Column robots and Warwolves, as they have a significant presence here.

The best tactic to use here is to stay on the main roads and pull enemies to you until you've hunted here awhile. As you advance in level, move deeper into the canals or higher up on the ridges to fight the bigger mobs. Some of the foes in this zone fly and will pursue, but not many. One thing to note about this zone, as well as Brickstown, is the sniper activity. While snipers do exist in the other city zones, the Crey and Nemesis snipers are a serious threat in the higher-level city zones. They are capable of delivering a great deal of damage from an unexpected front,

which can be devastating to wounded or ranged Heroes who are short on hit points. Always keep an eye on the skyline, looking for figures standing or kneeling on the ledges to avoid being surprised.

Resources

Name	StL	Origin	Location
Phillipa Meraux	6	Natural	In Liberty Town, SE
Peter Stemitz	6	Magic	In Liberty Town, NW
Tina Chung	6	Tech	In Williams Square, in Plaza
Jenny Firkins	6	Science	At Red River, NW
Jose Escalante	6	Mutant	At Blackstone Hills, E
Cadao Kestrel	7	Magic	Just East of M. Harvey Medical Center, Red River
Anton Sampson	7	Tech	In Liberty Town, SW
Ginger Yates	7	Science	At Blackstone Hills, SE
Numina		Task For	In Williams Square, in Plaza
Infernal		Trainer	In Williams Square, in Plaza
Mark IV (Tech)		Store	In the Gaspee, S
Penny Preston (Mutant)		Store	In Liberty Town, S
Agent Six (Natural)		Store	Under the Gaspee location marker
Exit to Talos Island			North
Exit to Eden			Southwest

Neighborhoods & Villain Groups

Neighborhood	Levels	Villains
Hutchinson Park	37 – 39	Devouring Earth
Liberty Town	31 – 36	Rikti, 5th Column, Nemesis
Williams Square	31 – 33	5th Column
Red River, The	34 – 36	Circle of Thorns, Crey, Nemesis
Blackstone Hills	37 – 39	Devouring Earth
Gaspee, The	37 – 39	Crey, Nemesis, Circle of Thorns
Louis Forest	34 – 36	Circle of Thorns, Devouring Earth

BRICKSTOWN

Levels

Security Levels 30 to 38

Physical Description

Densely populated middle-class area, lots of brown-stone buildings. The center of the zone is dominated by the Ziggurat, the supervillain prison and surrounding security areas.

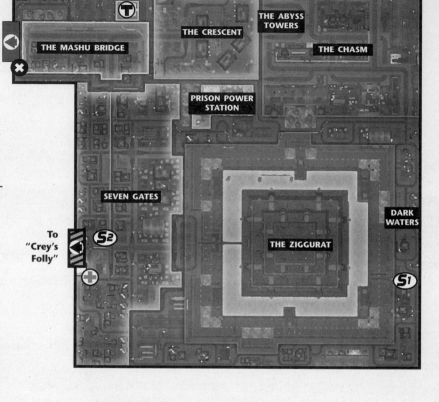

THE MASHU BRIDGE

To Independence Port

THE CRESCENT

THE ABYSS TOWERS

THE CHASM

PRISON POWER STATION

SEVEN GATES

To "Crey's Folly"

THE ZIGGURAT

DARK WATERS

T Monorail Station

+ Hospital

S Store

X Trainer

Safe Zone Entrance

Hazard Zone / Trial

Stores

S1 Holsten Armitage (*Science*)

S2 Serafina (*Magic*)

Mission Doors

Office	Abn Off	Ware	Abn Ware	Tech	Sewers	Caves	5CB	CoT
12	9	28	7	5	52	10	13	9

Background Story

The signature landmark of Brickstown is Ziggursky prison. This mammoth structure is most often called "The Ziggurat," and was constructed to hold prisoners with powers that would allow them to easily escape from normal jails. Other nicknames for the prison, used most often by those within its walls, include "The Brick House," and "The Big Zig."

Ziggursky Prison and Brickstown both lie above a series of natural caverns, and could theoretically be destroyed if those caverns were collapsed. The Freakshow are aware of this weakness and have already made several failed attempts to do just that, in order to free their brethren held within.

Hunting Tips

While lower level than Founders', this zone is slightly harder to hunt in due to the density of the spawns and the ferocity of the enemies. This place is crawling with Freakshow Juicers and Stunners and 5th Column Vampyrs, which are great for experience but challenging for you if you're unprepared. The Juicers and Stunners fly and pursue frequently, and the Vampyrs have several Hold, Slow and Root powers that make retreat impossible, so even just moving through the zone to explore it could result in an unexpected trip to the hospital ... and that's no fun for sightseers.

However, for a prepared group, this is a fantastic zone to street hunt in, with plenty of spawns to keep the experience flowing in. As with any densely populated zone, crowd control is an important survival tactic, because following a runner around a corner could easily add another group to the melee at the worst possible time.

As mentioned in the Founders' Falls section, Brickstown is also crawling with Crey snipers, so watch the building tops for enemies trying to get you centered in their crosshairs.

Resources

Name	StL	Origin	Location
Allison King	6	Magic	S of Crescent (no neighborhood)
Neal Kendrick	6	Tech	Next to Brickstown Infirmary (no neighborhood)
Lou Pasterelli	6	Science	Along the southeast wall
Merisel Valenzuela	6	Mutant	In front of warehouse north of the Ziggurat (no neighborhood)
Gordon Stacy	7	Natural	At the south middle wall
Colleen Nelson	7	Mutant	In "The Crescent" east of the monorail station
Steven Sheridan	7	All	To the right of Brickstown Infirmary
Manticore		Task For	Near Independence Port tunnel (no neighborhood)
Swan		Trainer	Near Independence Port tunnel (no neighborhood)
Holsten Armitage (Sc)		Store	In warehouse east of Ziggurat
Serafina (Magic)		Store	Seven Gates
Exit to Independence Port			Northwest
Exit to Crey's Folly			Southwest
Greenline Monorail			Northwest

Neighborhoods & Villain Groups

Neighborhood	Levels	Villains
Mashu Bridge	30 – 32	5th Column, Crey, Freakshow, Prisoners
Crescent, The	30 – 32	Crey, Freakshow, Prisoners, 5th Column
Prison Power Station	30 – 32	Freakshow, Prisoners
Dark Waters	33 – 35	Freakshow, Prisoners
Seven Gates	30 – 35	5th Column, Crey, Freakshow, Prisoners
Ziggurat, The	33 – 38	5th Column, Crey, Freakshow, Prisoners
Abyss Towers, The	30 – 32	5th Column, Crey, Freakshow, Prisoners
Chasm, The	30 – 35	5th Column, Freakshow, Prisoners

HAZARD ZONES

Hazard zones are sections of the city that have been isolated for one reason or another and have controlled access. This means that for you to enter a given hazard zone, your Security Level must be at least as high as the lowest listed level or you will not be able to enter. Given that being a sidekick only raises your Combat Level, a sidekick can not enter a hazard zone if his Security Level is not high enough, even if he's attached to a Hero who can. Spawns in hazard zones tend to be much larger and closer together, designed for groups of six to eight Heroes, and the police drones are only present at the zone entrances. Additionally, each hazard zone has at least one monster roaming it. Monsters are large enemies that typically require a group to take it down, as they have a lot of hit points and are capable of dishing out vast amounts of damage.

PEREZ PARK

Levels

Security Levels 7 to 14

Physical Description

A large forest surrounded by city buildings. At one end of the park is a large lake with rivers branching from it.

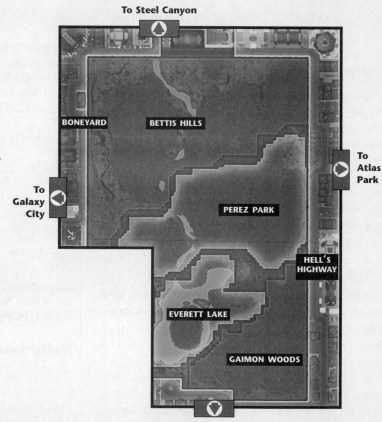

Mission Doors

Office	Abn Off	Ware	Abn Ware	Tech	Sewers	Caves	5CB	CoT
5	15	0	0	10	13	50	0	0

Background Story

Nestled near the center of the city, the park borders Atlas Park to the east and Galaxy City to the west. Also connected to this paradise lost is Skyway City to the south and Steel Canyon to the north.

Perez Park was once an idyllic retreat from hectic city life, and home to many areas where families would picnic or simply relax in the sun. Tree-lined walkways meandered through the park and were often populated by couples taking romantic evening strolls. The Gaiman Amphitheatre show-cased outdoor performances (including those by the acclaimed "Paragon City Players"). Everett Lake provided a lovely splash of cool blue water, while the nearby Bendis Lake House was popular among the crowds for its famous burgers.

Recently, the tranquility of the area has been shattered. Perez Park is now infested by many different villains — all with varying agendas. Not only has the area become a favored spot for the dark rituals performed by The Circle of Thorns, but Vahzilok, Clockwork and others are often spotted there. The biggest problem the park has, however, is that it's become a focus of the gang wars in Paragon City.

Two groups of thugs, the Hellions and the Skulls, have intensified their conflicts here. Both of these gangs are connected to more powerful organizations, but no one has been able to conclusively determine their benefactors. One thing's for certain, — anyone caught in Perez Park at the wrong time is likely to get caught between these two vicious groups during one of their many skirmishes.

Hunting Tips

Perez is one of the most difficult zones to traverse, and that is only partially due to the spawn density. The center of the park consists of a maze of "tun-nel-like" paths through the forest, and the over-head map does not reflect these "tunnels," which means you can spend a lot of time wandering around, pretty much lost, just to find a mission waypoint that's "somewhere" in the middle, all the

while trying to deal with the Vahzilok and Circle of Thorns enemies that live there. If ever there was a zone that defined the need for the Teleport Friend power, this is it. Leapers can bounce over the top of the canopy, and fliers can fly, but since they can't pop down through the dense covering of the trees, they are also forced to drop to the ground and roam through the "tunnels." Since the map doesn't show where you are or where you've been, sometimes the best solution is to use the old maze tactic of putting your right hand on a wall and fol-lowing it, making all right turns, until you're where you want to be.

Street hunters will enjoy the veritable cornucopia of targets here, as pretty much every faction at this level spawns somewhere in this zone, and in very large groups. Starting on the streets outside the walls, work your way through the armies of Skulls and Hellions, being careful to not aggravate other groups in the densely spawned area. As you advance, move within the park walls and fight the Circle of Thorns, Clockwork, Lost and Vahzilok that can be found there. Hydra are also excellent to fight, though care must be taken to watch for the Kraken, the hydra monster that roams Everett Lake.

Resources

Name	Location
Exit to Steel Canyon	North
Exit to Galaxy City	West
Exit to Atlas Park	East
Exit to Skyway City	South

Neighborhoods & Villain Groups

Neighborhood	Levels	Villains
Gaiman Woods	9 – 12	Clockwork, Hellions, The Lost
Bettis Hills	7 – 11	Circle of Thorns, The Lost, Hellions, Vahzilok, Skulls, Clockwork
Hell's Highway	7 – 10	Hellions
Boneyard	7 – 10	Skulls
Everett Lake	9 – 14	Hydra Men, Clockwork, Circle of Thorns

BOOMTOWN

Levels

Security Levels 11 to 19

Physical Description

A destroyed urban area, once boasting a vista of skyscrapers and massive office complexes, but now a smoldering, debris-littered battlefield.

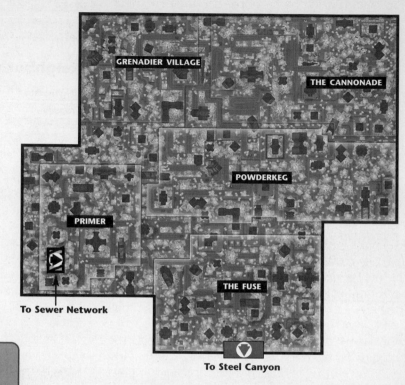

GRENADIER VILLAGE

THE CANNONADE

POWDERKEG

PRIMER

THE FUSE

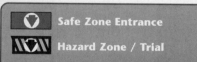
To Sewer Network

To Steel Canyon

	Safe Zone Entrance
	Hazard Zone / Trial

Mission Doors

Office	Abn Off	Ware	Abn Ware	Tech	Sewers	Caves	5CB	CoT
0	25	0	0	0	20	0	0	0

Background Story

Boomtown is as dead as Steel Canyon is alive. Choked with smoke, flames and debris from the Rikti attack, this area took the brunt of the damage to the city. Skyscrapers as tall as those found in Steel Canyon lie toppled and broken, stumps of concrete and steel jutting into the blackened sky like rotting teeth. Train tracks lie twisted and deformed, while burning and broken carcasses of cars can be found in alleys, rubble piles and even tossed into the remains of park trees, a testimony to the savage fury of the attacks in this region. Huge craters, many still smoking, dot the landscape, contributing to the area's apocalyptic feel.

Given the chaos that reigns here, the city's law enforcement officials have walled it off and are fighting a stalemated battle with its denizens, a menagerie of the city's villain population.

Hunting Tips

This is a great zone for hunters who are coming out of Steel Canyon and dislike the confined spaces of Skyway. With lots of wide open spaces, the spawns are not dense at all, and there are many factions here to choose from. The zone is relatively easy to get around in, especially once you get used to it, so the only real downside is the fact that, with all the rubble and debris around, it can be hard to spot a spawn until you're right upon it. However, perceptive Heroes will spot the NPC chatter that is the telltale sign of most villain groups, or the audio cues for those mobs that do not speak, like the Clockwork. Hunting here is relatively simple, with lots of room to engage enemy groups at range, break them apart and manage them. Babbage, the Clockwork monster, roams the Grenadier neighborhood, so be on the lookout for him if you're hunting in that area.

Resources

Name	Location
Exit to Steel Canyon	South
Exit to the Sewer Network	West

Neighborhoods & Villain Groups

Neighborhood	Levels	Villains
Grenadier	14 – 20	The Lost, Clockwork, Outcasts
Cannonade, The	14 – 20	Clockwork, Trolls, Outcasts, The Lost, Vahzilok, 5th Column
Powderkeg	11 – 17	Clockwork, Trolls, Outcasts, The Lost, Vahzilok, 5th Column
Primer	11 – 17	Clockwork, Trolls, 5th Column, Outcasts
Fuze, The	11 – 13	Clockwork, Trolls, Outcasts, Vahzilok

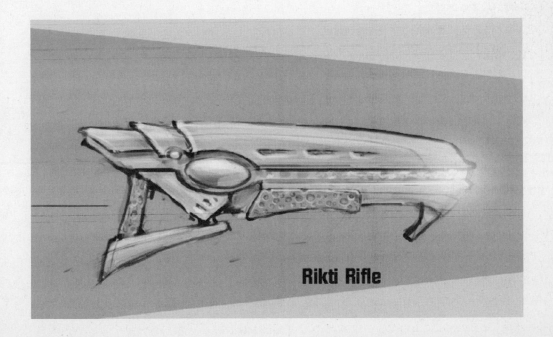

Rikti Rifle

DARK ASTORIA

Levels

Security Levels 21 to 29

Physical Description

A dark, foggy cityscape with abandoned buildings and vehicles strewn everywhere covers the vast majority of Dark Astoria. At the northeast corner of the zone, an enormous desecrated cemetery looms.

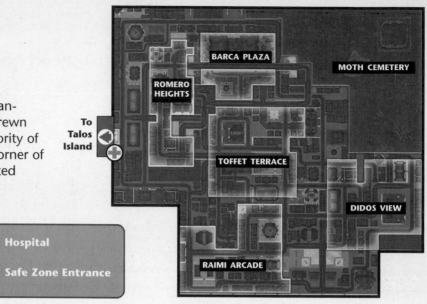

Mission Doors

Office	Abn Off	Ware	Abn Ware	Tech	Sewers	Caves	5CB	CoT
0	43	0	6	0	12	12	12	6

Background Story

Once an idyllic commercial center, much like Talos Island and Steel Canyon, this area thrived as people bustled about their daily lives. Even the presence of the pastoral Moth Cemetery did not detract from the beauty of this area. The Rikti invasion came and went, and the people in this peaceful neighborhood were relatively untouched by the devastation. However, while the Heroes of Paragon were busy rebuilding the city, the trickster god of the Banished Pantheon stumbled upon something ... beneath the sod and graves of Moth Cemetery lay an ancient god, far older than those of the Pantheon, and far more powerful. Wishing to use this power to release him and his fellow gods, he ordered all of his followers to invade the area and seize control of it.

The city authorities and Heroes, already reduced in number and staggering from the Rikti onslaught, had no choice but to relinquish the area to the Pantheon and wall it off. Within the walls, the army of Husks and Shaman ravaged the zone, tore the ground apart and sacrificed every man, woman and child in their efforts to wake the god Mot, but all their efforts were in vain. To this day, Lughebu's soldiers search for a way to wake the sleeper, while the spirits of those who once lived there wander about, unable to sleep.

Hunting Tips

"Skyway with fog" describes most of this zone, as it has many of the navigational challenges of Skyway City with a tenth of the visibility. However, the spawn density is far sparser than Skyway's, so navigating the zone while you can't see fifty feet in front of your face is not quite as dangerous as it sounds. Outside of Moth, in the city portion of the zone, the hunting is pretty much the same as Steel Canyon, with sparse spawns of large groups to compensate for the poor visibility.

Inside of Moth, however, different tactics need to be used. The spawns are higher level, more powerful and denser. Enemies will pop up out of the ground when you step near them and quickly surround you. Massive chasms, filled with Shaman and Totems, must be navigated around and in. Mausoleums, hillocks and fissures hide spawn from view until you're right upon them. And Adamastor, the Banished Pantheon monster, roams this area with impunity. Careful planning and crowd control is required in the cemetery to avoid drawing the attention of more than one group at a time, or being ambushed by a hidden group you weren't expecting.

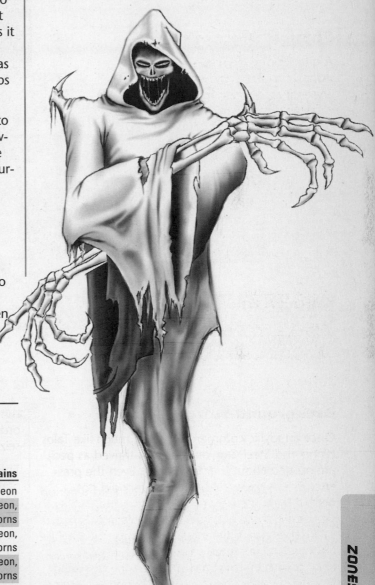

Resources

Name	Location
Exit to Talos Island	West

Neighborhoods & Villain Groups

Neighborhood	Levels	Villains
Moth Cemetery	27 – 29	Banished Pantheon
Dido's View	24 – 26	Tsoo, Banished Pantheon, Circle of Thorns
Raimi Arcade	21 – 26	Tsoo, Banished Pantheon, Circle of Thorns
Toffet Terrace	24 – 26	Tsoo, Banished Pantheon, Circle of Thorns
Barca Plaza	24 – 26	Tsoo, Banished Pantheon, Circle of Thorns
Romero Heights	21 – 26	Tsoo, Banished Pantheon, Circle of Thorns

CREY'S FOLLY

Levels

Security Levels 30 to 38

Physical Description

A giant sewage disposal or treatment facility appears to cover a vast majority of the area. The large lake of water seems extremely dirty, if not toxic, and the facility itself appears well worn.

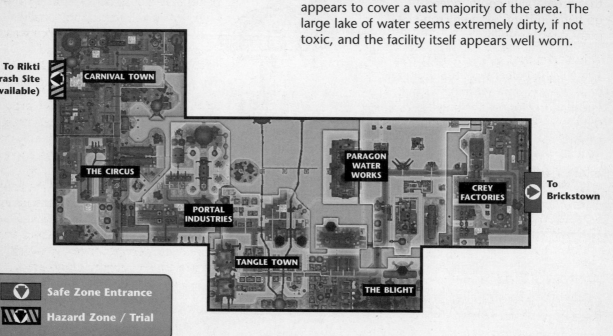

⬇	Safe Zone Entrance
〰⬇〰	Hazard Zone / Trial

Mission Doors

Office	Abn Off	Ware	Abn Ware	Tech	Sewers	Caves	5CB	CoT
0	9	5	52	0	20	0	0	0

Background Story

In the early 1900s, Paragon City entered a period of intense industrialization. Corporations quickly accumulated land near Paragon City's profitable port and converted it into a veritable ocean of manufacturing. Warehouses, factories and sweatshops dotted the once pleasant neighborhoods. Dark clouds billowing from myriad smoke stacks created a permanent noxious fog. Engineers quickly converted the streams and rivers into canals that swept away the constant flow of industrial waste. Paragonians nicknamed this area "Venice" for these omnipresent watercourses.

In the 1940s and '50s, increased awareness of the environment provided the impetus for change in the zone. Slowly, new technology allowed corporations to change their previous methods and cut down on the pollution in the area. While the zone would never become an area for family living, it no longer posed an imminent threat to the health of the city. Saying that one worked in "Venice" no longer carried the connotations of dismal and deadly working conditions. In fact, the area became the poster-child of the '70s environmental movement; it was held up as proof that profitability could indeed go hand in hand with environmental responsibility.

This all changed with the Rikti War. The alien invaders targeted a Crey facility in the area in their initial assault. The resulting explosion not only devastated the Crey labs, but also created a strange element that poisoned the area. A greenish miasma now lies as a thick mist everywhere. The once clean waters that made the area famous are now filled with brackish muck. During the war, the area was quickly abandoned; it no longer had any strategic use.

Hunting Tips

This is the roughest of the hazard zones for many reasons. All of the enemies are not only high level, but complex in their attacks, with multiple power sets and damage types available to them. Add to that the fact that many of the Freakshow and Crey enemies will take flight to pursue you, and Devouring Earth foes will pop up out of the water with no advance notice, and you've got a truly hazardous zone on your hands. Unlike zones such as Independence Port or Talos Island, where the water can be a refuge, here it is very dangerous because enemies literally appear out of the water. In other zones, if you see the spawn and see them turn towards you, indicating you've partially drawn aggro, it allows you the chance to back off before being attacked. Here, that delay is invisible to you and when they pop up, they do it to attack. Consequently, the water is best avoided unless you're actively looking to fight Devouring Earth.

Crey, Rikti and Nemesis are always fighting it out in the factory areas, especially on the catwalks between the smoke stacks — this zone is very much a three-dimensional one, combat-wise, especially given Crey's propensity for taking flight to flee from or chase you. There's nothing special about the tactics here, beyond being aware of spawns occurring above you while you fight. Additionally, many of the buildings and catwalks are decorated with Crey and Nemesis Snipers, always looking for ways to reduce the Hero population.

The Circus and Carnival Town are "Barter Town" mazes of sheet metal and debris that are extraordinarily difficult to traverse on the ground and full of very densely spawned groups of Freakshow. If at all possible, pull the Freaks out of the area to fight instead of engaging them on their own turf, because it's virtually impossible to spot the spawns hidden behind and under things until you step into them, at which point you've doubled your enemy numbers.

Resources

Name	Location
Exit to Brickstown	East
Exit to the Rikti Crash Site	West

Neighborhoods & Villain Groups

Neighborhood	Levels	Villains
Paragon Water Works	31 – 36	Crey, **Devouring Earth**, Freakshow, Nemesis, Rikti
Blight, The	34 – 36	Crey, **Devouring Earth**, Rikti
Tangle Town	34 – 36	Crey, **Devouring Earth**, Nemesis, Rikti, Freakshow
Portal Industries	34 – 36	**Devouring Earth**, Freakshow, Rikti, Nemesis
Carnival Town	37 – 39	Freakshow, **Devouring Earth**, Nemesis, Crey
Circus, The	37 – 39	Crey, **Devouring Earth**, Freakshow, Nemesis, Rikti
Crey Factories	31 – 33	Crey, **Devouring Earth**, Freakshow, Nemesis, Rikti

TRIAL ZONES

Trial zones are exactly like hazard zones above, with two exceptions: no random monsters roaming around, and a defining mission as the basis for the zone.

FAULTLINE

Levels

Security Levels 14 to 19

Physical Description

An enormous metropolitan area torn apart by an earthquake. At the southern end, stands a giant facility resembling a hydroelectric plant.

Background Story

The Overbrook Dam was an amazing step forward for Paragon City. It began a new area of prosperity for the city. The Overbrook sprawl naturally spread from the area and was quite prosperous until the earthquake hit. Now Faultline is an area of chaos and destruction under constant siege. Many different villain gangs want to control the dam for their own purposes. If this is ever allowed to happen, it will be a huge blow to the peace and safety of the entirety of the City of Heroes.

The Trial

The Faultline Trial is initiated by accessing the terminal in the dam at the far end of the zone from the entrance. To be able to participate in this trial, you must be at least Level 14 and you and your teammates must all be in the same Super Group. This trial is designed for twenty-five Level 19 Heroes *or* thirty-five Level 18 *or* fifty Level 17 Heroes.

The trial room is vast — and mostly water. Four pylons stand toward the front of the trial, connected by a pathway that zigzags between each. A building stands on a narrow strip of land to one side of the feeder river at the far end of the trial. This building and the four pylons are subject to attacks from villains. Each structure has a set amount of hit points; at 0, they

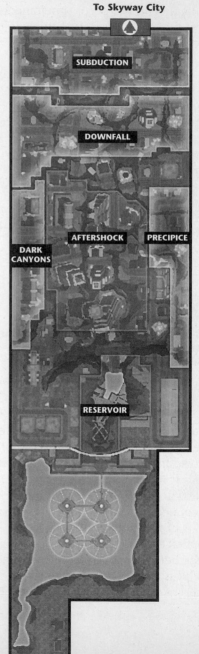

begin to smoke, and are considered "destroyed."

Waves of minions and lieutenants attack the pylons; a boss-level villain lies in wait at the far building. Depending on the size of the Super Group, the attacks will progress from one pylon to another — until eventually the building is targeted — or the attacks will occur simultaneously, so that the group has to spread itself thinly in order to defend each location.

You must successfully defend 3 of the 5 structures (that is, prevent them from being "destroyed") for 45 minutes.

Defeated Heroes appear at the entrance of the trial and can immediately join back in the fighting, without having to run back from the hospital.

The reward for this trial is a medal on your ID card, a large Experience Point bonus, and a special Enhancement that modifies two or more powers/effects and is valid at +/- 5 levels instead of the normal 3.

Hunting Tips

The most difficult zone in the game to traverse, Faultline is virtually impossible to navigate effectively without fly, leap or teleport. Large groups of Vahzilok and Clockwork roam the broken streets, while the Circle of Thorns dominates the dark recesses of the massive chasms that rip through the area.

Tactically speaking, this zone can cause some serious headaches. With only two types of terrain available for fighting in, block-sized "islands" and narrow crevasses, there is no room to run without falling off a cliff and/or running through another group of enemies. The good news is that there are a lot of places to perch and attack mobs at range with little-to-no way for them to close the distance between you, and very few of the enemies in this zone can fly, the exception being the Daemons summoned by the Circle of Thorns.

For the trial, go for a good mix of melee archetypes and don't focus on the size of the group as much because the villain spawn will match the group size based upon a pre-determined balance … to a point. So, if you're a Level 17 Hero, you need to plan on bringing 49 Level 17 friends because the trial will be spawning enough to deal with 50 of you. You can certainly bring less, but expect the fight to be a lot rougher. Load up on Inspirations and bring folks who can fight for long periods of time on low Endurance because 45 minutes is a *long* time to be constantly fighting. Don't burn Inspirations or Endurance on resurrecting people, both because there's no need to do so (as they respawn just down the hall) and more importantly if you resurrect someone (or yourself) in the midst of the fighting, you're very likely to be quickly defeated again and just add more debt. Click "OK," take the free Heal and Endurance recharge, and run down the hall to rejoin the fight.

Resources

Name	Location
Exit to Skyway City	North

Neighborhoods & Villain Groups

Neighborhood	Levels	Villains
Subduction	11 – 13	Clockwork, Vahzilok, Circle of Thorns
Downfall	11 – 17	Clockwork, Vahzilok, Circle of Thorns
Aftershock	14 – 20	Clockwork, Vahzilok, Circle of Thorns
Dark Canyons	14 – 20	Vahzilok, Circle of Thorns
Precipice	14 – 20	Clockwork, Circle of Thorns
Reservoir	18 – 20	Clockwork, Vahzilok, Circle of Thorns

TERRA VOLTA

Levels

Security Levels 23 to 29

Physical Description

A polluted landscape populated by numerous industrial facilities. A giant aqueduct adorns the center of the zone and massive cooling towers dominate the southern end.

Safe Zone Entrance

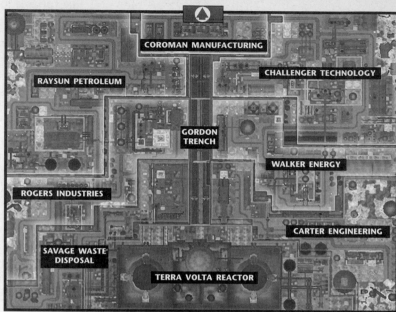

To Independence Port (exit on roof)

COROMAN MANUFACTURING

CHALLENGER TECHNOLOGY

RAYSUN PETROLEUM

GORDON TRENCH

WALKER ENERGY

ROGERS INDUSTRIES

CARTER ENGINEERING

SAVAGE WASTE DISPOSAL

TERRA VOLTA REACTOR

Background Story

As paragon city expanded in the 1950s, its power needs continued to grow. The city's forward thinking planners conceived of a plan to provide efficient energy to meet the city's projected growth well into the next century.

Construction began in 1955 and was completed in 1959. The first super villain attack occurred 14 hours after the Terra Volta plant went online. The entire project had been plagued and delayed by interference from super villains, setting a precedent of sorts which would be continued throughout Terra Volta's entire history of operation.

Beset from all sides, the city's Heroes and the selfless efforts of it's municipal workers are the only force that can keep the Terra Volta complex from falling completely under the near-constant attack from multiple villain groups. Meanwhile, the aging reactor continues to pour out power to keep the city running.

The Trial

The Terra Volta Trial is initiated by accessing the terminal near the cooling towers at the back of the zone. This trial is for up to eight Heroes who are at least Level 23, with no Super Group being required. Upon entry, the group leader is given a Coolant Gun. The players progress through four rooms — each filled with villains — before reacing the "core." If the Heroes attempt to run past the foes of one room, they'll be followed into the next.

Once you reach the fifth room, the climactic room, you find the reactor under constant attack.

Villains keep spawning again and again around the large room. The reactor core itself is in a central glass-walled room. There are four possible entrances to the core — the group must defend these doors while the Hero with the Coolant Gun enters the core and attempts to deactivate it. Once the Hero has done enough "damage" with the gun, the attack stops and the trial is over.

Defeated Heroes appear in the first room instead of the hospital.

The reward for this trial is a medal on your ID card, a large Experience Point bonus, and a special Enhancement that modifies two or more powers/effects and is valid at +/- 5 levels instead of the normal 3. Additionally, the radiation from the reactor has "mutated" the Heroes such that they can reselect their Archetype, powers and power sets. Enhancements are put into a "special bag" for this process and reallocated when done. Unallocated Enhancements are lost.

Hunting Tips

While not as difficult to traverse as some zones, the horseshoe shape of Terra Volta (around the Gordon Trench and Reactor) and massive walls make getting where you want when you want somewhat difficult without fly, leap or teleport. Terra Volta is essentially a war zone, with large groups of Freakshow fighting Sky Raiders, Sky Raiders fighting Devouring Earth, Lost fighting Freakshow, and so forth. Everywhere you turn, there are big mixed-villain groups going at it, all of which will turn and suddenly become friends against you if you draw their attention. The spawns are not dense, but they are big, and the buildings and fences frequently hide spawns until you're too near to avoid them. If you're hunting Freakshow, just walk around — they're everywhere and isolated enough to make pulling them apart easy. Sky Raiders are always either on catwalks, roofs or the alleys between buildings, again in large spawns, far apart. The Lost are always underneath things or hiding away, like

cockroaches, and the Devouring Earth stay in the destroyed sections, fending off the other factions from trying to push them out.

Given that the trial only allows 8 Heroes, it's imperative that you pick a good balance, because the team is going to take a *serious* beating. Any ranged Heroes had better be there for crowd control and be able to sustain that effort for a long period of time, without running out of Endurance halfway through. With no room to maneuver, no room to get airborne, and little room to avoid melee from villains, this is definitely a mission for more durable Heroes. The doors in the final room are close enough that people from one can step over and help those at another, but all four doors need to be protected. The person with the Cooling Gun needs to focus on his task and not be distracted to help teammates, so pick someone who can devote his attention without affecting the entire team.

Resources

Name	Location
Exit to Independence Port	North

Neighborhoods & Villain Groups

Neighborhood	Levels	Villains
Carter Engineering	28 – 29	Freakshow, Sky Raiders, Rikti, Devouring Earth
Terra Volta Reactor	28 – 29	Freakshow, Sky Raiders, Rikti, Devouring Earth
Savage Waste Disposal	28 – 29	Sky Raiders, Freakshow, Rikti
Walker Energy	26 – 27	Freakshow, Sky Raiders, Rikti
Gordon Trench	28 – 29	Rikti
Rogers Industries	26 – 27	Freakshow, Sky Raiders, Rikti, Devouring Earth
Challenger Technology	23 – 25	Freakshow, Sky Raiders, Rikti, Devouring Earth
Raysun Petroleum	23 – 25	Freakshow, Skyaiders, Rikti, Devouring Earth
Coroman Manufacturing	23 – 25	Sky Raiders, Freakshow

EDEN

Levels

Security
Levels
36 to 40

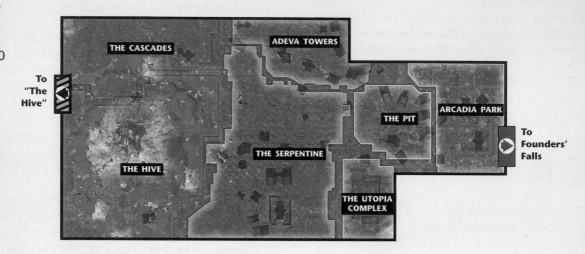

Physical Description

Large commercial area covered with dense foliage and falling buildings. To the southeast, an abandoned Crey facility. To the west, spires protrude from what appears to be a giant anthill.

Background Story

Once, Eden was a beautiful suburb of Paragon City called Woodvale. It was the prime location for families to set up residence. There were many parks and it had easy for drives into the country. This proved to be its undoing. Offended by the encroaching urban sprawl, the Devouring Earth launched a massive assault on Woodvale. The creatures destroyed many of the buildings and other man-made objects. The rest they buried or left in ruin, driving all the previous inhabitants into the city proper. Now, Eden is a sprawling wilderness, with nature slowly taking over completely. If the spread of the forces of the Devouring Earth is not stopped, it could soon begin to swallow other parts of the city.

The Trial

In the neighborhood called The Hive there are spires that resemble termite mounds or ant hills. Within the largest of these is a cavern that contains an open well, above which hovers the Spirit of the Woodsman. The task of the Heroes is to keep the Spirit alive while wave after wave of villains attacks it for 30 minutes. This is a mission for 8-50 Heroes, all in the same Super Group, all level 36 or higher.

Defeated Heroes appear in a side chamber in the mound and can quickly rejoin their teammates.

The reward for this trial is a medal on your ID card, a large Experience Point bonus, and a special Enhancement that modifies two or more power attributes and is valid at +/- 5 levels instead of the normal 3.

Hunting Tips

This zone is second only to Faultline for difficulty of maneuvering. Two-thirds of the zone is similar to Boomtown and relatively easy to move about in, but the middle third has all of the worst aspects of Perez Park, with tunnel-like pathways through the forest that are filled with large groups of Devouring Earth to block your path and become aggressive on you as you round the corner into them.

Crey and Nemesis are sprinkled about the zone, primarily in the front and the abandoned complex, but the vast majority of the enemies here are the Devouring Earth. The spawns are large and sporadic, with some areas having very tight groups, and others very sparse. As with Boomtown, the rubble frequently hides spawn until you're right up on them, and given the dangerous nature of the spawn, this is not an area you want to be surprised in. So keep alert, use solid crowd control, and don't chase those runners.

Eden is the most difficult trial in many ways. First is obviously the power level of the enemies involved. Then there is the literally uncountable number of spawns. And lastly is the fact that the primary objective of every spawned enemy is to launch attacks at the Spirit of the Woodsman until they are attacked by you, which means someone needs to be watching for spawns and every single enemy must be engaged the moment it spawns. 30 minutes is a very long time to keep something alive, especially when everything that appears in the room has destroying it as their primary objective until they are interrupted. While logic may indicate a Blaster or Controller could use an area-of-effect attack in the spawn area to draw the spawned enemies' attention, that logic tends to break down when you consider that every spawned enemy will then turn its aggro to the Blaster or Controller, at least until they are dead from the withering barrage, then the enemies will return their attention to the Woodsman. The most effective method is to use a Tanker, preferably one with the Provoke power, as all it takes to disrupt the AI is the slightest bit of annoyance. The Tanker can then, in turn, soak up as much damage as possible while the other Heroes dispatch the now distracted enemies.

Resources

Name	StL	Origin	Location
Exit to Founders' Falls			East
Exit to The Hive			West

Neighborhoods & Villain Groups

Neighborhood	Levels	Villains
Arcadia Park	33 – 34	Devouring Earth, Nemesis
Utopia Complex, The	33 – 34	Crey, Devouring Earth
Adeva Towers	35 – 36	Devouring Earth, Nemesis
Serpentine, The	35 – 36	Devouring Earth
Hive, The	37 – 39	Devouring Earth
Cascades, The	37 – 39	Devouring Earth
Pit, The	35 – 36	Devouring Earth, Nemesis

SEWER NETWORK

Levels

Security Levels 36 to 40

Physical Description

Extensive labyrinthine sewer network.

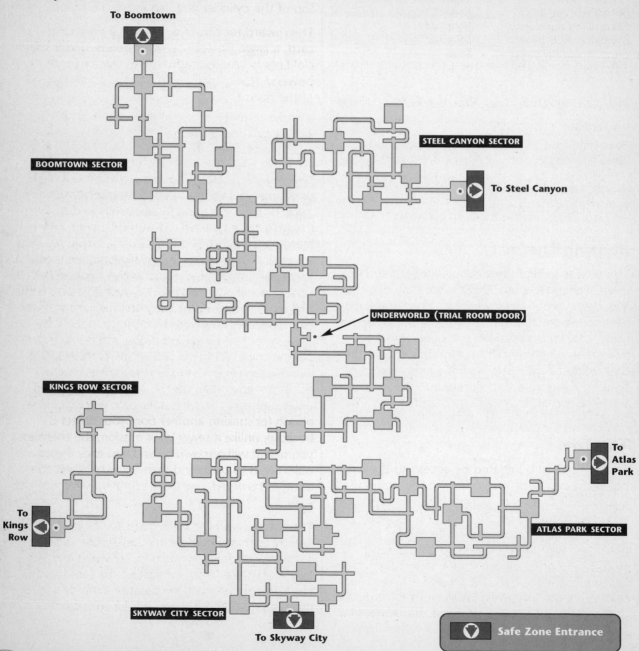

To Boomtown

STEEL CANYON SECTOR

BOOMTOWN SECTOR

To Steel Canyon

UNDERWORLD (TRIAL ROOM DOOR)

KINGS ROW SECTOR

To
Atlas
Park

To
Kings
Row

ATLAS PARK SECTOR

SKYWAY CITY SECTOR

To Skyway City

▼ Safe Zone Entrance

Resources

Name	StL Origin	Location
Trial Room Door		Center
Exit to Boomtown Sewer		North
Exit to Steel Canyon Sewer		Northeast
Exit to Atlas Park Sewer		Southeast
Exit to Skyway City Sewer		South
Exit to Kings Row Sewer		West

Neighborhoods & Villain Groups

Neighborhood	Levels	Villains
Boomtown Sector	37 – 40	Tentacle, Amoeba Men, Rikti
Steel Canyon Sector	37 – 40	Tentacle, Amoeba Men, Rikti
Underworld	38 – 40	Vahzilok, Rikti, Tentacle
Kings Row Sector	35 – 38	Tentacle, Warriors, Rikti
Skyway City Sector	37 – 39	Vahzilok, Tentacle, Warriors, Rikti
Atlas Park Sector	35 – 38	Vahzilok, Amoeba Men, Tentacle

Background Story

The sewers of Paragon City are very old and very deep. The most recent levels were built over the top of the ones from the previous century. Lately there has been a great deal of monstrous activity in the sewers, and many Paragon City workers have been attacked or abducted. There is a rumor that at the deepest level of the sewers lies a great beast of some kind, but no one that has ever searched for it is known to have returned.

The Trial

The Sewer Trial is initiated by accessing the terminal at the center of the zone. The trial room itself is a cylinder filled with labyrinthine walkways that descend into a murky pit. Hydra Men fiercely protect the passage downwards; the Heroes must fight their way through. Should enterprising Heroes leap or fly by the Hydra Men, they will follow the Heroes to the bottom and join their master against the intruders. The Heroes must defeat the Hydra head at the bottom of the cylinder in

45 minutes to complete the trial. This is a mission for 8 Heroes, levels 36 and higher.

Defeated Heroes appear in a side chamber at the top of the cylinder and can rejoin their team.

The reward for this trial is a medal on your ID card, a large Experience Point bonus, and a special Enhancement that modifies two or more powers/effects and is valid at +/- 5 levels instead of the normal 3.

Hunting Tips

To get to this zone, enter the normal Sewer Network from any of the entrances above ground, then immediately look around for a small metal door. Go through it, and it will take you down to the Abandoned Sewers. As with the Sewer Network, this zone is essentially one incredibly long sewer door mission. By incredibly long, we mean that your group could spend twelve hours in this zone and still not see all of it. If your objective is the trial room in the center, your best bet is one person with Teleport Friend and Invisibility just running straight to it and avoiding all the introductory combat, because your group could spend three hours just fighting their way to it. If your goal is experience and adventure, then enter at one door and make getting to another door your objective. The reason for making another door your object is because, unlike a sewer door mission, the enemies you defeat will respawn behind you and, if your objective is to go in and then come back out the door you entered, you will be fighting your way out as well.

The spawns are high-level, good sized, and spaced exactly as they would be in a sewer door mission, so the risk of drawing additional enemies accidentally is very low. When navigating, be careful when you come to intersections because a group of enemies can be sitting just around the corner and

catch you unprepared. It is also wise to frequently check for targets as you walk along, as there are Hydra Tentacles all over this zone that pop up out of the water to attack.

For the trial, bring a solid, well-balanced group as there will obviously be a lot of fighting. Defeat all the Hydra Men because if you don't, they will fol-low you down and complicate the big fight at the end. They don't respawn, so getting rid of them is the best solution. In the final area, the group can not all focus on the head because the tentacles spawn fast and furious and will dispatch the Heroes one-by-one. The best solution is to delegate the head to one or two of your team while the rest fend off the tentacles.

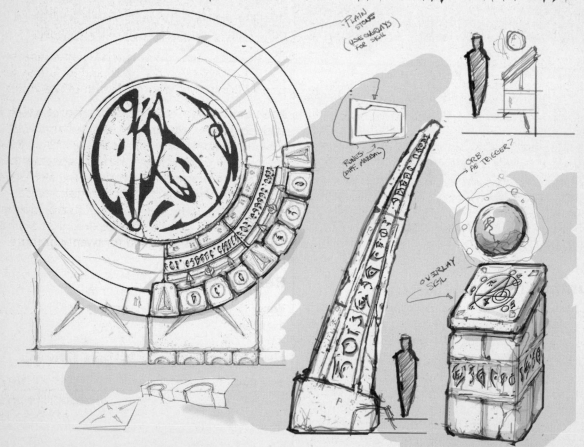

THE HIVE

Levels

Levels 38+

Physical Description

Rocky area with termite-mound spires and hills. A huge crater resides near the center that houses the Amoeba that is Hamidon. An Abandoned Crey facility perches in the northwest corner.

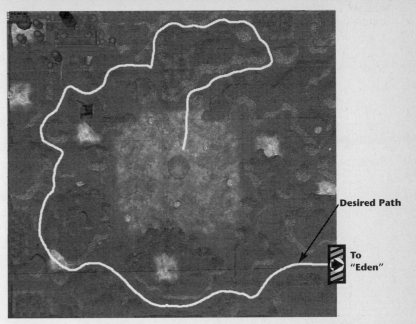

Desired Path

To "Eden"

Hazard Zone / Trial

Background Story

The Hive is perhaps one of the most dangerous areas in all of Paragon City. It lies deep within the wild untamed regions of Eden and contains many forces of the Devouring Earth. Few Heroes have ever ventured in without being defeated and none have explored the Hive in full. It is strongly recommended that Heroes venturing into the Hive be fully prepared and travel in as large a group as possible. In addition, only those with superior tactics will have a chance of success in this deadly complex.

Hunting Tips

Bring friends. Lots of them. First off, the front door has a pair of Level 40 monsters, which will take at least two groups to defeat. The zone is adorned with several such groups that you will need to navigate through before you arrive at your destination. Additionally, the Devouring Swarms that hover about the zone are nothing like the normal Devouring Earth Swarms you've encountered before. They do a *lot* more damage, do not fly away (they just stay and eat you), and

can not be shaken off of you no matter where you go or what you do, up to and including teleporting/jumping/flying the length of the zone.

The Hamidon is a giant amoeba, part of which is sticking out of the ground here. He can not be truly defeated, but he can be pushed back, which is your goal if you're here. He's in the center of a group of three types of Mitochondria, all Level 40 archvillains, with the nucleus being the actual Hamidon. These assistants do not move, can not be pulled solo, and must all be fought as a group. This encounter is designed for twenty or more Level 40 Heroes.

Resources

Name	StL	Origin	Location
Exit to Eden			South

Neighborhoods & Villain Groups

Neighborhood	Levels	Villains
The Hive	40 – 42	Devouring Earth Monsters and Archvillains

ZONES

MISSION ZONES

Mission zones are dynamically created zones that are personalized for you and your group. There are nine different types of locale, each with its own character and optimum tactics.

GENERAL TACTICS

Some suggestions that apply to all mission zones:

◆ Just because you complete your objective does not mean the zone is empty. Take the time to make sure you've cleared out all the enemies, as those are easily accessible targets for experience and drops that you don't want to waste.

◆ When you are ready to leave a completed mission, you don't have to find your way out — just click on the green Mission Complete text at the top of the screen and you'll instantly leave the zone.

◆ Mission objective objects — the glowing objects present in some missions, usually called *glowies* — are not always easy to find. They are frequently small and stashed in corners and behind things, so as you move through a mission area, make sure to explore it thoroughly on your first pass. Otherwise, you may find yourself at the end of the mission zone and missing a few glowies, which means you and your team must now back-track through the entire area, searching in every nook and cranny, to complete your mission.

◆ Likewise, make sure that you explore the area well enough to get a good, clear mission map without major gaps. In particular, make sure you get a strong outline of the walls in large chambers, to ensure that you're not missing any small or obscured passages that might lead somewhere interesting or important.

OFFICE

The office maps range in size from very small to huge and multi-level. They contain a standard corporate office environment, with cubicles, office equipment, vending machines, and so forth. Lots of stairs and catwalks adorn many of the areas, and many enemies can become aggressive across these spaces. Simply because you cannot see the target does not mean it cannot see and attack you. To travel from floor to floor, find the elevator rooms and check the bright green arrow, indicating which way the elevator goes (up or down, always found in separate rooms). There will also be a sign on the wall saying what floor you're on. Not all office missions go up, but instead start on a higher floor and go down. Pay careful attention to which direction you entered a floor so you know which direction to exit it, either to advance through the mission or exit the zone. The glowies on these maps can be inside cubicles or in side offices, even under desks and other furniture, so prepare to spend some time searching, especially for the smaller ones, like bombs. Many of the corners on this map are tight, so take care when going around a corner or at an intersection lest you run unprepared into a group of enemies. The rooms are large enough to fly in, but many of the hallways are not.

One thing to note, the office and abandoned office maps are the most common ones used by the AI for ambushes, due to the ledged nature of some of the layouts. When entering one of these maps, make sure to move through the first hallway cautiously, as there may be a ledge above your head filled with enemies that are aware of your presence and will drop upon you the moment you appear beneath them.

ABANDONED OFFICE

The abandoned office maps are exactly like the office maps above, except in disarray and slightly darker, due to lights being out. Same floor plans, same layouts, the only difference is the shabbiness and the state of disrepair of the items and furniture. The elevators look and behave exactly the same as on the office maps.

WAREHOUSE

Warehouse missions are always flat and single-level, though there are some catwalks and upper decks in the large rooms (sometimes connected by upstairs hallways). The areas are always big, large enough for fliers to escape melee range most of the time. The rooms are filled with crates, forklifts, shelves, office furniture and other things typically found in a warehouse. Glowies on this map are frequently behind stacks of crates or inside cubicles, so careful searching will be required to find all of them. The corridors are wide enough that it's relatively easy to navigate them without too many surprises.

ABANDONED WAREHOUSE

Abandoned warehouse missions are identical to warehouse missions. The only difference is the disrepair of the fixtures and the slightly darker lighting. Shelves are knocked over, things are broken and dingy, and so forth.

TECH

Tech maps are straight out of any televised space drama, with futuristic lighting and fixtures and lots of blinking, flashing and pulsing lights and sounds. Otherwise, these maps function the same as office maps. The elevators function the same, though there are only three per room instead of four, and the maps are frequently vertical, going up or down, as with office maps. One difference,

while Office maps usually only have one elevator going into a floor and one going out, Tech maps often have two, or sometimes three, elevators going out of the level, each one leading to a different area of the mission. Also, be on the alert for very narrow hallways hidden almost invisibly behind walls — this is a map type where thorough mapping is crucial.

SEWERS

Sewer maps are composed of green, dingy, tubular passageways connecting large rooms, frequently with catwalks and walkways above the ground. Massive pipes spew green liquid about, the same green liquid that's on the floor of every room and tunnel, while roaches gather in small clusters everywhere. These maps almost always simulate multiple levels by having downward sloping tunnels, with the objective usually being at the "bottom." However, the maps rarely cut back on themselves underneath, so the net result is that they are essentially flat. The glowies on these maps are usually quite visible, even at a glance. The tunnels and intersections can be a bit tight and spawns are frequently just around the corner, so exercise caution when moving about in these areas. The tunnels and rooms are both large enough for most fliers to avoid melee range. Just in case you're wondering, there's no penalty for wading through, or even fighting in sewage (except where it falls from above, and can obscure your vision — sometimes enemies hide under sewage cascades).

CAVES

Cave maps are much like the sewer maps, in that the tunnels are rounded, they empty into large rooms, and generally slope down without cutting back underneath so they map out flat. However, the tunnels are much smaller in diameter and are very crooked — visibility down the tunnels is limited, and running into hidden spawn is more

common. Also, the rooms can be much larger than sewer rooms, having as many as five levels of catwalks and floors in them, providing massive chambers in which to fight. As with the sewers, the glowies tend to be easy to find. While the chambers are frequently large enough to fly in, the corridors are not only too tight to fly in, they're frequently too tight for two huge Heroes to walk through side by side, which means melees tend to be fast and confined. The more fragile Heroes who have to be close to the frontline to be effective (i.e., healers) need to be careful not to get stuck between enemies, walls and their allies, or they may find themselves taking a beating and unable to retreat from it. If you're trying to make a quick retreat, watch out for tight turns and jutting rocks that can reach out and say "gotcha" at crucial times.

5TH COLUMN BUNKERS

5th Column Bunker maps are just like cave maps, except that they are much better lit, and the large, cavernous rooms are filled with modern stairways, consoles and futuristic machinery, complete with blinking lights and sounds. The glowies can be almost as hard to find as on warehouse maps, as they might be hidden among the machinery and consoles. Tactically, these mission maps are similar to the cave maps. The built-up parts of these maps can be very

complex, with multiple levels and many catwalks. But don't worry about the many gun emplacements … the 5th Column doesn't use them against Heroes.

CIRCLE OF THORNS LAIR

Circle of Thorns Lair is the home city of the Circle of Thorns, sunken beneath the earth. This ancient city is somewhat similar to the cave maps, but with some important differences. The vast caverns are filled with buildings, rope bridges, catwalks and spires. The tunnels are straighter and torchlit, and the intersections tend to be larger and easier to spot enemies in. There are large, glowing, circular portals that teleport you to other areas of the map when you step through them. Tactically, these maps are very similar to the 5th Column Bunker maps, except Circle of Thorns Lair areas tend to be more symmetrical (if there's a chamber down the left passage, there's probably one down the right too, and branching chambers tend to meet up again, eventually). Some of the larger and higher-level chambers can be really awe-inspiring — and devilishly hard to explore completely, so take your time.

STORES

Stores are where Heroes purchase Inspirations and Enhancements, and come in two forms: buildings and stand-alone NPC contacts. Additionally, each of your contacts can also provide a few Enhancements suitable to your level and Archetype, though not nearly as many as will be available in a store. The type and level of Enhancements a store sells is dependent upon the level of the zone it's in and the Origins it serves. See the various zone descriptions (pp. 244-263) for exact locations of stores.

The stand-alone merchants are either the very lowest-level stores (the various anonymous Freedom Corps reps) or the very highest (the named individuals who are the sole source for highest-level Enhancements for each Origin). Actual storefronts serve the mid-level Heroes.

Top-Level Stores

The NPCs that constitute the top level stores in the game (your only reliable source for level 30, 35 and 40 single-Origin Enhancements) work very differently than the retail stores that serve the mid-levels.

There's one top-level store contact for each Origin, three in Founders' Falls and two in Brickstown. They can be tricky to find, but this guide makes that task a whole lot easier, since they're keyed out on the City Zone maps. Each of these NPCs specializes in Enhancements for one Origin. They also sell Generic Enhancements and dual-Origin Enhancements related to their specialties, and Heroes of other Origins can complete their assignments and do business with them.

Each of these NPCs is a unique individual with a highly individualized appearance and a personal background story. Furthermore, each one will ask Heroes they've just met to perform a single mission on their behalf. This mission must be successfully completed before you can do business with them as merchants. As missions go, these tend to be short, and they're not the most difficult around (though they're not trivial). Once you've completed the mission, the NPC will appear on your map as a contact.

These five merchants are flagged below with NPC after their Origin.

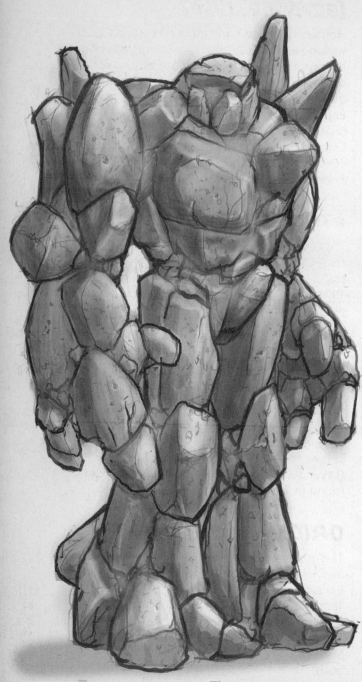

AGENT SIX (NATURAL, NPC)

Agent Six is a special agent for the US Government. She wears a tight-fitting black outfit, and is found in a hard-to-spot back alley. She sells all Technique single-Origin and some dual-Origin (Natural/Magic and Natural/Technology) Enhancements (Level 30, 35 and 40 Enhancements) after you perform a mission for her. She can be found in Founders' Falls.

BIOTECHNIX (MUTANT)

BioTechniX sells Power Five Secondary Mutation single-Origin Enhancements at a premium. It also sells all Genetic Alteration and Focus dual-Origin Enhancements (Magic/Mutant and Mutant/Science). This store has branches in Talos Island (Level 25 and 30 Enhancements) and Independence Port (Level 25 and 30 Enhancements).

COOKE'S ELECTRONICS (TECH)

The store sells Power Five Gadgets and Invention dual-Origin Enhancements (Natural/Technology and Science/Technology) at a discount, and the Generic Training Enhancements at a normal price. This store has branches in Steel Canyon and Skyway City (Level 15 and 20 Enhancements at both).

DEIMOS INNOVATIONS (SCIENCE)

This store sells Power Five Genetic Alterations, Inventions and Experiment dual-Origin Enhancements (Science/Mutant and Technology/Science) at a discount, and the Generic Training Trainings at normal price. This store has branches in Talos Island and Independence Port (Level 25 and 30 Enhancements at both).

EXARCH INDUSTRIES (TECH)

The store sells Power Five Gadgets and Invention dual-Origin Enhancements (Natural/Technology and Science/Technology) at a discount, and the Generic Training Enhancements at a normal price. This store has branches in Talos Island and Independence Port (Level 25 and 30 Enhancements at both).

FREEDOM CORP BASIC (GENERIC)

The tech inside can sell any of the Generic Training Enhancements at a discounted price. This store has branches in Steel Canyon and Skyway City (Level 15 and 20 Enhancements at both).

FREEDOM CORP SPECIAL FORCES (GENERIC)

The special forces of Freedom Corp sell Power Five dual-Origin Enhancements at a premium. They also sell all Generic Training Enhancements. This store has branches in Talos Island and Independence Port (Level 25 and 30 Enhancements at both).

FUTURE DYNAMICS (NATURAL)

The store sells Power Five Relics and Gadgets dual-Origin Enhancements (Natural/Magic and Natural/Technology), and the Generic Training Enhancements at a normal price. This store has branches in Talos Island and Independence Port (Level 25 and 30 Enhancements at both).

HOLSTEN ARMITAGE (SCIENCE, NPC)

Holsten claims to be from the future, a future where Paragon City was destroyed by the Rikti. He says he escaped back to a time where he could prevent the tragedy. He asks the Heroes to perform a task, and afterwards sells all Experiment single-Origin and limited (Science/Mutant and Technology/Science) dual-Origin Enhancements to them (Level 30, 35 and 40 Enhancements). He can be found in Brickstown.

IMAGE, INC. (NATURAL)

The store sells Power Five Relics and Gadgets dual-Origin Enhancements (Natural/Magic and Natural/Technology), and the Generic Training Trainings at a normal price. This store has branches in Steel Canyon and Skyway City (Level 15 and 20 Enhancements at both).

MARK IV (TECH, NPC)

Mark is a prototype Artificial Life Form, on the run from the Crey Labs that created it. It will sell all Cybernetic single-Origin and some dual-Origin (Natural/Technology and Science/Technology) Enhancements after the Hero performs a mission (Level 30, 35 and 40 Enhancements). It can be found in Founders' Falls.

ORION LABS (SCIENCE)

This store sells Power Five Genetic Alterations, Inventions and Experiment dual-Origin Enhancements (Science/Mutant and Technology/Science) at a discount, and the Generic Training Enhancements at normal price. This store has branches in Steel Canyon and Skyway City (Level 15 and 20 Enhancements at both).

PANDORA'S BOX (MAGIC)

A salesclerk behind the counter sells Power Five Relic and Focus dual-Origin Enhancements (Mutant/Magic and Natural/Magic). They also sell Generic Training Enhancements at a normal price. This store has branches in Steel Canyon and Skyway City (Level 15 and 20 Enhancements at both).

PENNY PRESTON (MUTANT, NPC)

Penny is a young girl, barely 13 years old, although she is wise well beyond her years. She is a mutant "catalyst" who has the ability to trigger specific secondary mutations in Heroes. She needs a task performed for her before she can sell the Hero Single Mutation and dual-Origin (Magic/Mutant and Mutant/Science) Enhancements (Level 30, 35 and 40 Enhancements). (Even if you're not a Mutant Hero, Penny is worth checking out, because she's the only child NPC in the game.) She can be found in Founders' Falls.

SERAFINA (MAGIC, NPC)

Serafina was a Genie, owned by the magic Hero called Sirocco. Sirocco died in the Rikti war, but before his death, made one last wish of Serafina, that she would help the Heroes of Paragon City. She granted the wish, but in doing so she lost most of her Genie powers, keeping only her communication lines to the Entities. This enables her to sell all Entity single-Origin and some dual-Origin (Mutant/Magic and Natural/Magic) Enhancements (Level 30, 35 and 40 Enhancements) to Heroes, after they perform a favor for her. She can be found in Brickstown.

SUBGENETICS (MUTANT)

They sell the Power Five Genetic Alterations, Focusing Devices and Secondary Mutation dual-Origin Enhancements (Magic/Mutant and Mutant/Science) at a discount, and the Generic Training Enhancements at normal price. This store has branches in Steel Canyon and Skyway City (Level 15 and 20 Enhancements at both).

TABITHA FABISH'S (MAGIC)

A salesclerk behind the counter sells Power Five Relic and Focus dual-Origin Enhancements (Mutant/Magic and Natural/Magic). They also sell Generic Training Enhancements at a normal price. This store has branches in Talos Island and Independence Port (Level 25 and 30 Enhancements at both).